EL TEL WAS A SPACE ALIEN
The Best of the Alternative Football Press Volume 1

edited by

Martin Lacey

with material from

Lennie Lawrence
Chelsea Independent
When Sunday Comes
Leyton Orientear
The Elmslie Ender
Arsenal Echo Echo
Blue Print
Eagle Eye
Flashing Blade
The Pie
The City Gent
Heartbeat
Just Another Wednesday
Tired And Weary

First published 1989 by
Juma, Trafalgar Works, 44 Wellington Street, Sheffield 1

ISBN 1 872204 00 7

fanzine history

In the beginning there was *Sniffin' Glue*, the archetypal fanzine chronicling the punk explosion of 1976-77. *Sniffin' Glue* was badly written, badly laid out and overpriced, but it was important, and eventually legendary, because it was the first, and for a time the only. It wrote about something nobody else would touch, and as a result built a circulation and reputation out of all proportion to its literary qualities. Editor Mark Perry knew that. When the established music press started falling over itself to give punk the sycophantic saturation coverage it didn't need *Sniffin' Glue* had had its day. He quit, at the top.

There were imitators and successors, none of which really came close: *48 Thrills*, *Ripped and Torn* in the early days, then hundreds upon hundreds who took up the torch, for the most part with a steadily declining relevance.

My own involvement with fanzines started early in 1979 when, living in Sheffield, I published the first issue of *New Musickal Excess*, later known as *NMX*, reporting the vibrant local music scene and covering the emergence of such bands as Cabaret Voltaire and the Human League. *NMX* lasted for three and a half years and 24 issues, making it a real veteran among fanzine, few in this fickle and volatile market getting into double figures. When the Sheffield scene went into decline I took off, living in Cornwall, and Canada before eventually going back to my roots, London. Somewhere along the line I'd become a printer. I started a new magazine called *'Overground'*, an eye-boggling publication which was a non-starter commercially, but generated a lot of interest in the printing, which I had achieved working weekends in the Soho printshop where I was employed. By the end of 1984 I had a solitary A4 press running after hours in a semi derelict shed at the back of some shops in Upper Clapton Road, turning out such titles as *Next Big Thing*, *Raising Hell*, *A Pack Of Lies* and *Snipe*.

Now, many readers of football fanzines, many editors of football fanzines for that matter, may wonder what all this has to do with their product. The connection becomes clearer if I point out that the editor of *Snipe* was one Mike Ticher. Mike Ticher did not invent the football fanzine. There were one or two independent club based magazines around before the first issue of *When Saturday Comes*, *Off The Ball*, which emerged simultaneously must take an equal share of the credit, and of course *Foul*, sadly neglected and forgotten until excavated and canonized by the same Mr. Ticher recently, was doing a similar thing in the seventies. Nevertheless the part played by *When Saturday Comes* in proving it could be done and in nurturing, publicising and encouraging a unified scene based on mutual respect and common aims cannot be overstated. Issue 1 of *WSC* was intended as a free giveaway with Issue 2 of *Snipe*. But the new magazine struck a chord, interest was phenomenal and *Snipe* was soon consigned to history. Within a few issues *When Saturday Comes* had outstripped the printing facilities I could offer and from there it has gone from strength to strength.

My own magazine, *The Elmslie Ender*, started in the spring of 1987. In my teens I reported Wealdstone matches for a local freesheet, the *Harrow and Ealing Post*, and I had fond memories of *Long Ball Down The Middle*, an irreverent magazine published by the Wealdstone Supporters Club from the mid seventies. Initially I suggested reviving this institution, but could raise little interest. I did, however, come across one or two people willing to contribute to an independent publication. *The Elmslie Ender* is now eleven issues old, a modest but thriving magazine, typical of the genre.

explosion

Since 1985 more than a hundred independent football magazines, mostly devoted to a particular team, have appeared - to put an exact figure on it is pointless as new titles appear literally every week - and though it's early days for most of them very few have packed up. The reasons for this phenomenal success story are twofold. Firstly, running a football fanzine is both easy and rewarding. My experience of trying to sell a music fanzine is of an uphill struggle to persuade an audience who are cynical, apathetic, like to think they've seen it all before even if they haven't and would probably rather spend their last 50p on a drink. By contrast, football fans are just that - *fanatics* - and if somebody's taken the trouble to write about their team they'll buy it, and if it's any good - most fanzines are - they'll come back for more. Potential sales depend on the size of the club, but even first issues tend to sell several hundred, and from the supporters on the terraces the response is likely to include offers of help and contributions, letters of encouragement and agreement, even reasoned dissent, which is equally welcome. Now practically every team in the Football League has at least one fanzine devoted to it; some have several; even some non-league clubs have two.

The second, more important reason for the growth is that fanzines are *needed*. The initial inspiration for most of them is likely to have been at least in part the sterility of the official matchday programme. The programme is bound by protocol to maintain a sporting, neutral tone, which is enough on its own to create a void for fanzines to fill - a place to print all those crude and sarcastic jokes about rival teams. The programme is not bound by anything to be an out and out PR tool for the club, but often that's what it is. Voices of dissent, criticism of players, management or board decisions are strictly excluded. There is no forum for fans to express their real opinions and concerns. Ground safety ? Behaviour of the police ? Ticket prices and allocations ? Forget it. According to the programme everything's wonderful, and in the directors box it probably is.

the scum

Dissatisfaction with the popular press also fuels the passion of the fanzines. Since the majority of sports page readers don't actually go to matches arguments and scandals are given prominence while the true, glorious nature of the game barely gets a look in. But if the back pages are bad, the front page is worse. The media have shamelessly pursued a policy of equating football fans with hooliganism.

The truth is violence at football has long been in decline: in the seventies I used to watch Watford from time to time and no Saturday passed off without a punch up somewhere along the line. I remember hundreds of Plymouth supporters running the length of the pitch to fight with Watford fans, with minimal interference from the police, Millwall followers taking over Watford town centre, blockading the station and throwing Watford fans off trains. It was, sadly, accepted as part and parcel of the game, strictly local paper stuff. Even at Wealdstone, a derby with Barnet or Wimbledon was unlikely to pass off entirely peacefully. The turning point in more than one respect was Heysel. Disasters sell papers. Suddenly hooliganism was big news and every minor incident was likely to be blown up out of proportion and used to discredit football as a whole.

The idea that football fans are hooligans seems to have taken root, not just with Joe Public but with those who should know better. At football matches the police can exercise powers and behave in a manner which would cause public outrage if inflicted on any other section of society. Firstly there's the arbitrary suspension of civil liberties for travelling supporters. Thinking of arriving early to take in the local sights, have a meal, perhaps a convivial drink with rival supporters? If the police identify you as football supporters they can invariably find an excuse to 'hold' you until you can be escorted directly to and from the ground with other supporters.

Depending on the place and the occasion police are often friendly, helpful, efficient and sensible. In some places and on some occasions however the police maintain 'order' by simple intimidation, responding to any movement, singing or chanting with random ejections for trumped up offences such as 'pushing' or 'bad language'. Their justification will be that crowd surges are dangerous and chanting enflames rival fans. Very occasionally this may be true, but rarely if ever is either likely to be as dangerous or inflammatory as the actions of the police charging into a crowd to perform their own brand of hooliganism. Sometimes the biggest thugs are in uniform.

There is no point whatsoever pretending football hooliganism doesn't exist or that it's not a problem and fanzine writers have as much enthusiasm as anyone for getting rid of this tiny but persistent element that attempts to spoil the game for everyone. Segregation is sensible. Police are essential. Where consensus breaks down is on what constitutes hooliganism and who the hooligans are. Too often it seems the police believe the answer to the first question is 'supporting your team', especially away from home, and to the second, all of us.

As if having the police against you isn't bad enough football fans now have to contend with the wrath of the government too. The Football Spectators Bill is such a totally unreasonable, unfair, unworkable and in the end downright malicious piece of legislation that one can only assume it is the government's tacit intention to deliberately kill the game of football as we know it, as a mass spectator sport. Mrs. Thatcher regards our national game as our national embarassment and wants to stamp it out.

ID

As already stated, violence in grounds is almost extinct, partly as a result of segregation and close circuit television, but also because of a genuine introspection and maturing of attitudes among football fans since Heysel, and a growing intolerance among the majority for the minority of troublemakers. Where violence occurs it is usually well away from the ground. Identity cards will not prevent home town gangs from waylaying visiting supporters; it is perfectly conceivable also that violent gangs will travel away to cause trouble even if excluded from the match itself, that's always assuming anyone determined to enter a football ground can in practice be banned. False identities are not hard to arrange. What might do something positive to reduce hooliganism is requiring proven offenders to report to the police or attendance centres on match days. Instead the government is making football and football supporters accept the cost and inconvenience of a futile attempt to deal with a problem which afflicts society as a whole. The game is the victim of hooliganism, not the cause.

So why pick on us? We live in a violent age. Hooliganism is everywhere, in Friday night mini-riots in quiet country towns, in drunken rampages on the Costa Brava, at rugby and cricket matches too. Going to a football match is safe compared to walking through some of our city centres at chucking out time. Drink related violence is endemic in pubs and clubs up and down the country. So do we hear plans for identity cards to be shown before entering licensed premises? Plans to combat theft from shops with shoppers' ID cards, convicted shoplifters being banned from supermarkets and shopping centres? No. The government may have scant regard for civil liberties but they know what would cost them votes. Football fans are a minority, easily victimised, and votes lost will be compensated by votes gained from the wider public who interpret this as a strong stance on law and order, never mind the real consequences.

If football fans thought for one moment that the scheme would magically rid the game of the unwanted element they would probably put up with the inconvenience. But on top of doubts about its effectiveness there is a fear that many loyal law abiding supporters will end up banned as a result of flimsy or fabricated police evidence. Even more sinisterly, it will give clubs the means by which to enforce their own bans against anyone they regard as undesirable. Fanzine writers perhaps?

Inconvenience is probably too mild a word to describe what's coming. Many travelling supporters have experienced horrendous queues and frightening crushes as a result of inadequate provision for visiting fans. Such things can only get worse. Nobody is quite sure what the result will be when 20-30,000 or more spectators have to have an identity card checked before gaining admission to the ground, but it's obvious entry is not going to be speeded up. It is barely conceivable that anything could have made the Hillsborough disaster worse, but in view of the circumstances which immediately preceded the tragedy it is clear that had the ID card scheme been in force the likelihood of such an incident would have been greatly increased.

reaction

So the game we love is under attack from all sides. Football fanzines, along with the Football Supporters Association have been the loudest, sometimes the only voice leaping to its defence. You might think that all sections of the sport would be grateful. You would be wrong. Football fanzines have received a massive thumbs up from the paying supporter and positive publicity in abundance from the more enlightened sections of the media. Football authorities and the clubs themselves have been a lot cooler. Now, though occasionally a football club chairman might make himself a nice nest egg from some sneaky property deal for the most part chairmen and directors are not in it for the money. Many, possibly most, are involved because they love the game and/or club, just like the fans. A highly visible minority however appear to have bought their way in to satisfy an egomaniacal desire for power and publicity. Inevitably clubs tend to keep fanzines at arms length. To grant official approval by selling a magazine formally on club premises might be seen as taking responsibility for the contents, which would be absurdly reckless. But a club governed by directors of the first sort will recognise that fanzines are run by the most loyal and devoted supporters who want nothing more than a successful team and a secure future for the club in which they can play a part. Sheffield United's *Flashing Blade* received a letter of encoragement and appreciation in response to their first issue. *Heartbeat* have had an entirely positive response to their efforts despite the fact that it is the most partisan and....well, crude of the contributors to this book. Hearts officials must have a sense of humour! This is not the case at some clubs, where fanzines have been greeted with threats, bans and outright hostility. This is presumably attributable to a paranoid fear of power being usurped by the peasants, or the threat of being *found out*. Thankfully as fanzines have become popular and established clubs have been forced to bow to public opinion and at least take them seriously. Things are improving, slowly, though for the most part football fans can still not count on the clubs they follow to defend their interests. For years supporters have poured their money in through the turnstiles, far outweighing the contributions of corporate sponsors or TV companies, but have rarely been granted an inside voice. The fans can be told (and have been) without forewarning or consultation that their club is on the brink of extinction, is going to 'merge' with a rival club, is going to build houses on the ground and share with another team many miles away, is going to build executive boxes on the favourite standing terrace, is going to change the club colours, kit or badge. Nobody who goes to football matches can be in any doubt that a football club is more than the grass, concrete and steel of the ground, or the players, staff and directors who inevitably come and go and are remembered for varying lengths of time and with varying degrees of fondness. It is more than a limited company with shares, assets and balance sheets. It's more than part of the community it takes its name from. It's a community in itself, something ethereal, almost spiritual, with the ground, the name and the colours among the sacred tenets. But in recent years a breed has arisen with scant respect for this tradition, who think owning shares gives them the right to treat a football club as their personal plaything. That should never be tolerated and fanzines have played a part in pursuing and exposing the guilty parties, and at most clubs fanzines are the only effective watchdogs, who can and will speak out when a club is being taken away from the people. Fanzines *care*.

about this book

The idea for this book is not quite original. A similar project was planned by an established publishing company about a year ago, and I was asked to contribute to it on behalf of *The Elmslie Ender*, but for reasons I've never fully understood the plans fell through. However, it seemed like a good idea, and since by the end of 1988 Juma, as we are now known, was printing nearly thirty different football fanzines on a regular basis I decided I was ideally equipped to assume the mantle of editor. I now hear I am not the only one embarked on such a venture, but this is hopefully the first book of its kind, and as far as I know the only one which is distributing its profits between the contributing fanzines. It is impossible to claim the selection herein is the definitive 'best'. Probably half the fanzines currently on sale I've never even seen. I've simply chosen my personal favourites, which I think form a reasonable cross section. I should say here that it has taken an immense amount of hard work to get this book together, but I would be lying. The enthusiasm and co-operation of my fellow fanzine editors has made it a very simple task, and sifting through the back issues to agree on which extracts to reproduce provided hours of pleasure. A few of the contributors originally invited to participate agreed to do so but failed go come up with the material in time. These will hopefully be included in a Volume 2 which will follow before too long. Only one magazine actually refused to be involved. I may have made a mistake in describing this work as a 'coffee table' book, which seemed to conjure up an image of its pages being drooled over by guffawing yuppies with no comprehension of the reality behind it. The letter declining my invitation also complained that the questinnaire sent to potential contributors was like something out of *Shoot*. Indeed one of the fanzines which has contributed did so on condition the questionnaire could be consigned to the bin, and the word *Shoot* was mentioned several more times. *Shoot?* In an effort to find out why this august journal is so reviled I actually went out and bought a copy. Had it been taken over by the Paedophile Information Exchange ? Merged with National Front News? No, *Shoot* is much the same as it ever was, making the cardinal mistake of assuming that because someone can play football they also have something worth saying, but generally depicting football as positive and exciting, just like the fanzines but to a different audience. After all, where would we be without childhood heroes? Not still watching football I bet.

It's taken six months to produce this book, from conception to binding. The extracts have been written over a period of years and should therefore be read with one eye on the historical context. The material from *Chelsea Independent* was first published during two seasons which saw relegation followed by second division football. *Blueprint* (Manchester City) was likewise covering a second division team. Both of these astutely predict their respective sides will win promotion. By contrast a note of pessimism may be detected in the selections from *Leyton Orientear* and *Eagle Eye* (Crystal Palace), while at the time of writing both clubs have reached their respective play-off finals. It should be remembered however, that deep down all football fans are optimists, otherwise they wouldn't come back for more. Just like gambling on horse racing, football fans gamble with their emotions every Saturday. It's an escape. Whatever your problems - parents, children, school, work, the bank manager, the threat of global destruction by nuclear war or ozone layer depletion - for 90 minutes once a week you can believe that nothing matters except 22 idiots kicking a ball around. That's magic, and if by any remote chance you haven't come to appreciate it yet I hope reading these extracts will instil you with some of the sense of excitement, passion and devotion which makes football great. See you behind the goal !

MARTIN LACEY

postscript: hillsborough

Saturday 15th April we had guests staying so I decided not to make my usual 300 mile round trip to watch Wealdstone but stay home in Sheffield and entertain. I completely forgot there was an F.A. Cup semi-final on and, driving out for a pub lunch in the country, took the road through Hillsborough. Going out of town, on the route which would be followed by the Nottingham Forest supporters, the road was reasonably clear, but heading the other way the traffic coming over the Pennines formed a solid queue stretching half way to Barnsley. It was 12.45. Returning some time after two police roadblocks were stopping and searching vans and minibuses carrying Liverpool fans. It was not surprising they arrived late.

We got home shortly after three and caught the tragedy unfolding on television. I switched off when they said 'There *are* fatalities'. I didn't want to hear more. Perhaps there were a couple dead, no worse than a car crash, was it? Later, listening to the car radio on my way to Tesco for some late shopping I was almost in tears as the enormity of the disaster sank in.

I guess my reactions were the same as football fans everywhere: shocked, frightened, bewildered, saddened, and later angry too.

Printing of this book was well underway. I considered suggesting to the contributors that the royalties from this book should be donated to the disaster fund, then changed my mind. Within a couple of days the fund stood at over £1m: the drop in the ocean we could add seemed irrelevant and in any case money is now likely to be the least of the problems faced by the victims. In an age where charity seems to have replaced justice and responsibility in making financial provision for the alleviation of misfortune I have no doubts these mass fund raising efforts are necessary. But they are a macabre and by now well established ritual, not immune to publicity seekers, public image boosters and those who wish to buy off their conscience without having to think about the reality. A sticker saying 'All Proceeds to Hillsborough Disaster Fund' would have no doubt done wonders for sales of this book, but then a lot of people with no right to do so would have been profiting from it - printers, booksellers, transport companies, paper suppliers etc. I could scarcely believe my eyes when I saw the Daily Mirror were using the Hillsborough disaster as the basis of a TV ad: a voice so insincere it sounded like it should be plugging "20 Slushy Greats from K-Tel" informed us how much Mirror readers were going to raise for the fund and smugly congratulated the paper on its 'sympathetic' coverage. I can think of several words to describe pictures of people being crushed to death. 'Sympathetic' is not one of them.

So the profits from this book will, as originally intended, be divided among the contributing fanzines, many, possibly most, of which have already made some sort of direct contribution to the disaster fund. Attention must now turn to the future, and ensuring it never happens again, and as the voice of terrace supporters the fanzines have a vital role to play, if only they can make the authorities listen. Though this book has concentrated more on the humourous side most fanzines started with the intention of expressing serious opinions on the state of the game. How many times have I read the objections to 'safety' fences, erected by clubs with no regard whatsoever for the safety of the fans, nor even in some cases for whether the fans behind them would get a proper view of the pitch? One can only assume that when the inquiry has done its job a fair bit of criticism will be aimed at the police. What happened outside Hillsborough was bad planning capped by one big fatal error. But these were simple human failings for which it would be wrong to bear any malice and as with all human errors it is impossible to say categorically the same situation couldn't arise again. What happened inside is a different matter entirely. When fans started climbing the fences to escape the crush the police shoved them back, maybe to their deaths, according to some reports laughing as they did so. While these police were clearly not aware of the gravity of the situation it is inconceivable that they didn't see there was real danger and distress. Had they been dealing with anyone except football fans their response would undoubtedly have been different. How many times have I read in fanzines bitter complaints about the contemptuous way football fans are treated by the police? All we've ever asked for is the normal respect, help and protection that all members of the public should have a right to expect. Apparently at Hillsborough that was too much.

In the aftermath a lot of sentences will begin with the words 'if only....'. Perhaps they could all be replaced by one sentence: If only the police, clubs and football authorities had listened to what the fans could have told them.

Inevitably there will be repercussions which we'll have to live with, like it or not: some all-seat stadiums, standing capacities drastically reduced with higher prices following. The way we watch football may be changed. But even allowing for human error on the day Hillsborough could have been perfectly safe with minor modifications which now appear all too obvious - if there hadn't been a fence round the pitch, if there'd been a fairer ticket allocation, if the turnstile-capacity ratio had been higher. No-one wants to congratulate themselves on predicting a disaster. Nobody is saying 'I told you so'. But never again need any fanzine editor feel guilty, reticent or apologetic about taking an unpalatable message and ramming it down the throats of those who have in the past tried to dismiss us. If they won't listen now the blood of the next disaster will be on their hands.

chapter 1

LENNIE LAWRENCE

charlton

LENNIE **LAWRENCE**

Sept. '88   No.1   (50p)

EEYORE SCORES!

(ANYTHING'S POSSIBLE WITH THE WOOLWICH)

LENNIE'S LOVELIES

COMIC STRIP ACTION

WIN A VIDEO!

SEE INSIDE

--PLUS--
PLAY THE CHARLTON LOTTERY AND WIN A PORTAKABIN
--AND MUCH, MUCH MORE--

LENNIE LAWRENCE

Issue 2   January 1989   50p

CAN'T STAND UP FOR FALLING DOWN

CARL LEABURN'S SOCCER SKILLS

GREENWICH COUNCIL NAME NEW VALLEY SITE !

EXCLUSIVE!!!

DIXON - A PORTRAIT OF POWER

NEW BIOLOGICAL FORMULA

INCLUDES FREE PROGRAMME !

MAGAZINE TITLE: LENNIE LAWRENCE

EDITORS NAME: ADAM PETERS

AGE: 19   OCCUPATION: STUDENT - Degree in Football (seriously) at East London Poly.

DO YOU/HAVE YOU EVER SUPPORTED ANY OTHER TEAM? NOT REALLY

MOST MEMORABLE MATCH EVER: CHARLTON v LEEDS, ST. ANDREWS, MAY 1987

MOST MEMORABLE SEASON: AUTUMN

ALL TIME FAVOURITE PLAYER: CARL LEABURN

WHAT SORT OF CAR DO YOU DRIVE? DON'T LIKE CARS - if it's over 7 miles I catch a train, if less I walk.

YOUR FAVOURITE MUSIC: VELVET UNDERGROUND, DOORS, MICHELLE SHOCKED, KATE BUSH, AND BIZET.

FILMS/TV: THE PRISONER, HANCOCK AND ANYTHING PRETENTIOUS

FAVOURITE CLOTHES: CHEAP AND BLACK

POLITICAL LEANINGS: LEFT OF CENTRE, RIGHT OF LENIN

WHAT PLAYER WOULD YOU MOST LIKE TO SEE PLAYING FOR ENGLAND (SCOTLAND/WALES IF RELEVANT)? ~~STANLEY~~ ~~DIEGO~~ ~~MARADONA~~ STANLEY MATTHEWS

LENNIE LAWRENCE

I think it was Virgil who once said, "Always begin an article with a classical quotation, it makes you seem literate." It's probably safe to say he wasn't talking about football fanzines at the time. He may have been, but if he was, he would probably have said something different.

The average half-time lasts around twelve minutes. Very few programme editors have worked this out, or at least very few supply a product that can last that length of time. The programme is, of course, the only real souvenir you can have of a particular game (if you really want a souvenir of a game lost 3-0 in the pouring rain). As far as reading material goes though, the programmes are sadly lacking. In all but a few cases, adverts dominate, and the remaining space is filled up with jaded cliches, misspelt names, and boring photos.

This dearth of reading material, together with a lack of a medium through which supporters could communicate, has given rise to this so-called "fanzine phenomenon". David 'Luton' Evans recently warned supporters that, under ID cards, they will need to be at the turnstiles by 2.15, to be in the ground by kick-off. This will mean an even greater need for the fanzine movement.

Football, apart from being a funny old game, and a game of two halves, is, for many people, something akin to a religion. I myself was a late convert, with no interest in the sport whatsoever until my teens. There was no tradition of, or dedication to, the sport within my family, despite the fact that my father played two games for Red Star Belgrade in the sixties. Any "Who do you support then" sessions at school were always parried with "Liverpool" (the only club I'd ever heard of!).

But in 1983 I discarded boring Liverpool and decided to adopt a club properly. Avoiding the poncy haircuts of the First and the park cloggers of the third and fourth I picked Charlton Athletic, the Second Division team with the nicest name! Another year passed before I discovered that Charlton was in London (I thought it was a Manchester satellite town, like all the other Athletics). I soon started going to home games, then away games etc. My lack of a lifelong devotion to the club hasn't prevented me from standing dewey-eyed at the Valley gates, wistfully wishing the return of the days of Bartram, Leary et al.

Last summer I found myself on the outskirts of Stoke. At first I thought it was just a bad dream, but there I was. I followed the signs to the City Centre, but all I could find was a Woolworths, a supermarket and three seedy video shops. There was a Tourist Information Centre though, so I popped in. "Excuse me, mate. Where's the city centre?" I asked. "You're in it," was the curt reply. How that city can support two football teams, and why one of them's called Port Vale, are two of the biggest mysteries of the Twentieth Century. Whether the city could still support two clubs when ID cards arrive is, perhaps, less of a teaser.

Individual clubs, and football as a whole, must survive any attack made on it (ID cards being the single biggest threat). For dedicated football fans, every ground is a temple, and the main place of interest in the town; every result is important, even the most insignificant of Sunday pub matches (they all mean something to someone). Football must survive. The emergence of the fanzine movement, and the FSA; campaigns at Fulham, QPR, Charlton, Spurs, York, Leeds, and elsewhere; the expansion of Supporter Power: these all reassure me that football will survive. The passion of its followers should ensure that. Every fanzine is a refection of that passion.

After all, if football does die, what else is there to do on a Saturday afternoon? Shopping, whilst a bind at any time, is positively suicidal on Saturdays. No other sport has anything approaching the same interest value. Of course, theres always fishing, DIY or train-spotting. Or I suppose we could watch Grandstand.

Personally I'd rather be strip-searched at Carrow Road any day.
ADAM PETERS

THE JIM·MELROSE STORY

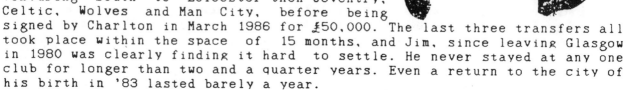

In keeping with our policy of breaking tradition, we bring you a "Where are they now?" column that instead of telling you that an old defender from the 60s now runs a sports shop in Dartford (don't they all ?), we catalogue the career of a more recent exile. In this case, one Jim Melrose.

Born in Glasgow in October 1958, Jim was playing for non-league non-entities Eastercraigs, when he was signed by Partick Thistle (aged 17). He made 112 league appearances for the club (scoring 31 goals), and gained Scottish under-21 caps, before venturing south to Leicester then Coventry, Celtic, Wolves and Man City, before being signed by Charlton in March 1986 for £50,000. The last three transfers all took place within the space of 15 months, and Jim, since leaving Glasgow in 1980 was clearly finding it hard to settle. He never stayed at any one club for longer than two and a quarter years. Even a return to the city of his birth in '83 lasted barely a year.

For his part, Lennie had signed Jim to score some goals in the push for promotion, and that he did (5 in 11 games), helping the club into the First Division in the process. The following season he scored 17 goals in 35 games, included a hatrick (two poaches and a lob) against Everton, a nine-second goal against West Ham, and two against Ipswich that forced the Voice Of The Members Terrace to declare "I won't call you a hommux again, Jim". A promise that lasted till the next game (against Leeds). Bryan Robson sang Jim's praises (in 'Shoot' magazine) but a few weeks into the next season Melrose was packing his bags.

He still had one more opportunity to demonstrate his great ingenuity. In the game against Forest (on the opening day) he ran into the penalty area, and stopped, not knowing what to do next. Rather than taking a shot at goal (which they would probably be expecting, naive as Brian's boys are), he merely waited for the inevitable challenge, and consequent penalty. Why was this great artiste allowed to leave ?

First Division goals have always been something of a luxury at Charlton. Our current golden boy, Andy Jones, looks about as dangerous in front of goal as a packet of mashed bananas. Yet Jim scored 17 times in one season, and all of them in the other team's goal. Why was he sold ?

Because he wouldn't move house is the simple explanation. He was still living in Manchester and commuting to London every week. Hardly an ideal situation, but perhaps there was something more ?

THE JIM·MELROSE STORY

He was sold along the traditional Lawrence transfer lines; strikers to Leeds, midfielders to Gillingham, defenders to Bristol City. He moved quietly to Leeds for £50,000, then even more quietly on to Shrewsbury (Bremner wasn't impressed, and preferred Pearson), where he would have sunk into obscurity, had he not found himself on the wrong end of a punch from Swindon (now Stoke) heavyweight, Chris Kamara.

It would take great provocation to cause a player to punch another after the final whistle. Before the whistle it's "all part of the game". But after, it's assault in front of a lot of witnesses (even at Shrewsbury). Kamara originally claimed he had been racially taunted by Melrose, a claim he later dropped (for the "good of the game " perhaps ?)

Either Kamara didn't like the look of him (but Jim's such a sweetie ?), or he was annoyed at Jim's superior skill (chortle), or he was provoked verbally by Jim, racially or otherwise. If he just wanted to release his pent up agression, why didn't he just hit the referee like everyone else.

Perhaps there is something about Jim's attitude that prevents him from settling anywhere. Eight clubs in eight seasons is not a record to be proud of (at least, not unless the sales are for purely financial reasons).

One thing is certain. Wherever he may end up, Jim will always be remembered here for his hatrick against Everton, his goal against West Ham, and his dive against Forest.

Discovered in the VIP car park after the Spurs game ...

FOOTBALL IDENTITY CARD
Conditions of Use

In this document, "card" means the annoying piece of plastic you don't really want, "cardholder" means you, and "Colin Moynihan" means small, squeaky bastard in a suit.

1) This card permits the cardholder to view, on production of the correct monies, a game of English league or cup football, providing that:

   (a) The game involves the club at which the cardholder is registered.
   (b) The machinery that inspects the card is fully operational.
   (c) The card hasn't been cancelled.

2) Cards can be cancelled for a number of reasons:

   (a) Accidentally,
   (b) Because of an offence committed within the ground.

3) Offences can include:

   (a) Swearing,
   (b) Cheering,
   (c) Looking a bit funny.

4) Cards can also be cancelled if the cardholder:

   (a) Commits an offence outside the ground (for instance, double parking),
   (b) Does something the club doesn't like (this can include chanting "sack the board").

5) Cancelled cards can only be reinstated if the cardholder:

   (a) Is very rich,
   (b) Is very influential,
   (c) Has photos of the Minister of Sport in a compromising position with a camel.

6) The following people do not need cards to get into a game:

   (a) Police officers,
   (b) Members of the board,
   (c) Rich People,
   (d) Players and officials,
   (e) Other persons impersonating one or more of the above.

7) If your card has been cancelled the only ways you can get into a game are by:

   (a) Becoming, or impersonating, one or more of the above,
   (b) Becoming either a cabinet minister or a member of the Royal Family,
   (c) Stealing someone else's card.

8) This card remains Government property. It may not be defaced, mutilated, or disposed of in any way other than by being thrown at a member of the opposition.

9) This will of course result in the card being cancelled.

10) You voted for us, remember.

LONDON STANDARD 25th August 1989

Charlton win!

CHARLTON 4 LUTON 2

Charlton kicked off their first home game in their new compact Valley ground in flamboyant fashion. Lee took the kick off, passing to Jones who chipped the ball sweetly over Mr.King's window box, straight into the path of the postman who hammered the ball home off his front wheel.

This sent spectators in the Main Stand (No. 17b) into raptures, and ruptures, as two elderly gentlemen fell out, landing on the balcony below. Charlton dominated the next twenty minutes, with Stuart, Walsh and a telephone box combining well in midfield to set up some good chances. The second goal didn't come however till the 27th minute when a mis-hit shot by Andy Peake (well, aren't they all ?) sped towards the corner checkout before cannoning in off the frozen food counter.

Despite constant pressure from Luton and a young boy who wanted to play with his kite, Charlton held their two-goal lead till the interval.

Shortly after the re-start, a controversial incident occured. Running backwards for a high header, Charlton captain Shirtliff accidentally knocked over an elderly lady in the area. Examination of her personal possessions revealed that she was, in fact, born in Luton, and a penalty was awarded. Harford cooly placed the ball on Mrs.Sanderson's head on the doorstep (penalty spot) where she lay unconscious before hammering the ball (and a pair of false teeth) into the back of the net, destroying a good crop of tomatoes, much to Mr.Eeyore's dismay.

Charlton swiftly restored their two-goal lead, Lee stealthily climbing the Hendersons' trellis, pursued by two Luton backs, before depositing a ball on Jones' unsuspecting head. The crowd, expecting the usual vertical header in front of goal, were shocked to see the ball hit the back of the net. Mrs.Hallwood tried to cheer the Luton 'keeper up with some of her home-made lemon tart.

With eight minutes left, Lee capped a superb personal performance by dodging three defenders and slotting a ball through to Reverend Hallwood, who rounded the laid-out figure of Les Sealey, to score in an empty net. A late goal from Newell, resulting from a defensive mix up between Mark Reid and a park keeper, was little consolation for Luton.

On a fine summer's day the main worry for the Charlton fans was the length of the queue for Mrs.Johnson's toilet.

Mark Stuart clears from a crowded area

AND AWAY THEY GO

Brief Appraisals of the careers of departing superstars.

MARK STUART

Scored a few goals. Spent the rest of the time being a useless bastard on the left touchline.

PAUL MILLER

Was always either in the team or on the transfer list. Scored at Chelsea, Gobbed at Jackson, Punched and kicked everyone else. Could always pick out an opposition striker with a 50 yard back-pass. Won't be missed.

DAVID CAMPBELL

Hasn't gone yet.

Simply correctly predict the remaining 1,534 scores in the football league, together with the total weight of the League management (sic) committee. You could win £100,000. Yes, £100,000. That's right £100,000. Five zeros.

Simply collect the vouchers from the next three crappy programmes, and send your entry to:

God we hope no-one wins this, The box in the corner, Portakabin no.3, Selhurst Park, Miles away from SE7, London.

Q. How do you confuse a Charlton forward ?
A. Put him in his opponent's penalty area

Q. How many Charlton fans can you fit in a mini ?
A. All of them.

Q. What's the difference between the team coach and an open goal ?
A. Andy Jones doesn't always miss the team coach.

OUT & ABOUT IN Greenwich AND DISTRICT

The start of a new occassional series, in which we will be highlighting some of the strange visual quirks, that set our Greenwich homeland apart, from the grey block called Croydon.

No.1. The Woolwich Ferry

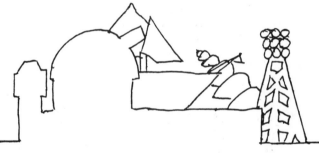

This weird sign appears along the approach to the ferry (South side). What does it mean ? Anyone au fait with their Highway Code will know that a red circle signifies a restriction, e.g. no cycling, no ten ton trucks etc. Clearly, therefore, this sign is here to warn drivers that they will not be able to use the ferry if their car is on fire.

Anyone with a better solution, or a similar photo (it doesn't have to be in Greenwich) - the usual address. Incredible prizes for funny photos/explanations.

THE PROFESSIONAL FOOTBALL HOOLIGAN

Tired of being a respectable supporter ? Bored of the drudgery ? Drive to the game ? Sit in the members' stand with a couple of kids ? Where's the life in the that ?

Haven't you ever wanted to do something a little more interesting ? Something a little more exciting ? At that dinner party in the evening, wouldn't you like to say something more than "went to watch a football match", when asked to detail your day. Wouldn't you rather say, "Me 'n' the kids went down the Palace, we got 'old of this couple of Arsenal lads, and we kicked their bloody heads in. Then we got really pissed, and shoved our bums out of the sun-roof on the way home." You wouldn't? Oh.

Wouldn't you at least like to break the routine ? To acquire that feared and respected label of HOOLIGAN - Enemy of this nation, and the whole free world. Glorified in the press, savaged by politicians, it's a great life. And it's so easy.

Below is a list of various hooligan acts. Do the act, and collect the points. Underneath you'll see the number of points you need to acquire various different statuses of thug. Start collecting now. Available from police stations where you see this sign:

1) Try to take a can of coke into a game (2 pts)
2) Cheer for your team in the Members Stand (5 pts)
3) Wear a turquoise stripey shirt (3 pts)
4) Watch your team away from home (8 pts)
5) Support Millwall, Leeds or Chelsea (10 pts)
6) Call one of your players "bloody useless" (12 pts)
7) Look at a Police Officer - by accident (3 pts)
                              - on purpose (6 pts)
8) Go to a football match (1 pt)
9) Watch the game from somewhere other than Directors, Executive or Press Box (19 pts)

*Less than 20 - You're not a football hooligan. You're probably Richard Collins, or one of his mates.
*21-30 - You're a fully-fledged hooligan. Your attendance at games is itself evidence of that. You will have to carry a Hooligan Card from the middle of next season onwards.
*31-40 - A card on it's own is not enough for your kind of thug. You should be branded on the forehead.
*41-50 - You are responsible for the Heysel Stadium disaster, and the behaviour of the British in Dusseldorf and Ibiza. You should serve a minimum of three years.
*51-58 - Castration is the only way to deal with your sort of thug.
*59-64 - Bring back hanging and National Service.
*65 plus - Get rid of that shirt.

And remember, you've got to hurry. ID cards will be with us soon All you'll be able to then is mug or kill other fans to steal their cards, and that only gets five points.

CHARLTON *SOCCER*SKILLS* ATHLETIC

All the great players have their own special moves, copied by admirers from generation to generation; Stanley Matthews' shuffle, Johan Cruyff's shimmy, Tony Adams' hand in the air. Here are a few of the Charlton squad's little manoeuvres, that you would be strongly advised not to include in your own repertoire (or coaching mannual).

ANDY JONES

① "OWCH-SOMETHING-JUST-HIT-ME-ON-THE-HEAD."

CARL LEABURN

② FLAP FLAP FLAP TRUMP FLAP

"I'VE-JUST-LOST-AN-AERIAL-DUEL-WITH-TERRY-GIBSON."

MARK STUART RIP*

③ *rest in plymouth

"I'M-MAKING-SPACE."

CARL LEABURN (again)

④ "OH-DEAR-I'VE-JUST-FALLEN-FLAT-ON-MY-FACE-IN-FRONT-OF-GOAL-(AGAIN)."

PETER SHIRTLIFF

⑤ uuuaaargh!! CRASH

"I'M-SORRY-HAS-THE-BALL-GONE"

PETER SHIRTLIFF (again)

⑥ ① NORWICH CITY F.C. butties BUTTIES

"WELL-WHERE'S-THE-F***ING-COACH?"

Q. What is the difference between Carl Leaburn and a hatstand?

HOW TO GET TO: SELHURST PARK (from S.E.London & Kent)

BY BUS: Number 75 buses are like Robert Lee: They're slow, and they don't appear very often.

BY TRAIN: The short journey to Croydon from Kent is a simple one, which can involve as few as four changes, each specially designed so the train you want to catch leaves a minute before the arrival of the one you're on. Explore the stations of South London, the Palace way.

BY TAXI: Just get in and say to the driver, "take me to the dullest, greyest, poxiest, most featureless lump of cement in the world." Telford and The Dell are out of the way of most local taxi firms, so you'll either end up at Selhurst or the National Theatre.

LENNIE LAWRENCE: THE MAGAZINE THAT'S NOT AFRAID TO BE A LOAD OF CRAP

A. Buy Lennie #3 to find out - out in April.

chapter 2

CHELSEA INDEPENDENT

chelsea

the
CHELSEA INDEPENDENT

issue 2   August 1987   price 20p

CHELSEA INDEPENDENT SUPPORTERS ASSOCIATION

EXCLUSIVE

THE
TOMMY LANGLEY COLLECTION

inside this issue

SHOULD JOE BE CAPTAIN ?

A TRIBUTE TO DOUG ROUGVIE

JADE IS THE COLOUR

ARE CHELSEA DOING ENOUGH TO SAVE THE BRIDGE ?

plus much more

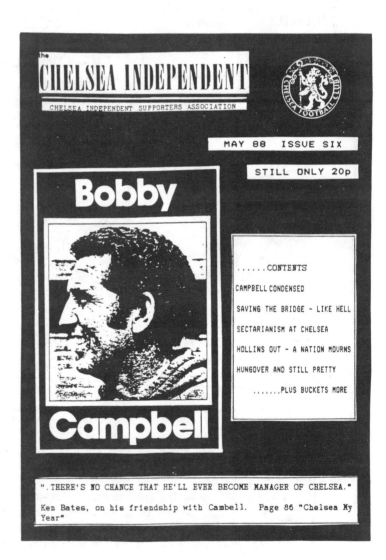

the
CHELSEA INDEPENDENT

CHELSEA INDEPENDENT SUPPORTERS ASSOCIATION

MAY 88   ISSUE SIX

STILL ONLY 20p

Bobby

Campbell

......CONTENTS

CAMPBELL CONDENSED

SAVING THE BRIDGE - LIKE HELL

SECTARIANISM AT CHELSEA

HOLLINS OUT - A NATION MOURNS

HUNGOVER AND STILL PRETTY

......PLUS BUCKETS MORE

".THERE'S NO CHANCE THAT HE'LL EVER BECOME MANAGER OF CHELSEA."
Ken Bates, on his friendship with Campbell. Page 86 "Chelsea My Year"

The Independent got off the ground around April 1987 when 'Crocodile' Mike Ticher sent out a clarion call to the hordes of Blues fans he knew. So, about eight of us met up in this noisy little pub near ULU which became our watering hole for some time. Immediate reasons for the meeting were the imminent bulldozing of the ground by Marler - we felt that truly independent supporters' clubs at Fulham and QPR had helped stave off, or at least postpone, such wonderful steps forward as mergers and yuppie flats, so it seemed only natural we form an independent supporters club (the CISA) and create the Independent as its mouthpiece.

Of course, the general and oft-quoted afflictions of the game - racism, violence, egotistical and insensitive administration at clubs and authorities etc etc etc - were also prime motivations. We've now (March 1989) been tilting at windmills for 11 issues and many terse put-downs by Ken Bates. What has been most invigorating about the whole thing is not that there are many fellow fans who think like us (because it's not necessarily true), but that there is so much diversity of view - it has taken the fanzine 'movement' to give this great bubbling mass of anger and humour an outlet and an edge.

PETER COLLINS

CONTRIBUTOR   Peter Collins

AGE   26

OCCUPATION   Journalist

DO YOU/HAVE YOU EVER SUPPORTED ANY OTHER TEAM Soft spot for Wealdstone
(I'm seeing a doctor)

MOST MEMORABLE MATCH EVER Ooer! How about Bolton 0, Chelsea 1 (1983);
and Grimsby 0, Chelsea 1 (1984)

ALL TIME FAVOURITE PLAYER Patsy Nevin

WHAT SORT OF CAR DO YOU DRIVE   Volkswagen Ozone-Eater

YOUR FAVOURITE MUSIC   Wire, Scott Walker, Pere Ubu, Cabaret Voltaire
(and more)

FILMS/TV   Come and See (dir. Elem Klimov), King of Comedy
(Scorsese); What the Papers Say, Shelley.

FAVOURITE CLOTHES   My Bros t-shirt

POLITICAL LEANINGS   Confused and demoralised left.

WHAT PLAYER WOULD YOU MOST LIKE TO SEE PLAYING FOR ENGLAND
(SCOTLAND/WALES IF RELEVANT)

I really couldn't give a stuff about England (and I'm English);
Scotland? How about giving Durie a try? Wales? JPR Williams.

Nick Brown by Peter

Peter by Steev

CONTRIBUTOR   Mick Allpress

AGE   26

OCCUPATION   Product Manager

DO YOU/HAVE YOU EVER SUPPORTED ANY OTHER TEAM   Lincoln City

MOST MEMORABLE MATCH EVER Lincoln 2, Stoke City 1 (League Cup 1975 or 6)

ALL TIME FAVOURITE PLAYER   Pat Nevin

WHAT SORT OF CAR DO YOU DRIVE   Company Car

YOUR FAVOURITE MUSIC Punk and soul

FILMS/TV   Bilko, Chigley and Apocalypse Now

FAVOURITE CLOTHES   Cheap ones

POLITICAL LEANINGS   Left

WHAT PLAYER WOULD YOU MOST LIKE TO SEE PLAYING FOR ENGLAND
(SCOTLAND/WALES IF RELEVANT)

Pat Nevin (for England); Nigel Clough

(PS...My favourite meal when recovering from illness is chicken and
cashew nuts with chips)

Mick Allpress. by Steev

Paul by Peter

CONTRIBUTOR   NICK BROWN

AGE   21

OCCUPATION   CIVIL SERVANT

DO YOU/HAVE YOU EVER SUPPORTED ANY OTHER TEAM? WEALDSTONE

MOST MEMORABLE MATCH EVER   Bolton (CA) 1-0 '83, Sheff W. A) 4-4 McGF

ALL TIME FAVOURITE PLAYER   RON HARRIS

WHAT SORT OF CAR DO YOU DRIVE   A CRAP ONE

YOUR FAVOURITE MUSIC   VARIED

FILMS/TV   Only Fools & Horses, Minder, M. Caine Films,

FAVOURITE CLOTHES THE ONES I WEAR

POLITICAL LEANINGS   VARIED

WHAT PLAYER WOULD YOU MOST LIKE TO SEE PLAYING FOR ENGLAND
(SCOTLAND/WALES IF RELEVANT)
ME ! PAT NEVIN- SCOTLAND, JOEY JONES-WALES!

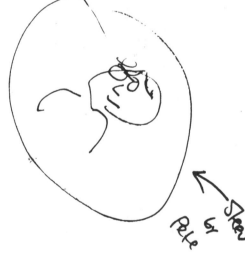

Pete & Steev

No photos — but we did these abstract
drawings of each other in the car on
the way back from Ipswich. It was
dark and the car kept moving.

MAGAZINE TITLE: *CHELSEA INDEPENDENT*

EDITORS NAME: *PAUL ROBERTS*

AGE: 23   OCCUPATION: *STUDENT*

DO YOU/HAVE YOU EVER SUPPORTED ANY OTHER TEAM? *NO*

MOST MEMORABLE MATCH EVER: *BRAZIL 4 SCOTLAND 1 1982.*

MOST MEMORABLE SEASON: *83-84*

ALL TIME FAVOURITE PLAYER: *PAT NEVIN*

WHAT SORT OF CAR DO YOU DRIVE? —

YOUR FAVOURITE MUSIC: —

FILMS/TV: —   *WHAT IS THIS, SHOOT?*

FAVOURITE CLOTHES: —

POLITICAL LEANINGS: —

WHAT PLAYER WOULD YOU MOST LIKE TO SEE PLAYING FOR ENGLAND (~~SCOTLAND/~~ ~~WALES IF RELEVANT~~)? *ROY AITKEN*

~~EDITORS~~ NAME: *STEEV BURGESS*

AGE: *MATURE*   OCCUPATION: *RETIRED CIVIL SERVENT (STUDENT)*

DO YOU/HAVE YOU EVER SUPPORTED ANY OTHER TEAM?
INTERNAZIONALE - MILANO

MOST MEMORABLE MATCH EVER: *CHELSEA VS F.C. BRUGE - ECWC 1971*

MOST MEMORABLE SEASON:

ALL TIME FAVOURITE PLAYER: *PETER OSGOOD*

WHAT SORT OF CAR DO YOU DRIVE? *GO-CART (ONCE A YEAR)*

YOUR FAVOURITE MUSIC:

FILMS/TV: *BRAZIL / THE PRISONER*

FAVOURITE CLOTHES: *BLACK ONES*

POLITICAL LEANINGS: *OUTSIDE LEFT*

WHAT PLAYER WOULD YOU MOST LIKE TO SEE PLAYING FOR ENGLAND (SCOTLAND/ WALES IF RELEVANT)? *PAT NEVIN / TONY DORIGO*

A TRIBUTE TO THE GREAT DOUG ROUGVIE

An era will end this coming season as Chelsea take to the field without Doug Rougvie, a man feared by Blues fans everywhere, and regarded with affection by wrestling buffs the world over. The gentle giant signed for Brighton and Hove Albion, where he will link up with old Chelsea favourites; Dale Jasper, Chris Hutchings and Robert Issac - as well as new assistant manager Martin Hinshelwood - as the Seagulls consolidate their push for Fourth Division status. According to Hinshelwood, Dougie may be in line for Brighton's captaincy, and is likely to be playing at centre-back, a position from which, as all Chelsea fans are aware, the gentle giant inspires such confidence.

Predictably, the move brought an angry response as Rougvie's fans flooded the Fulham Road to protest and an extra policeman had to be called upon to disperse them both. Throughout West London grown men were seen to cry with relief, whilst on the south coast fans queued to throw themselves off the Brighton pier.

Rougvie - or "Rubbish" as the Shed came affectionately to call him - moved to the Bridge from Aberdeen in July 1984 for a fee of £150,000. Brighton paid £50,000 for his services. Opinion is divided as to his true worth, though it is clear to most that £50,000 is the closest to zero. In a three year spell at the club Dougie played 99 first-team games for the Blues, bringing new meaning to the word finesse and making Chelsea fans long for the sure touch and delicate manner of Mickey Droy, a man who could frighten the ball out of the penalty area.

Like many others Doug Rougvie has written himself into the Stamford Bridge folk-lore. Who will forget the amiable Scot's displays at left-back? In this coveted position Rougvie became so well acquainted with the pitch, that there was talk of switching him onto the groundstaff. At centre-back he was a model of consistency, magnificently partnering Colin Pates or Joe McLaughlin and dispossessing them at every opportunity. And what of the punch that laid low John Fashanu during the 0:4 defeat at the hands of Wimbledon? Will the like ever be seen at Chelsea again? I fear not.

His pre-match warm-ups have now become legendary, yet hardly seemed necessary to achieve Dougie's standards, and who could doubt his love of a challenge. Remember how he conceeded a penalty at Hillsborogh denying Chelsea an historic win, just so he could have another crack at them. For many of us however Doug Rougvie's finest moments came in the heady atmosphere of a Full Members Cup Final at Wembley, as he single-handedly attempted to wrest the trophy from Chelsea's grasp in the dying moments of the game. Surely it was only the fact that we were playing Manchester City that foiled his valiant attempts to give away three penalties.

Dougie will be sorely missed, particularly by opposing forwards - there may never again be so much space in a Chelsea defence - but also by the scores of Blues fans who thrive on the hours of frustration and despair he gave them, a commodity rarely in short supply in this part of London. But what Chelsea have lost, Brighton have gained.....

Pete Collins.

GREAT HIPPIES OF OLD

No 1. - Tommy Ord, April 7th 1973 vs Stoke.

The idea that the 1960's didn't end until about 1974 is well supported by the evidence of Tommy Ord's full debut for Chelsea. Amidst a very nasty injury crisis, (which waylayed Webb, Hutchinson, Garner, Garland, Kember + Locke), many youngsters were drafted in to fill the gaps in the latter stages of the 1972-73 season. Of course these youngsters were prone to be susceptible to the latest fashions of the day, far more than the older generation of stars. Tommy Ord was the most unfortunate example. Obviously he had suffered from a bout of post-60's liberalism and decided, late on in the day, to become a rampant hippy. He carried out his conviction superbly. With an already classically ugly face he emerged from the tunnel (in those days a portacabin - no East Stand, remember) with his greasy hair dragging along behind him.

At the sight of him old men cried into their Bovril (3p) at the apparent demise of their once proud club, whilst women vomited openly in the stands. At one point during the warm-up, Tommy raced to the bench in an instinctive attempt to wear his tank-top with the two big stars on and had to be restrained by Ian Britton's wig.

However what was to come was worse. As the match progressed, Ord tucked in on the right side of midfield with greater and greater effort. As people looked up from their programmes (5p) in the twentieth minute, Ord unleashed a ridiculously spectacular right foot 'banana-shot', (as they were called in the 70's). It flew perfectly into the top corner of the net, from a distance of 20 yards. Ord raced over in triumph to the three workmen

Picture taken from Chelsea F.C. Who's Who (see review)

The reinforced lens needed to capture Tommy's looks has led to this deterioration in the quality of print

building the East stand, pausing only to check a possible magic mushroom patch on the far side of the area. Hippydom had arrived at Stamford Bridge, 1-0.

In great Chelsea tradition Stoke went on to score three times, but with the majority of the crowd still hallucinating from Ord's appearance and goal, everyone went home delerious. 1-3.

Perhaps Ord's most lasting impression was the introduction of the stupidly long hair cut and tank-top which plagued Chelsea and their impressionable fans, until they were rescued in the late 70's by those nice skinhead people, some of whom you can still see today.

NEXT ISSUE: Roger Stonefree.

Adam Porter

CUP OF NO CHEER

A sanguine MARTIN BOOTH takes our annual early Cup exit philosophically...

That long haul back from Barnsley gave plenty of time to contemplate Chelsea's truly abysmal record in the FA Cup since we won it in 1970.

Looking back, no wonder the bookie grinned and offered me the ludicrously generous odds of 66-1 when I went down after the Ipswich game to back the lads to win at Wembley.

He must have done his homework. In 19 seasons since 1970, Chelsea have crashed out in the third round seven times, in the fourth seven times, the fifth three times, and have only reached the quarter-finals twice.

In the interests of good local relations, the Blues have only beaten one London side (Palace in '71) but have gone out to local rivals seven times.

And since the Spurs game in 1982 Chelsea have failed to get beyond the fourth round. Yup, no wonder the bookie grinned.

The irony is that 1970 was the climax of 20 years of glorious cup-fighting by the lads. After semi-final appearances in the early '50s, 1970 came at the end of a six-season run when the Blues had got at least as far as the sixth round.

Old reputations die hard, and on the morning of the Barnsley game two of the Daily Express's four pundits tipped Chelsea to reach the semis this season.

Since 1970 memories of Chelsea in the FA Cup fall into three categories; great victories, hard-fought exits and Oh-Christ-don't-remind-me defeats.

Who can forget Mickey Droy's double as we came back to beat Sheffield Wednesday 3-2 in 1975, Clive Walker's two against Liverpool in 1978, Peter Rhoades-Brown's first goal for about a century that helped beat the Scousers again in '82 and Kerry's four at Wigan just four years back?

Then there was Ossie's goal that wasn't enough to beat Arsenal in 1973, the epic 3-2 loss to Palace in front of 54,000 we would have won the Cup that year if we'd game in '82 (I'm still convinced we would have won the Cup that year if we'd won that day) and the ten-man fightback against Liverpool in 1986.

But they are dwarfed by memories like Orient in 1972 and 1978, Birmingham two in 1975 (they played with ten defenders and still beat us), Southampton two years later, Wigan in 1980,and those friendly boys from Cold Blow Lane in 1985. (Man United last year hardly counts. Crap as we were, at least it was a big name that knocked us out. The way we were playing, Bognor Regis would have fancied their chances.) And now Barnsley.

There is no-one to blame for all this. Ken Bates rightly pointed out we have had some rotten luck with Ted Croker's blue velvet bag recently, not being drawn at home since Liverpool in 1986. And the only person more or less constantly connected with Chelsea over the last 19 years is Peter Bonetti, and it seems a bit rough to blame him. After all, we still have to put up with people rubbishing the Cat's whole career because of one performance in Leon.

Still, there is always the chance of getting to Wembley in the Russell Grant Trophy, a tournament of such stature it makes the Simod look like the European Cup. Never mind. If the lads get through, we'll be there.

And at least the odds on us for the FA Cup should be excellent next year.

ARE YOU FIT TO BE A CHELSEA FAN ?
A QUIZ BY *MICHELLE A. BINFIELD*

A quiz to test your mettle when it comes to following the Blues. Answer the questions below and match your answers against the charts at the bottom.

1: Following our recent defeat at Bournemouth, which of the phrases below are you most likely to have uttered?

(a) 'I've heard there are quite a few nicely situated grounds in the third division';
(b) 'We'll be OK once Joe's back in the side';
(c) 'We miss Pat Nevin';
(d) 'In the light of our injury list and the bad luck we had, I don't think we should get too alarmed'.

2: Reading in your Spurs News Daily Mirror that Chelsea are to ground-share with QPR next season, what do you do?

(a) Take up watching crown green bowling;
(b) Imagine what a nice atmosphere there'll be in a smaller stadium and thrill to the fact that it's so close to the Wogan studios;
(c) Write to the Independent claiming that it would never have happened if we hadn't sold Pat;
(d) Ignore the article as coming from the pen of a brain dead Spurs fan.

3: Dobby Campbell buys Jimmy Case to 'add some necessary steel and ex-perience' to the side. Do you:-

(a) Apply for shares in the St John's Ambulance Company;
(b) Tell everyone who'll listen that Micky Hazard always did seem to get knocked off the ball too easily;
(c) Mutter 'he's no replacement for wee Patrick' and pour yourself another whisky;
(d) Thank your lucky stars that he won't be able to kick lumps out of us again.

4: Which phrase best sums up why you support Chelsea?

(a) It's cheaper than buying a cane, some handcuffs and a set of stocks, and you do have this little problem that needs rectifying....;
(b) We are a lovely side to watch and, given a year or so, we'll be back on top of Division One;
(c) Pat Nevin used to play for them (sniff! sob!);
(d) Either: 'They're *my* team', or 'Someone has to'.

5: What did you do when you heard news of Nevin's transfer?

(a) Send in your Go For Goals pledge (well, it won't cost much now, will it);
(b) Recall Kevin McAllister's goal v. WBA in the Members' Cup and remind yourself what a promising player he is;
(c) Move to Chester;
(d) Shed a tear (or two) and start praying we don't get Everton in any of the Cups.

6: If Chelsea had to adopt a new anthem, which should they choose?

(a) The theme from *Laurel and Hardy*;
(b) *So You Win Again*, by Hot Chocolate;
(c) Any Cocteau Twins record;
(d) *The Only Way Is Up* by Yazz and the Plastic Population.

Mostly a's: *'The unjustified pessimist'*. I know that supporting the most frustrating team in the land is sometimes an ordeal, but your pessimism is a bit extreme. I bet you were in heaven when we had Dublin, Wood and McLaughlin in the same side.

Mostly b's: *'The unjustifiable optimist'*. Are you naive, or just incredibly stupid? Whatever, we think you should learn to expect a wee bit less from CFC. Either that or expect quite a few disappointments.

Mostly c's: *'The Mike Ticher section'*. Your name is either Clare Grogan, Mike Ticher, or my mate Rachel Burford.

Mostly d's: You're far too sensible to be a Chelsea fan.

LUXURY FLATS IN SW6

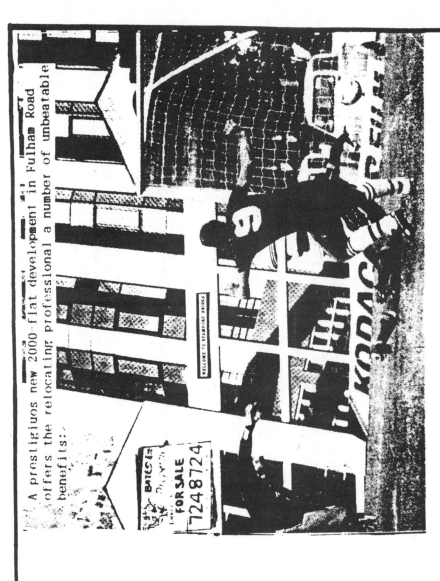

A prestigiuos new 2000-flat development in Fulham Road offers the relocating professional a number of unbeatable benefits:-

* 3 bedrooms

* all mod cons

* a large recreational area, with goal-posts for the children (access may be restricted on Saturdays)

* superb catering facilities (pity about the food !)

* interesting Edwardian public conveniences

* community singing every weekend

* extremely loud and tannoy system (including boring DJ)

* police escort to and from Fulham Broadway Underground station

* free Panini stickers !

* call Bates Estates for a mouthful

We won't be there too long

Blinking back the tears meant I didn't see much of the utterly predictable aggro after the Middlesbrough game at the Bridge.

However, I do recall dimly that the Boro fans were the first on the pitch And taunted the home fans with antics that will no doubt be forgotten when Fleet Street harks back to the latest chapter in the thick volume of Chelsea followers' misdemeanours. And weren't the police unbelievingly slow getting to the away end, and shouldn't the terrace gates have been stewarded and locked? Also I wish Sports Ministers could keep their gobs shut until they know the difference between a corner flag and a goal post, and have been to a few matches.

No matter. What remains is that we are the boys in blue in Division Two again, and who's going to bet we won't be there too long? Already we can plan ahead to the delights of trips to Oldham, Shrewsbury and jaunts by the sea at Brighton and Bournemouth. But it's going to hurt all the more because we got used to going to places like Anfield and Old Trafford. That we adapted so quickly to life in the upper echelon was yet another testament to the team that John Neal built, who went everywhere with a never-say-die attitude that made you feel you belonged with the big boys and had always been there. When you went to a party and introduced yourself as a Chelsea fan, they didn't snigger and make cheap jokes anymore. Well, o.k. they did, but you could laugh back in the knowledge that you had a team to do the business and make you proud to follow them. The team John Neal brought up in 1984 had the makings, not just to clone the mid-table antics of the likes of Southampton etc. but of a side capable of winning things. A bit of fine tuning, a judicious signing or two and we would be up there.

Three years after that first great season back in the top flight the heart has been ripped out, the indomitable spirit has gone and all that is left is the club's name, us loonies who would still love Chelsea if they played in the Vauxhall Conference, and Ken Bates. Our beloved Chairman must, of course, take a large share of blame for the unthinkable happening. He gave the best contract in English football to the wrong manager and was too proud to sack him until it was too late.

I have mixed feelings about slagging Bates. I was at a supporters' forum in December '82 at a time when Chelsea were storming down the Second Division table. Bates stood and told 200 of us Chelsea would be one of the top six sides in the land within 5 years. All 200 of us laughed. Grown men wept at the idiocy of the idea. This was, after all, the time when Mike Fillery was giving new meaning to the word idle. Yet in less than 3 years old Cap'n Birds' Eye (some relation, surely?) had made it come true. A pity he forgot to tell us the sequel.

Since then he has presided over a disastrous decline, slagged off the fans in unforgivable programme notes - like those that greeted the faithful on a rotten wet night at the Watford game - and left many suspicious about how committed he really is to the fight against the Yuppie-come-latelies who want us out of the Bridge. And John Hollins? He was John Neal's best signing of the summer '83. His spirit galvanised that new team and made them sweat blood for a blue shirt. But from sergant-major to general is a big step and Hollins simply couldn't do it. It is no secret that his man-management skills were zero. As a coach he could lead by example. As a manager he had to give orders, and I doubt that any Chelsea team, before April this season, went out with the faintest notion of tactics that would help it to score more goals than the other side.

We've been relegated with a side that we know can play football. At rare moments this season Chelsea produced skill and verve that faceless robots like Wednesday and Southampton could never dream of. But we still went down, from a First Division filled, as Bob Paisley rightly said, with some awfully average teams. Will you remember Luton, Norwich and Coventry in 12 months' time? No, but the bastards will all be going to Anfield next season.

Of course the players must take the blame too. If they had shown May's commitment during February and March we could have spent a month sun-bathing instead of watching the play-offs. But too often they seemed to release that they were wasting their energy by being played out of position. Durie, Hazard, Kevin and Clive Wilson and, criminally, Kevin, were all used in wrong positions, for most, if not all, of the season. Spackman, Speedie and Mickey Thomas have never been replaced, and our full-backs are great attackers. A pity they can't defend.

It's hard to pick out the worst day. Not winning a single London derby was bad and made for some difficult Monday mornings at work, but the manner of defeat at Arsenal, Q.P.R. and especially West Ham was painful. Being out-classed at Everton was a sobering eye-opener. Our pathetic attempt at an off-side trap being sprung by mighty Southampton at the Dell will stick in the mind, though the score will merge with all the other 3-0 hammerings. Our Cup exit at Old Trafford, a spineless collapse without a shot on target against a very ordinary United, sticks in the throat. Were we really as bad as I remember? (yes - ed.)

But Oxford was the ultimate, it summed up the season. In 30 years time when I think of 1987-88, I will think of Oxford. The opposition made Watford look like Brazil. Jesus, they made us look like Brazil in the first half when the Blues scored three super goals and it looked as if that epic record-breaking run was over. Half-time, 3-0 up against the most inept side I have ever seen, I wondered, how can we possibly balls this up? Ever up to the challenge, the lads responded magnificently and caved in to a team whose four goals that day so exhausted them that they couldn't score again for 6 games. Oxford was the day we knew we were in deep trouble.

Yet despite this catalogue of mediocrity, a season when every major test was failed and Chelsea honed their capacity for snatching a draw from the jaws of victory to a fine art - those points dropped at Charlton and Coventry - 40,000 turned up for the Middlesborough game. If the Bridge had been empty it would have been no more than the club deserved. But 40,000 turned up and the reception when the team ran out was genuinely moving. It made you wonder what would happen if Chelsea ever won anything again.

More than one person 'up north' has confessed to me this season their amazement at the size and passion of Chelsea's support. Support unrivalled in London and indeed anywhere outside Merseyside and Tyneside. What a pity that, as we all know, Chelsea seem destined never to put it together at the top level - the only possible reward for that type of support. We had a team that could have competed at this level, but now they are has-beens and so consequently the team is being broken up.

Another moment that summed up the season. Indeed the whole Hollins era, for me, came halfway through the second half at Old Trafford in the Cup. Over 10,000 Chelsea fans travelled up, (my car broke down - it took me 8 hours) and were being rewarded with a show of mind-numbing inadequacy. Suddenly everyone stood and clapped and cheered. My companion at the game, not a football expert, asked: "why the applause?" I pointed out that our subs were warming up, Pat Nevin and Nicky Hazard, the two most talented players at the club. My friend, mystified, turned and gave me the quote of the season: "So why are they on the bench?"

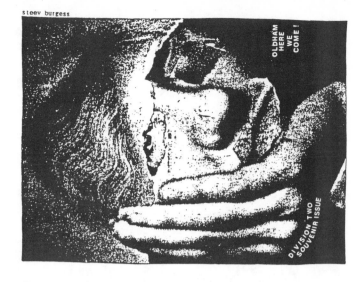

steev burgess

OLDHAM HERE WE COME!

DIVISION TWO SOUVENIR ISSUE

THOSE PROGRAMME BLOOMERS –
Colin Pension's Top 10 Mistakes

1. v. Blackburn – Check out that 'Blackburn' badge – it's Blackpool! Nice one Colin.

2. v. Leicester – *Bridge Banter*(!) happily informs us that Clive Wilson is to make his 50th appearance for the Blues that evening. Sorry Colin, Clive was suspended after his sending-off at Barnsley.

3. v. Walsall & Leicester – Swindon tickets £4.50? Come off it, Col, I paid £4 for mine.

4. v. Blackburn – It's *Bridge Banter* again, this time telng us that Ian Porterfield scored the winning goal in the 1978 Cup Final. That'll come as some surprise to Roger Osborne!

5. v. Leicester – Great Games From The Past rewrites history as Chelsea beat Leicester 3-2 in the 1985 League Cup Final.

6. v. Man City – the long-serving Norman Medhurst becomes Norman Meadhurst. What a send-off.

7. v. Leicester – turn to page 30, those wonderful statistics. Bearing in mind that the goalscorers are printed in bold type, check out the Barnsley game. Yes, we beat them 10-1! Hands up if you left before the end.

8. v. Leicester – that invaluable list of kit sponsors still includes the retired Steve Vicks. Ian, David and Kevin should have their money back.

9. v. Blackburn – page 27 welcomes hordes of Lancastrians to the Bridge and asks them to remain calm at the end of the match 'for, although the ground may appear empty there could still be considerable congestion in the Fulham Road.'

10. The price. £1 – surely the biggest mistake of all.

ANYBODY WHO went to Germany this year for the European Championships will have noticed the wildly exaggerated claims made by the English media. Combine this with the "riot" at the 'Boro game and the Government has the perfect excuse to impose a 100 per cent membership scheme.

Yet the facts of the European Championships are these:–

* Of 300 English fans arrested. only 29 – less than 10 per cent – were charged with an offence.
* Over 800 Germans were arrested during the two weeks.

The German police have different approaches to trouble – their tactic is to sweep up any potential trouble before it gets out of hand, meaning that more people are arrested than in this country. The offender is then kept inside for a few hours before being released.

It is also disturbing to note that several journalists were offering groups of fans money to start fights.

Over 20 companies have now written to Colin Moynihan. the Minister for Sport, suggesting ways of issuing identity cards. The scheme which is due to start in time for the 1989-90 season, following Parliamentary legislation. will cost anywhere between £2 million and £20 million. Those most affected will, of course, be those who do not attend regularly – the likely result is that the "floating fan" will be scared off and attendances will fall.

The national membership scheme will also involve the computerisation of every turnstile in the country – the likelihood of such big names as Halifax. Crewe. Chester City etc being able to afford this looks grim. Soon after the introduction of the scheme. such clubs could fold – clearly, the only institutions which will be able to afford supporting the idea will be the "Big Five".

Of course, you will still be able to travel away, but with Luton's ban on away fans proving popular with the Government. and the latter's interference (can they really deny it?) with the FA inquiry into the 'Boro game. it seems likely to me that a "home-only" situation will arise within a couple of years.

A national membership scheme for football is the first step in a National ID programme. Already the Government is experimenting with ID cards for pubs. allegedly to crack down on under-age drinkers and violence. What price. by 1990. a curfew to go with your card – I suppose the streets will be safe!

Such schemes are not far off. The only way to stop them is at the beginning – say NO now to the national membership scheme. Every supporter should write to his or her local MP. telling him or her that supporters should be consulted and that supporters' representatives be co-opted onto the Government's working party. which now only includes members from Government, police. the FA and the Football League. WE are the people who put more money into the game than any of the so-called sponsors (over £60 million through the turnstiles last season). It is the majority of well-behaved supporters who will pay the price for the actions of a few.

The London branch of the Football Supporters Association will be taking further action to quell the authorities. To find out more go to the FSA's next meeting on the first Thursday of the month. the University of London Union. Malet Street, WC1.

NICK BROWN

AN AFTERNOON IN THE COUNTRY (CENSORED VERSION)

Here is a story of old I shall tell
Of three Chelsea geezers called Twigs, Baz and Del
One day we proceeded to Norwich away
Where most of the locals looked dodgy or gay.
They wore sensible shoes and flasks of tea
And also flared trousers that swung at the knee.
In Norwich, the country air was breezy and rich
Then a donkey called Joe led the Blues on the pitch,
The game did commence at a frantic old pace,
There was no Nicky Hazard, so no one found space.
I thought that the first half wasn't that good
But what can you expect with players like wood.
In the second half of the game. the goals just went in
One bloke said "My season ticket's straight for the bin".
As we sat there dejected, sad, pissed off and bored
Some prat announced the time that each goal was scored,
We had come all this way to this poxy old hole,
And we hadn't even managed an effort on goal,
How we lost to these farmers I really don't know,
So we all cried together – "Hollins must go"
We had every right to complain. moan and whine
Because Norwich were unlucky not to get nine,
After the match we headed for the train,
The feeling was mutual. never again,
How poor Nicky Hazard was not in the team,
And we want the greatest. yeah we want the cream,
We won't go again if our best player won't stay,
But we already have tickets for Derby away.

Derek Carpenter, Peckam.

(Pity about the heterosexism, but a nice effort nonetheless)

CHELSEA FANS have given their verdict on the Sun's recent telephone poll by giving owner Rupert Murdoch this message:

BOG-- OFF

The vote on your super soaraway Independent's Sun Crisisline was 100-1 in favour of the antipodean newspaper magnate being thrown into Sydney Harbour with lead weights tied to his ankles.

The Crisisline 'phones never started ringing as thousands of loyal Blues fans tried to contact us, only to find we'd taken the phone off the hook.

Originally, we aimed to canvass the views of SUN JOURNALISTS on the merits of Murdoch and his editor Kelvin MacKenzie, but an incredible 100% could not master the use of the telephone, lending credence to speculation that all their stories are made up in the pub.

Taking a leaf from the Sun's book, we made up our own SENSATIONAL results:

* An AMAZING 99% of you agreed that a 6,000 year old fossilized dog turd could produce a more informative, less biased paper than Mackenzie;
* A stilll more MIND BOGGLING 1% thought that even Colin Benson could do a better job;
* An UNBELIEVABLE 100% of Chelsea fans agreed with the proposition that Rupert Murdoch's TESTICLES should be wired into the NATIONAL GRID. 99% of you offered to do it!!
* A STATISTICALLY IMPOSSIBLE 104% of you phoned in to tell us that you don't exist!!!!

And the critics were unanimous in telling Murdoch how he should run his 'newspaper'. Frank, who stands in the Shed every week, even when there's no game, told us: "I think Murdoch should allow the workers to take control of the nespaper so it reflects the popular will of the masses and can play a serious role in bringing about world socialism."

Sid, a loyal Blues fan of two minutes standing, exclaimed: "Murdoch should swallow twenty-five kilograms of swarfega, and then bog-off.".

One thing is for sure — Chelsea fans say MURDOCH MUST GO.

PAUL CANOVILLE : A TRIBUTE

I write to you so that you may give a mention to a former Chelsea player who has had to quit the game because of injury, Paul Canoville. Despite his efforts in a four year spell at Chelsea the action packed Bridge News and Club Programme could not spare even a small col umn as a tribute.

Any self-respecting Chelsea fan will remember, with disgust, his one minute debut when he came on as sub at Crystal Palace to a chorus of boos, hisses and racist chants, from his own fans - he had the misfortune of being Chelsea's first black player. But who could forget how the idiots suddenly forgot he was black when he scored soon after at Fulham and estabilished himself on the left wing, even scoring a hat-trick against Swansea in a 6-1 victory to firmly estabilish himself as a crowd favourate.

After we won promotion he made more memorable performances, for me the pick being the opening day of the 84/85 season and the roasting he gave Viv Anderson at Highbury, followed 6 days latter by the kicking he gave John 'muppet' Bailey of Everton in a televised match! But his greatest moment came in the Milk Cup match at Sheffield Wednesday on January 30th 1985 when he stepped off the bench to inspire Chelsea's revival after trailing 3-0 at half-time, only for Dougie to wreck his finest moment with a typically non-sensical lunge at an oppanant. Nevertheless will we ever forget his triumphant sprint to the half way line after scoring our fourth goal.

Although he occassionally showed a remarkable resemblance in style to Clive Walker in that he could outpace three defenders only for his cross to land in the Fulham Road, he was a good servant to Chelsea with a never-say-die attitude. Would it now be too much to ask Chelsea to stage a benefit match to help him out now that his career has ended so prematurely?

Kelvin Barker
Shepherds Bush.

Thanks for your letter Kelvin - I remember Paul as a player who was gifted with a tremendous talent, a talent Chelsea never managed to fully develop. A trait that is sadly all too evident at the club now (said to give me the opportunity to talk about Roy Wergle). Considering we have twice had the player on our books he hasobviously impressed somewhere, and judging from his limited appearances on the pitch I can see why. He possesses amazing talent and one day will score THE BEST GOAL YOU WILL EVER SEE - as he finally beats that sixth man and rifles in a 30 yard shot. Perhaps his unwillingness to shackle down to a set role, i.e. defend, has caused Bobby Cambell to think that he can afford to let Chelsea's most gifted player go. I find that depressing and a parallel to the fate of Paul Canoville.

So why don't the Club play Reading as a pre-season friendly, with the gate given to Paul?

THE 1987/88 SEASON ENCAPSULATED

OXFORD AT HALF TIME

OXFORD AT FULL TIME

GREAT GAMES FROM THE PAST.   NUMBER 2

Chelsea v. Middlesborough - Graham's Goal.

I'm sure most readers will remember Graham Wilkins with affection, a player who delighted in trying to dribble the ball out of his own penalty area. In my memory he is permanently identified with the glorious 1978-79 season, when as you will recall Chelsea menaged to record all of 5 victories. Five. Count 'em. 1-0 away at Wolves, 4-3 home to Bolton (Flashers match), 3-2 away at Man City, and 2-1 at home to Birmingham were the first four, the last two inspiring foolhardy hopes of achieving 21st position at Easter. By the time it got round to the fifth win however, we were well and truly down.

Glamourous opponents on April 21st 1979 were Middlesborough, a team that already had put seven past Chelsea that season, and 12,000 die-hards, their senses numbed by a season of inconceivable incompetence, were at the Bridge ready for more humiliation. This was the year, don't forget, when that immortal combination of; Nutton, Sitton, Bannon and Britton had led us to such triumphs as 0-6 at Nottingham Forest. For some reason I got to the ground about 10 minutes late, and finding the Shed closed, had to stand in splendid isolation under the score board at the away end, the smattering of Boro' fans collecting in the pen by the East Stand. This was unfortunately to deny me a clear view of the glorious event.

As I recall, Gary Stanley put us ahead, only for Boro' to equalise. It began to look as though the familiar pattern of defeat was about to be followed. But midway through the second half, the ball came to Graham, on the right hand edge of the Boro' area - not wishing to take the chance of controlling it with that immaculate left foot, he shot first time with his right, and the ball sped past the keeper into the bottom corner, almost as if it were going were intended. Pandemonium! For the first and only time the cry went up, "Theres only one Graham Wilkins". Twelve thousand people muttered simultaneously "Thank Christ".

Later in the game Chelsea were awarded a penalty. Surely the impossible couldn't happen twice in one game, that Graham Wilkins would score and we would win by two goals? Hysteria all around the ground, people fainting and crying, the more restrained of us making desperate mental notes of how we would tell our grand children. Surely it was too much to ask? It was. Langley, ever reliable from the spot missed. But still, we had had enough excitement for one day.

For the record that was not the only goal Graham scored in his career at Chelsea. I remember well how he deftly turned a cross into his own net, for the winner, in the 89th minute of a game with West Ham two years later. However, his goal for us will live long in the memory. They were bleak years, but men of Graham's talent did their best to liven them up. Where would we have been without them to give us a good laugh every week? Isn't it about time the ninth Wilkins' brother was given a run out in the youth team?

Mike Ticher

WHEN SUNDAY COMES
ISSUE 2   AUGUST 1988
40 PENCE

UGLY

Inside THE Liverpool fanzine
Craig Johnstone Cup Shock
Super League And......More

the magazine was started because loads of others were and it was something i wanted to do there are no real problems at anfield, but the amount our fixtures are mucked about with is a pretty large pain, i also try and point out anything that is wrong and i hope to entertain people, i also print all letters and articles i'm sent, unless i don't like them and there are quite a few different views in it these days. not much more to say really, read the examplesand send me your money.

WHEN SUNDAY COMES

ISSUE 3 OCT 1988 40 PENCE

IAN WHO?

LIVERPOOL SIGN UNKNOWN WELSH DUSTMAN

INSIDE: Loads more out of date stuff

MAGAZINE TITLE: When Sunday Comes

EDITORS NAME: Ian Tilley

AGE: 20 (21 on 10/5/68)   **OCCUPATION:** Clerical Assistant.

DO YOU/HAVE YOU EVER SUPPORTED ANY OTHER TEAM?
I like to watch Woking struggling to get out of the Vauxhall Opel Div.1.

MOST MEMORABLE MATCH EVER: lots, err "84 European Cup Final, one since
I started going '88 FA Cup Final . BAD memories.

MOST MEMORABLE SEASON: all time predictable - 1987/88.

ALL TIME FAVOURITE PLAYER: I love them all?? Peter Beardsley.

WHAT SORT OF CAR DO YOU DRIVE? NONE.

YOUR FAVOURITE MUSIC: The Undertones, The Wedding Present, The Ramones.

FILMS/TV: Gregory's Girl, American Werewolf, Footie, even the watch, Smith + Jones.

FAVOURITE CLOTHES: Snorkel Parka, Pullover, T-shirt, Jeans, D.m's.

POLITICAL LEANINGS: anyone who seems to be doing it for someone else.

WHAT PLAYER WOULD YOU MOST LIKE TO SEE PLAYING FOR ENGLAND (SCOTLAND/WALES IF RELEVANT)?

I wouldn't mind seeing anyone actually playing for England, especially John Barnes.

How about Neville Southall?

Seriously, Gary Ablett's gonna be good, hang on? is he English??

SKIPPY GOES HOME

AS CRAIG JOHNSTON LEAVES FOR AUSTRALIA, HERE'S A TRIBUTE TO ONE OF MY FAVOURITE PLAYERS

I was looking forward to the Cup Final, hoping Nigel Spackman and Gary Gillespie would both be fit, especially Gary - not the world's luckiest man, and wondering whether Mr.Dalglish would pick Jan Molby or Ronnie Whelan to sit next to Craig on the substitute's bench. Then one morning a few days before the game, I'd been at work a little while, and Eddie placed the paper on my desk, and it told me Craig was going back to Australia.

When I started to go along to games Craig became my favourite player. He was really exciting to watch, not short on skill, and gave 100% everytime, he fully deserved the glory of scoring what was effectively the winner in the 1986 F.A.Cup Final. Bob Paisley summed up my feelings in his book, with the following text.

1,2,3,4....Craig Johnston knows the score.

....

Craig is very much a crowd pleaser. They admire his industry, his courage and his dedication to the cause. They enjoy his turns and his drag - backs and his dribbles. They can identify with him and his feelings for Liverpool Football Club. You would think he had grown up on The Kop judging by the effort and eagerness that spill out of him every Saturday afternoon.
Most players hate running, the hard graft of chasing up and down for 90 minutes. Craig loves it, he's like one of those toys with the long-life batteries, you just switch him on, put him on the pitch and watch him go, and he's still going strong when the other batteries have long since run out. He's the proverbial 110·per center, a very strong and single minded character, he certainly puts his heart and soul into that number 8 shirt every weekend and you can ask no more than that of any player.

....

Craig used to pull on the Red shirt of Liverpool with such pride, realising the great honour being bestowed upon him. It seems however, that Craig pulled on the famous Red for the last time in Alan Hansen's testemonial, and his last goals were in the 5-1 win at Sheffield Wednesday on May 7th.

Craig issued this short statement just a few days before the Cup Final.

"I have fallen out of love with football, I have started to hate some aspects of it and I know this is the right decision for me and my family."

Craig has twice before stated a desire to leave Anfield, but it seems that this time the situation will not be resolved, the frustration of not being able to hold down a regular place could be a major factor in this.

It was debateable as to whether or not Craig was suffering a loss in form, but when Ray Houghton arrived from Oxford, he was no longer a regulsr, and had to settle for any shirt he could get, all to often this was the 12 or 14.

From now on it will be the shirt of an Australian photographer that Craig wears, and i'm not glad to see him go.

In all Craig Johnston played 272 times for Liverpool, although too many of these were as a substitute. In this time he scored surprisingly few goals, just 40 all told. But some of them were priceless. (ask Mr. Mimms).

GOODBYE AND GOOD LUCK.

YOU WILL BE GREATLY MISSED.   CHEERS THEN

IsupportLiverpool,myNumber is...

Was it a government ploy, or just coincidence? Just as we were about to get seriously wound up about everyone having to join a national membership scheme, the "Super League" debate comes along and we forget all about it. It may have risen to the surface again by now, but at the time of writing it seems to have sunk, so here's a few lines to refresh your memories.

The idea seems to be that everyone will have to show their "Football League Membership Card" to gain entry to games, and this is of course going to stop taxi drivers dying from heart attacks brought on by hooligans in Mediterranean resorts. A major flaw in the plan is that it is such a major infringement on civil liberties. Could it lead to "Waitrose Supermarkets Membership Cards" with convicted shoplifters having theirs confiscated? And then there's Mr.Smith down the road who only goes to The Mersey Derbies, it's a bit of a pain in the neck for him so he may not bother anymore. And how is someone as forgetful as The Princess of Wales going to remember where she put her card? When Cup Final day comes around. What happens when that Non League side just down the road from Leeds gets drawn away to Wolves in the Cup? (how's that for media bias). Will non members be able to get in the away end? Or your average fan forgets his card because he had to rush to the game? Many of us have forgotten our season tickets before. How are they going to check 50,000 cards at the big games anyway?

It may stop some people from travelling to games if they know they may not be able to get in, but there are ways around most things, people still go to Luton (including some Luton fans), and when Chelsea were banned a few years back stadiums rang to the chorus of "We're not here, we're not here, we're not here". The hooligan will certainly still cause problems outside grounds, especially if he travels and can't get in, and in case you didn't realise the majority of problems are outside the grounds anyway.so all that happens is more hassle for the real fans.

You see Mrs.Thatcher, hooliganism is societies problem, not footballs.

THE SECRET OF SUCCESS

Over the last few seasons much has been written about the secret of Liverpool's continued success. Most of these theories, however, have been as wide of the mark as a Brian McClair penalty, but now, for the first time, the real truth can be revealed.

The hypothesis about to be outlined is not the result of years of research by eminent professors of psychology, nor has it been reached by endless hours of studying videos of every Liverpool match (or watching Match of the Day Live - same thing really !). It was instead formulated simply by looking at any team photo from the last ten years.

Liverpool's triumphs are due singularly to the sheer ugliness of their team. When Alex Ferguson recently ranted about intimidation at Anfield, he was not referring to any actions by the crowd or any physical contact on the pitch but was instead incensed by the overwheming revulsion his players had felt in being confronted by the most daunting collection of human disfigurement seen in public since Slade last appeared on Top of the Pops.

The jewel in Liverpool's crown was undoubtedly one Ian Rush Esq., a man so hideous he would cause opposing centrebacks to literally vomit before matches at the prospect of having to closely mark him, and here was the reason for the man's apparernt devastating pace. What defender was going to be in any sort of state to sprint having recently puked their raw steak all over the dressing room floor.

On Rushes departure as a peace offering to Juventus (recent reports from Italy talk of severe problems with stadiums being flooded with half digested spagetti) Liverpool were left with the almost impossible task of replacing him. They first went for the obvious remedy of commissioning Madame Tussaud's to consruct an identical replica of Rush which subsequently arrived but like most waxworks John Aldridge suffered from a severe lack of mobility and first touch control.

Not daunted by this early setback the unrivaled Liverpool scouts finally came up trumps when in the back streets of Newcastle they came across the Geordie answer to Quasimodo in Peter Beardsley. Beardsley, a man so dedicated to his task he actually had his teeth removed in an effort to increase his undoubted ugliness.

Paul Walsh...
    Wasn't ugly enough?

The inability to reach these exacting standards has been the downfall of many a good player at the club. For instance, Paul Walsh, a fine striker at Luton and by no means an oil painting himself, in struggling to establish himself sported some of the most ludicrous hair cuts in history in an attempt to worsen his physical appearance but all in vain and he had to resign himself to the fact that he would never be grotesque enough and left for pastures new.

Other clubs have tried the same policy to a lesser extent, and not without success, surely it is no coincidence that Chelsea's brief flirtation with the upper reaches of the First Division corresponded with Doug Rougvie's presence in the team, and indeed Brighton's promotion challenge must have been aided in no small amount by his appointment as their captain. Surely the effect he must have on the referee at the toss-up is worthy of an official protest by opposing clubs.

The great Leeds team of the early 70's appeared to possess much the same philosophy as Liverpool with players such as Billy Bremner, Eddie Gray and - well, the whole team really if

CONTINUED OVER

the truth be told. However, seeds of doubt as to whether the ugliness of Don Revie's team was intentional or not were sown in many minds by his famous "no sex on the night before a match" ruling - as if there was any likelyhood! Also who could forget Nobby Stiles and the part he played in England's World Cup Winning side, in spite of German protests that he should be outlawed under the Geneva convention.

So until there is a radical change of approach from the other clubs Liverpool's domination will continue. Watford's solution to the problem, by playing 11 blind players so they could not witness the horrors of the Merseyside team appears not to have paid off this season, perhaps they should have returned to useing sighted players against the rest of the opposition . The only way for the other clubs appears to be to play Liverpool at their own game and to search the back streets and basement bars for their own sorry speciman of human facial abomination.

For some reason the authors of this article wish to remain anonymous, however michael and paul did assure me that they know nothing of the article in "Off The Ball" Issue 10 that this one bears a remarkable resemblance to, it is new to them, and hopefully to many of our readers.

1274   LIVERPOOL - THE LEAN YEARS   1986

Although the records are pretty sketchy, it can be safely assumed that Liverpool did not win anything during the 1274/1275 season.

Attendances were low, as most supporters did not know where the ground was, and since the death of Thomas Aquinas half way through the season, Mercantile Ye Credite, a local company, had withdrawn its support. So from being the Crown Prince of clubs, Liverpool dripped to a mere matt of their former gloss, and the whole staff had to eat candy. The captain of the side at that time, one Kenneth of D'g'l'sh senior and a man of few words, does state in his aftermatch journal that, "Eeh...". Unfortunately, historians have failed to discover the meaning of this word, despite intense archeological, psychological, neurological and Jim Rosenthal and so can only assume that it conveys that 'Sick as a liverbird. Over the moan. Taking each Hanseatic League match as it comes effect that we now know so well.

Throughout the following 710 seasons, Liverpool did manage to plummet to second place on a number of occasions (one), but not until 1985/86 did the team find itself in unheard of territory. Due to the world accidently falling off its axis, Liverpool were in second place behind Everton on 21st February 1986, but true to history, they sauntered past their local rivals to take their 708th title, and despite a close victory over Norwich in the FA Cup 3rd round, they took the pitch in the final after an hour's play, to overcome them again, in a rush. The season ended in disappointment however, as a solitary double was achieved and the League Cup, now sponsored by some large trees, evaded their grasp. Two dubious, outside the penalty area, blatantly biased, offside, own goals contributed to their overall defeat. Q.P.R., shocked by this gift, failed to turn up for the Final and Oxford finally won more than a canoe slalom.

Despite losing again this light year, Liverpool are once more the team to lose to, and are striving for the 'Quintoquadagintillion', another record in terms of One followed by 138 zeros, 1000000000000000000000000000000000000000 000000000000000000000000000000000000000000000000000000000000000000000000000000000 00000000000000000000000 trophies.

No doubt Kenneth of D'g'l'sh senior would appreciate the comment made by his canny descendant in reply to that age old question, "What is the Liverpoolsecret?", when the current incumbent intoned, "Eeh..."

Nuff(ink) said.

'WE ONLY SING WHEN WE'RE WINNING'

The Kop...It's all gone quiet over there.

If Mirandinha is given stick for the darkness of his skin, then Barnes is really in for a hard time isn't he. Probably not, but only because he's wearing a Liverpool shirt. Most of these racists are fickle and inconsistent - part timers. They can be silenced, so don't just stand there, say something.

All mankind are equal. Racism is sick and unfunny, tell the racist near you how wrong they are, and you should get through. If the Kop becomes intelligent and fair minded about this one I shall be impressed.

POLICE WHO HAVEN'T A CLUE

A special mention to whoever was in charge for both the games at West Ham United, if anyone was, after the League game we went over the pitch, through the main stand, and ended up with the home fans, hardly reassuring. The Cup game brought a journey home trying to dodge the helicopter searchlight, escape from London? They decided to use metal detectors as well, Mark's keys and coins aren't made of metal, interesting. I guess there's only one way to deal with crowds of hooligans, what about football fans, better organisation wouldn't be a bad idea, a constable was gestured by a superior to open the second exit, after the fans had been suggesting he do so for a few minutes.

P.S. Rather a dissapointing result in the cup as well.

Many of the bad points I make about the Kop here are common to all football crowds, a few are unfortunately unique to this home terracing. Many of the points will only refer to the middle third of the Kop, and perhaps the lesser half of this, but this is where most of the "noise" comes from.

I had been told, like everyone else, of the legend that was 'The Kop', so when I first went to Anfield I made straight for the most famous part of the ground. I wanted to savour the great atmosphere at the centre of the Kop, the crowd surges, the endless defeaning chanting, striking fear into all opposing teams. I wanted to stand amongst one of the most intelligent, fair minded and humourous crowds to be found at any football ground.

Something was wrong, it would have been an effort to find any atmosphere to talk of, and far worse than that, a perverse sense of humour, and often fair minded only when Liverpool were winning. Worse of all, racism was abundant, I was not aware that I was to expect this more in Liverpool than in many other places.

Eventually I became too frustrated with the constant pushing, and the lie that this was something special. (I'm also dead short and couldn't see anything). I moved to the left, near the back, there's plenty of room and a good view, now I observe the centre of the Kop, and do not associate myself with it. So what observations have I made?

UGLY RACISM

You'd have thought that the arrival of John Barnes would at least shut up the racists (and get rid of those that really meant it), but even if some people stopped going, others still thought it funny, and of course lots of mindless idiots still join in. My case in point, this season, Liverpool v Newcastle United, a young Brazilian, Francisco Ernandi Lima da Silva, scores in front of the Kop, he gestures to the Kop, Johnny Barnes is injured, so he's not playing, and the chanting starts, 'You Black ...I wonder if his parents weren't married, anyway, how Barnes felt sitting in the main stand I don't know, I guess Mirandinha was confused, he must surely be the lightest 'black' person ever to appear at Anfield.

ACTING BADLY

Seeing as I got a rather gut-turning picture I thought I'd go into detail on a point that could go in the yet more examples bit. Millwall played some decent stuff at Anfield, and picked up a couple of nasty injuries, an example is on your right. How did the Kop act when Ian Dawes lay injured shortly before being carried off? Well I may (not) surprise you that it wasn't too clever. Or is "Who's the actor in the blue?" funny?

Could Liverpool lose their fair play title?

'MUNICH'

I'll probably do a whole article about this in the next Issue, but for now...I'm told this chant only began about 10 years ago, and from my experience I hope it has gone through a peak. It goes beyond having a go at the fans of one of the teams you want Liverpool to beat the most. How would someone feel if they'd lost a close relative in the Zeebrugge disaster, and someone came up and started telling jokes about second hand lorries falling off the backs of ferries. It's not funny is it, 'ha, ha missis, your son just fell under a train'. The Munich air crash saw wives and children lose husbands and fathers, and parents back home were told of their sons deaths.

Hardly something to joke about or taunt with, if the Manchester United fans do start by taunting the Liverpool fans with 'Shankly 81', surely the reply should be to chant 'Shankly' back, they must dream of ever getting a manager that good/successful.

MORE TALES OF STUPIDITY

Could be a bit of a list this, firstly we have the inability to decide whether or not a player is liked, I don't mind people slagging off players, as long as they don't decide they like them when they score, for me, no one could replace Craig, and no one plays for Liverpool if they haven't got some ability. There also seems to be a poor knowledge of London, I used to think that only West Ham were cockneys, it now seems the bow bells can be heard in Wimbledon and Watford. It's like calling someone from Birkenhead a Liverpudlian. Of course it is becoming embarrassing the number of times that the away fans out-sing the Kop, but they add silliness to injury, with their sarcastic applause. I never thought I'd hear 'You're not singing anymore' quiter than those that it was being sung to, but the Kop managed it against Millwall, or was it Middlesbrough, or.. I always manage to stand in front of those with limited vocabularies, I'm sure swearing can be avided, even in the heat of the moment. The appeals for penalties are well known, but don't miss the more obvious ones. Why only cheer for the opposing team when their goalie runs to the Kop, how about when they come out, at least good play doesn't go unnoticed. So how about a bit more noise, as I write, the day after the 4-1 at West Ham they really need it, there seems to be enough noise at away games, don't tell me the London Reds are louder.

Dear Mr. Tilley,

Thank you for your letter requesting permission to sell your football magazine on InterCity trains.

I regret to inform you that you are not allowed to sell this magazine on my scheduled InterCity trains or any relief service thereto.

I have no control over the activities undertaken on trains chartered by individual football clubs and you should approach those organisations should you wish to operate on these trains.

Yours sincerely,

R.J. SANDERS.
Area Passenger Manager.

Ed. The story behind this one, thrown off the train for breaking all kind of sub and bye-laws, and plenty of BR rules, I guess selling a magazine is pretty way out behaviour. Although this particular guard wasn't half a rotter.

LIVERPOOL FC 1992

JAN MOLBY - Has not been available for all the season as he has achieved a life-
times' ambition in winning the RAC rally, closely followed by Merseyside Police.

IAN RUSH - Sold to Juventus for £8 Million in the 1990 season and repurchased
for £100, 000. (Terry Venables, who is now celebrating his second season in
charge of Juventus says "Life is not as easy as they said it would be in the
Italian 3rd Division North").

GARY ABLETT and JOHN ALDRIDGE have both retired after becoming involved in one
of Liverpool FC's greatest footballing moments during the Simod Cup Northern
Section 3rd Round Qualifying tie, when Ablett hit a 40 yard ball down the line
and Aldo controlled it first time!

   The career of ALAN HANSEN is still on a knife edge and the club are hoping
his 92nd knee operation will be a success.

   JOHN BARNES and BRUCE GROBBELAAR have had a busy season on the international
front. Barnes has just returned from England's crunch World Cup qualifying tie
in Afghanistan (where we achieved a great I - I draw) and England's manager,
Barry Hearn Enterprises was quoted as saying "John has the potential to produce
the goods in an England shirt, but we must be patient". Let's hope his 200th
appearance for England next month will be the turning point. Bruce has also just
returned from being on duty for his country - Zimbabwe are at war with South
Africa and Bruce is recognised as one of the great commanders (not of the penalty area!)

   STEVE McMAHON is facing a court room battle with the lawyer of a Mr. N.
Whiteside from Manchester who claims that Steve's tackle was high, McMahon totally refutes the claim. (PS Whiteside leaves hospital next week and doctors say
he should soon be able to remove the collar on his neck!)

   RON WHELAN, who this season scored a hat-trick in the last five minutes to
win the Reds the Milk Cup at Wembley is the season's leading goalscorer with 3.

   PETER BEARDSLEY - is still performing solidly at right back in Dalglish's new
IO man containing away team formation although modelling committments have cur-
tailed his appearances.

   STEVE NICOL - has moved to Rangers being purchased by Graeme Souness for £I5
and an exchange deal involving Gary Stevens total fee estimated £I5, 000, 000 -
(Stevens has since been transfered to Everton in an exchange deal for JIM BEGLIN,
his leg actually, which was left in the dressing room the last time he played
at Goodison).

   RAY HOUGHTON - recovering in hospital after putting the proverbial IIO% into
a game for the first time, KENNY DALGLISH is in the next bed, recovering from
the shock of Houghton trying for once.

   BARRY VENISON breaks down in tears during training, claiming that he simply
can't face 40,000 people after the mess the barber made of his perm, he is told
to have it cut short as he did when the same thing happened in I989.

P.S. I am really a Liverpool supporter, but if you can't take the mick out of your
own team, then who can you? Answer, Everton, Man. Utd, Forest, Wimbledon etc.

                                                          Cheers, Mark Jeffery

The Merseyside FSA has a bevvy with Bob Paisley

   Sorry to bring you this report so long after the event, but here is an
example of what The F.S.A. gets up to.

                              Merseyside F.S.A. branch meeting 14/3/88
Guests: Mr. Sid Moss and Mr. Bob Paisley. Liverpool F.C.

   Branch information and dealings were kept very much to a minimum in order
to ensure that our two guests were to be allowed as much time as they needed
to address the Branch, but those issues that were raised were of some
importance, we wrote letters to all three local League clubs, Tranmere
Rovers, Liverpool and Everton asking them to give us details about selling
arrangements for away matches, a complaint had been received from a member
complaining that when they tried to buy tickets for certain away matches
they were told that they weren't on sale at that particular time, but the
next time they tried, all tickets for that particular game had been received
and sold , so we asked the clubs if they wouldn't mind giving us some idea
of when they receive their allocation and up to what time do they sell them.

Liverpool Echo 11/2/88

Another matter that was brought up was the trouble outside Goodison Park and the surrounding area during the Everton verses Middlesbrough F.A. Cup replay, which resulted in one fan being slashed across the face and almost losing his eyesight, a couple of days later on, after he had had emergency treatment at a local Hospital, he was visited by a member of the Merseyside Branch who is also an Everton Supporter, and was made aware of our best wishes for him. The result of this incident is that the Branch have now written to Merseyside Police asking them if they would like to send a member of the force along to explain their policy of Policing night matches.

The branch also sent a letter of thanks via Liverpool City Solicitor Mr. Harry Livermore to the anonymous businessman who put up the bail for the remaining defendants in the Heysel trial.

A letter of complaint was also sent to Manchester City, after their poor handling of both travel and seating arrangements at the F.A.Cup 6th Round Tie between Man. City and Liverpool at Maine Road, people travelling by coach were stopped 2 miles out from the ground and forced to walk the remainder of the way in torrential rain, as if this wasn't enough they then found that when they got to the ground they were left to find their own way to their seats, as there was no sign of any Stewards, this meant that people were left to find a seat where ever they could, regardless of what row or seat number was on their ticket, this included families, as well as groups.

Once we had dealt with this business it was on to the main part of the evening, the first to speak was Sid Moss, who is a member of the board of Directors, he gave us a brief insight to how the Club works: There are 8 Directors, which include the Club's Solicitor, Mr. Tony Ensor, and the Accountant Mr. Corkish, he then went on to explain that each member of the board has specific duties within the club, and it can cost a fair amount of money, so a sort of general warning to anyone who is on, or was thinking of joining, the board at their local club. Beware, there are alot of overheads, and in Liverpool's case these are very high, because of this he said, not many people are in it for the money. We were then told in slightly more detail than in the past about how they discovered the hole in The Kop. Some years ago, when it became compulsary to make safety checks on the grounds, Liverpool were the first club to receive a Certificate of Safety, but rather than leave it at that, they then went on to make sure that they tested the Crush Barriers around the ground more regularly than they normally have to, he explained that they have a Strain Machine which thay put on the Barriers and test them like that, this time as usual, they tested one or two that had been standing for a few years longer than the others, but while they stood the test it was felt wiser to place new ones at certain points around the Kop, when they set about this they started to drive a pile into the ground in order to strengthen it for the barrier but the pile just completely vanished from sight so upon further investigation it was discovered that there was a sewer running right through the Kop, and that it was washing the ground away underneath, and that the whole lot could have collapsed at any time at all during the season, causing great catastrophe and a horrifying loss of life. The rest of the story has been well told elsewhere, but while the work was going on 24 hours a day Liverpool F.C. were served with a writ from a nearby resident who had complained about the constant noise and disturbance, some people from the club went to see her to try to get her to change her mind, but she wouldn't, but in between her complaining and the writ being served she went away on holiday, therefore giving them just enough time to continue until she got back, by just working during the day in which time the Club could just about manage to complete the work within the time the Football League had allowed them.

After a short break it was the turn of Bob Paisley, he told us that he had guided Kenny Dalglish along from his early playing days with Liverpool, right up to the present and his decision to go into management. He was then asked if he thought that the present Liverpool team was more defensive than any of the past teams, he said that it wasn't really anymore defensive than any other team in the past, that it just seemed that way, "A team's still got to balance no matter what style they play, It's still very much a team game, that aspect hasn't altered, it's just that it might seem as though the game has gone more defensive."

Once again he reiterated his claim that the present First Division was not as strong as it had been in the past, and that it could do with cutting down a bit, he was then asked what he thought about the Leeds United team of the early 70's and the Liverpool team of today. "Leeds were a team full of good individuals, where as this present Liverpool team are a real team, in as much as they all play to each other and not to one particular player", when he was asked about the sweeper system, and whether or not it was his or Kenny Dalglish's idea, he was a bit cagey, and he wouldn't really say whose idea it was, all he would say was that "Kenny always knew who he was playing against", as if to say that Kenny Dalglish played the sweeper system only against certain teams , and when or if he knew it would work. Next came the almost inevitable question "Would you make a move for Ian Rush if he was to become available again?" Once again he never went into too much detail but said that he thought the board would listen very closely to any proposition concerning the possible transfer, and that Liverpool still have the option of first refusal if he should ever consider returning to England again. "How did your being left out of the 1950 F.A. Cup Final affect your decisions later in life as a Manager, when you had to make the same sort of choice yourself?" "That stood me in good stead later on in life, especially when it was my turn to leave a player out for an important match or a Cup Final, knowing just what it was like myself meant that a player would understand how I felt when I had to tell him he wasn't playing". Later on, Bob Paisley made a very interesting statement when he was asked about how playing in Europe put too much strain on players after a hard season at home as well as possible International matches, he definitely agreed that it did and that it wasn't very beneficial to the players who were always expected to be on their best form at all times for both Club and Country, and he went on to say that

he doubted very much that Liverpool would have won the Double in 1986 if they had still been playing in Europe, or that the present team would have been anywhere near as successful as they had been if teams were still allowed to compete in Europe.

Barry Stone.
Merseyside F.S.A.
Branch Committee.

EDITORS BIT: So the F.S.A. does do some good things. It comes as no surprise that Sid Moss said that most people aren't in it for the money, this of course means that some are, and he may well be one of them. I was shocked though that Bob Paisley, a great man it has to be said, is in favour of a premier league, something I don't consider to be so great. Of course there are no stunning revelations from either men, but I hope this gives some helpful info, and is also a good advert for The F.S.A.

Mr. Paisley, Is it true that you don't care about the smaller clubs?

Merseyside F.S.A. meets at the Triton Public House in Paradise Street, Liverpool City Centre on the second Monday of each Month.

London F.S.A. meets at the University London Union, Malet Street, near Goodge St tube stop on the first Thursday of each month.

All are welcome to these meetings.

Further details can be obtained by writing to, The Secretary, F.S.A. 59 Oakwood Road, Halewood, Liverpool. L26 1XD.

OBVIOUSLY, THERE'S ONLY ONE

News was filtering through from the westerly outpost of Carlisle that they had un-
earthed a star of the future. An eighteen year old who possessed refreshing skills and
scored goals in the hard world of the third division.
Of course the Cumbrians were rubbing in the fact that
they'd snatched a talented youngster from right under
the noses of Newcastle United. A kid born and bred on
Tyneside who had previously been a trialist at St.
James Park and who was later to cost the club
£125,000 to bring home.

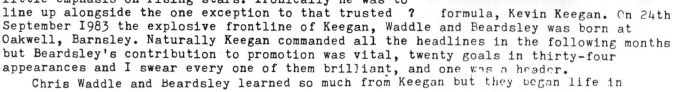

Peter Beardsley - Carlisle, Vancouver Whitecaps,
Manchester United back to Vancouver and then
Newcastle United. The conversation raged as to
whether he would be a success, but he was the right
type of signing. United had for so long relied on
players in the 'twilight' of their careers with
little emphasis on rising stars. Ironically he was to
line up alongside the one exception to that trusted ?   formula, Kevin Keegan. On 24th
September 1983 the explosive frontline of Keegan, Waddle and Beardsley was born at
Oakwell, Barnsley. Naturally Keegan commanded all the headlines in the following months
but Beardsley's contribution to promotion was vital, twenty goals in thirty-four
appearances and I swear every one of them brilliant, and one was a header.

Chris Waddle and Beardsley learned so much from Keegan but they began life in
Division One without their 'father figure'. This time Waddle grabbed the limelight with
his explosive burst's, out of the play for so long he would suddenly create havoc and
invariably scors. Arthur Cox used to say that "Waddle was no good to you unless he had
the ball", he was right, in fact he was fortunate on occasions not to be arrested for
loitering with intent at St James' Park, meanwhile Beardsley worked tirelessly for the
team, creating space, chasing balls and defenders and bringing others into play with his
impeccably perfect passing. Still he found time to score seventeen goals which
remarkably included a tap in and some penalties plus an unforgettable hat-trick against
the Mackems.

Unfortunately Jack Charlton was manager ? and he and Waddle didn't hit it off so
Chrissie decided to depart for pastures new, which in a way was the best thing that
could have happened to Beardsley. He was now totally released from the shadow of Keegan
and Waddle and for that matter, thanks to the supporters, Jack Charlton who in one
season had almost destroyed what Cox and Keegan had built. Peter himself admitted that
he would have went the same way as Waddle if Big Jack had stayed in charge.

As it was Beardsley was now the player who the supporters "hung their hats on".
Those who were not transfixed with Keegan and Waddle knew Beardsley was also England
class and in the nine months building up to Mexico he was to prove it. Nineteen goals
this time, just when you thought you'd seen everything, the following week he'd pop up
and amaze you further, every goal sheer brilliance. It wasn't only the goals though, he
covered every blade of grass week in, week out. One moment particularly stands out,
playing Barnsley in the second round of the Milk Cup, United were pressing for a goal
and had a corner at the Leazes End. Beardsley took up his usual position on the edge of
the box only to see the ball cleared over his head and towards Ian Walsh, the Barnsley
striker, who went wide with the ball but before he'd reached even a suitable crossing
position, Beardsley had sprinted back to cover United's laboured defenders and made a
challenge that resulted in a Newcastle throw. Beardsley always made a point of
applauding the fans at the end of each game and was subsequently always last off the
pitch, that season I'm sure those who used to leave early stayed behind to show their
appreciation of his performances he recieved a standing ovation after every game, win or
lose. I've never before or since seen that level of consistancy over forty-two games.
The last game of the season was at Leicester, United were to finish eleventh which to us
is 'dizzy heights' it was also mainly down to Beardsley. That day some five thousand
supporters travelled to Filbert Street not only to celebrate that lofty position but to
give Peter a send off. He'd been included in the squad for Mexico, something which had
given the whole area a lift. The reception he was given at the end of the game, after a
two-nil defeat, was something I'll never forget. As usual he came over to say thanks for
the support and he was greeted with chants of "Mexico, Mexico" he must have stood for
five minutes clapping and waving.

His exploits in the World Cup have been well documented and to this day those are my
proudest moments even though I was a million miles away. Glued to the TV and watching
the 'Pride of Tyneside'- who played for my team-play on the worlds biggest stage was
MAGIC, I still cringe when I see that moment when he put the ball one way past the

Paraguayan defender and then run round the other and then hit his shot over the bar. What a goal that would have been!!

He returned from Mexico no-longer 'our' Peter, the whole world had shared him. He also returned to a club that had not built on the previous seasons progress and subsequently struggled. Beardsley now a marked man did not reach the height's of the season past but was still head and shoulders above the rest, all bar one young man called Paul Gascoigne. The two had combined so well before Peter went to South America and continued in that vein, until the pressure and an injury got to Gascoigne. Gassa (as he was known before he found fame) was to miss most of the campaign leaving Beardsley with the responsibility of digging the team out of the mire. The goals didn't flow which resulted in accusations that he wasn't trying, other players at the club became unhappy at the preferential treatment he recieved, (children) and envious of his 'goody goody' image. The team fell deeper into trouble and at the end of February was rooted to the bottom of the Division. Beardsley had scored only four goals and was being crucified for it in the press. A few days after a defeat at Wimbledon (the point where it looked like there was no return), I attended another Beardsley 'Talk In' at a Workingmens club on Tyneside. As usual Peter was honest and forthright and told the audience that when his contract expired in FIFTEEN months time he would leave if the club were in a similar position but he pointed out that, who knows? the club may have won something afterall, who could have envisaged the teams plight after the encouraging signs the season before. At this point a fan stood up and shouted "Peter, get yourself away to Liverpool, you're too good to be wasted at this club" there was a massive cheer and most of the audience got to their feet and applauded. Here was a man who was worshipped by the fans, the same fans who knew he would never achieve the success he deserved with his hometown club. He would be missed so much, but that was the depth of feeling for him.

The following Saturday Beardsley scored a vital winner against Aston Villa and then the return of Gascoigne brought new hope. Paul Goddard started to hit the net regularly and then, just when survival looked possible Beardsley limped off in a game against Manchester United. Newcastle still went onto win with ten men. The following day speculation was mounting that Peter had played his last game for Newcastle. Relegation and losing Beardsley was unthinkable, fortunately the team got the points needed to survive. The rumours of Beardsley's departure persisted and at the final game of the season against Forest Beardsley's name was chanted in the hope that it would not be good bye.

Two months later it was, after a drawn out saga, much debate and bitter words Peter was sold. Stuff the fans! I for one would rather have watched an international class entertainer for one more season than see a poxy new stand for the bussinessmen. Some at the club did not stand up to the belief that he was the best and should not be sold, others have said he wanted to go, fair enough you don't pass up the chance to join the best club in the world. This though would not have occured if he played for an ambitious and successful Newcastle United.

After winning a championship medal and on the eve of the '88 Cup Final Beardsley was the focal point of a documentary analysing Newcastle's failures and mismanagement on BBC Two. He recollected the '74 Cup Final when Newcastle returned from Wembley 3-0 losers but were greeted by a quarter of a million people on the streets of Newcastle. He said that he wanted to be part of something like that and which he would have given his right arm to do. That is also something I would have given my right arm to see, pity some did not share that dream.

Stephen Brennan.

We've all watched the rest, well the Liverpool supporters amongst us have. My commentary on his time at Anfield may appear in the next Issue. I shall be writing this in return to Steve for this article. Unless there are two Steve Brennan's writing for fanzines in Newcastle, this man is one third of the team which writes...
THE MAG, Newcastle United's fanzine, 50p, A4 SAE.
404 Warwick Court, Gateshead, Tyne and Wear. NE8 IEY.
A most impressive effort, humour and serious articles, racism, monetarist board, buy it, etc,

PETER BEARDSLEY

LIVERPOOL 1
MAN UTD 0

Grobbelaar

Nico

Venison

Gillespie

Molby

Whelan

McMahon

Barnes

Houghton

Aldridge

Beardsley

Spackman

Rush

Although it is easy to pick John Barnes as Man of the Match, with his fairly impressive ball skills, with a team performance as impressive as this, when each player could have won the award on his day, picking out one player is unfair. From Bruce Grobbelaar, with that amazing first half save from Anderson's header, through the whole team, to Aldridge, who is a better player after spending the summer months practising his ball control, everyone gets 10 out of 10. One last thought though, isn't it strange, even ridiculous, to be in the situation where the manager can take off last seasons leading scorer, and replace him with a multi million pound player?

The game at Old Trafford will be the best one to win, but this was worthy of a certain degree of celebration. Much credit goes to Nigel Spackman, who played so brilliantly after coming on as an early substitute for a rather badly injured Steve McMahon. His performance was matched by all of his team mates, except Ian Rush, who only showed glimpses of the ability he has, having come on for the last quarter, to replace a tiring John Aldridge

SING ME AN OLD FASHIONED SONG

Or, better still the realities of the Kop sound today. In a previous article in this fine 'zine some of the widely held myths of the Kop were thankfully dispelled, all credit to the author for highlighting some of its more uglier characteristics.

However, the Kops attitude today is more complex than it first appears to the average hack looking for a story to slag down Liverpool with. Having been a regular supporter on the Kop for a number of years now I like many others noticed a distint quietening from the ranks of this most hallowed of terracing. The seeds of quiteness were sown some time back and its roots have grown slowly but deeper over the years."How? Why?" you cry, "Treachery!" you scream. But before you rip this page out and use it to burn my house down, read on. I believe one reason for the quietness, ironically, is that the Kop has been a victim of the teams own success. For example, who has not been to the match recently (circa 83-87) and has been lacking any great anticipation, excitement, or passion for the approaching match, because you know quite simply that the opposing team will be swept aside in typically clinical fashion, after a few minutes token opposition from the other team. This is not meant as an attempt to attack Liverpool as a boring, mechanical team, because we are not, remember Arsenal have not won the League for eighteen years. If anything it only goes to show how many of todays middle/low level placed league teams fail to meet the exacting high standards of quality, that Liverpool continually set, especially in the previous seasons. Please note that my comments are not a direct criticism of these clubs managers etc(apart from Ferguson and Harvey-ed)... but more of a reference to the way in which funds are unavailable to them. and club. and ultimately the fans, but that's another story.

To return to the problem. You may well remember however many a shock win from a visiting team, but if you remember this then you will also most probably remember the far better atmosphere on the Kop. This was due quite naturally to the need, the urgency to recover, to equalise, to win. The ground no longer sits back (sic) but now gets behind the team, it is at such times that they say, it was just like the old days. Personally, and I am sure many will agree with me that the best place to hear the Kop in full voice is ironically away from home. Because on the Kop terracing at Anfield it lacks the impetus, the passion,since everyone expects everyone else to start the songs and chants, everyone expects the roar to occur naturally and instantly when the occasion requires it, so we fail to attempt to start it ourselves. So in my opinion to fully appreciate the atmosphere and energy fans can generate, and the affect this has on the team, it is best alas, to visit an away fixture. It is at these occasions that the full nature of the Reds support is brought out. At these events there is a sense of a need to sing and get behind the team, to support them away from the comparitive security of home. This unique atmosphere is even more prevelant at the 'big' games. For example, most recently at Villa Park against Arsenal in the Littlewoods Cup, 3rd round, 2nd replay. Here the vocal support was almost continuous and almost certainly a contributing factor to the Reds brilliant win. That is not by any means the only example. Who could fail to forget the atmosphere at Hillsborough for the F.A. Cup semi against Notts. Forest - fewer supporters but a far greater voice, or against Southampton at White Hart Lane, again with fewer supporters. Or (the list is endless) against Man. Utd at Goodison 85, when the display of support our supporters showed, won the praise of their then manager, Big Ron.

So in effect the Kop is hopefully merely dormant, requiring a good kick up the R's to rewaken it's obvious true potential (another St. Etienne should suffice). The Kop as it was, is now best seen at the away fixtures and rarely at home. Probably at no better away venue than at Wembley for a Cup Final. Liverpool and the supporters have big aspirations, we thrive best on the big occasions, therefore it is not surprising that a mid-season game against a mid-table team at mid-week fails to ignite the Kop's passion. I make no apologies for such a biased article against home support. I only wish it was not so, and that the Kop soon puts me right.

The author of this article signs h??self as 'Moog'.

chapter 4

LEYTON ORIENTEAR

leyton orient

THE ALTERNATIVE ORIENT
SUPPORTERS MAGAZINE

AUG. 87 no.10 30p

Leyton
ORIENTEAR

LEYTON IS BACK !!!

...and there will be many who will feel a little regret at the
dropping of the name 'Clapton.' To them I would say it is a perfectly proper
and natural thing for any football club to desire to identify itself with the
borough or township in which the ground is situated. A first-class football club
should always be in the forefront of a town's recreational and social activities ...
we look forward with confidence to a successful and prosperous Leyton Orient
F.C. . . . 'Clapton Orient F.C. is dead, Long Live Leyton Orient.'

Leyton Orient programme notes - 28.9.46.

THE ALTERNATIVE ORIENT
SUPPORTERS MAGAZINE

INSIDE: ■ NORWAY TOUR REPORT
        ■ ORIENTEAR POLL RESULTS
        ■ MEMBERSHIP SCHEMES
        ■ PLUS THE USUAL STUFF

JAN 88   No 15

LEYTON
ORIENTEAR 30p
The Alternative Orient Supporter's Magazine.

Frank Clark gets up to face another hard day at Leyton Orient -
a similar routine as Greavsie in his Tottenham days. But Frank
recovered in time to collect his Bell's bottle for being their
Manager of the Month - Congratulations - any chance of a tipple
for the lads in the supporters' bar?

INSIDE

·Lock up yer members.
·Going up - Will we, won't we.
·Musical raves from the grave.

FEB 88 No 16

LEYTON ORIENTEAR 30p
The Alternative Orient Supporter's Magazine.

A TRIBUTE TO
PETER ANGELL

MAR 88 No 17

LEYTON ORIENTEAR 30p
The Alternative Orient Supporter's Magazine.

REVEALED!

The Secret Diary Of
Frank Clark (Aged 43¾)

APR 88 No 18

LEYTON ORIENTEAR 30p
The Alternative Orient Supporter's Magazine.

How do you spell that, again?

R-H-I-N-O!

[photo by Skinny John]

INSIDE
TIGER TALES
OPINION POLL
THE POLICE & ORIENT

MAY 88 No 19

LEYTON ORIENTEAR 30p
The Alternative Orient Supporter's Magazine.

YIPPEE!! We can still make it via the dreaded play-offs
Eddie Lewis, Cyril Lea, Sid Bishop & Joe Elwood
put a spring in their step to mark the occasion

INSIDE: ■JOHN SMITH ■HOMELESS SHRIMPERS ■THE
MAGNIFICENT 7

OCT 88 No 22

LEYTON ORIENTEAR 30p
The Alternative Orient Supporter's Magazine.

SHOULD I STAY OR SHOULD I GO?

FRANKIE, FRANKIE GIVE US A WAVE....

NOV 88 No 23

LEYTON ORIENTEAR 30p
The Alternative Orient Supporter's Magazine

Would the boo-boys abuse this man?

LAURIE CUNNINGHAM SCORES THAT GOAL AGAINST
HULL IN THE 1976 LEAGUE CUP . . . SAY NO MORE

INSIDE
●ANTI-FASCIST ACTION - RID FOOTBALL OF NAZIS●
●FAREWELL TO RODNEY - A BETTER-LATE-THAN-NEVER TRIBUTE●
●REVEALED: COLIN MOYNIHAN TALKS RUBBISH●
▷SPOT SID THE SURREALIST AND WIN A FRENCH LOAF◁

DECEMBER 1988 No 24

LEYTON ORIENTEAR 30p
The Alternative Orient Supporter's Magazine

'WHERE ARE THEY NOW'
Sgt SIDEBURNS IS FOUND AT LAST!

Sgt Sideburns has not been seen at Brisbane Road this
season - but we've found him! The police officer - famed
for ejecting West Siders for daring to vocalise their
support - was spotted recently, with fellow officers,
leaving the barbers after the weekly facial hair perm!

JANUARY 1989 No 25

LEYTON ORIENTEAR 30p
The Alternative Orient Supporter's Magazine

WATCH OUT — HERE COMES...

DON'T MENTION THE MONKEY!

POSTPONED DUE TO CONTINUED INTEREST IN THE F.A. CUP
- UNLIKE OURSELVES

HARTLEPOOL

DON'T SAY WE DIDN'T WARN YOU!

LEYTON ORIENT v HARTLEPOOL UTD, LEYTON STADIUM, 28:01:89

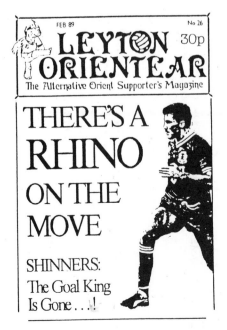

FEB 89 No 26

LEYTON ORIENTEAR 30p
The Alternative Orient Supporter's Magazine

THERE'S A RHINO ON THE MOVE

SHINNERS:
The Goal King
Is Gone...!

Form 1

MAGAZINE TITLE: LEYTON ORIENTEAR

CO-EDITORS NAME: GARY WINCH

AGE: 28   OCCUPATION: BT CLERICAL OFFICER

DO YOU/HAVE YOU EVER SUPPORTED ANY OTHER TEAM? NO

MOST MEMORABLE MATCH EVER: ' W BA FACUP 3rd RD '85 2-1

MOST MEMORABLE SEASON: 82-83 AVOIDED RELEGATION TO 4th!

ALL TIME FAVOURITE PLAYER: PARSONS | COMFORT | GODFREY

WHAT SORT OF CAR DO YOU DRIVE? NONE

YOUR FAVOURITE MUSIC: SMITHS | COSTELLO | AFRICAN

FILMS/TV: OBSCURE SUBTITLED | DOCUMENTARIES | YOUNG ONES | FRENCH + SAUNDERS

FAVOURITE CLOTHES: T-SHIRTS GAUDY PATTERNED EFFORTS

POLITICAL LEANINGS: LEA OF KINNOCK

WHAT PLAYER WOULD YOU MOST LIKE TO SEE PLAYING FOR ENGLAND (SCOTLAND/WALES IF RELEVANT)? ALAN COMFORT

Form 2

MAGAZINE TITLE: LEYTON ORIENTEAR

CO-EDITORS NAME: STEPHEN HARRIS

AGE: 26   OCCUPATION: CIVIL SERVANT

DO YOU/HAVE YOU EVER SUPPORTED ANY OTHER TEAM? USED TO WATCH HASTINGS UNITED, (BUT ALWAYS BEEN AN O's FAN

MOST MEMORABLE MATCH EVER: ORIENT v ARSENAL FA CUP SEMI-FINAL

MOST MEMORABLE SEASON: 77-78

ALL TIME FAVOURITE PLAYER: STEVE PARSONS

WHAT SORT OF CAR DO YOU DRIVE? BICYCLE

YOUR FAVOURITE MUSIC: ROY HARPER / POGUES / BILLY BRAGG / MODERNITY FOLK MUSIC

FILMS/TV: ENGLISH FILMS. DON'T WATCH TV MUCH

FAVOURITE CLOTHES: I'M NOT A TIDY DRESSER.

POLITICAL LEANINGS: LEFTISH / GREEN

WHAT PLAYER WOULD YOU MOST LIKE TO SEE PLAYING FOR ENGLAND (SCOTLAND/WALES IF RELEVANT)? STEVE CASTLE (ORIENT)

Form 3

MAGAZINE TITLE: LEYTON ORIENTEAR

EDITORS NAME: DAVE KNIGHT, THOUGH THERE'S FIVE OR SIX OF US WHO MAKE EDITORIAL DECISIONS, I JUST CO-ORDINATE IT.
OCCUPATION: SOCIAL WORKER

AGE: 33

DO YOU/HAVE YOU EVER SUPPORTED ANY OTHER TEAM? NO.

MOST MEMORABLE MATCH EVER: VS. MIDDLESBROUGH IN F.A. CUP '77/'78 IN (6TH. ROUND - O's WON 2-1 AND PLAYED IN THEIR ONLY SEMI-FINAL -

MOST MEMORABLE SEASON: 1969-70 - 3RD DIVISION CHAMPS AND '73-'74 WHEN WE MISSED PROMOTION TO THE FIRST DIVISION BY ONE POINT.

ALL TIME FAVOURITE PLAYER: TOM WALLEY

WHAT SORT OF CAR DO YOU DRIVE? VAUXHALL CAVALIER.

YOUR FAVOURITE MUSIC: DEXYS, TOM WAITS, POGUES, FALL, NEW ORDER, LOU REED, SOME COUNTRY MUSIC AND SOUL.

FILMS/TV: DON'T WATCH MANY T.V. PROGRAMMES, BUT LIKED 'YOUNG ONES'. I LIKE TOO MANY FILMS, BUT I GUESS "CASABLANCA", "APOCALYPSE NOW" AND "THE COLOUR PURPLE" ARE 3 FAVES.

FAVOURITE CLOTHES: NOT THAT BOTHERED

POLITICAL LEANINGS: LEFTISH, I SUPPOSE. SOME ANARCHIST STUFF APPEALS TOO.

WHAT PLAYER WOULD YOU MOST LIKE TO SEE PLAYING FOR ENGLAND (SCOTLAND/WALES IF RELEVANT)? IT'S NOT THE INDIVIDUAL PLAYERS THAT BOTHER ME REGARDING ENGLAND, IT'S MORE THE UNADVENTUROUS STYLE OF PLAY. I'D LIKE TO SEE PLAYERS ENCOURAGED TO BE IMAGINATIVE AND ATTACK MINDED - WELL, I CAN DREAM, CAN'T I?

Form 4

MAGAZINE TITLE: LEYTON ORIENTEAR

EDITORS NAME: TOM DAVIES

AGE: 18   OCCUPATION: STUDENT

DO YOU/HAVE YOU EVER SUPPORTED ANY OTHER TEAM? NO

MOST MEMORABLE MATCH EVER: ORIENT 2 TORQUAY 0 (85-86 NEW)

MOST MEMORABLE SEASON: 1977-78

ALL TIME FAVOURITE PLAYER: ALAN COMFORT / JOHN QUERSIE

WHAT SORT OF CAR DO YOU DRIVE? NONE

YOUR FAVOURITE MUSIC: SMITHS / BILLY BRAGG / WEDDING PRESENT / POGUES

FILMS/TV: ALTERNATIVE COMEDY - THE STUFF (BLACKADDER ETC)

FAVOURITE CLOTHES: FAT FROG & T-SHIRTS

POLITICAL LEANINGS: LEFT OF CENTRE

WHAT PLAYER WOULD YOU MOST LIKE TO SEE PLAYING FOR ENGLAND (SCOTLAND/WALES IF RELEVANT)? ALAN COMFORT

LEYTON ORIENTEAR

The Alternative Orient Supporter's Magazine.

Fellow Londoners often question O's supporters on their choice of club, given the amount of choice there is in 'The Smoke'. I've no idea how it came about for me.

My grandad was a Clapton Orient fan during the twenties so perhaps I inherited a faulty personality trait from him. My dad, though, was a Chelsea man but as we lived in Leyton and he thought 1st division crowds were too much for his little son it was to Orient he took me one fateful day in September 1966.

At the time I counted myself as a Spurs fan, idolising Jimmy Greaves (how times change!), but though O's lost that first game 0-1 something had been kindled inside of me. There was a friendliness and humour about the place, and Spurs gradually faded from my horizons. Here was a club that needed my support - buckets were passed around the terrace (no, not for being sick in, but to collect pennies for survival). It was also like joining an elite club. The players had a kind of honesty and spirit in adversity that endeared them to my heart and no one, bar the elite few, knew who the hell I was talking about when I went on about the skill of Mal Slater, the tough little winger Terry Paine or the vision of Dave Metchick. Cliff Holton was the only name they recognised. Anyway, I lived in Leyton. The O's were my hometown team.

Little did I know just how severely my support would be tested over the next 22 years. One third division title, one F.A. Cup semi-final appearance, a close run promotion bid for division one in 1974 and, er, um, no that's it. On the negative side I've witnessed two relegations which have seen us down to the fourth, many seasons of struggle and a couple of close shaves with bankruptcy. Hardly awe inspiring is it? But for some reason (mental health probably) I still keep coming back for more along with 2000 or so fellow sufferers.

However, in 1986 after conflicting statements in the press from the Board, another shave with extinction and reading 'Off The Ball', a few of us decided that rather than write to the local press about our feelings of unhappiness at how OUR club was being run, we could try and start a journal for O's fans. So Leyton Orientear was born and my kitchen became a magazine's office.

That first issue was severely critical of affairs at the club, and we were invited to meet Frank Clark to hear their responses. We of course used the info gleaned as the basis for no.2 and the ball had started rolling. Since then the magazine has created a momentum of its own. Starting with just 100 copies of no.1, we have now grown to a circulation of 1500, which ain't bad considering the average home gate is around 3000.

But, what I've enjoyed most is the way O's fans have supported the whole thing with letters, articles and chat.

The magazine has had to remain totally independent of the club who regard us with what they call "resigned tolerance". Leyton Orientear is banned from sale anywhere inside the ground, the club shops and the supporters club bar. We have to sell in the street. I shall never understand football clubs' attitudes to supporters' initiatives. We are, after all, football fans with the clubs' interests at heart, and we are the major reason for there being football clubs in the first place. Without supporters there would be no clubs. It's not as if we even threaten those who control the game and the clubs. They have to answer to no-one. Their position is unassailable. All we can do is put forward our views and possibly embarass those who use their power poorly. I would have expected clubs to welcome supporter involvement, but I've now learnt that even at a small, homely club like Orient there are those who cherish their positions so much that even a little, amateurish magazine like ours is viewed as anti-establishment and controversial in some way. Or maybe they are all just severe paranoiacs.

But we still keep supporting the O's. Why? Well, I think the friendliness between the supporters is one good reason, and I particularly enjoy the optimistic pre-match drink-up in the bar and the group therapy which takes place in the same place afterwards. This is when we shout and scream at each other about who was to blame for another disappointment. Was it the manager? Was it the team? Or was it one particular player? Various theories are supported and attacked with great vigour. Threats to life and limb are made, but never carried out and 3 hours or so later everyone goes off having agreed nothing but feeling a lot better. These passionate debates ease that dreadful depression which every football fan has experienced. Orientear just cribs ideas from and fuels further debates.

The last few seasons have been an unmitigated disaster for the Leyton team, staff and supporters. In 1982 we lost our second division place under Ken Knighton (Frank Clark was only his assistant then). After a season of struggle in the third Ken got, or was pushed, out. A better season followed but in 1984/85 we continued our slide into the fourth. Frank Clark guided us throughout this difficult time, and is still with us now in our annual fruitless search for promotion. In fact, each year we slip a little bit further away from those coveted top spots: 5th in 85/86; 7th in 86/87; 8th in 87/88 - it's all a bit disheartening, but gates were up over last season, we had a good cup run and did occupy top spot on two occasions during the first half of the season. Things have deteriorated this season and we are now fearful of seeing the O's stuck in the "Basement" long term with the added fear of one day finding ourselves fighting for our league place. However, we do still enjoy our football.

Playing in the lower divisions may lack glamour, but it is relatively easy to meet with opposing fans and enjoy a drink together. If anyone out there is considering a visit to Leyton Stadium please get in touch with us. Doing an alternative footy magazine makes all this even easier and we've had great days out in Birkenhead (Tranmere), Stockport, Rugby (where we joined the locals in their cheese throwing competitions), Rochdale, Grimsby, Wolves, even Cambridge, and many others. All have involved meeting opposing fans. We've also hosted other fans in Leyton. Through the fanzine network we were able to organise an Anglo-Scottish tournament with Queens Park supporters and their magazine, The Web. Our football team has played against the Peterborough Effect, Bournemouth fans and West Brom's 'Fingerpost' mob. Fans of York, Exeter, Carlisle and Colchester have all shared a pint or several in our club bar. Leyton Orientear has certainly helped us in our relations with other fans and it's great to have a whole day and night's activity based around your team's fixture on any particular weekend. It's been worth doing it for that reason alone.

The magazine has made several suggestions to the club through its pages and, though we don't claim the whole credit for various developments, we feel that the magazine has put supporters' views over and some have been acted on. Such developments include the change of name back to Leyton Orient, a highlights video of last season, greater availability of replica kits, toilet improvements, the birth of the Football In The Community scheme which has just started at Leyton Orient and a better policing policy on racism at the ground.

The other great thing about doing the magazine has been meeting bundles of O's fans. There's now about ten people who are regularly involved in Leyton Orientear, who I hardly knew before the magazine. We have Rupert, Sarah, Sid the Surrealist and The Stranger doing regular columns, Skinny John, a keen local amateur photographer, taking original photos for us to use, Mike Finch, a compositor by trade, doing the artwork for us, and Tom Davies, Gary Winch, Neal Arnold, Dave Chapman and Steve Harris all regularly writing articles, reports etc. and helping to make editorial decisions. On top of that there are countless individuals who have written pieces, sent in items of interest and helped in selling the finished product. We've even made a bit of cash and have been able to sponsor a player, a matchball and a charity football tournament. We've also made a donation to the Supporters Club Development Scheme. In fact a whole social scene has been created just by the magazine's existence. I've certainly enjoyed being a part of all that.

But, the thing that really makes all this happen is the love of Leyton Orient - a club who are continually up against it. Any small victory is a cue for mighty celebration. F.A. Cup wins against Chelsea ('72 and '78), W.B.A. in '85, Oldham away in '86, Spurs in the Milk Cup in '85 etc. etc. prompted great spontaneous drink ups. These moments are highly cherished. They are what makes it worth the bother. Now, we just long for our first promotion since '69/70. The trouble is that we seem to be a long way off at the moment.

The set up at O's doesn't seem too encouraging at present. The club have announced a £200,000 loss recently, two directors have resigned, there's talk of a takeover bid, rumours about players' unhappiness over training with the assistant manager, Brian Eastwick, and a defence which is set on self destruct. What the future holds is uncertain, but Frank Clark is currently running the show as Managing Director, with the chairman away in Africa. He's Tony Wood, a businessman based in Rwanda, who looks like Compo from Last Of The Summer Wine. The fans are getting restless as rumours fly around, but there is no doubt that some bright enthusiasm is needed. The club feels stale and almost satisfied with a nice cosy place in the fourth division. That won't help us climb out of the basement Division.

Leyton Orientear continues to print fans' varying views and brings the rumours out into the open. The club continues to regard us with resigned tolerance, but seems more friendly than a year ago. However, we still have no access to the players or staff, can't sell the mag in the club shops or ground, and are kept at arms length. Leyton Orientear, if it can maintain its popularity with O's supporters, will, however, be around for a long time yet.

DAVE KNIGHT

Out And About In...
FOOTBALL'S BASEMENT.

In this article we try to give you a quick trip around some of the fourth divisions stadia. Hopefully, the piece will also give a flavour of what it is like to follow a club like the O's - the misery and the euphoria. So here goes. We start with probably the worst trip of last season, another 0-0 draw at Colchester.

COLCHESTER: Membership schemes, long way from station, rubbish ground where we never win. In last 3 league meetings we haven't even scored a goal, and when we did score in the Freight Rover, we lost on penalties. Still, when they had an away end it was like standing on scaffolding and you worried about jumping up and down in case some change fell out of your pocket and disappeared between the wooden planks.

SOUTHEND: Never win. Used to have a nice away end til the bulldozers moved in. Pretty boring place. Lost 1-5 there once with Cadette, who we had just sold to them getting 4 of the goals. Plenty of pubs and an exotic train journey from Liverpool St. via Romford, Billericay etc. - exciting stuff.

PETERBOROUGH: Always freezing when we play our seemingly annual Christmas match there. Got the longest stand in League. Orient's Donuts beaten up two years ago. Great shopping centre.

ROCHDALE: Stevie Castle's favourite ground - he always scores there - got 4 two seasons ago. Dubious toilets with no roof, but at least you can watch the game while relieving yourself. No tea last year, but good pub with dodgy jukebox. No Ladies toilets - Sarah had to use the men's with a guard placed on the entrance. Great town for a good drink.

HARTLEPOOL: Not much of a place. Sexist pubs that won't serve women, good kebab joint in town, snowball fight with their supporters in Feb. '87, but don't mention the monkey. Good view of North Sea with old ships and boats in the harbour. Plenty to distract you from the football - can't be a bad thing.

BURNLEY: Last game of '86/'87 season and a crucial match to them and a massive, vocal crowd were there. The finale was very emotional and the Turfites treated us like kings. The best stadium in the 4th and one of the best towns - the Boot was an awe inspiring pub in '87 with lads painted in claret and blue singing their hearts out. The most enjoyable O's defeat I've ever witnessed. This year the weather was awful and the crowd much thinner. The only laugh to be had was seeing Gary come in late, so spoiling his 100% record.

WREXHAM: Nice away end, if you sit - terrible if you stand. Bit of a dodgy place but the ground is near the station. Best programme in the 4th, largely because it is the only official programme to ever mention Leyton Orientear including our own one. The supporters club is also the only one I know of which is inside the ground.

CREWE: Nice station, but what about the town. One of the best chip shops in Britain is opposite the ground. The mushy peas and curry sauce are second to none. We were 2-0 up in '86, but lost 2-3 - sick. Awful fence at away end.

NORTHAMPTON: Meccano Stand. About a million miles from the station. Called off on New Years Day '86. Three sided crap ground. I've heard that the away end is now so bad, they only charge £2 to get in. Still it's the only end I've been in where there's birds' nests in the toilets.

PORT VALE: Coldest day ever for football, and the worst game ever to match. Nowhere near anywhere. Not in Stoke, but Burslem. One good thing - they knocked Spurs out of the cup.

TRANMERE: Always a good trip. Brilliant ground. Birkenhead is a great place to visit as a football fan, and the Vittoria Vaults or Piggy's as it's known locally is one of the best and most friendly pubs I have ever found. A game at Tranmere is party time. Ferry across the Mersey in May '87 and took a long hike to the ground. Great wins in '86 and '87, but defeat in '88, but every one a cracking day and night out. Going there in '88/'89 is the only good thing about not getting promoted. Birkenhead is just full of nutty pubs and nutty people.

Where a bottle of spring water spilt on the pitch can get your game abandoned - The Shay, Halifax.

ALDERSHOT: Train from Waterloo and a walk through town. Good kebab joint. Lots of paras and squaddies - I was once moved on from a chip shop at gunpoint by a swarm of these types. It's like playing football in the back garden when you get into the ground. After the match you can expect to be taken Orienteering (!) by the local Bill as they lead you over a Krypton Factor assault course in the forest at the back of the ground.

CARLISLE: Miles from anywhere. Historians and culture buffs (imperialist bastards) can visit the castle or the museum. Used to be in the First Division. Dodgy Indian near station.

CAMBRIDGE : The Pits! Awful away end - ten steps behind the goal at Colditz. Lose 120 balls every game. Yomp through fields of rhinos to get to the ground. Loads of bikers (not the Easy Rider types, more Rick Astlet lookalikes). Will go down in O's history as the scene of Mike Conroy's only full game, featuring his awful cross, shot or pass, or whatever it was, when in the clear in '88 - a real rare old gem.

TORQUAY: Membership scheme (BOO!). Nice quaint ground, right near Babbacombe which is full of old fogies. Always a draw.

HALIFAX: Always go in Shay Hotel pub. Good chips in town. Friendly and lots of fun, but probably the worst pitch and a poor ground. Another Orient graveyard - we never win there They beat us 4-0 in '86, when most people would say,"Only Halifax concede 4 goals at Halifax." Great views of the Dales.

EXETER: Street lights for floodlights. Awful away end. You just come across the ground without it showing itself to you. Long walk from station. Excellent kebabs near ground. Morris dancers in town centre.

HEREFORD: Homely town, as they say. Good pubs in town. Nasty mob. You can taunt the S.A.S. or walk through cattle markets. Len Weston Stand not recommended for vertigo sufferers.

WOLVES: A dodgy place. Graffitti welcomes away fans courtesy of Wolves Subway Firm. Main stand 150 miles from pitch. Fine old stadium, great club tradition, gold shirts, Derek Dougan, Steve Bull, blah, blah, blah. Still it is near Darleston, home of the Spring Head, the only pub in the midlands with O's stickers behind the bar. This place is a second home for some of us who use it regularly as a half way stop on any trip up or down the M6. One of the best chip shops in the world is just round the corner from the Spring Head - a great place.

STOCKPORT: How many times are we going to go there? Scene of great cup battle in the mud in '88, and a nice place when the Man. Utd yobs aren't out cockney bashing. Also where Dino danced with a hooligan to avoid being hit.

FULCHESTER UTD: 250,000 capacity. No admittance fee. Just shout streams of abuse and impersonate favourite 'VIZ' character.

LIVERPOOL: Why do we always win here? (Dreaming). Referees are not influenced by the home fans, who are all locals from as close as London. Poor away end. Promoted to Division One with us in '62, but have had a less exciting time than us ever since. Still, both our teams play in all red. Dodgy kebab near station.

SCARBOROUGH: Another meccano, pre-fabish type ground. No away end cover, and if it rains, you're knacked, as the police take away your brollies, telling you that they are offensive weapons. A pretty crappy place. Almost as crappy as their board of directors, who barred the O's team from a post match drink on our last visit.

Collectors' Corner

SCUNTHORPE – A collector's item now they've moved. The best away end in the division – roof and no fence, but we don't talk about our last trip there.

NEWPORT: Another collector's item. One of the most depressing grounds I've ever visited – a club in it's death throes – very sad.

LEYTON: Not a bad ground, but the supporters are severe manic deppressives. However, the playind surface is magnificent. Here we see a Colchester player going down to try and discover the secret of the best kept pitch in the League.   [photo by Skinny John]

GRIMSBY: Scene of the Steve Parsons leg breaking incident of '81, back in our 2nd division days. On our last visit, the away facilities were pretty bad - a corner section with big fence and miserable police. Cleggy is a grand old place. Take a stroll along the prom. Take in the sea air, eat chips and mushy peas. Pubs aren't so good. Nice beach near ground.

LINCOLN: Nice cathedral. Apart from that, the whole place was so boring, I fell asleep. Mick also got a ticket for not having road tax, but the disc had fallen off the windscreen. Since their departure from the League, they have built a pretty reasonable stand.

DONCASTER: Not much of a ground left, but a wonderful town. Check out the White Swan with the tallest bar in Britain, The Castle and the Mason's Arms. All are around the market. Try chips and mushy peas from Rothwells in Copley Road next to Discontinued Records, the best record shop in the world. One of the best away trips.

SHEFFIELD WEDNESDAY: The way they're playing, they'll soon be down with us. We played them in the cup a couple of years ago. The strict police escort, the hour spent driving around Sheffield, the complete refusal of the police to allow any of us to wander around and sample the local brews, and the "straight on the coach" policy after the game made this one of my worst trips ever. The police were well over the top. If this is what first division football is about, then I don't mind staying out of it.

WOODFORD: Scene of a 1st round cup tie. More of a roped off allotment round the back of some houses than a football ground. The mud helped us out when an own goal looked certain, and we won 1-0.

ENFIELD: We won't talk about this cup tie but a nice non league ground. The away end's burger bar is a disgrace. The queue was 80 minutes long - we know cos one mug actually waited. Meanwhile, friends of the burger man got theirs quick through a side window. Enough to provoke a small riot when you're starving hungry.

STOKE: Nice ground, poxy view for away fans. It was like watching a game through a cheese grater. Still, the scene of a fine Littlewoods Cup win, our first in a penalty competition, and the joyful singing of "Mills Out" - even the Stoke fans joined in.

OLDHAM: A rearranged cup tie in a January freeze up meant taking a day on the sick and suffering exposure in our heaterless Allegro. A great 2-1 win warmed our hearts though.

BUCKINGHAM: Another tiny little 1st round ground. A man patrols the riverbank, carrying a keep-net for ball retrieval. He was kept busy. Meanwhile, the Milton Keynes skinheads, who turned up for a spot of cockney bashing, were a pain and one or two of our fans needed stitches. How stupid can you get?

LEYTON ORIENT: Home of London's greatest soccer soap opera. Frank Clark is expected to keep us going down here till the next century. Watch Rhino in footie boots as he charges around, share a beer with the goalie, applaud the fine quality of the pitch, jeer the poor quality of the team, unlees you come to see the annual demolition of Rochdale (8-0 - I can still hardly believe it!). Follow the O's fortunes in Leyton Orientear.

PINKY AND PERKY

RUPERT WRITES

Why do some men want to become a directors of football clubs? Most of these men appear to be successful in business so maybe they have more money than sense. More likely they are on a ego trip, all be it an expensive one. Have many have supported 'their' club man and boy?

Why is it then that these successful businessmen appear to be unable to run a successful (successful being defined as having a bank balance in the black) football club? Of the 92 league clubs how many are in the black? Let's be generous and say 30. That leaves a hell of a lot of directors running their clubs to the wall, at a guess around 360 of them. Why should their business be successful and their football club not? What difference is there between running a fish shop and running a football club? Too much difference? Okay them how about between a cricket club and a football club. See much difference? No neither do I. But I don't see any cricket clubs in financial difficulty.

Possibly cricket clubs look after their members better. Possibly the word members is the key. Every 'season ticket holder', which after all is what every member is gets invited along to AMG's, and gets told of the movement of players and ground improvements each year. A far cry from the way a football season ticket holder is treated.

More disturbing is the current trend for football clubs being owned by limited companies. At first it seemed that these companies were to become saviours of the less well off clubs but it now seems that the reverse is true, Charlton being an example. Who would like to guess at the future of Newport County now that it is out of the league and in the hands of a director that owns a building company? The writing may be on the wall for this sort of arrangement if the current trend of borough councils is continued. Greenwich Borough Council for example has, and they say will continue, to block any building on land marked 'sports ground' in their borough plan. That kicks into touch any wholesale development of the Valley. The same is true of Newham Borough Council when Grand Metropolitan tried to build on the home of Clapton FC's Spotted Dog ground.

In Orientear we have tried to impress on the newer supporter some of the antics of the Orient board in the past. We have been criticised for doing so. To rake over history is not constructive we are told. The directors we are told are making a effort by meeting the supporters on match days in their own supporters 'hut'. It's wool-over-the-eyes time again folks.

But should you believe that your directors do care and do learn from their mistakes bear in mind that in 10 years time there will be a totally different board room line up. Don't believe me? In the 'line up' in the Orient programme of March 4th 1978 there is not one name on the list of directors, manager and backroom staff that appear in the programme ten years later. Maybe I'm getting old and cynical but I don't believe that directors care one jot about the supporters of 'their' clubs. If they did they would recognise and value the alternative magazines that have sprung up around the country. Long may we continue to have a voice in football.

Meet The Manager

Full name: Name omitted to protect the innocent
Nickname: Frankie Moscow
Name you use to shake off the police: If I told you that I'd never be able to use it again.
Born: Yes, at an early age.
Where: In Newcastle so as to be near my mother.
Sex: Silly question.
Previous clubs: A six iron and a wood.
Schoolboy achievements: I scored behind the bikesheds once.
Most memorable match played: In the Rose & Crown, I finished 151 with treble 19, treble 20 and double 17.
Actress you'd most like to get your leg over: No comment.
Interests: 11% in the Abbey National and 10% in Nationwide.
Car: Raleigh
Bike: Austin Rover like Tebbit rides.
Skateboard: Don't be daft I'm a roller skate man.
Dislikes: Leyton Orientear.
Favourite food: PAL, it gives me a shiny wet nose and glossy coat.
Biggest disappointment: Brian Clough signing a further two year contract for Nottingham Forest in May this year.
Best signing: Me - as a football manager.
Second Best signing: Me again - this time as managing director.
Ambitions for your club: To finish higher in the league than last year, and the year before that, and the year before that and the the year before that.
Person you would most like to interview: Margaret Thatcher - preferably through a medium.

Orientear columnists: Rupert writes......and Sarah says..................

SARAH SAYS...

I am a relative newcomer to football and my experiences only relate to Leyton Orient Football Club. Early last season I was dragged down to Brisbane Road under protest by my friends Neal and Jeremy and was determined not to enjoy myself. I had always detested football and had fallen victim to the side of football that the media love to present to us. I prepared myself for a barrage of sexist, macho, drunk and marauding football supporters - certainly no place for a woman I thought. I was pleasantly surprised to find little evidence of this and more amazed still that I had a brilliant time and have been to virtually every home game and several away trips since. The atmosphere at Orient is a very friendly one and would in football jargon be described as a 'family atmosphere'. Perhaps the day I most enjoyed last season was when Leyton Orient played Nottingham Forest in the FA Cup on my birthday. The atmosphere was fantastic with 20,000 in attendance and not a hint of trouble - and we nearly beat them.

I find it difficult to convey my enthusiasm for football to other women and it is a source of great amusement to my friends and family. However women friends that I have persuaded to come down the Orient have all enjoyed themselves and have wanted to come again. The atmosphere is not intimidating and I would quite happily go to a home game on my own. Unfortunately not all clubs are as friendly as Leyton Orient and I am sure that if my first taste of football been at Leeds United then I would not be so enthusiastic.

I felt that I wanted to express my experiences and enthusiasm to other women to encourage them to come to Orient. I wrote a letter to Leyton Orientear asking if they could do anything about a sexist advertisement in the programme. The advertisement concerned motor insurance and has a picture of a woman in a bikini with 'Stone Motor Polices Cover the Best' emblazoned across her breasts. I am sure that it is this sort of attitude which puts women off football. I also asked if there could be some sort of women's contribution to Orientear and the result was "Sarah Says". As yet, the column has not developed very far as it began late in the season but the response has been favourable.

There has been a great deal of support for the removal of the Stones motor advertisement and the club has been approached. We had a letter from the Leyton lesbians and offers of contributions from other women. I am hoping to do some work over the summer and have articles about women's teams and do an interview with a professional woman footballer from the 1930's. I will also do a survey of women's toilet facilities at away grounds - Rochdale has the worst record so far. I had to squat in the men's urinals with Jeremy guarding each entrance!

I think a lot has to be done for women to penetrate the male bastion of football and make football more accessible to women. In these days of supposed equality it is a sport like may others, played, managed, coached and largely supported by men. Until recently I did not realise that there were any women's football teams - do we ever hear about then or see them on Match of the Day? I do not know if the situation is any different now but would hope that education was more progressive, but certainly when I was at school it was always hockey and rounders for the girls and footy and rugger for the boys. It seems strange as hockey is a lot rougher than football - I think they were just afraid that we would be better than them. To challenge the position of women's involvement in football means challenging the sexist nature of our society and is part of a wider debate.

At grass roots level, I feel that it is important to make football more accessible to women in the local community both as supporters and players. I think this has already begun at some clubs and I can use Millwall as an example. They have a women's football team and provide a creche on matchdays for people attending the game or for people to shop while their partners are at the match.

I think Leyton Orientear and football fanzines in general can act as a valuable forum for supporters to express their views about the club and football in general and criticise negative aspects about the club like sexism, racism and lack of facilities. They can in turn put pressure on the club to bring about changes which supporters want. For women I hope we can suggest a women's team for Leyton Orients and facilities like those offered at Millwall. I still maintain that if Frank Clark was woman we would not still be floundering in the fourth division.

Sarah Tabor

THE SEASON SO FAR...

You may be wondering what I've been up to during the last few months. Well, I've been busy writing headlines for the Sunday Sport and speeches for Nigel Lawson, and I've also been buying some teabags.

On the football front, it's been a strange season for Leyton Orient. We began with 0-0 draws with Crewe and Stockport, which is a suburb of Greater Manchester with a bridge like structure carrying railway or road over valley, river etc. i.e. viaduct. Crewe has ex-O, Andy Sussex, with haircut. We then lost 1-3 to Hereford - the home crowd wasn't happy.

Anyway, Kylie's new album is a real winner, full of bouncy tunes to get you moving. I think we should all "Do The Locomotion".

ONIONS

The following week we were beaten 1-0 at Hartlepool. The home fans taunted us with chants of "Yuppies, Yuppies" and a rendition of Eastenders' theme tune. We replied with,"We've got better regional stereotypes than you. Leyton, Leyton" and followed up with a continuous bhuddist mantra whilst flicking dessicated onions from our burgers. A few days later we lost 1-4 at Rotherham, who have ex-O, Tony Gre-alish, with beard.

THE OXO MURDERS

After our 3-0 defeat at Torquay, who have dog with teeth, I stopped off for dinner with the Oxo family, who are Fulham fans. I have known them for many years. They are a charming couple with wonderful children. Various comments were made as hilarious witticisms were exchanged across the table.

The children confided in me, and told me of their hatred of the Renault 14 couple and their plans to sabotage their new car, thus causing them to meet a sudden and horrible death. They also told me of their plans to drown Nanette Newman in a vat of Fairy Liquid. It goes much further!

EXCITING NEW GAME

If you get bored on one of those long away trips, you can play this exciting new game. It's called desert island refs, and is similar to the radio show, "Desert Island Discs". You have to choose the 3 referees you would like to have stranded on your desert island to officiate any matches you might have. My three would be; K.A.Redfern of Whitley Bay, M.J. Bodenham of Sussex, and Anita Harris.

THE EFFECT OF CIVILISATION ON THE PEOPLE

Ian Juryeff scored the 4th goal in our 4-0 win over York, and it could easily have been more. The crowd were happy, and after further wins against Stoke and Colchester (8-0), they talked of going to San Fransisco with flowers in their hair. After our 2-2 draw with Burnley, we were stopped in the street by a large mob, who asked us,"Where are you from? Who are you? What do you think of Kylie's new album?". We realised that they were the Burnley Royal History Re-enactment Society as they proceeded to re-enact Lady Di's marriage to Prince Charles in 1981 at St. Paul's Cathedral.

OXO FAMILY ACID HOUSE SHOCK!

My financial advisor told me some shocking news the other day. It concerns the Oxo family, who I told you about earlier. After Fulham's 5-1 over Aldershot, one of the mischevious children took an Oxo cube and carefully slit open the foil wrapper. After inserting a tab of Ecstacy, mum unwittingly put it in the evening meal. Later, as they were seated in the lounge watching the hilarious "'Allo 'Allo", they started dancing around the furniture shouting "Gravee, Gravee..". After this, they visited the Renault family, but far from murdering them, they ended up having sex with them. Let this be a warning!

KIDNEYS

I was strolling down the road after our 4-0 win over Exeter, when I saw a man wearing a microwave oven. He stopped me and said,"Sid, you're crap. You are not a surrealist. You do not express the sub - concious activities of the mind. You're a sham. I am defrosting my kidneys". I gave him a teabag. Goodbye

* Tottenham - 2 points deducted.

Looking Forward...

BY THE STRANGER

If Colin Moynihan has his way this will be my last season of wandering around the Football League grounds, because I certainly won't subscribe to a national membership scheme which is an infringement of civil liberties. They can stuff it. I'll watch non league football.

The Football League should follow the example set by the Scottish National Party who won a great victory by telling people not to pay the poll tax. Well, the League should tell the Tories to leave soccer alone and concentrate on Henley and Badminton, and all the other toffee nosed sports. Football is the sport of the working classes, not rich fat idle bastards, sitting in their boxes, sipping wine and scratching their cobblers.

The Football League should also be trying to do something about the current standard of soccer, which is at an all time low. The game is now played at such a frantic pace that skill is at a minimum, and any player showing a modicum of ability is clobbered by the thugs masquerading as footballers. The ball spends most of the 90 minutes in the air, thanks mainly to the likes of Wimbledon. Anybody who thinks Wimbledon have been good for the game is blind. It's up to the authorities and the club managers to get the game back to it's entertaining best.

I think all players, coaches and managers should read the book written by Duncan Edwards, one of the greatest players ever, who tragically died in the Munich air crash. Duncan's book, called "Tackle Soccer This Way" is a gem - an instuctional book with a wealth of sound advice and tactics. In the following months I'll relate some of it's excellent advice. As a taster, especially for Wimbledon fans, Duncan says this about ariel ball:"If you stand on the terraces on a Saturday afternoon and a player balloons the ball higher than anybody else has done, weep for him. Don't cheer - the player has just plunged into the depths of the game".

Only a few trips to face this time. Barry's excellent comments on players to watch, which have been very accurate, follow my comments.

ENFIELD - F.A.Cup, 19th November: Just up the road. A ground I've never been to, but I used to go fishing at Enfield Locks.
BARRY'S FORM: A possible upset. We might win but a draw is most likely.

CAMBRIDGE (A) 26th November: From one non league ground to another. The club with the worst away end in the world. If you've ever wondered what prison is like, Abbey Stadium will give you a good idea. Comes complete with it's own wardens.
BARRY'S FORM: Old George Reilly has returned and his ariel power has to be feared.

LINCOLN (H) 3rd December:
BARRY'S FORM: A side running into form. Excellent win at Burnley. Watch Gamble and Sertoni.

GRIMSBY (A) 17th December: Well, actually, Cleethorpes. Usually windy here. Don't expect to see any deep sea trawlers on the river, they've all gone. Just a few inshore boats fish from this once great fishing port. A few good pubs. The bar on the railway station used to be good. It may still be. The ground is good and the away end is better than most. An interesting place if you have the time. Visit Grimsby Docks - you can still get the feel of what it used to be like.
BARRY'S FORM: Another side getting some recent good results. Could be dangerous. Don't write them off. Alexander, who signed from Barnet, is now finding his feet.

In between these games we have a couple of delightful Freight Rover Sherpa Van Trophy cup ties. Reading at home (yawn) and, yes, that wonderful town of Aldershot again. It will be just my luck that when I become a non league fan, the Shots will drop out of the League.

Totally Scunned

Scunthorpe Utd. 3 Leyton Orient 2

S****horpe '88, and aftermath: A terrible game and a turning point in last season's campaign.

I really don't know what to say. There's only one team in the league that can screw up the way we can. From the moment the Orient self denial squad, encouraged by the great performance vs. Hartlepool, set off up North, we were confident of another 90 minutes severe suffering, but until the last 4 minutes something strange was happening - we were winning. "Don't worry" thought Frank,"I think I can pull this one out of the bag." Off came Hull, on came Harvey. We collapsed and they won. Mind you, they brought on a decent substitute with 5 minutes remaining.

It was a stupid bloody game anyway. The weather was horrible, and most of the Scunny nutters seemed asleep as we took the lead when Castle's shot was handled by Lister (it was a good save), and the Woodford Bridger tucked in the penalty. The pitch and the game, however, were a complete joke. Scunny piled on the pressure and Wells had to save us on a number of occassions with a blinding string of saves. Half time came, along with a dinky little tea trolley, which rolled down to our end to serve some dodgy tea.

We looked to be cruising it in the second half. Juryeff latched on to a poor back pass to make it 2-0, and a 3rd goal looked on the way. However, clinging on seems to be too boring for Frankie's merry men. The worst substitution in Orient history 10 minutes from time (did Frank the game was over?) and Wells' return to normal service ensured a close finish. Then Steve Johnson came on for Scunny and Wells gifted them an easy smash-in goal. 1-2 with 3½ minut-

es left - it could only be a consolation goal. Our lads in yellow, ably motivated by our excellent manager, collapsed. Whatever happened to team spirit and discipline. Wells booted a loose ball along the ground straight to a Scunny, who lobbed it back in over Wells' head - 2-2! We'd have to settle for the draw. I don't want to talk about their 3rd goal, but the 200 odd O's fans gave a loud series of "Clark Outs". I give up with this crappy team, and unless they SORT THEIR LIVES OUT, going up is out of the question. Oh yeh Frank, we're definitely good enough to go up. Such a well lead, determined and organised side. I think I'm just gonna stick my head down the toilet. AAAAAAAAAARRRGGGGH! Let's hope the cab driver takes them all for a dip in the Humber.

Tom Davies

SCUNTHORPE POSTSCRIPT

REGGIE LOOSES HIS RAG!

Reg, Leyton Orientear's on the spot, roving reporter, managed to get down to the dugout from his seat in the stand between the last goal and the final whistle - no mean achievement (the man should have an Olympic trial). Anyway, he managed to get an in depth interview with Frankie at the moment of truth. It went something like this:

Reg: You're ****ing Idiot, Frankie.
Frank: **** Off!
That just about sums it all up. Time to go yet Frankie?

Ode To Scunthorpe

Rollo and Mike Sheridan sent in this poetic masterpiece, which, they say, was not originally for publication, because, "it is filled with the raw stuff of human experience from soaring ecstacy to the darkest depths of despair. It was," they felt,"altogether too overwhelming an experience to unleash even on a public whose senses were numbed by continued exposure to Esther Rantzen. But no, I have a duty to art. Publish and be damned. Here it is then, in all it's awesome majesty :

A Scunny Thing Happened...
OR
Almost Drowned At The Old Show Ground.

'Twas on a rainy Saturday
To Sc******pe we did go.
We thought we'd see a football match,
Instead we watched the O's.

The rain ran down the windswept pitch,
We shivered in the stand
On soaking soaking seats with peeling paint,
Cold coffee in our hands.

Then out came all our gallant lads
In yellow shorts and shirt.
Their hearts ablaze, their eyes aflame,
They paddled through the dirt.

Steve Castle's shot flew from his boot
Exactly as he planned.
A Scunny jumped up on the line
And stopped it with his hand.

"A penalty!" we all agreed,
The referee did too.
Steve Castle hit it from the spot
and in the net it flew.

Then Juryeff with subtle skill,
The second goal he scored.
It really gave us quite a thrill,
Oh, how we did applaud.

We sang and cheered, we jumped about,
We chortled in our glee.
We joined the queue to celebrate
With one more cup of tea.

We thought that we were bound to win.
We'd played them off the park.
It seemed no one could stop us now
Then up stepped Frankie Clark.

"A substitution I shall make,"
He said,"This just won't do.
Now, who has had a decent game?
Oi, Alan Hull, it's you!"

"Get off the park", bold Frankie cried
"Let's make a game of it.
I'll send Lee Harvey on instead,
He always plays like s***".

Four minutes left, the clock ticks fast.
The Scunnies needed three.
They'll never do it - yes they did,
The rest is history.

I'll not watch this lot anymore,
No, not another match.
I'll bang my head against a wall,
It doesn't hurt as much.

Eat yerself fitter

The food sold at football grounds is notoriously bad, and we at Leyton Orient have, by no means the worst (the story springs to mind of the refreshment stand in the away supporter's enclosure, first game of last season, at newly 'Maxwell-ised' Derby County where, with the emphasis on cost-cutting, the attendant found his hut still full of pies left over from the previous season. The dutiful attendant re-heated the pies and sold them to the starving hundreds of Arsenal fans, resulting in record queues for the toilets during the game), it is by no means the best.

Leaving the rolls sold in the Supporter's Club out (cheese or ham – at a fair price), and concentrating on the (un)fare supplied within the hallowed walls of Brisbane Road, the hamburgers and hot dogs (sorry, JUMBO SAUSAGES), come to mind. Vastly overpriced and, by all accounts vastly below standard (makes me glad I'm a vegetarian!). The attendants are, especially in the West Stand, some of the rudest characters I have come into contact with across a counter (with the West Stand's 'Fat Fryer' really taking the biscuit – or the putty-textured roll as the case may be!) leading me to stop buying their provisions on principle alone. That's without looking at the conditions in which the food is prepared.

The range of sweets available is hardly mind-boggling (Kit-Kats), but at least the O's caterers don't sell bloody 'Yankee Bars'!!! (If you're not familiar with this particular culinary delight, they are sort of thin Mars Bar imitation which I have never seen on sale anywhere outside of football grounds).

Tea and coffee at football stadii has an individual quality, unique unto itself – drink it too soon and you'll remove your tongue with one sip.

Until I started going in the West Stand the worst tea I had the misfortune to drink was at Elland Road, where tea, coffee and Bovril all came from the same pipe, leaving each drink tasting of all three. But the tea from the West Stand bar is the pits. If they ask you: "One or two?" they don't mean sugar lumps, they mean dunks of the teabag.

If you drink the West Stand tea, drink it black (or piss-colour as the case may be), as the milk defies description

If you don't fancy that, then there is 'Orient Champagne', or BANANA FIZZ – a delicious concoction of additives that taste worse than it's plastic bottle.

Nobody is expecting Haute Cuisine at football matches, but in these hi-tech days of microwaves, etc, surely somebody could throw something together that resembles food – fresh sandwiches shouldn't be too hard. Until then I'll stick with my 'Veggyburgers' in wholemeal rolls and my 'Thomas the Tank Engine' flask of tea. And you wonder why they call me Skinny John!!!

Issue 21 (Sept. '88)

Fat Fryer – the sequel

Dear, oh dear! What have I started? It seems my harmless little article in issue 21 has created something of a 'Frankenstein's Monster'! One little line, referring to the guy that sells hamburgers in the West Side as the 'Fat Fryer' has led to nearly everyone I meet wanting to talk about his hamburgers. I have even been accosted in the Supporters' Club by two poor souls defending both his hamburgers and his style of service (including a certain typesetter from this very fanzine, and an editor of 'When Saturday Comes' – a particularly sorry case – who claims that these burgers are – and I quote – "The best I've ever had.") There's no accounting for taste, is there?

As for old 'F.F.' himself, he seems to have acquired a certain fame, which, if not quite of Michael Jackson stature, ain't half bad for a hot dog (sorry, JUMBO SAUSAGE) seller. Old F.F. takes it all in his stride (or waddle, as the case may be). He hardly bats an eyelid whilst walking past a North Bank in full voice with "You're so fat it's unbelievable", or "There's only one Fat Fryer".

The West Side's takings must have risen dramatically over the last couple of months as people go to see this 'Larger Lout' in action – slapping down burgers, arms, grease and sweat flying, swearing at customers. Quite a sight – though not one for the squeamish!

Don't get me wrong, though. He can't be all bad and I don't wish to sound too vindictive. I mean, any man with bigger tits than Ian Juryeff deserves at least a degree of respect!

So, as we await the flood of 'Fat Fryer' T-shirts, books, LPs, films, etc, that go with such notoriety, give him a friendly wave and shout, "Hello Fat Fryer", as he carries his cardboard boxes full of the afternoon's takings round the pitch at the end of the game – I will.

SKINNY JOHN

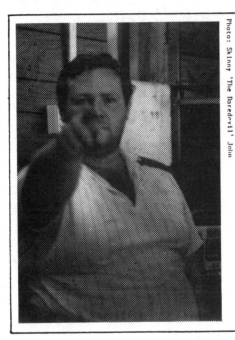

Photo: Skinny 'The Daredevil' John

BRISBANE ROAD SUPERSTARS PRESENT

MY BURGERS NEED YOU

–THE FAT FRYER–
requests your custom
at the
–WEST SIDE BURGER BAR–

Issue 23 (Nov. '88)

Fat Fryer in Orient take–over shock!

Just before Christmas, the Daily Mirror (I always think it's so kind of Robert Maxwell to produce a paper for the hard of thinking, don't you?), ran the 'exclusive' that one Julian Lloyd-Webber was to buy Leyton Orient for £1million. We now bring you the full story – EXCLUSIVE to Leyton Orientear.

That's right folks! Just when you thought it was safe to go back in the West Stand . . .

We have it on good authority that the world renowned gourmet chef, Mr Fat Fryer, has bought Leyton Orient! A source (sauce?) close to Mr Fryer, who's friends just call him 'Fat', has revealed that he has, in fact, been paying the club's former chairman, Tony Wood, in weekly instalments for some time. This surely must account for those large cardboard boxes he used to carry from the West Stand to the East every game. It also explains why he suddenly stopped! We can therefore only conclude that Mr Fryer is now definitely the outright owner of the club.

"Now he's the boss, we are going to see some changes!" said my source, who after being threatened with a bread roll has chosen to remain anonymous. "The name for a start."

'Lay-it-On Oriental Take-away Food Centre' is to be the new name, the South and East sides of the ground becoming the largest Chinese take-away in the world.

"The new I-D cards will be out," continued my source, inbetween bites of Jumbo Sausage.

"Everybody will be force fed one of these as they go through the turnstiles- too busy in the toilet for the rest of the game to even think about hooliganism."!

Other sweeping changes around Brisbane Road are expected to be a new playing strip for the team – the most likely to be F.F.'s personally favoured 1972-C&A look. Also it'll be bye, bye Frankie! "Mr Fryer will insist on a healthy looking manager to set a good example to the team" – Ron Atkinson, perhaps?

The only current team member who's place is assured is Ian Juryeff. "Mr Fryer is very impressed with his physique" – the new signings are likely to be Jan Molby and Paul Gascoigne to aid the O's return to fatter fortunes.

Well, there it is – remember where you read it first!

SKINNY JOHN

Issue 26 (Feb. '89)

SOD THIS FOR A LARK
or FIRST OF THE SUMMER WHINE

Orient 1 Peterborough 0

I must admit to being one of those people who
finds it hard to get into football this early in the
season - although normally manage to drag myself along
to these summery events. However, this year, today's
spectacle was my first taste of professional football
of the season, having missed Tuesday's cup game by
falling asleep in the armchair and then finding I
couldn't be bothered to rush round the corner in time
for the kick-off.

Today I must admit, even though I'm a loyal long
standing supporter, to feeling pretty apathetic at the
kick-off - pissed-off by half-time and wishing I hadn't
bothered - and totally bored with the whole bloody
thing by the end.

Highlights of the game were:-

i The new chairman's striking resemblence to 'Compo'
and the way that he seemed to enjoy football and
cheer and smile.

ii The result.

iii Seeing lots of people I hadn't seen since last season
especially Spud who said he'd been on the wagon for
3 weeks: but there again maybe he was winding me up.
And Mick who'd come 440 miles to see this!

iv Pushing in the queue for non-alchoholic drinks at
half-time without being elbowed.

v The 2nd half - although the 1st half was far worse.

Lowlights of the game were:-

i The 2nd half - although the 1st was far worse.

ii The lumps of 'stuff' in the tea.

ii Three bloody quid to get in!!!!!!!

iv The poxy programme which is thinner than last year's
and with more adverts.

v The first, I mean only, goal - mainly because I was
looking the other way.

vi Thinking it's a long way to next summer!

All in all, during the close-season I'd forgotten
how crappy 4th division football was - but there again
I can remember thinking the same last year and the
year before..... but it usually gets better or at any
rate, my enthusiasm grows and I become dead keen or
maybe brainwashed or something and last the full season
through ice and snow........ I suppose I will again
this year...cos I'd be lost without something to cheer
and moan about.

Cheers, see you next week!

Match report from Orientear No.1 (Sept. '86)

AWAY WE GO! :- TRAVELLING WITH THE O'S

BY GARY WINCH

AWAY TRAVEL.

As any loyal fan will know, following your team around the country means travelling thousands of miles during the season. The 3 main modes of transport being car, coach and train, each has it's own pros and cons.

TRAVELLING BY ROAD

Our wheels usually mean the cheapest trips, with 5 bods in a car, petrol costs can be split. It also means you can arrange your own itinerary and visit any services, towns etc. on our journey. One of the main disadvantages is the possibility of breakdown. I know of a few instances where supporters have spent the after-noon stuck in a layby watching the world speed by instead of the super O's.

Coach travel works out slightly more expensive, but the Supporters Club run a reliable service and a coach to every game. Also, you are amongst Orient fans and can get involved in long debates about the best team in Leyton (who said Leyton Orient?).

I occasionally travel on the supporters' coach and look out for coachloads of other supporters from rival clubs and make disparaging remarks up and down our motorways, and spend a small fortune on sustenance courtesy of T1IF, Granada, little Chef etc. Still, if you win the sweep by predicting the scoreline it might pay for a buttered roll.

A popular pastime with some football fans is to look out for coachloads of other supporters from rival clubs and make disparaging remarks and gesticulate wildly e.g. "Be off with you, rascals!" - wave aside with back of hand.

One of the downers with the Orient coach is the choice of entertainment. It is not always ideologically sound. Barry Manilow, Rod Stewart, Queen, Chas and Dave etc. leave something to be desired!!! Not forgetting such highly original comedians as Jimmy Jones, who is racist and sexist, Bernard 'fat gut' Manning, who I find about as funny as child abuse, although going to Torquay we watched the Comic Relief video which was really terrif!

TRAVELLING WITH B.R.

Another feature of rail travel is that you often meet interesting characters and supporters of other teams, sometimes the teams themselves and even our own Orient players (autograph books at the ready-"It's for my brother, sister, grandma etc.). We once met 2 Swindon players; Paul Roberts (I'm sure O's fans are familiar with him) and Chris Ramsey, who played for Brighton in the F.A.Cup Final in 1983 vs. Man. Utd. and

we had a long chat as they waded through about 27 cans of lager. We have bumped into them on a few occasions since and they remember us as "the Orient Fans".

B.R. Buffet cars are infamous but convenient. You can usually have a beer when you fancy, even if they do charge about £8 a can.

One of the joys of rail travel is the scenery - plenty of green bits and a few yellow bits as you whiz past looking for famous landmarks. When you go through Milton Keynes, everyone looks out for the concrete cows, not forgetting the locals in their bikes, waving and commenting,"Milton Keynes, it's quite nice really!'"

Of course you are bound by B.R.'s timetables and some trains run at strange times. My favourites are:

00:15 Birmingham New St.-Euston (Walsall Feb.'83 lost 0-2)
20:40 Taunton-Paddington (Exeter Feb '84 won 4-3)
23:50 Euston-Manchester (Rochdale May '86 won 4-1)
00:30 Manchester-Euston (Stockport Mar '87 drew 2-2)

But this can get a bit boring at times, how about....

ALTERNATIVE MODES OF TRANSPORT

Our old friend, British Rail, offer the most expensive form of travel even with Railcard discounts, but at least you can come and go as you please to some extent. You can plan your trip so you arrive ridiculously early and explore the towns / cities' various tourist traps e.g. shopping centres, chippies, pubs etc.

A group of us were thinking about travelling to an away game in a totally different manner - pushbike, C.5, longboat up the Grand Union Canal, but finally decided on Space Hoppers.

Gary on his way

So far there are 20 of us going to North-ampton on 11.4.87 by space hopper, that is the inflatable rubber balloons with a face painted on the front and two tentacles to hold on to as you bounce along happily. We will need to check with N.T.F.C. for parking arrangements etc.I don't envisage any difficulty taking the M.1, as I haven't seen any signs saying "Space Hoppers Prohibited". This will, in fact, be a sponsored Space Hop for a very worthy cause, "Save The Flip Flop". This is a new pressure group recently formed to look after the interests of flip flop wearers, who have been attacked by successive governments and have put up with vicious smear campaigns in the press and media. Flip flops are most fashionable items in alternative footwear. We recently held a mass demonstration through London and it was hoped to bring the place to a standstill, but only 7 people turned up and the public hurled abuse at us, "Get your hair cut!", "Bloody pseudo-revisionists!" "Go back to Milton Keynes",etc. We must be pretty close to a Police State, when we have to put up with this sort of thing. I believe it is time for us to come out of the shoe shop and wear our flip flops with pride. Bastards! Please get in touch if you want to sponsor us. If we are still in with a chance of promotion at the end of the season, as I'm sure we will be, we shall be leap frogging to Burnley. Thankyou.

COMPO PUSHES THE BOAT OUT

Compo (2nd from left in our picture) and the board demonstrate their own alternative transport -executive style- as they float up the Lea for another away trip. They don't look too happy, but then, it's a long paddle to Southend, or, perhaps they are just worried about getting into deeper water than that they are in already.

'Orientear-ache' is the letters section. We receive many spoofs and this one purports to be from Robert Maxwell. We have no confirmation as to the truth of this!

→

THIS IS YOUR CAPTAIN SPEAKING!

STOP ME IF YOU VE HEARD THIS ONE BEFORE

Paul Shinners.

SPOT THE DIFFERENCE

A rare Black Rhino

I'm just getting really fed up with this team. O.K., so we've been up near the top for most of the season so far, but we haven't established ourselves when we should really be way out in front. Every time we've had a chance to go top, Leyton Orient have (deliberately?) blown it - games vs.Hartlepool, Exeter, Wrexham, Cambridge and Swansea all illustrate the point. Particularly as between the last two listed we thrashed Rochdale 8-0, which was brilliant.
I don'tcare how many astonishing and impressive stats. we get bombarded with in the programme, once again we are making a total cock up. We seem to do this EVERY season without fail, yet the same stupid mistakes are made. Any other team would have been full of confidence   for the match at Swansea, but no not us. Instead, we played like a bunch of monkeys with no organisation or cohesion. What on earth do we do in training?
In my opinion we have got the players. Comfort is probably the best winger in the fourth. Godfrey, despite his faults, can still turn in useful performances and get vital goals. Smalley, Day, Dicko and Howard are all fine defenders and Hull up front is an excellent prospect. Nugent too looks good, but Shinners, well, he's a two month wonder (September and October 1985). Nevertheless, there is no reason or excuse for us not going up. We're constantly told how we are geared to going places, but are we? I'm certainly getting impatient, perhaps too impatient.
Why are we allergic to going top? Why don't we ever put together a really good run of 5 or 6 wins? Why haven't we got a really strong central midfield player? Why is Shinners playing? (Aren't we fickle). Why is that banana fizz drink they sell at the refreshments bars so horrible? Why is my new Leyton Orient scarf falling to bits after only 2 months? All mysteries of the Orient (unbelievably tedious and journalistic phrase) which remain unsolved.
SAVE THE BLACK RHINO! As we've got one in the team (Shinners) I think it's only fair we start sending hatemail to the current president corrupt of
ZAMBIA   . Put pen to paper now.
                                        Tom Davies.

From issue 13 (Nov. '87)

Dear Leyton Orientear,
                This is Captain Bob here, the saviour of British and international soccer. As you know, the League Mismanagement Committee leave a lot to be desired, namely, me - The Lord Robert Bloody Maxwell! I am, of course, a lifelong socialist. Anyway, I have decided to take over your fanzine, and indeed Leyton Orient Football Club."Maxwell Orient" has a certain ring to it. I'm sure you'll agree. £48 sounds like a nice round figure.
I have always been a fan of the O's. Who can forget the double winning side of '61? Then of course, our famous trio of Hurst, Peters and Moore of '66, never forgetting Charlie George and the other Charlie, Mr. Nicholas, who scored both goals in our Littlewoods cup triumph over Liverpool last season. There are so many fond memories, never forgetting that you only joined the League in 1977 and now stand proudly in the First Division. It was a shame that Orient had to move away from The Valley and share Millwall's Selhurst Park, but I will build a fine stadium in our native West London and we will be twinned with my other favourite team, Lichtenstein Rovers. Our new multi-purpose stadium will be, er, multi purpose. The snack bars will sell Maxwell tea and coffee, also Maxburgers, which will be fried in my very own fat, which I shed in workouts in the gym, at only £9.50 each.
On the staffing side, I have a few people in mind. My youngest son will be a director, likewise my daughter. My wife will make an excellent physio. My nephew is a great goalkeeper and my young God-daughter is a natural left back. There's nothing wrong with having a family club, it just depends whose family! However, the present programme sellers can remain - no one can accuse me of nepotism. With regards to the Orientear, I will do for the magazine what I have done for the Mirror. We will have some more photos i.e. Lady Di's new hairstyle and dresses, me mixing with famous sportsmen around the world etc. We will have bigger, BOLDER headlines with more exclaimation marks !!!!, and regular columns! by soccer experts! like Jim Davison and! Jonathan King!!
I understand that a certain gutter press paper magnate made a bid for Orientear last year. You will understand that I am a different sort of man altogether. I treat my staff fairly and will usually give a month's notice before sacking a couple of thousand people.
You will understand that mine is the only way forward, so do not argue. I am a reasonable man and look forward to your agreement to my proposals. If you print any of your sarcastic comments comments after my letter, I shall have no choice but to instruct my lawyers to take legal action and sue you for a tidy little sum.
                Yours

                Bob Maxwell
P.S, I am of course a lifelong socialist.

chapter 5

ELMSLIE ENDER

wealdstone

the elmslie ender

WEALDSTONE SUPPORTERS MAGAZINE
ISSUE 5   MARCH 88   FORTY PENCE

the elmslie ender

AN INDEPENDENT VIEW OF WEALDSTONE

ISSUE 9   FEB./MARCH 1989   50p

 ALL MAGAZINE !

INSIDE YOUR SOARAWAY CONTROVERSIAL ELMSLIE ENDER:
GROUNDSHARING EXCLUSIVE - IT'S HALIFAX!
GMVC GROUND SURVEY. WHEN HASTINGS WALKED OFF.
AWAYDAY TO BANBURY. CLOCKSIDERS REPLY.
ALL THE USUAL RUBBISH (and I don't mean the team).

LOCK
UP
YOUR
SHEEP
Here
come
Merthyr!

EDITORS NAME: SUDHIR RAWAL

AGE: 25   OCCUPATION: CHARTERED ACCOUNTANT.

DO YOU/HAVE YOU EVER SUPPORTED ANY OTHER TEAM? CHELSEA

MOST MEMORABLE MATCH EVER: WEALDSTONE v BOSTON UNITED - FA TROPHY FINAL

MOST MEMORABLE SEASON: 1984/85 - WEALDSTONE'S DOUBLE WINNING SEASON

ALL TIME FAVOURITE PLAYER: ALAN CORDICE

WHAT SORT OF CAR DO YOU DRIVE? XR2

YOUR FAVOURITE MUSIC: HEAVY ROCK to ROCK (ie anything from Scorpions through to Thin Lizzie)

FILMS/TV: Comedy / crime thrillers + Particular film has got to be 'the Great Escape'

FAVOURITE CLOTHES: ANYTHING BUT JEANS

POLITICAL LEANINGS: CENTRE - RIGHT

WHAT PLAYER WOULD YOU MOST LIKE TO SEE PLAYING FOR ENGLAND (SCOTLAND/WALES IF RELEVANT)?

no-one in particular, but anyone who can play football, pass etc rather than hoof the ball around ie Adams.

EDITORS NAME: MARTIN LACEY

AGE: 29   OCCUPATION: PUBLISHER OF THIS BOOK

DO YOU/HAVE YOU EVER SUPPORTED ANY OTHER TEAM? ARSENAL - TILL I WAS 11
CHELMER FLAMES (ICE HOCKEY)

MOST MEMORABLE MATCH EVER: WEALDSTONE v SWANSEA F.A.CUP 86/87 - don't know why!
DOING THE DOUBLE OVER WIMBLEDON IN 74/75

MOST MEMORABLE SEASON: 74-75 - WHEN I FIRST WENT TO AWAY GAMES

ALL TIME FAVOURITE PLAYER: GEORGE DUCK

WHAT SORT OF CAR DO YOU DRIVE? VAUXHALL ASTRA & FIAT 127

YOUR FAVOURITE MUSIC: PATSY CLINE, BLONDIE, RAMONES, BUZZCOCKS, WIRE, R.E.M., GEORGE JONES, JOY DIVISION + LOTS MORE

FILMS/TV: REPO FOR THE SKY, A TASTE OF HONEY, CARRY ON FILMS, CLOCKWORK ORANGE, TERRY & JUNE

FAVOURITE CLOTHES: LYNCH MOB T-SHIRT + ANYTHING EXCEPT BLUE JEANS

POLITICAL LEANINGS: LABOUR - BUT FAITH SEVERELY TESTED BY HAVING TO DEAL WITH SHEFFIELD CITY COUNCIL

WHAT PLAYER WOULD YOU MOST LIKE TO SEE PLAYING FOR ENGLAND (SCOTLAND/WALES IF RELEVANT)? VINCE JONES, JOHN FASHANU

the elmslie ender

AN INDEPENDENT VIEW OF WEALDSTONE

A visit to many non-league grounds, even in the higher ranks, can be something like standing in a muddy field with all the atmosphere of outer space. A visit to Wealdstone is nothing whatsoever like that, which is why at the age of eleven I stopped describing myself as an Arsenal supporter. The problem with Arsenal was that nobody else in my family liked football and the tortuous trek across North London to Highbury was considered too fraught for me to make on my own. But a couple of miles down the road I found the alternative and I haven't felt the urge to visit Highbury for eighteen years.

Wealdstone have rarely numbered among the giants of the non-league game. Eighty-nine years have brought them three league championships, two Wembley finals and a mere two F.A. Cup victories over Football League opponents. Home crowds have not averaged four figures for the past fifteen years. What Wealdstone do have in their favour is a hard core of extraordinarily loyal, fanatical and vocal fans. You'll find us wherever Wealdstone play, whether it's a local derby with Enfield, a rainy night in Gateshead or Macclesfield, even a pre-season friendly or Middlesex Senior Cup tie. We may not always outnumber the home supporters but it's rare indeed if we don't make more noise. At home too, Lower Mead, ramshackle though it may be, is a perfect football fans' ground, terraced on three and a half sides, with substantial covered areas behind each goal, including the Elmslie End, a cavernous long shed with a downward sloping roof which almost overhangs the goal. Home games are not always magic, but just occasionally, usually on a soggy Tuesday night when nothing much is at stake but something intangible gels, the crowd succeeds in firing up the players and the action on the pitch spurs the crowd on some more, then the passion, partisanship and sheer hysteria can barely be surpassed at any football ground in the country.

History: Founded 1900; Athenian League champions 1952; joined Isthmian League; won Amateur Cup 1966; Joined Southern League 1971; promoted to Premier Division 1974; founder members of Alliance Premier League 1979; relegated 1981; won Southern League 1982. Recent events start here. In 1984/5 Wealdstone became the first, and so far only, team to achieve the non-league double, winning the Gola League (now GMVC) and F.A. Trophy. There was only one way to go from there, down. Rival fans would assert that Wealdstone's triumph came in a poor season. Certainly the double winning team were past their best, and but for the Gola League's bizarre points system of three points for an away win but only two for a home win (since abandoned) Wealdstone would actually have finished third behind Nuneaton and Bath. The team was not strengthened, slumped to mid table in 85/6 and narrowly avoided relegation in 86/7. Manager Bryan Hall resigned and moved to upwardly mobile Yeovil Town, followed by several players. The Elmslie Ender made its debut.

The magazine was not a reaction to the depressing events on the pitch - as football fans we are all used to the ups and downs - but the inertia which seemed to grip the club at boardroom level. Wealdstone were sinking obviously and inexorably and nobody seemed to care. Also as printer of the early issues of 'When Saturday Comes' I witnessed the beginnings of the fanzine explosion at first hand and felt it was a matter of pride that Wealdstone should have their own magazine.

87/8 dawned and things got worse. The new manager, Colin Meldrum, proved totally useless. At one stage Wealdstone were totally unable to field a team of eleven professionals and had to call up two players from the Supporters Club Sunday league team. By October they had not won a match and he was sacked, whereupon Wealdstone promptly beat Enfield 1-0. Appointing another manager was clearly a mistake. The next incumbent was Terry Burton, formerly a coach at Arsenal, now something or other at Wimbledon. He lasted fourteen games, none of which were victories.

BRITAINS MOST BANNED FOOTBALL MAGAZINE !

As if being relegation certainties by December wasn't bad enough there was an even darker cloud on the horizon. Wealdstone won the Alliance Premier League two years before the introduction of automatic promotion to Division Four, but they wouldn't have qualified in any case because the ground would not have met Football League requirements. As long as I can remember there have been plans for a new ground; in the seventies it was going to be on the same site, but since it was clear this would not be economic in the eighties it was planned instead to sell Lower Mead, long earmarked by the council as the ideal spot for a supermarket, and build on a cheaper location. Property developer and builder, David Morritt, who became chairman at the beginning of the decade, for a long time looked like the man to achieve this. But land is scarce in Harrow and nobody wants a football ground on their doorstep, so despite surface optimism nothing happened.

Happier days: Wealdstone players show just what they think of the 'sacred' Wembley pitch. The familiar face on the left is Vince Jones. Though tremendously popular with the fans he could never hold a regular place at Wealdstone. He was transferred to Wimbledon for a derisory sum, went straight into the first division side and....the rest is history, as they say.

However, Wealdstone's Wembley triumph came on the day of the Bradford fire, and in the ensuing climate of safety consciousness the capacity of Lower Mead was repeatedly cut, from 9500 (the record crowd stands at over 13000) to 3000, no big deal in itself since the last time Wealdstone attracted over 3000 spectators was in 1979. Morritt claimed, however, that £150,000 worth of improvements were required to prevent the ground being closed altogether, and it would be pointless to spend this money when a new stadium was being built, so we were told the club would groundshare with either Harrow Borough or Barnet for the '88/9 season. But rumours suggested the cost of the improvements was being vastly exagerrated, the implication being that Morritt wanted Lower Mead vacant for whatever reason. At this point people began to wonder just what his motives were and whether there was any prospect of a new ground ever being built.

Worse was to come. The story broke in the 'Harrow Observer', and was quickly seized on by the national dailies, that Morritt had put in an offer for Watford and planned to move Wealdstone in at Vicarage Road. This would have been tantamount to a death warrant for the club. As it happened the plan was a non starter: Watford rejected the deal and Elton John cancelled the sale. But Morritt's goose was cooked. Though he controlled enough shares to remain chairman of Wealdstone if he so desired, a combination of legal moves and pressure from club members and supporters culminating in a pitch invasion and demonstration persuaded him it was time to leave. Vice chairman Alan Clifton took over at the top, promising a new era of optimism and co-operation, specifically supporters representation on the board, a new ground within a year, no groundsharing, and money for new players. One year on the coup has only partly fulfilled expectations. At the time of writing (March '89) the site for the new ground has yet to be publicly announced. Groundsharing has been in the air again, though looks unlikely for '89/90, and while Tony Jennings has spent freely on new players the team is currently nearer further relegation to the wastes of the Southern League lower divisions than it is to regaining its place in the GMVC. But at least Wealdstone F.C. will survive, something which for too long we couldn't say with confidence.

As for the Elmslie Ender, through all the disasters it grew in sales and stature, the biggest break coming from the unlikeliest source. In issue 3 I penned a paragraph slagging off Dagenham after they'd beaten Wealdstone 3-2 at Lower Mead with a last minute penalty. It was the sort of insignificant whingeing all football fans partake of after losing a local derby, though it also touched on a genuine grievance against the East London club, Wealdstone fans having twice been involved in wasted trips to matches which had been called off. However, the editor of a Dagen-

A group of Wealdstone supporters display their usual sense of decency and restraint at an away game.

ham supporters' magazine pointed this out to Dagenham officials. Now, the Elmslie Ender is an independent magazine, and to this day we have not had any complaint from Dagenham F.C., or been asked by anyone to explain, justify or defend our comments. Dagenham complained direct to the GMVC Management Committee, who issued us with an ultimatum: apologise or they would instruct all their member clubs to ban the magazine from their grounds. Though agrieved we apologised. They banned us anyway, first from the 22 GMVC grounds, then, since by this time Wealdstone were assured of relegation, from every ground in the feeder leagues, a ridiculous 212 in all, giving rise to our proud boast that the Elmslie Ender is Britain's most banned football magazine. And all because we spoke up for Wealdstone fans!

The Elmslie Ender has never shrunk from criticism of events on the field, such that it has been re-christened the 'Elmslie Abuser' by some. But anyone who could watch the team they love being dragged through the mud and made a laughing stock and remain entirely positive about it should be editing a club programme. It has been our misfortune to publish our magazine for two years which have seen almost nothing but disaster. We have nevertheless retained a sense of humour and done our best to rally support even in the darkest moments. Wealdstone are limping along on home crowds of 5-600, but can still find 100 supporters cheering them on at a typical away game, something pretty much unique at this level.

The official attitude to us at Wealdstone has been necessarily cool. After the original Dagenham complaint we were summoned to the club office and warned that unless we agreed to the Supporters Club taking over the Elmslie Ender, or at least taking responsibility for the contents, we would no longer be able to sell it in the ground. This would have been easy, as my co-editor is on the Supporters Club committee, but it would have meant compromising our independence, something we were not prepared to do. In any case by this time the club was preoccupied with its internal ructions, so we largely ignored the advice and continued to sell until the end of the season, when Wealdstone were forced to impose the ban dictated by the higher authorities. Indeed, with optimism worthy of King Canute, Alan Clifton wrote to us specifically banning any further publication of the Elmslie Ender. The only changes we have made are to include the word 'independent' prominently on the front and sell on a corner outside the ground. Sales have boomed! Unofficially our relations with the club are perfectly cordial. In fact my co-editor Sudhir Rawal also contributes to the matchday programme, while one of the supporter-directors, Toby Jackson, is an occasional contributor to the Elmslie Ender. In short, we get along fine.

There's certainly a lot to be said for supporting a 'small' club, and though we all wish Wealdstone could be not quite so small, should you ever be at a loose end for a game to watch you will find yourself most welcome here. A word of warning though: you'll come back for at least eighteen years!

MARTIN LACEY

MARTIN SAYS......

Well, back for another season of agony and ecstasy, lets hope a bit less of the former than last year. And if you believe Aaron Gransby in the Harrow Observer (bearing in mind of course that he's a Harrow Borough supporter) this is definitely our last here at Lower Mead and there's nothing can be done about it, the council having decided in their wisdom that the place is unsafe. To be honest I have myself many a time wondered just how safe the Elmslie End structure is, and as for the main stand only the fire authorities are qualified to comment. And yes, Mr.Morritt is perfectly justified in saying he won't spend a six figure sum bringing the ground up to standard when he's in the process of building a brand new ground. But as I write, in mid July, the proposed site for the new ground isn't even for sale as far as anyone knows and a lot of people won't have total faith in the masterplan for the future until the floodlights are up and the first match at the Morritt Stadium kicks off. After all, there's been no shortage of ambitious plans in the past, as long as I can remember in fact, that have come to nothing.

Make no mistake, ground sharing would kill the club. If we couldn't get 500 to some of our home games last season how many are going to turn up for 'home' games at Barnet? And how can we hope to win new fans this season, even if things go well on the pitch, when there won't be football at Lower Mead in '88-89 ? We might be able to make do with ground sharing for one season at a pinch, but any longer and the people of Harrow, who haven't exactly flocked to watch the Stones of late anyway, are going to forget Wealdstone F.C. exists. Wealdstone belong in Harrow and nowhere else. So, Mr.Morritt, the life of this club is in your hands. Don't let us down. Get your shovel out and get building!

Looking back now.....the final word on the end of last season. Was it a mirage or did Enfield really bring nearly a whole coachload of supporters? Of course it had been well publicised in advance that they would have adequate police protection. I wonder who they're supposed to need protection from though? And did I say ade-quate? The number of 'boys in blue' on hand looked more like they were planning for a full scale civil war rather than Wealdstone v. Enfield. Still at least the police did what they were supposed to i.e. keep rival supporters apart. Last time I went to Enfield (1986) the police arrived three quarters of an hour after all the trouble (which was started by Enfield supporters) and responded by randomly ejecting Wealdstone fans and threatening gbh to anyone who didn't want to lick their boots. Somebody at Southbury Road has obviously sussed that it's cheaper to dial 999 than arrange sensible police cover in advance.

As for our match with Barnet, the all-ticket arrangement was a fiasco. It seemed perfectly reasonable when it looked like Barnet would either be celebrating the championship or needing points to clinch it from that match and a capacity crowd was on the cards, but it was obvious at least a fortnight in advance that Barnet had blown it and the game was going to be a total anti-climax. Surely the all-ticket arrangement could have been lifted then, or at least it could have been better publi-cised that tickets would be available on the day.

And I see my plea for an end to the racial abuse got a BIG response at the Enfield and Barnet games (yes, I'm being sarcastic now). I'm not going to start sounding like a scratched record so I'll say no more on the subject. Maybe Santa'll bring some of you some brains for Christmas.

What does this season hold? At least things can't get worse.....can they? No, from now on it's up and up. It's always sad to see old faces depart, but in all honesty the only one we're going to miss on the field is Steve Tapley. To think of OUR player of the season coming back in Enfield colours! I'm sure he'll get a real warm Lower Mead reception! Mark Graves? A nice bloke and all that but he hasn't really looked capable of performing at this level since before he lost his place to Andy Graham in the double season. We wish him all the best of course. Promisingly we've still got Pat McCarthy, Steve Hatter and Byron Walton, new faces who brought a glimmer of hope at last in the spring. And new heroes....Barry Lowe - he may look like he's got lost on the way to collect his pension but did you see the way he ran rings round those young Chelsea wimps? And Mike Perry - a few more goals like the season's opener won't go amiss. What to aim for this year? Realistically, half way in the league; a decent run in the Trophy; getting past the first round in the F.A.Cup. No matter, I'll still be cheering the team on next April, digging up my souvenir piece of turf at the final match.......

the elmslie ender

40p

NUMBER TWO
AUG/SEP 1987

COLIN MELDRUM SPEAKS ★ WEALDSTONES FIRST PROFESSIONAL MATCH ★ AWAYDAY TO ALTRINCHAM

Issue 2 - August 1987
'At least things can't get worse',
we predicted naively!

Phil Jackson and Don Cross against Altrincham.......glory for them but shame for Wealdstone
Photo by Lee Glenn.

DISGRACE ! says Sudhir Rawal

Two supporters club players have represented Wealdstone F.C. in G.M.Vauxhall Conference matches this season. The two, Don Cross and Phil Jackson started the match against Altrincham; Cross started against Runcorn with Jackson on the substitutes bench; Cross and Jackson were both substitutes against Welling United; Cross was substitute against Telford United.

A club of Wealdstone's stature should never have got in such a position. How can a club which performed the non-league double just two years ago be in such a state that it has to rely on Supporters Club players to make up a team?

No disrespect to the two people concerned, who performed magnificently at Altrincham, but too many people were let down. The 100 Stones supporters who travelled the 200 miles to Altrincham had made the trip to see Wealdstone F.C., not SFC Wealdstone, who could be seen on a Sunday morning at Whitchurch and Headstone Lane.

Everyone appreciates the club had injuries and suspensions, but one player was on holiday and another could not get time off work. If they want to fart around in the season that's their problem, but they should not be playing football at a club of such high standing.

The name of Wealdstone has been blackened, and for such a stupid reason. Can you imagine the same happening at Barnet or Enfield?

The early season form has been absolutely diabolical. The performance at Welling was the worst I have seen by a Wealdstone side in years. It was painful to watch. Welling are a poor team but they pulled us to shreds. Even the good players performed badly.

the elmslie ender

NUMBER THREE
OCT / NOV 1987

40p

OUR BEST EVER CUP RUN....WEALDSTONE'S FILM STAR FAN.....AWAYDAY TO CHELTENHAM....
PROBLEMS AT SCARBOROUGH....81/82 REVISITED.....PROGRAMME SURVEY.....and lots more...........

THE SEASON SO FAR   by Martin Lacey

So it's goodbye Colin, hello Terry. Undoubtedly the truest thing said about the affair was that it was a mistake appointing Colin Meldrum in the first place. He never gave the slightest sign of being a success. Quite honestly, it was embarassing to watch some of our performances, seeing the players running around with no tactics, no co-ordination, no ideas. Especially since the players we've got aren't a bad lot by any means. We all know the squad lacks strength in depth, and one or two, only one or two, are not good enough for this level. But basically we have a team which, if not capable of bringing the championship back just yet, should certainly be able to hold its own in the GMVC, with the right leadership of course. It was all so predictable too. Nothing at all happened in the close season to suggest there would be any improvement on the dire form at the end of last year. The alarm bells should have been ringing non-stop, and throughout the pre-season friendlies they certainly were. At least it seems unlikely our best players will join a mad rush to join Colin Meldrum at his next club!

Miraculously crowds appear to be up on last year (the invisible man must be bringing all his relations), hopefully the rot will be stopped before total disillusion sets in and some success can still be salvaged from the rest of the season. The uncertainty over Lower Mead, the continued existence of the new ground only as a pipedream and the prospect of ground sharing hang like a nasty black cloud over us all, but the sacking of Meldrum proved that the powers that be here still have their hearts in the club. It would have been so easy to let him go on till it was too late.

It was quite a shock to arrive at Cheltenham and find the team playing in blue and white. Combined with the unfamiliar sponsors name it suggested someone had left the kit at Lower Mead and had to borrow Cheltenham's spare set, but no, we really are back in the old blue and white again. Now, changing a club's kit or colours is a serious matter. These things mean a lot to the fans and some clubs have got in the habit of changing strip design, if not colours, every season as a matter of course.

Supporters are rarely consulted and the changes are usually a marketing ploy designed to extort as much money as possible from the long suffering and ever shrinking army of fans who want to be seen in the right kit and have the latest souvenirs, and the players end up looking berks in their dinky diagonal textured stripes. But in Wealdstone's case the move is the right one. The club played in blue and white for eighty odd years until somebody with scant respect for tradition decided blue and yellow was 'in'. I was in Canada at the time, so Imissed the reasoning behind it but always vaguely assumed the club was offerrred some surplus Wimbledon kits at a knock-down price, or else was trying to set up a sponsorship deal with a custard manufacturer. I got used to it, even replaced my trusty blue and white scarf with a blue and yellow one a couple of years ago. But blue and white is a return to pride and tradition, an acknowledgement that Wealdstone F.C. has a history pre-Morritt dynasty, and one day our decade in blue and yellow will be seen as merely a minor aberration forgiveable in view of the harsh times in which it was perpetrated.

the elmslie ender

WEALDSTONE SUPPORTERS MAGAZINE
ISSUE 4   DEC/JAN. 87/88   FORTY PENCE

With a lot to say about HOOLIGANISM in general and TAMWORTH in particular, plus END OF THE CORDICE ERA, Awayday to RUNCORN, the day DAVE BASSETT WAS SENT OFF at Lower Mead and all the usual moaning.

Issue 4 - December 1987
One win, four managers and out of the F.A. Cup. What next?

MARTIN MOANS !

Walloped at Welling.... destroyed by Dagenham..... Just when you thought things couldn't possibly get worse, they do : TAKEN APART BY TAMWORTH! Yes, we were kidding ourselves when we thought Wealdstone could live on the same pitch as the mighty West Midlands Leaguers - the class difference was just too great. Quite honestly our players looked like reluctant participants in a Sunday morning kickabout, quite unconcerned about the result, and if that's what they think of the F.A.Cup it's high time they f***ed off and let somebody else down. Soon Sunday morning in the park will be the only place they can get a game (and here I'm probably doing SFC an injustice). Can't they get it through their heads that there's actually several hundred people that PAY to watch them play, and a sizeable band

that follow them around the country and cheer them on even when things aren't going well. They don't deserve it. Maybe the players think we're just a bunch of eccentric nutcases, and after Tamworth I wonder myself about our sanity. But it's our money that keeps Wealdstone going, gives them shirts to wear and a club to play for. At least we deserve the respect they can give us by giving 100% EVERY week. And while we're about it, for a special award for apathy, incompetence and pure unbridled cowardice can I nominate.....no, not the Wealdstone team....
THE STAFFORDSHIRE CONSTABULARY. There were easily enough police on duty to enforce some rudimentary segregation. Instead they were content to let the thugs hold sway- at one stage the Wealdstone supporters were actually protecting two terrified Special (i.e. part-time) constables from the hooligans. I watched most of the game with the Tamworth SUPPORTERS, which seemed like the safest place to be and they were openly ashamed of the hooligans and apologetic for the police lack of action. As they pointed out, the thugs would not be seen at the ground again till the next cup run.

Since that fateful day things have hardly got better - stuffed at Stafford, embarassed at Enfield....chastised by Cheltenham....buried at Barnet.... and very nearly yomped over by Yeading!

HICK COPS COP OUT !

Apart from the continued dismal run the main talking point since the last issue was the scenes that took place at Tamworth in the F.A.Cup. We were fairly beaten on the pitch - the players managed to contrive the worst performance of the season, and there have been some bad ones! This incompetence was nothing compared to that of the police and the administrators of Tamworth though. I'm not a knocker of the police - I'll leave that to the loony lefties, Martin, - but the total lack of action was unbelievable. When I got into Tamworth at 11 in the morning my companions and I were confronted by the police at the railway station. A plainclothes policeman was backed up by a transit van load of policemen. He said there had been rumours circulating that we were bringing 800 supporters - that we haven't got 800 supporters at the moment! Did the police attempt to ask either club how many fans we would bring? Tamworth were told on three occasions by Pete Braxton that he expected only 200 supporters to travel. If we had taken 800 fans I can only imagine the riot which would have ensued. What did take place was disturbing enough. It was Tamworth's biggest game since 1969, but at kick-off time only 6-8 policemen were inside the ground. Just at this time the pubs closed and two hundred drunken yobbos walked in. The inneffective and undermanned police did nothing. They did nothing when these thugs attacked Stones fans behind the goal. The thin blue line was not the police segregating rival supporters but the Wealdstone supporters protecting the police from getting their heads kicked in, no matter that we were likely to get OUR heads kicked in.

No attempt was made to segregate supporters either before or after the initial trouble. Contrast this with the Metropolitan Police. You may accuse them of overkill, but it's effective. When was the last time we had trouble at our ground? For the Lincoln match the notorious Lincoln Transit mob didn't even make it into Harrow. They were stopped and turned back miles before they reached the ground. Incidentally, one of these van carried thugs has just been jailed for five years for his hooligan activities.

Back to Tamworth. Even when the modern day equivalent of the SPG turned up they were limited in their actions by a weak kneed inspector. These SPG types are evil looking.They have DM type heavy boots, blue overalls and black dots which go under the guise of hair. If they had been let loose the thugs would have been unceremoniously dealt with in a few moments, fair justice. Yet the inspector was happy to allow things to go on. Fearing that if they were sent in the game would be abandoned he was quite happy for the linesman to have fireworks thrown at him, to be kicked as he attempted to run down the line and to be continually spat upon. What did he want to happen? A firework up the linesman's arse? The linesman couldn't do his job properly and the second goal would not have stood if he was able to run down the line.

The game should have been abandoned, and it was fitting that Colchester United beat Tamworth 3-0 in the first round. The F.A. are just as bad. Up until now no action seems to have been taken. It will probably be no more than a note in the programme about the little boys not doing it again. They are unlikely to be able to read it, let alone take heed - that's if they turn up at the Lamb Ground again this season.

The local newspaper shares some blame in hyping up the game. It made us out to be all conquering heroes who would be so difficult to topple. All conquering? Two years ago maybe - but not now. The same paper said after the game how wonderful their fans were. What?!!! Did they fight well? Did they run onto the pitch on umpteen occasions in a particularly graceful manner? Did they throw their fireworks with commendable accuracy? What a pillock! A final postscript: our friend the police inspector thought the crowd trouble was very minimal, and that the police controlled the game very well. What more can you say.

SUDHIR RAWAL

SINCE LAST TIME......... by Martin Lacey

'As most of you know, (in fact as most of you knew before I did), since last issue the 'Elmslie Ender' has become **controversial**. As author of the 'offending' comments, about which no more will be said, I can assure all concerned that no malice was intended. Nevertheless we have been threatened with being banned from the terraces both at Wealdstone and every ground in the league if we don't tone down our act. In effect we have been asked to submit to censorship, which poses a real threat to the existence of this magazine. For the time being we continue. Yes, we will be more careful. But no, if people who wield power without having any idea what it's like to be a real fan on the terraces think we're going to pay up and shut up they've got another thing coming.

Well, David Morritt's takeover of Watford appears to have been a 24 hour wonder. I can't deny the idea brought a smile to my face, not because I'd like Wealdstone to play at Vicarage Road, but because for one night Watford's fans must have had nightmares at the prospect of their team ending up playing in blue and white and called Wealdstone and Watford Hornets F.C. or something similar. Now that the farce is over the question on everyone's lips is 'what now?' Plans for a new stadium in Harrow are obviously getting nowhere otherwise, presumably, the bid for Watford would never have arisen. Perhaps the council could tell us if there's actually the slightest prospect of planning permission for a new football ground being granted anywhere in the borough. It would be bound to face stiff opposition from local residents practically anywhere. Right now it looks certain that if Wealdstone F.C. is to exist next season it will have to exist at Lower Mead, which means the safety repairs will just have to be done, at a cost of anything from £2.50 to £250,000, depending on whose estimates you believe. Can I go further and suggest a plan so bold and radical that I realise many people will think I'm being flippant. How about staying at Lower Mead permanently? Mr. Morritt has put quite a lot of money

into Wealdstone over the years. It seems clear he now wants his money back by selling the freehold to the ground. Why? He is a rich man, rich enough to come up with £2m to buy Watford overnight it seems. So why not put money into bringing Lower Mead up to Football League standards? The main stand side would have to be completely rebuilt, but there's room there for a few shops, flats or office blocks to pay for it. The other three sides of the ground need only modest alterations. Access is good. Segregation no problem. And it's a great ground to watch football on. In my opinion it's high time someone looked at it positively.

OK, what's been happening on the pitch? Our last chance of something to cheer about this season went predictably out the window with the Trophy tie against Telford. For ten minutes we were all over them. Then Telford scored......then they scored again..... then again, and they spent the rest of the match laughing at us. I can't remember feeling so utterly let down since we lost 5-0 at home to Enfield in the F.A. Cup about ten years ago. Telford's fans put up a good show, but where the hell were they when we went to the Bucks Head for a league match earlier in the season? Sat at home waiting for a cup run. A word too for Kevin Charlton, their goalkeeper. Over the years he's taken every shade of abuse from Wealdstone's fans but he always stays good humoured and ready for a chat. At the end of the match, when the rest of the Telford players went to applaud their supporters he stayed to give us his compliments, out of sympathy more than anything I suspect. He must reckon by the time Wealdstone are playing at the same level as Telford again he'll be well past retirement age. Perhaps they'll give him a job in P.R. Finally, they were selling red plastic clowns noses in aid of Comic Relief at the turnstiles. I noticed by the end of the game several of these had been thrown on the pitch. A more apt comment would be hard to find.

the elmslie ender

WEALDSTONE SUPPORTERS MAGAZINE
ISSUE 5   MARCH 88   FORTY PENCE

INSIDE YOUR SOARAWAY CONTROVERSIAL ELMSLIE ENDER:
GROUNDSHARING EXCLUSIVE - IT'S HALIFAX!
GMVC GROUND SURVEY. WHEN HASTINGS WALKED OFF.
AWAYDAY TO BANBURY. CLOCKSIDERS REPLY.
ALL THE USUAL RUBBISH (and I don't mean the team).

Issue 5 - March 1988
Disasters on the pitch take a back seat

In a surprise move last night, David Moppitt, millionaire builder turned football ground buyer, made a £72.63 bid to buy out Halifax Town's board of directors. 'I have always wanted to be chairman of Halifax', said Moppitt from his base in America, 'I saw the highlights of their 4-0 defeat by Notts. Forest and was impressed by their general standard of play and the overall set-up seemed custom-made for the 21st century'.

A source close to Moppitt stated, 'David is believed to be trying to purchase any ground that Stuart Pearce has scored at, but I refute the allegation that he is going to build blocks of flats on the grounds concerned and call them Pearce Mansions.'

Our reporter Aaron Glumsby, caught up with Moppitt in his 17th floor penthouse office suite on the former site of the now defunct Miami Dolphins stadium, now renamed Moppitt Towers.

Mr. Moppitt outlined his plans. 'I had always said that my intention was to get the best for Willesden Football Club and to achieve league status. By moving to Halifax we immediately overcome the problems concerning the state of Lowe Mead Stadium. We would be playing in a stadium already enjoying league status. As I always look to the future there would be some priorities to attend to. For example we would need to build a new ladies toilet in case Vauxhall-Opel take over the sponsorship of the Barclays League.'

Asked if he thought his co-directors and the club members would share his enthusiasm, Moppitt commented, 'As you are aware my fellow directors Mr. Macaroni and Mr. Cluck are lifelong supporters of the club who rarely miss a game, they may be difficult to persuade. The vice-chairman, Mr. Clifftop, is behind me 100%.

'As for the members, if they are upset I am sure the offer of a good deal on one of my new properties in Rochdale or Newport would appease them. Anyway, I could outvote the lot of them.'

Back home, supporters club chairman Roy (Mein) Kamp was furious. 'What a carve up, sod me, the bastard, bless my soul, blow that for a game of soldiers, good grief, whatever next, where is Halifax?' he exclaimed.

Supporters club secretary Rick DuGod was equally surprised. 'It comes as a complete shock, can you get there by train direct from Watford Junction?'

Meanwhile we are getting reports from our foreign correspondent that an American based British millionaire property developer has put in a bid to buy Juventus.

Another source close to Mr. Moppitt said, 'I believe this bid to be from David, however it is unlikely to go through as there is no bar under the main stand.'

It is of course a rule of the General Motors Vauxhall Conference that there must be a bar within throwing up distance of the pitch.

Source unknown, I'm afraid.

By TREVOR HAYLETT

NON-LEAGUE Wealdstone United have made an audacious take-over bid for First Division Watford.

They want to buy out ~~~~~~ in with Wat~~~~

THE BASTARD! Not only is he threatening to move us all to Watford without any consultation, but he's changed the name of the team without telling us. Either that or the Daily Mail are displaying their usual standardsm of informed, accurate journalism. Wonder if it's the same reporter who visited Enfield Town F.C.?

Issue 6 - April 1988
Morritt has resigned,
relegation beckons.

WHAT ABOUT FOOTBALL ?

Like most supporters, I suspect, I don't give a toss who's chairman or what his motives for holding that position are. That's under normal circumstances. That's if we can have a competent team and a secure, well planned future. I don't think Wealdstone supporters are particularly demanding. We are grateful for the success we've had and don't underestimate David Morritt's role in bringing it. But now there's been three years of meteoric decline, and whatever criteria you base your judgement on Morritt has failed, failed abysmally. We are playing in a condemned stadium, with no definite prospect of a new ground despite years of promises, we are facing relegation as a result of bad managerial appointments and lack of investment in the team, and the club is losing money largely due to poor attendances. (Regular readers will be familiar with my criticisms of the club's failure to launch any significant PR or advertising to interest local people even when offerred free help to do so).

Alan Clifton has offerred David Morritt an honourable, reasonable way out, suggesting that he should take over as chairman with David Mor-

ritt staying on the board of directors. Surely if Morritt has the interests of Wealdstone at heart he would accept this? But he has said he will be chairman till his dying day. For who's benefit? Certainly not ours.

The first shots in the battle for control were fired at the Supporters Club AGM on March 7th which was addressed by both Morritt and Clifton. Morritt set the ball rolling by wagging his finger and warning everyone that he didn't appreciate nuisance calls to his home in the early hours. Then he complained that he hadn't been invited to sit in on the meeting from the start, thus missing interesting facts like the Junior Stones Club have twice as many members as the supporters club proper, and the Elmslie Ender contributed the magnificent total of £5.80 to club funds last season (I should point out that this only takes into account Issue 1, and we have really high expenses, and beer's gone up and, er....). Anyway, David should join the Supporters Club next season. Basically, he stumbled, floundered, forgot what he was talking about, contradicted himself over the Watford affair (saying 1. that he never intended to do anything behind the supporters' backs but the Watford deal was investigated, discussed and rejected before it ever reached the press, and 2. that he realised only relocation in the Borough of Harrow was acceptable but he still considered the Watford deal could have been a success, for financial reasons), got everyone's backs up by constantly referring to Wealdstone as 'my club', exposed himself to ridicule by suggesting one of the benefits of the Watford deal would have been that Wealdstone members would have been able to watch Watford free when Wealdstone were away, apparently oblivious to the fact that most of the supporters present actually go to away games and would rather travel to the other end of Britain to watch Wealdstone than see Watford. Most disturbingly of all, he declared that he **didn't know** how much Wealdstone F.C. owes him. Thi was stretching credibility a bit far.

The challenger, Alan Clifton, read a prepared statement which had been given in advance to David Morritt. Basical-

ly he said what everyone wanted to hear. Make him chairman and there would be a fantastic new ground in twelve months, supporters representation on the board and no groundsharing under any circumstances. The only thing that could possibly be said against his plans is that it all sounded too good to be true. Nevertheless, there is no faulting Clifton's track record, dedication and abilities. The vote of 36-1 in favour of a motion of no confidence in Morritt summed up the prevalent feeling.

Of course it meant nothing. Morritt controls the shares and can stay on if he wants to. I wouldn't pretend to understand the complexities of the legal situation and the various moves currently going on. If you believe half of what you read in the Harrow Observer the club is heading for total anarchy. I only hope somebody takes responsibility for paying the players.

While the future existence or non-existence of Wealdstone F.C. is clearly a bigger concern than whether we drop down a division it is nevertheless slightly disturbing that in this debate football has hardly been mentioned. It would have been comforting if either Morritt or Clifton had attempted an explanation of why a club supposedly sitting on £7 million is plunging towards the Southern League.

MARTIN LACEY

The Final table...........

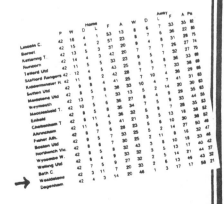

chapter 6

ARSENAL ECHO ECHO

arsenal

There are 21000 pieces of A4 paper locked in 6 white boxes somewhere between the Sheffield printers and my home in Guildford, Surrey. I've taken the day off work and along with my stapler aimed to unite them into hundreds of 24 page magazines in time for the forthcoming home match.

It's 4.30 and they should have been here over five hours ago. Princess Anne has just had four private letters stolen from Buckingham Palace. I'm worried. I must wait and wait, growing more impatient by the minute.

With luck this article, indeed this book, will be read by someone in the 21st Century. It would be great to think that the *Arsenal Echo Echo* will still be going, tackling the major stories - "Why have Manchester United sacked manager Vinny Jones?" "Is Ossie Ardiles really the right man to take over as Chairman of the Football Association?"

The *Echo Echo* has been strong enough to survive a turbulent childhood. Most kids would be mentally scarred from such a terrifying start - early rejection, arrest by the police, getting banned from Highbury and continually being folded in half and shoved in someone's back pocket, but the *Echo Echo* has, to the end of the 1988/89 season at least, survived all that.

I often wish I could honestly claim that the magazine sprung out of discontent for something or, more excitingly, someone at Arsenal. But unfortunately it wasn't. It just seemed a great thing to do.

After putting it all together with the aid of typewriter, glue, scissors, photocopies etc., I faced the prospect of an enormous printing bill. Luckily I bumped into someone who could photocopy 1250 copies, after working hours, cash in hand and with all the nudge-nudges and wink-winks-my-son thrown in free, which was just as well because there were plenty of those.

Tuesday November 3rd 1987 and Chelsea are the visitors to Highbury. Along with a friend we arrived at the Mecca of football hours early (so we left Brisbane Road and went to Highbury instead).

"Right, let's start selling," "Yes, let's." Although neither said anything we shared similar thoughts - How do we sell it? It was dark, everyone was rushing about, no-one apart from me, my friend and nudge-nudge wink-wink geezer knew anything about the magazine or even types like it, and with a picture of Lester Piggott on the front page, I think even Victor Kiam would have struggled to flog it.

Two hours later we'd sold about 12 and at 30p each that was £3.60. We were laughing. After squeezing the remaining 687 through the turnstiles we entered the ground.

At half time I tried to sell on the North Bank. Someone bought one....and then the bloke behind also wanted a copy....and the bloke next to him. Suddenly it's , "'Ere mate I'll 'ave one", and "Ay, over 'ere". Things were looking up. What's more Arsenal beat Chelsea 3-1.

THE NON-LAUGHING POLICEMEN

The two policemen approaching me a few weeks later weren't going to buy a copy. They weren't even going to pick one up, browse through it and then ask if it's okay if they keep it for reference - "No, piss off fuzz, give us yer 30 pence". I'm glad I didn't say that. These two PCs were about to enforce the law: "Has the club given you permission to sell this 'ere magazine?" "They haven't said I can't", which was true, although unlikely to mislead even the greenest boy in blue. After being escorted across the North Bank to the club offices the assistant secretary David Miles made my double negative positively redundant and I was kicked out of the ground. The magazine was banned from Highbury for its forseeable life, which didn't seem very long; luckily I wasn't.

It's a rare experience that few can have known to be sitting in the bookmakers hearing the latest score from a match taking place barely 100 yards away. What's more, it was a bugger of an afternoon for the dogs in trap 6 at Hackney.

The press loved it. Not that trap 6 had been a bummer but that Arsenal could ban a magazine that was about....Arsenal, and had been put together by....Arsenal fans - the enemy within. Yours truly even appeared on ITV at 3.30....in the morning. Mind you a lot of people actually rang ITV to complain about the scheduling of the interview - mainly nightworkers.

The last year has been fairly incident-free and with ten issues now in circulation the *Echo Echo* has enough regular buyers to, if we maintain the standard, hopefully see us into the 21st Century.

P.S. The boxes eventually arrived at 6 o'clock.

GUY HAVORD

MAGAZINE TITLE: ARSENAL ECHO ECHO

EDITORS NAME: GUY HAVORD

AGE: 21   OCCUPATION: PIMP

DO YOU/HAVE YOU EVER SUPPORTED ANY OTHER TEAM? NO

MOST MEMORABLE MATCH EVER: 1979 F.A. CUP FINAL.

MOST MEMORABLE SEASON: 1979/80

ALL TIME FAVOURITE PLAYER: MALCOLM MACDONALD/LIAM BRADY/CHARLIE NICHOLAS

WHAT SORT OF CAR DO YOU DRIVE? HONDA ACCORD

YOUR FAVOURITE MUSIC: HOUSEMARTINS/ELTON JOHN/~~SASHA DISTEL~~ FRANK SINARTRA

FILMS/TV: ANY BY WOODY ALLEN/LAUREL + HARDY/MARX BROTHERS/DORIS DAY

FAVOURITE CLOTHES: JEAN'S (SHE DOESN'T MIND!)

POLITICAL LEANINGS: A FAT CAPITALIST/FASCIST PIG (BUT WITH A HEART, OF COURSE)

WHAT PLAYER WOULD YOU MOST LIKE TO SEE PLAYING FOR ENGLAND (SCOTLAND/ WALES IF RELEVANT)?

JOHN BARNES.

The
Arsenal Echo Echo
November   30p

- Pleat resigns . ●Hartley sacked.
- Venables goes missing in Florida.
- Ardiles deported back to Argentina

SPURS NAME NEW BOSS

"Ivring Scholar looked at my record and said:
'Lester, you're the man for Tottenham.'"

The
Arsenal Echo Echo
ISSUE 2   30p

STEVE WILLIAMS ATE MY HAMSTER

BRIAN CLOUGH ... fears

BRIAN CLOUGH was almost speechless last night.
    But it didn't stop him making this sensational claim: "Young Stevie Williams ate my hamster."
    "We were at a charity do for deaf and dumb refs. I went for a Jimmy Riddle and Stevie was looking after my hamster.
    "When I returned Stevie was just sitting there grinning.
    "It only takes a second to eat a hamster."

PLUS - INSIDE:
George caught spending a £5 note - police investigate. Paul Davis seen using right foot - Interpol alerted.

The
Arsenal Echo Echo
ISSUE 3 FEB./MARCH '88   30p

EDITOR ARRESTED
They did it on the North Bank

THE editor of the Arsenal Echo Echo has been arrested for selling the magazine on the North Bank.

   While you settled down to watch the match against Everton he was escorted around the back of the North Bank through a maze of corridors to the office of David Miles, the assistant secretary of Arsenal FC.

   Miles took one look at the magazine and said: "No, we don't want this sort of thing sold inside the ground."
   The police then took the editor to their offices at the Clock End, recorded his name and address and threw him out of the ground. He was warned that to re-enter would cause further problems.
   The club would be sending a copy of the magazine to their legal men.
   That Monday he telephoned Mr Miles and asked him to alter his decision. He wouldn't.

Inside – How we saved FA Cup

The
Arsenal Echo Echo
MARCH / APRIL '88   ISSUE 4   40p

ARSENAL OPEN CLOCK END EXECUTIVE BOXES

INSIDE: Read how Nigel Winterburn had his right-leg amputated to aid mobility

The
Arsenal Echo Echo
APRIL/MAY '88   ISSUE 5   40p

BEDLAM!
Bitter Bates
blasts big
block blow

KEN BATES..."Well gutted"

By MARK 'Scum' COOPER

KEN BATES, the world's biggest bighead, is set to stay at crisis club Chelsea - after a dream move to Arsenal fell through.

Bates was shattered by the news that his £3.5 million transfer to Highbury had been blocked. Fighting back the tears and visibly pulling at his beard, he told a half-empty press conference: "I'm well gutted, Brian."

Bates, 72, who last week rejected a move to West Ham, considering them to be in a sufficient mess already gulped: "I take great pride in making a once glamorous club the laughing stock of London. So why have I been denied the opportunity to inflict untold damage on another football

Continued on back page

Bully boy Bates big blow

Continued from front page
club? It would have been a great challenge."

Arsenal chairman Peter Hill-Wood was outraged: "I thought I was unpopular when I sacked Don Howe, but Ken is King of the cock-ups. It would have been an honour for him to replace me at Highbury."

TEA-BOY SHOCK

At Chelsea, the woes continue. Yesterday their tea-boy sued the club for £500,000 because his contract was not going to be renewed when it expired in ten years time. Fans' favourite John 'There's no crisis at this club' Hollins, who left Stamford Bridge in March, is widely tipped to take over. Meanwhile the tea-boy is set to become the new Wales manager.

The rest of the staff were horrified by the news that Bates would be staying at the club.

However, caretaker-manager-coach-tea-boy Wally Campbell said: "I'm sure we can continue to hate each others guts."

News of Bates's non-departure was broken to the team after their monthly training session, supervised by Woody Allen. "I'm off to Brighton" said one "I going to be a football player" said another.

But the last word was left to Kerry Dixon, speaking from his luxury yacht off Rio he said: "As Chelsea's centre-forward, I have absolutely no idea what's going on at the club."

The
Arsenal Echo Echo
SEPT./OCT. 88   ISSUE 6   40p

It's Bryan Robson

Robbo entertains the Old Trafford crowd with his new pre-match warm-up routine.

The
Arsenal Echo Echo
OCT/NOV '88   ISSUE 7   40p

KINKY EMLYN SEDUCED BY TORY TEMPTRESS

SEXPOT Tory MP Edwina Currie has spoken about her wild nights of passion with the ex-soccer star Emlyn Hughes.

Following the revelations of squeaky-clean Tom O'Connor and Frank Bough this time it's squeaky-voiced Emlyn.

Edwina tells of kinky Emlyn's 101% commitment in bed:

"He bought me a Leeds United shirt," says Edwina, "I had to pretend I was that great striker Allan Clarke - Emlyn loved to be dominated in bed."

"Clarke's nickname was Sniffer - but that's another story."

Edwina gave Hughes all the benefits she had to offer:

"I remember during one very passionate night, I wore an early 1970's Chelsea shirt and a pair of muddy boots. Emlyn thought I was Ron Harris. He would kick me in the shins and laugh - it was one of his wildest fantasies."

"Ron's nickname was Chopper - but that's another story."

"I was very sad when we broke-up," says Edwina. "But it was his fault. He had this bloody annoying habit of throwing his arms around me and saying 'Well done pal.'"

****
How do you confuse the Spurs coach driver?
Ask him the way to Selhurst Park.
****

The
Arsenal Echo Echo

DEC./JAN. 88/89   ISSUE 8   40p

Sex Bribe Shock

PAULINE....Pictured just before
Spurs appeal at the Football League.

HOW I SCORED FOR SPURS

Spurs shabby season has
plummeted to a new low with
the sensational revelations
that they SEXUALLY BRIBED the
Football League to win back
their two points.

These were deducted after
Spurs failed to fulfil their
opening fixture of the season
against Coventry. But
following an appeal they were
surprisingly given back those
points.

Cynics claimed that Tottenham had friends in high
places. However, they couldn't have been further
from the truth, Spurs friends were in LOW places –
the brothels of London.

Continued on back page

A prostitute rang the Echo Echo to tell the
whole sordid story. For safety reasons she was
simply known as Pauline;

"My pimp arranged a meeting with these two men
who I only knew as Irving and Terry. They said
they wanted me to do something unusual. Well, I
wasn't expecting these two to come up with
anything kinky I hadn't already heard before.
I've been on the game longer than Jimmy Sirrel's
been in it. But I must confess they did shock
me.

DON'T DIE OF GAZZA

Irving said he wanted me to go to the Football
League and present the Spurs case in their bid
to win back their two points. He said he'd give
me Gazza if I did. I said I had enough diseases
as it was without another I'd never even heard
of. But I thanked him nevertheless.

Irv got out his cheque book, it was a very
nice one covered with pictures of Mickey Mouse
and Donald Duck. "How much?" he said. "Ten," I
replied. Well, I'm not cheap you know

He said "That's okay," and I said, "Grand,"
because I was happy to do business with such a
nice man. But he looked up and screamed, "Ten
grand! I know Graham Kelly's not that exciting
but I'm sure you can do it for less than that."

CHUBBY CHEQUERS

It was then that Terry, the chubby one, tried
to calm Irv down by reminding him that it was a
very small sum compared to the money he'd wasted
on players. This seemed to cheer him up and he
wrote the cheque.

I then mentioned to Irving that Graham Kelly
had infact left the Football League and was now
the secretary-designate at the Football
Association. He became a bit abusive and said:
"Look love, I think me and Terry know a little
more about football than you. If we didn't then
Tottenham might as well be run by two old
tarts." I thought it best to keep quiet.

The rest as they say is history – Spurs won
back their two points, after I'd given a few old
codgers at the League the time of their lives."

The
Arsenal Echo Echo

FEB./MARCH 1989   ISSUE 9   50p

WE'LL TAKE EACH GAME AS IT COMES

GEORGE GRAHAM
EXCLUSIVE

"We're no counting any chickens yet....We'll wait until
May....It's a marathon no a sprint......You get nothing for
being top at this stage......It's not a matter of life or
death, it's more important than that....A bird in the hand
is worth two in the bush.....A nod is as good as a wink to a
blind man...You can take a horse to water but you can't make
it drink......Nice to see you, to see you nice......You
dirty rat....Frankly my dear I don't give a damn.....Hello,
good evening and welcome......Please yer self.....Aye, aye,
that's yer lot."

GOLDEN GUNNER
Leeeee Chapman

LEE CHAPMAN — Just the name sends a shiver up the spine.

What words can be used to do justice to his overwhelming influence on Arsenal Football Club? Magnificent? Revolutionary? Ahead of his time? A miracle from above? Or a bloody useless old fart? It's not for a humble journalist like me to decide.

Lee Chapman was many things to many people. To his adoring fans on the North Bank, he was affectionately known as Dougie, after another national hero Sir Douglas Barder — he was good in the air, but had two wooden legs.

To the spectators in the stands, who used to rattle their jewellery every time he got the ball, he was christened a 'Firkincunt' — which is Indian for 'Oh he of very much skill!'

It was while I was in India last year that I met a man who had actually seen Chapman score a goal, for Arsenal. Now as you will appreciate, for security reasons, I cannot name him or else he will be mobbed in the streets, trambled to death in the crowd's excitment and worse still, be asked to appear on Saint and Greavsie.

But for some very strange reason Lee's memory is not celebrated at Highbury. There are no Lee Chapman stands, no portraits adorning the boardroom and even the 'At least Lee scored with me' knickers have long been out of stock.

Perhaps, wisely, Arsenal have decide that just as the Busby babes has over-shadowed Man Utd's future, so the celebration of Lee Chapman maybe just too daunting a prospect for some of the younger players.

The closest he came to etching his presence on the corridors of Highbury was when a marble bust of himself was made and placed in the entrance. But unfortunately some prat called him Herbert instead of Lee and it couldnot he changed.

Even his arrival in that never-to-be-forgotten summer of 1982 was something very special.

Because Arsenal and Stoke couldn't agree on a fee for him, the matter went to a transfer tribunal. So we had to pay half a million pounds for Chapman. Not bad for a footballing genius.

The press reported that Terry Neill offered £300,000 and Ritchie Barker wanted £800,000.

The Echo Echo can reveal that both these figures are wrong.

Neill infact offered £1million and Barker said: 'You can have him for nothing.' So the tribunal settled on a middle fee of £500,000.

GOALS GOALS GOALS

Lee's impulsive need for a new challenge meant he stayed at Highbury for just one and a half years. But what times they were.

The goals just rattled in.

Four goals in 23 league games made him one of the most feared strikers in Europe, nay the world.

Dixie Dean's record of 60 goals in a season was in danger. Had Lee not missed half of his first season I feel sure he would have grabbed the remaining 57 goals he needed to re-write the history books.

Then came that dark day in December 1983, when Lee joined Sunderland.

Despite the suddeness of the move Arsenal fans hold no grudges. Each time he returns to Highbury the fans bite back the tears, get the hankies out and sing, as one:

"Leee Chap-man..is a very good player...is a very good player."

THERE WILL NEVER BE ANOTHER LEE CHAPMAN

TERRY VENABLES can bring Diego Maradona AND the Championship to Spurs.

That's the astonishing verdict of the man who knows him best — Allan Harris, Tel's No. 2 at Barcelona and Queens Park Rangers.

Harris is Venables' closest associate ...

IS ALLAN HARRIS ANY RELATION TO ROLF HARRIS?

NO MORE HEROES ANYMORE

ONE of the saddest days of my childhood was when I discovered that Roy Race, he of Roy and the Rovers, did not exist, and was no more than a fictional character, a cardboard cut-out. It may sound corny, but it's perfectly true.

A similiar mood of deception swept over me when I heard that Charlie had finally left Highbury, for Aberdeen.

I've long ceased believing in Roy Race, but I hope I never stop believing in players like Charlie Nicholas.

Both men were heroes. Stars. They had glamour. Aroused excitement. Performed the unperformable.

In the last 10/15 years only three players have been Roy Race to me - Malcolm Macdonald, Liam Brady and Charlie Nicholas. Macdonald and Brady have been gone since 1980. So in eight years I've had one.

One star in eight years wouldn't sell many tickets at one of the top theatres in the the country.

Charlie Nicholas is the juggler. He holds the crowd spellbound, as he rotates eight hoops. They cheer and shout fervently. The promoter smiles wealthily. But unfortunately, Charlie often drops the hoops, so the boss decides to sack him.

His replacement is someone who never drops the hoops, but can only juggle three at a time. The audience have seen genius, erratic it may have been, they don't want to watch predictable mediocrity. The show closes.

When we said goodbye to Charlie, we said goodbye to flair, imagination, raw excitement and colour. Surely, everything that football should be.

I hope we haven't said goodbye to all that, for ever.

Charlie couldn't tackle, he 'bottled it', he couldn't head, he couldn't run as fast as Groves, or for as long as Talbot.

So why the hell did we buy him?

In one of Woody Allen's films, Broadway Danny Rose, Allen is sitting in the back of a taxi with a woman. He turns to her and says: "You're so beautiful I can't keep my eyes on the meter.'

In much the same way, Nicholas did things that made you forget, or even care, what the score was. He was/is a one-off. Unique.

But we bought Placido Domingo and get him to sing Spandau Ballet, we bought Laurence Olivier and put him in a Carry On film, we bought Rembrandt and made him paint the fence.

Petrovic. Just that name makes you realise that Nicholas is not becoming a Highbury outcast, but infact joining a special group of rejects along with Petrovic, Alan Hudson and one of its founding members, Peter Marinello.

Did Petrovic 'bottle it' aswell? Could he not head either? Did he not sweat blood and guts? Give 101%?

Is there really no room for the likes of Petrovic and Nicholas at Highbury, or even in English football? There's got to be, there must be.

I want class. I want excitement and unpredictability. Without it going to football would give me no more than the feelings I get commuting to work, doing the washing-up or watching someone juggle three hoops.

Groucho

THE OLD DAYS!

I have been watching Arsenal now for many years.

I haven't missed a single match since 1892, home or away.

I am also a very keen follower of the reserve team, having missed just three matches since they were formed, although I do confess to having been absent at a few youth team games.

Our younger fans won't remember the great team of the 1930's, I'm more certain today than I've ever been that that was the finest side ever to play in red and white, or even orange and green for that matter, because that did happen once. We were playing Sheffield United at Highbury and weeks of constant blizzards had left most of London 25 feet deep in snow, but our undersoil heating meant the game went ahead.

It was a fantastic match, the Gunners were 4-0 up at half-time. But in the second-half Sheffield United played with their willies hanging out of their shorts and won 5-4.

Am I a crank?
Fred Fogey
Enfield.

GREAT SUPPORT

I think the Gunner is a fantastic programme. I think everything about Arsenal is great, the players, the manager, the stadium even the toilets. I love the offside trap, queing for the tube and paying extra for big matches.

Although I've been to every home match this season I didn't get a ticket for the Littlewoods Cup Final but it was a very fair way of doing things.

I also think it's a terrific idea that we should pay £1 for a souvenir programme to celebrate getting to Wembley, baring in mind that most of us still have some money left from our trips to Hillsborough and Goodison earlier in the competition.
Keep up the good work boys.
Kevin Connolly
Islington

PEN PAL WANTED (1)

I'm a desperately poor Russian boy who has managed to smuggle this letter out of the country. I would like to write to an Arsenal fan who can tell me what is happening at Highbury. Please also send me videos of recent games (VHS or BETAMAX, no problem) and recordings of Stuart Hall's match reports for my new CD player.
Yuri Bloodytakequinnov
Moscow
P.S. Is it true that you still wear flares?

PEN PAL WANTED (2)

Hello everyone in Arsenal land. My name is Anna, I am living in Norway. I like to travel very much and go to Highbury when I can. I'm heavily into bondage and Panini stickers, but not at the same time. You can get in contact with me by ringing my sister, 'Heaving Helga', who has stuck her telephone number in every phone box in London.
Anna Banner
Oslo

PROGRAMME'S NEEDED

I wonder if anyone can help me. I would like three programmes that I failed to get because I was ill and forced to miss these games:
West Ham v Bolton 1923 FA Cup Final
Manchester United v Sheff Wed 1958 FA Cup
England v West Germany 1966 World Cup Final
I will pay postage.
Gus Geezer
Godalming

FANS!

I would like to strongly condemn the morons that stand on the North Bank and sing their filthy songs. "We can see you sneaking out" and "Can you hear so-and-so sing" is grossly offensive to our many deaf and blind fans.

"You're supposed to be at home" is deeply upsetting to the homeless, and our crippled fans should not have to listern to "Walk on". Lads, cut it out, or else me and my scissors will make sure you'll never be able to "Score in a brothel"
Wendy Whingebag
Vycombe

GORY GORY DAYS

BY AL FRESCO

The date is Febuary 21st 1989. Ailing North London "giants" Totteringham have called an extraordinary meeting to discuss the club's plight - stuck near the foot of the Division One and with a desperate relegation battle on their hands.

Manager El Tel Venerables wipes sweat and aftershave off his forehead. "Just give us the dosh, Irv, and I'll buy you a successful team," he says.

Chairman Irving Scholastic shakes his head. "I've bought you Gasbox and Stewpot; what more do you want? I'm not made of money. Well, I am actually, but it's all locked up in a Channel Islands investment company."

El Tel suggests. "Rushy, he's the bloke. What a striker! Beg Liverpool to let him go."

Scholastic disagrees. "He wouldn't come here - he likes the ball played into the oppenent's half of the field." "You know," says Irv, "I wasn't that bothered about not winning things as long as we kept getting publicity."

El Tel sniffs, wipes away a tear. "Yeah, but even Loadsamoney has stopped telling jokes about us now. Ah, let's go for a walk."

Outside the crumbling facade of a once proud stadium a local senior citizen is selling newspapers. Rumour has it that it's Wild Bill Nickelperson, ex-Totteringham manager. Other sceptics say the chaps only claim to fame is an appearance on a Chas N Dave video.

"Paper, guv?"

Scholastic offers a 20p coin. "Keep the change," he says to the vendor, then to Venerables. "What's the back page say, El Tel? Break it to me gently....."

El Tel scans the page, stumbling over words of 5-letters or more. At last, he cringes. "I'm sorry, oh great one, I've failed you - there's not a mention of us. It's all.....Arsenal, top of the league again."

"Even after we've lost 5-0 on consecutive Saturdays?"

"Yes."

"Even after the East Stand collapsed?"

"Yes."

"Even after our coach driver got lost on the way to a home match?"

"Yes. I think our share prices get a mention on the financial pages."

Scholastic scrates his nose. "What was the attendance at the last game we turned up for at White Hart Lane.?"

"Eighteen."

"Thousand?"

"No, Irv, hundred."

"Even Barnet get more than that. We must do something to get back in the slimelight. Yeah, I've got it - A new star to bring the crowds flocking back. Oh, I can see it now. We'll be so popular we'll have to play our home games at Wembley."

At last a genuine smile replaces the tight-lipped smirk on El Tel vacuous face. "Who is it, this saviour?" he pleads. "Is it Maradonut? We tried to get him before, you know. Or Ruud Pushandpullit?"

"No," Scholastic replies, "neither of them. This man will cost us thirteen million but he's a real thriller and he moves so well off the ball."

"You don't mean?....."

"Exactly. Michael Jackson."

"But he's B-A-A-D."

"So are we, Tel. Now get on the blower."

....to be continued.

STEVIE WILLIAMS sings

LOVE SONGS

```
***********TIE A YELLOW CARD AROUND THE OLD OAK TREE*******
****YOU'LL NEVER WALK AGAIN*******************I KNEED YOU**
**GOOD GOLLY JOE WORALL**********BRUISING YOU**************
**********YOUR HIP BONE WAS CONNECTED TO YOUR LEG BONE*****
*HERE COMES THE REF AGAIN***************KING OF PAIN*******
*************YOU'VE LOST THAT NUMBING FEELING*************
**YELLOW CARDS OF TEXAS******SEE YOU LATER LESTER SHAPTER*
*******GONNA MAKE YOU AN OFFER YOU CAN'T REFUSE***********
```

With all due respect to Luton, any player who goes to Kennilworth Road at 30-years-old must realise that their career is heading in one direction. Yes, those cheeky Hatters did beat us in the Littlewoods Cup final, but any social climber worth his sea-salt knows the difference between Arsenal and Luton Town, especially in today's loadsamoney world of football.

So barring a remarkable about-turn, similiar to Wembley 88, Steve Williams is set to join the Nearly Men - nearly a regular international, nearly a top-class club player, nearly a very good footballer.

For many with less talent than Williams this would be a fine accolade...to have been an international, to have been a good club player and a good footballer. But to my mind, it's nearly an insult.

Mind you, he's joining a large group of under-achievers...Peter Marinello, Rodney Marsh, Peter Osgood, Alan Hudson and a bloke called Charlie Nicholas. Williams has won just six England caps...pathetic eh? Even Spurs' Gary Stevens has seven. Guess how many caps Hudson won. Two. Osgood? Four. Rodney Marsh? Nine. Ray Wilkins? Eighty-four.

How the hell can Ray Wilkins earn 78 more caps than Williams, play for three of the greatest teams in Europe (he did play for Chelsea though - Ed) and still not be able to touch Williams in terms of skill and imagination? Do we praise Wilkins for making a lot from a little or condemn Williams for making a little from a lot?

For much of his career Stevie has been a bloody idiot. He's been honest, direct and has never hidden his passion to win, sometimes outside the laws. While that's endeared him to us it hasn't impressed the nobs, and they're the ones that matter. Lawrie McMenemy apart, it seems to an outsider that messrs Robson, Howe and Graham have failed as managers. Failed to harness a rare talent and use it for the benefit of the side. So he's a hot-head. So he says things that are tactless and offensive. He's a bloody good player and that, at the end of the day, is all that should matter.

FIRST IMPRESSIONS

Williams, groomed at the Bernard Manning charm school, marked his arrival at Highbury in 1984 by criticising his new guv'nor Don Howe, for not putting him straight into the side for the game with Tottenham. "Why pay half a million pounds for a player and then stick him on the subs bench?" he asked publicly. Privately, his opinions were probably exactly the same. But because he dared to air his views he was deemed a trouble maker, a bad boy and the nobs don't like these sort of people.

For a period, when George took over, Williams suddenly blossomed again after he'd seemed set to go to Queens Park Rangers. His calming, yes calming, influence on our young side was a massive factor on our re-emergence as a side that was once again winning and, just as important, entertaining.

But it wasn't to last. Williams expressed his displeasure at missing out on the Littlewoods Cup final by staying at home. Roast beef, Yorkshire pudding and the omnibus edition of Eastenders before a cup final was never going to please George. The race was now on to see who would leave first, Williams or Dirty Den.

In the end Williams won. Meanwhile Den continues to go round putting people's backs up and annoying the nobs. Perhaps he'll soon join Stevie at Kennilworth Road.

DEC 1984

JULY 1988

HERB

GIVES IT TO YOU STRAIGHT

Jan Molby's jailing. Damn bad show. Don't want fat foreigners clogging-up our prisons. They come over here, fill our jails. Send them all home that's what I say. British prisons for British criminals. What sort of future is there going to be for the children of Lester Piggott and Peter Storey?

Those bloody Spurs spivs are at it again. First match postponed. Because of builders. I know they're not too keen on the Indians, but they love the cowboys don't they. All summer they had to fix their poxy ground. Nearly four months. My wife could have had half a baby in that time. If I was married. Spivs. The lot of them. Not women. No, Spurs. They're the real spivs.

I feel sorry for you lot. Trip to Spurs on the tube means a long walk. Fans have enough crap to put up with watching modern football. When I was the Guv I got those twerps at London Transport to move the nearest tube station right next to Highbury. Buggered if I was going to walk half a mile to work. And I got them to call it Arsenal. What do Spurs call their nearest tube station? Seven Sisters.

Then the Lilywhites turn-up late at Charlton. Why? A good friend of mine, who's been dead 14 years, told me why. Directors delayed the players tube journey until they could buy those cheap day savers. Then it was too late. Old Irv got panicky. Stopped a coach. Full of old codgers it was. Irv pointed his nose at the driver. Told him it was loaded. Everyone jumped off sharpish. Apparently, they got Bobby Mimms to drive to Selhurst Park. Enough said.

Up yours

Herbert Chapman

(HERBERT CHAPMAN)

SOUNESS SIGNS DANNY LA RUE

GLASGOW RANGERS boss Graeme Souness last night swooped south once more to pull off the sensational £750,000 transfer of Danny La Rue.

Said a delighted Souness: "We saw him at the London Palladium last month.

"He's just the type of person we want at Ibrox - he's English, very expensive and over the hill."

La Rue was just as happy: "I've heard a lot about the atmosphere at Ibrox. And the thought of playing in front of all those hairy Scotsmen is very exciting."

GOLDEN GUNNERs
John Hawley and Ray Hankin

My parents were going through that cynical middle-age period, of things aint being what they used to. Jim Reeves had been elbowed for Bow Wow Wow, Fred Astaire's career was on the slide after an unsuccessful switch to break-dancing and as for the youth of the day, well, they didn't know they were born. I didn't dare talk sport for fear of wave upon wave of geriatrics being mentioned; Tom Finney, Stanley Matthews, Fred Perry, Dennis Compton, the list was endless.

It was on a boring Monday evening, having sat through an hour's lecture on why comedy aint what it used to be, which coincided with the Mike Yarwood show, that I finally snapped: "If you want comedy funnier than old 'Bing and Bob', sillier than 'dear Groucho', and crazier than Chaplin I'll give it to you - come to Highbury tomorrow and see Hankin and Hawley, The H-Buns. They agreed to.

December 1st 1981, Arsenal v Liverpool, Milk Cup 4th Round. It was to be an historic night, it was to be first public performance by the H-Buns since their acrimonious break-up in the 70's, following months of success at the Elland Road Club. Would they be as good as before? Why are they joining up again, even the Beatles didn't dare that? Questions buzzed around an excited Highbury.

But as kick-off time approached, with my parents happily eating popcorn and taunting the Liverpool fans, a rumour quickly spread across the terraces that the H-Buns had had a blazing row and John Hawley had withdrawn at the last moment. He'd flatly refused to be the back end of the donkey or to tell the joke about not having struck any balls since he trod on the garden rake. This was confirmed to us minutes later over the tannoy: "My lords, ladies and gentlemen, we regret to inform you that ill-health has forced Mr John Hawley to pull out of tonight's show," but we knew otherwise, My Dad didn't reckon that this would have happened in his day.

Ray 'The show must go on' Hankin was substitute, I told my parents this meant he was the star attraction and would be on later in the evening. God, I hope he's good.

I needn't have worried. After half-time with the crowd bored and in desperate need of tomatoes to throw at the performers, it happened - Hankin emerged from the dug-out. He ran up and down the touchline and, without stopping, tried to take his tracksuit trousers off. Crash! How the crowd roared. Already he had them eating out of his hand.

As the linesman checked his studs he poured itching powder down the back of his shirt. Onto the pitch glided 24-stone Hankin with all the grace of Niall Quinn on roller-skates.

It was vintage comedy. What made it all the more funnier was the fact that Terry Neill and Don Howe brought him to Highbury in the first place.

RELIEF

The final whistle came as a great relief to us all, we could laugh no more. Hankin took a bow centre-stage and the whole crowd, especially my parents, roared their approval for one of the all-time greats. He may have been getting on a bit but he still knew how to make them laugh. "Do you get many like him at Arsenal?" my mother asked excitedly. I couldn't answer, laughter had gripped me once more as I recalled the incident near the end when he produced a ping-pong ball from Alan Sunderland's hair.

It was to be a bitter-sweet night, the first and last time he was to play Highbury. His contract was cancelled the following month after just one more appearance as substitute, in the replay at Anfield. His bust-up with Hawley had forced Neill to decide between the two - he chose Hawley, scorer of one goal for the Gunners but more importantly, two stone lighter.

Hawley had come from Sunderland earlier in the season. Neill heralded his signing as "only just the start" (we know what he meant now, but we didn't at the time). He went on: "We had a nice long chat and he is eager to join us." I'm not surprised. If someone was stupid enough to pay £45,000 for me and stick me in Arsenal's first team I would be prepared to have ago, and John Hawley felt the same.

He scored just three league goals but was not the same following the disagreement with Hankin, doing the "I say, I say, I say' jokes with Alan Sunderland and Brian McDermott raised few laughs.

Hawley's career was at rock-bottom. But worse was to follow - he joined Orient, on loan. It was the end. Brief comeback appearances at Hull City and Happy Valley of Hong Kong only illustrated that Hawley without Hankin was like Laurel without Hardy.

Guy Havord

GORY GORY DAYS Part 2

March 1989. The crisis at Totteringham Football Club deepens. Yet another defeat at Highbury; an early exit from the FA Cup at the hands of non-league opposition; and elimination from the Sherpa Van Trophy on the away goals rule - "you give away goals, you get eliminated".

For boss Terry "Suntan" Venerables even the offers of a return to Spain have dried up. The last such one was a phone call in January, the chance to manage El Pincho's Wine Bar XI in Marbella. Tel politely declined.

With Totteringham now 6 points adrift of fellow strugglers West Ham, both chairman and manager know time is running out.

Irving Scholastic looks at his lego model of the reconstructed East Stand. He shakes his head, demolishes it. "Too many red and white bricks," he explains.

Irv speaks again: "Well, future manager of England, what hope can you offer this week?"

El Tel shifts nervously in his chair. "I was reading in the TV Times the other week..."

Scholastic interrupts, "You, reading? Never!"

Terry continues, "Well, the wife was helping me with the big words. And I was thinking - no jokes please - that if we could just stop conceding goals we could get Gasbox or Stewpot to take a dive, Fenchurch puts away the penalty and voila - 1-0, three points."

Scholastic sniffs. "So you've found a goalkeeper in the TV Times, eh?"

"Yeah, that's right."

"I hope this is nothing like the Michael Jackson fiasco. I've never heard so much abuse! Good job most of it was in jive and I couldn't understand it."

Venerables warms to his theme. "This man," he says, "is more popular than Michael Jackson. In fact, Radio 2 - Bryon Butler & Co - love him. And he's got pedigree. At 19 he played in goal for Real Madrid."

Scholastic is out of his chair. "Yes, a dago! It's obvious. That's what we need, Tel. You're a whizz with Spaniards. We'll re-name the team Real Totteringham or Spurselona." He calms for a moment, "Hang on, who is this superstar goalkeeper?"

El Tel coughs. "Er.....Julio Iglesias."

"He's the one who did 'Feelings', nothing more than feelings' isn't he?"

"The very same."

Scholastic beams. "'Er indoors loves that song. We'll teach 'em to sing it on The Shelf."

"There isn't a Shelf anymore, Irving."

"Well, they can sing it at the Paxton Road or Park Lane End then. Who cares? This is better than poxy Chas 'N' Dave. A second singing Dago. It'll be like having Ossie back again."

"So I'll make a bid for him, Irv? He's in his 40's, I think."

"So are all the great keepers, you dolt! Shilton, Jennings, Zoff. It's a mature man's position. Yes, this club will make football a family entertainment again."

"A bit like Watford? - Riding high in the second division."

Irving purses his lips. "Yes, a little like Watford," he says, "but they've got a transvestite chairman......which gives me an idea."

AL FRESCO

TONY COTTEE: JUST HOW GOOD IS HE ?

A Scientific Approach

Most of us here at Highbury were bitterly disappointed that Mr T 'my decision was based purely on money' Cottee decided to go to Everton. In losing out on this glamorous transfer just what are we going to miss?

We here at the Merson Institute of Statistics and Hydrodynamics have done a scientific study of the Cottee phenomenon. The results are shocking, and those with a sensitive (or even sensible) nature are advised not to read any further.

All scientific study must be done as a comparison with the known universe. We use as our comparison, Mr P. 'Tintin' Groves, a familiar and well loved (well...) player.

```
##  FACT: P Groves   cost          25 000 pounds
##  FACT: T Cottee   cost       2 500 000 pounds
```

After months of complex calculation on fourth generation IBM mainframe computers we calculate that this means that Cottee cost 100 times more than Groves. The superstar Cottee is 100 times more valuable than the ordinary Groves.

But what does this mean in footballing terms?

Perriii scored approximately 9 goals last season (was it really so many?). This means that Cottee will score 900 goals next season! This averages out at nearly 18 goals a game, and is quite a good scoring rate really, even slightly better than Kevin Campbell's. Obviously Tony C will score 0 goals in some games, and over 40 in others....this is one goal every two minutes. This sort of scoring will be sorely missed at Highbury.

Another interesting factor about Peree 'I can also end my name in two Es' Groves is that he can run quite fast. He can do 100 metres in ten seconds. Our computers therefore predict that if Cottee is 100 times better (i.e. 100 times faster) he will be able to achieve speeds of almost 2,000 miles an hour!

This is fast enough to outrun an Exocet missile, never mind a lunging Terry Fenwick tackle. Colin Harvey admitted this was a big factor when they signed him: "The savings on coach transport will be substantial," he said.

So fellow Gooners, we have to agree, we certainly lost quite a good player when Cottee decided on money, sorry, I mean Everton. Any player who can score 500 goals a season and get to away matches anywhere in England, on foot, in under ten minutes, has got to be better than Martin Hayes.

But there is one small worry for all those optimistic Everton fans. Those of you who have seen Tintin score a goal will have seen Perry's impressive celebratory jump into the air after he scores. We estimate Perry jumps about four feet off the ground in celebration. Using the same calculations as were used in this analysis, we can expect Tony Cottee to jump over 400 feet whenever he scores one of his 900 goals. This may cause problems of recovery from the river at Forest and other such grounds...

TRUE FACTS FROM THE WORLD OF FOOTBALL

Not many people know this, but Alan Smith has a better goals per game ratio than T Cottee. Alan's is 0.37 per game over 200 league matches, and Cottee's is 0.35 per game over a similar number of matches.

Data supplied by the Merson Institute and the Imaginary Merson Boys.

BOOK REVIEW

ALEX JAMES - LIFE OF A FOOTBALL LEGEND by John Harding

unique in one respect. John Harding rightly calls him the first truly 'modern' player - performing a role rather than holding a position. James provided the ammunition for men like Bastin, Lambert and Jack as the Gunners swept all before them. It was fast, effective, and beautiful to watch.

Harding draws liberally from contemporary match reports and reminisces of family and friends to tell his story. Scepticism at the ability of one so small to handle pro-football was overcome and initial success at Raith Rovers and Preston North End - bundled unceremoniously over the border in a fast car! - led to Arsenal.

Incredibly Arsenal only secured James' services in 1929 through a part-time job arranged for him at Selfridges. As a legal way of offering him more cash, Chapman secured the offer of a 'sports demonstrator' post in Oxford St at £250 a year. Charlie Nicholas wouldn't have liked it, but James jumped at the chance.

Always headstrong and confident in his own ability, James often clashed with his autocratic manager and once went on 'strike' for more money when his Selfridges contract ended.

Indeed the unmistakeable thread here is of an endless search for financial security at a time of little or no commercial outlet for players outside the game. On retirement it led to failed ventures in the world of Pools and shopkeeping, and a coaching trip to Poland just a month before Hitler invaded.

James died in 1953 aged 51. In an era when the simply competent are feted by all and the merely good hailed as world class, you might dismiss the praise heaped upon Alex James. Could he really be that good? Read this book. Then you will know.

"ALEX JAMES" IS PUBLISHED BY ROBSON BOOKS AT £12.95.

WEE ALEX, arms buried in voluminous sleeves and baggy shorts flapping round his knees, darts across the Highbury turf with three baffled opponents gaping helplessly behind him.

Those Man City players left open-mouthed in the James' slipstream in October 1934 were not alone in failing to stop this wizard who gave life to Chapman's tactical plans. He could split any defence in Britain.

Pinning down the man who helped revolutionise soccer is a mite easier in print. From a tough beginning in impoverished Lanarkshire to critical acclaim in London, James' life mirrors that of many pre-war stars but is

HERB

GIVES IT TO YOU STRAIGHT

England in Saudi Arabia. Words fail me. I thought they had all the camels, not us. But those Johnnies at the FA love Bobby Robson. Dick Wragg says he's right behind him. Safer than being in front I suppose. Nice man, Wragg. My dad went to school with him.

   I should have been the England Guv. Wragg interviewed me twice during the 1940's. I'd been dead for 16 years. Unfortunatley that worked against me. Had it only been five years I would have got the job.

   Where's my bloody clock been? Arsenal said they were going to 're-locate' it during the summer. And they did - in a basement. And we have to wait until Christmas to see it again. Same could be said of Perry Como. Damn bad show. It's seen a lot of things that clock. I used to date women underneath it. But it rarely lasted. They got fed-up having to scale the Highbury walls to get there. Laddered their stockings. Strange fellows, women.

   Vinny Jones. A cad of the highest order. Plays at Wimbledon. So did Fred Perry, but he never kneed his oppenents in the goolies. Jones should be drummed out of the club. But Bobby Gould can't see what's going on. Blinded by his own eyebrows. Apparently Hitler only wanted to invade Britain to capture Gould's eyebows. Use them for his moustache. Luckily for us his eyebrow's scrambled old Jerry's radar system.

   Up yours

Herbert Chapman

HERBERT CHAPMAN

Mad   Deadly

World heavyweight boxing champion 'Mad' Mike Tyson spoke
last night of his fear over his forthcoming bout against
Paul 'Deadly' Davis, the Arsenal footballer.

Speaking from a New York sanitorium, 'Tyre-neck' Tyson,
25, was foaming under the armpits as he spoke of Davis:

"I saw on TV the damage he did to that guy and it scares
the crap out of me."

'Tyrant' Tyson, who's had to endure a torrid time from
the press who recently accussed him of being a homosexual,
added:

"I guess I respect Paul now. He's a good-lookin' guy
with muscular biceps, trim thighs and firm buttocks - I'm
greatly looking forward to our encounter."

Meanwhile, Tyson's manager Yoko 'Oh yes' Ono was busy
denying her protege is a weird, psychopathic, anorexic,
drug-crazed, wife-beating, Panini collecting poofter:

"Mike is a warm, full human being. Just because he is a
child of peace, he should not be persecuted for his
strange bald patch or lack of teeth. The man is an
artist."

Back in London, however, Davis's manager George
'Grizzly' Graham, was having none of it:

"Tyson's timid, he'll go to any length not to fight Paul
- punching lamp-posts, driving into trees, sleeping with
his wife - the man's a mess."

For his part, former England international 'Death' Davis
said:

"I had a pretty good work-out in the Southampton match,
my left hook's coming on a treat and I feel ready for
him."

                                        MARK 'SCUM' COOPER

20 incredibly boring things you already knew about. . . WEST HAM

1. West Ham ALWAYS play exciting entertaining football.

2. West Ham have had just four managers since the war.

3. John Lyall is the league's longest serving manager.

4. West Ham's most famous supporter is Alf Garnett.

5. Alf always says 'Up the 'ammers'.

6. But in real life Alf, Warren Mitchell, supports Spurs.

7. Upton Park is a small compact ground.

8. Despite what people think, West Ham's pitch is a lot bigger than most teams'.

9. West Ham's song is 'I'm forever blowing bubbles.'

10. West Ham nearly had the youngest player to score in an F.A. Cup final, but big bad Willie Young hacked down poor acne-face Paul Allen. (How many times have you heard that one?)

11. The whole of England should be grateful to West Ham, because they won the World Cup for us, thanks to Geoff Hurst and Martin Peters. (How many bloody times have you heard that?)

12. Billy Bonds was rejected as a youngster by Arsenal - Herbert Chapman didn't like his beard. (Now, that I've never heard)

13. All cockneys support West Ham. (zzzzz)

14. True cockneys are born within the sound of the Bow bells.

15. West Ham fans are very loyal. (Where's the bog?)

16. West Ham have groomed many managers - Malcolm Allison, John Bond, Bobby Moore. (Enough said)

17. There's never a crisis at West Ham. (Only three left)

18. West Ham are like the Christmas decorations, they always come down in the new year. (zzzzzzzzzzzzzz)

19. West Ham is in the east end of London.

20. West Ham's highest ever league position is 3rd. (Now, that is interesting)

(Size of gates 1) 9 feet 3 inches, 2) 17ft, 3) 12ft 6".
Quotes - 1D, 2G, 3F, 4H, 5C, 6A, 7B, 8E)

ALTERNATIVE QUIZ

What were the size of the gates for the following matches this season.

1. Arsenal v Liverpool (Littlewoods Cup replay)

2. Chelsea v Crystal Palace

3. Spurs v Nottingham Forest.
   (Answers at the bottom of the page)

Match these well known sayings with some of football's legendary characters.

1. Hic, minez a pint of Newwcazle brown pleeeeze, hic.

2. People tell me I'm too old, but it doesn't bother me - I'm going deaf.

3. Ref! Ref! Look at your linesman.

4. I thought we should have had three penalties and all seven of their goals looked offside to me.

5. There's no crisis at this club.

6. I think I've got the support of the man on the street. It's the men that live in houses that I'm not so sure about.

7. Okay, so the tackle was a little high, but did he have to clutch his forehead?

8. Is this the ladies?
   What do you think of this ladies?

A. Bobby Robson

B. Graeme Souness

C. John Hollins

D. Kenny Sansom

E. Bryan Robson

F. Tony Adams

G. Peter Shilton

H. Terry Venables

ANSWERS -

Is this the end for Tottenham?

\+ \+

The city of Nottingham hadn't seen anything like it for years - the return to England of Lee Chapman. Not since the funeral of another forest favourite, Robin Hood, had so many people lined the streets for a stiff.

Earlier, the myth of the thick Frenchman had been exploded when the bosses of first division Niort refused to pay Chapman's previous club Sheffield Ved the transfer fee until they'd seen him in action.

After the first training session Anglo-French relations hit an all-time low. Mrs Thatcher offered to pull out of the EEC AND drink a pint of French UHT milk, but it couldn't stop the return of Chapman.

Welcome home, Leeeee. British football hasn't been the same without you.

\+ \+

xxxxxxxxxxxxxxxxxxxxxxxxxxxxxxxxxxxxxxxxxxxxxxxxxxxxxxxxxxxxxxxxxx

HOW DO YOU TELL A PROSTITUTE IN TOTTENHAM?
SHE'S THE ONE WITH A PLEAT IN HER SKIRT.
x x x x x x x x x x x x x x x x x x x x x x x x
WHAT DO YOU CALL A CHELSEA PLAYER WHO PASSES THE BALL TEN YARDS?
GIFTED.

xxxxxxxxxxxxxxxxxxxxxxxxxxxxxxxxxxxxxxxxxxxxxxxxxxxxxxxxxxxxxxxxxx

MY FAIR BRADY

One can only think that those who questioned Liam Brady's parentage during the FA Cup match at Upton Park must themselves be lacking in some of societies important requirements.

Though it does seem strange that those without a brain should seek to ridicule the illegitimate.

After all, those born out of wedlock had no control over their status, but you did at least attend school for a few years.

It's just a shame that you weren't around when Liam played for Arsenal. Oh yes, he played for the Gunners, during the 1970's - when you were practising your three-times table and self-abuse.

Infact, Brady was not a bad player as I remember. Had you followed Arsenal then, you would no doubt have sung his name and hailed him as the King of Highbury. After he left this continued for some years.

Even if you did admire him then, you can't like him now because, after all, he's a West Ham bastard isn't he?

Why does he always stand next to me?

chapter 7

BLUE PRINT

manchester city

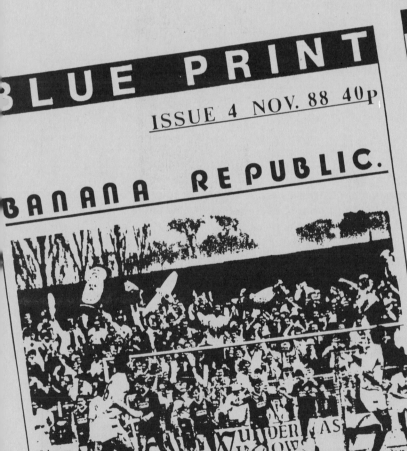

BLUE PRINT

ISSUE 4 NOV. 88 40p

BANANA REPUBLIC.

INSIDE:

ERIC NIXON INTERVIEW.
THE BANANA STORY—BLOWN OUT OF ALL PROPORTION.?
HAPPY 10th BIRTHDAY TO THE LEICESTER AND RUGBY BRANCH.
RESULTS OF TARBY COMPETITION.

PLUS: YOUR INVITATION TO THE BIGGEST FANCY DRESS
PARTY FOOTBALL HAS EVER SEEN, TO BE HELD AT
STOKE CITY ON BOXING DAY......

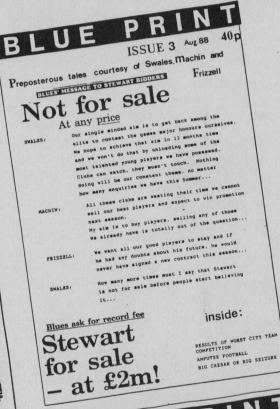

BLUE PRINT

ISSUE 3 Aug. 88 40p

Preposterous tales courtesy of Swales. Machin and Frizzell

BLUES' MESSAGE TO STEWART BIDDERS

Not for sale

At any price

SWALES: Our single minded aim is to get back among the
elite to contest the games major honours ourselves.
We hope to achieve that aim in 12 months time
and we won't do that by unloading some of the
most talented young players we have possessed.
Clubs can watch, they musn't touch. Nothing
doing will be our constant theme, no matter
how many enquiries we have this Summer...

MACHIN: All these clubs are wasting their time we cannot
sell our best players and expect to win promotion
next season.
My aim is to buy players, selling any of those
we already have is totally out of the question...

FRIZZELL: We want all our good players to stay and if
he had any doubts about his future, he would
never have signed a new contract this season...

SWALES: How many more times must I say that Stewart
is not for sale before people start believing
it...

Blues ask for record fee

Stewart
for sale
– at £2m!

inside:

RESULTS OF WORST CITY TEAM
COMPETITION
AMPUTEE FOOTBALL
BIG CAESAR OR BIG SEIZURE

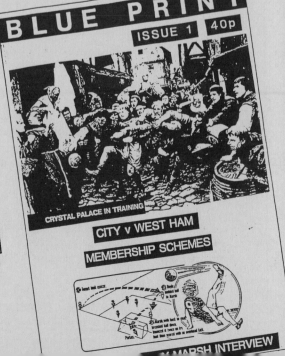

BLUE PRINT

ISSUE 1 40p

CRYSTAL PALACE IN TRAINING

CITY v WEST HAM

MEMBERSHIP SCHEMES

MARSH INTERVIEW

BLUE PRINT

When you're born in Manchester you're forced to make decisions early on in life. Red or Blue. The decision speaks volumes. "He's a Red him isn't he?" "Yes." - (pause) "Typical!"

It becomes part of your life - it becomes part of you.

There can be many factors that can try and influence this decision, like a family full of Reds.

My grandad was responsible for taking me to my first football (I use the term loosely) match at Old Trafford to see the world famous team, Bill Foulkes etc. I can't remember anything much about the game, only that my grandad felt it had been such a splendid day out I should have a reminder, a little keep-sake all of my own, a picture of the United team to go on my Supercar wallpaper. Shove it grandad.

This was what probably made my decision for me. Having United perpetually rammed down your throat, family, T.V., school, just made me and perhaps half of Manchester think, hold on, there must be something else.

Something else there was. My grandad bit his lip, relented and took me to Maine Road. But he didn't bite hard enough; his compromise only reached reserve team level. No matter, I was a Blue.

My City picture, Tony Coleman etc. was firmly stuck on, pre-Bluetak, next to a youthful Cliff Richard. Not all my decisions were the right ones.

Mum and Dad - Reds - finally gave in one birthday to my fervent requests for a plastic duffle bag with a strange, nondescript City player on the side - they had plenty to choose from.

It took a trip to Ashworth Valley with the cubs, a blazing Akela and a frantic fire to turn this player into a plastic monstrosity with legs five times the size of its body. I was itching to get home and write Neil Young next to it.

I was fortunate enough to start following City when the team was winning everything in sight. I've continued to follow them through thick and thin - Hair! I suppose the pinnacle of the teams success was the League Championship and my hair reached its own pinnacle a bit later with a rather resplendant Rod Stewart cut, with flares and platforms as essential accessories.

After many highs and lows, a couple of cup finals, a couple of Simod cup matches, Europe, Halifax, Championship near misses, Channon near misses, the pleasure of seeing the greatest footballer ever to grace any football pitch - Rodney Marsh - and the worst - Mike Walsh - relegation hit us. The first time it was a shock. The second time hurt.

The club have made many grave mistakes throughout the time I have followed them. The greatest mistake of all thpugh was to take their fans for granted, to simply use them as turnstile fodder.

Relegation gave me many things to think about, Shrewsbury on a Tuesday night for one. More than this though it led me to take a closer look at the club I loved and I didn't like what I saw. A lot of time was spent knowing things had to be said, knowing things had to be done but not knowing what.

An article in The Observer on football fanzines - I'd never heard of them before - gave me a start. John Dewhirst (City Gent) gave me the encouragement to carry it through and the enthusiasm of many City fans made it all worth while.

Getting the fanzine off the ground was easy compared with getting the nod from the club. To be fair to Swales, and it's hard, at least it was easy enough to get to talk with the bloke - but why shouldn't it be?

Two visits to see the secretary and the commercial manager later, an uneasy compromise was reached. They stated that they couldn't support it as it might affect programme sales - yawn - but then wished me all the best with it if I ever decided to print. I'd decided to print a long time before this.

No such compromise with the bloody chairman of the Supporters Club. Here was a person who supposedly had the interests of the clubs supporters at heart walking into our meeting with an air of indifference, barely looking at us, hardly listening to us and stating after a couple of minutes of his valuable time that he could never support it as it might criticise the club.

A bit of advice if you're thinking of doing a Manchester City fanzine - don't listen to anyone connected with the club or you'll never find yourself at some unruly hour frantically rubbing letraset while watching Prisoner Cell Block H.

BLUE PRINT

I sold the first issue at a night game stood on my Jack in Kippax Street. It took a bloke who staggerred up to me with his hands open slavering "Just take what you need, son" to help me realise that selling could be enjoyable. I had a smile on my face all night thinking of that bloke spending the entire game looking for the team sheet.

The first issue sold out in ten days, the re-issue followed suit - we were on our way.

I'd like to think that the issues to date have been diverse enough to interest all tastes and a commonality to twinge everybody's conscience. Material has ranged from translating football chants into Esperanto to identity cards, amputee football to share issues and who could possibly forget the fancy dress we organised at Stoke for Boxing Day, inflatables et-al.

I wouldn't say it's been all plain sailing though. It's time consuming and it's bloody hard work. A baby that grows into a monster. I would have been overwhelmed at the enormity of it all if it had not been for the loyalty of the people who have supported this venture and continue to do so.

The rewards have been many though and can perhaps be epitomised by the night game at Stamford Bridge where we stood with the Chelsea fans selling copies of Blue Print. Who said it couldn't be done.

It's early days for Blue Print. We hope we're getting it right - just hope the team follows suit.

MIKE KELLY

I started watching football as a teenager, went to a couple of City matches and was hooked for life. There's a certain spirit amongst the fans, they chose the 'unfashionable' team in Manchester so tend to be individualists. The humour and inventiveness in the crowd at Maine Road is marvellous to see. This is borne out in the success of the fanzine which has leapt from humble beginnings at Christmas 1987 to the prominence it enjoys now. Mike Kelly started the fanzine and controls the editing and content while I look after the finance and distribution. We are very different people with a different outlook on life but work well together as a team.

I see fanzines as a way of promoting football positively. They have helped to establish a network of contacts between the fans of different clubs and have given people an identity with the club they support. They have also given a valuable insight into other clubs and their supporters and have shown that the hopes and aspirations I have for Manchester City are exactly the same that other fans feel for their clubs. Above all the fanzines have given a voice to the people who care for their team. It is my hope that fanzines can bridge the gap that exists between the paying supporter and the club that he or she supports.

FRANK NEWTON

MAGAZINE TITLE: BLUE PRINT,

EDITORS NAME: MIKE KELLY

AGE: 31   OCCUPATION: SOCIAL WORKER

DO YOU/HAVE YOU EVER SUPPORTED ANY OTHER TEAM? NO

MOST MEMORABLE MATCH EVER: City v Sunderland F.A. Cup 1972-3 Round 5 Feb 24 Drew 2-2.

MOST MEMORABLE SEASON: This Season.

ALL TIME FAVOURITE PLAYER: Rodney Marsh

WHAT SORT OF CAR DO YOU DRIVE? Triumph Toledo.

YOUR FAVOURITE MUSIC: Early Punk Pistols, Clash, Buzzcocks, B-52s.

FILMS/TV:

FAVOURITE CLOTHES: Jeans & T-shirt

POLITICAL LEANINGS: Socialist

WHAT PLAYER WOULD YOU MOST LIKE TO SEE PLAYING FOR ENGLAND (SCOTLAND/WALES IF RELEVANT)? Steve Redmond.

MAGAZINE TITLE: BLUE PRINT

EDITORS NAME: FRANK NEWTON

AGE: 29   OCCUPATION: SYSTEMS ANALYST

DO YOU/HAVE YOU EVER SUPPORTED ANY OTHER TEAM? No

MOST MEMORABLE MATCH EVER: FA Cup Semi vs Ipswich at Villa Park 1981

MOST MEMORABLE SEASON: 1988/89, Banana season

ALL TIME FAVOURITE PLAYER: COLIN BELL

WHAT SORT OF CAR DO YOU DRIVE? BLUE FORD ORION DIESEL

YOUR FAVOURITE MUSIC: BLUES

FILMS/TV: BLUES BROTHERS,

FAVOURITE CLOTHES: JEANS + 'T' SHIRT

POLITICAL LEANINGS: BLUE

WHAT PLAYER WOULD YOU MOST LIKE TO SEE PLAYING FOR ENGLAND (SCOTLAND/WALES IF RELEVANT)? COLIN BELL

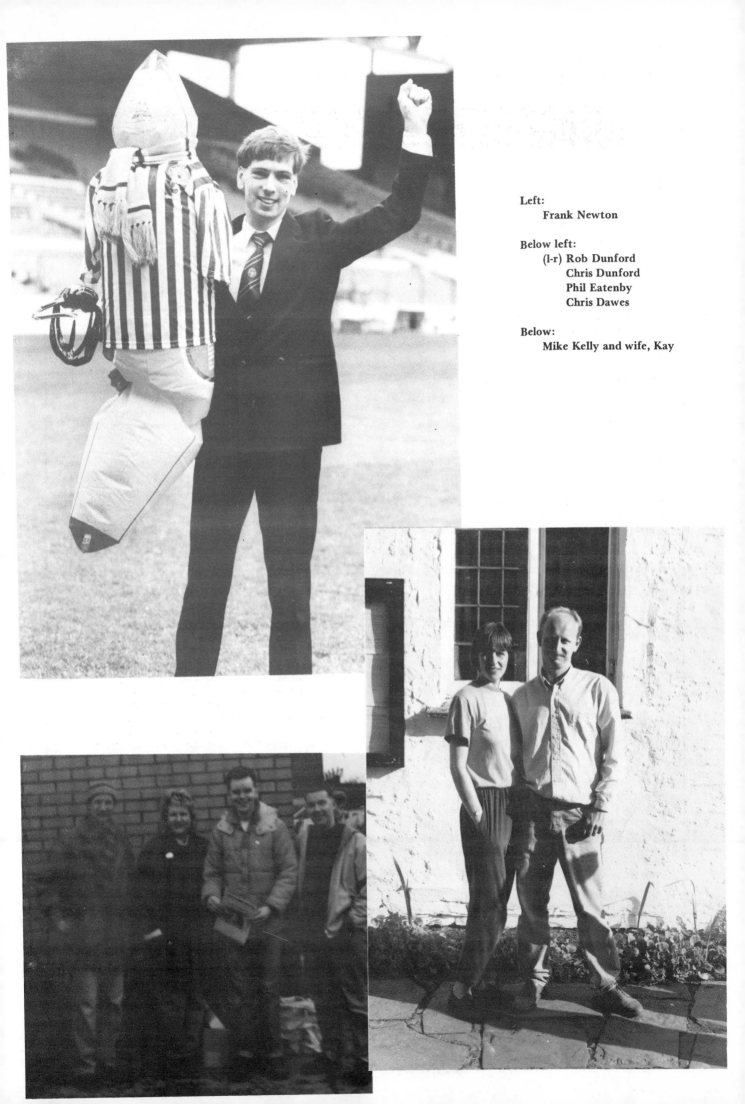

Left:
   Frank Newton

Below left:
   (l-r) Rob Dunford
        Chris Dunford
        Phil Eatenby
        Chris Dawes

Below:
   Mike Kelly and wife, Kay

YOU'LL BE BACK !!

There are a number of events that stand out in my memory during the ten years that I've travelled to City away games, and none more so than the final match of 1986/7 season.

City were lying third from bottom of the First Division, in the relegation zone. It was theoretically possible to reach the playoff's, but only the minor miracle of Charlton losing at home and City winning away for the first time in 27 attempts would achieve this.

Not much to be proud of, with this great club teetering on the brink of the Second Division. And yet an estimated seven and a half thousand City fans made the trip to Upton Park, West Ham (about the same number of Charlton fans who attended their home game the same day).

8 DEEP

I travelled down by car with a friend, and met up with another City fan who lived in London. We parked up and walked to a pub near the ground. There was the buzz of a big match in the air which I found strange in the circumstances. The first sight I had of something special was when we tried to get into the ground, only to find the queue at the visitors end stretching eight deep for about a hundred yards. It took nearly half an hour to get in, and looking round I saw that the queue was just as long as when I'd joined it. The mood was happy and expectant, very close to the atmosphere at the Cup Final in '81.

The team ran onto the pitch to a fantastic reception, there seemed to be blue and white everywhere. The game finally started, but I don't remember much of it, except that we were losing at half time and Liam Brady scored in the second half, the score finishing up at 2-0 to West Ham. But somehow the match or the score wasn't the important thing on that sunny day in East London, it was being there that mattered. The City fans just kept on singing as if we were winning the league.

WE WANT CITY

At last the final whistle blew. The result was academic in any case as Charlton had won their game, and City were relegated.

I stood on the terrace with tears rolling down my face, not wanting to move. The West Ham fans invaded the pitch, several thousand of them, and congratulated their team. Chants of we want City were not rewarded because of the mass of people on the pitch. I thought back to the Luton match two years previously and the angry scenes that followed. There could have been a bloodbath now as there was little to stop the huge City following from getting over the low wall at the front of the stand and invading the pitch themselves. Yet those fans were neither angry nor frustrated, but just waited patiently for a last glimpse of their team.

YOU'LL BE BACK.

It must have taken twenty minutes for the West Ham players to finally disappear, then their fans turned from the tunnel and walked across the pitch to the City end. The two sets of fans stood facing each other for a moment, then the West Ham fans were applauding us and we were applauding them. About ten thousand people stood there and clapped and cheered each other for several minutes. Then came the singing: "You'll be back" sang the West Ham fans "You're the pride of London Town" sang the City fans, and they stood there and cheered each other again. After a few minutes a scarf flew from the City end and landed in the West Ham group, then one came the other way, and soon the air was thick with scarves, shirts, banners and flags. At the front of the stand there was a sudden surge from both sets of supporters and they met at the low wall.... to shake hands, hug each other and swap badges, shirts, scarves and addresses.

We didn't get a last look at the team that day, but if they had come out they would have been treated like heroes.

I eventually left the ground nearly half an hour after the match had finished, knowing that I'd experienced something very special that afternoon. Football had won in an unexpected way, and that feeling will certainly live in my memory for a long, long time to come.

Frank Newton

STAY IN THE PUB

A match to grace any football pitch and every other cliche I can think of. Cast your mind back to the Cup-Final a joy to watch but what of that fiasco we had to endure before the game? A celebrity match. The word celebrity being used loosely. Where did they get them from? T.V. executives, producers comedians? I'll say they were, a bunch of them.

We had David Frost cavorting around the pitch as if somebody had stuck the key to his house up his bottom, some boxer who acted as if he'd tied his gloves to his feet and Jimmy Tarbuck who would have done himself more justice if they would have used him as the roller. Daley thompson appeared to be the only one who had been given coaching in how to kick the ball about the pitch.

What I want to know is, who actually sits down and thinks, I know, one hundred thousand people and millions around the world would like to see some middle-aged T.V. executive ruin the game we love? How does anybody arrive at that? The sad thing is for football fans that this debacle was an improvement on watching the policemen compete to see how high they can throw alsations over a wall before they (the dogs) catch their testicles on top of it. Or, as an alternative how many gymnasts it takes to jump on trampets before two meet in the middle. Why? At rugby league matches they have youngsters playing the length of the pitch before the game and watching them break free from a tackle and try and run the length of the pitch, their legs visibly

tiring and the crowd urging them on is part of the day, and I feel goes some way towards producing the healthy atmosphere that prevails at most rugby league games.

The debacle at Wembley proved one thing for which we can be grateful I suppose, and that is, it is possible to use a football pitch before a league or cup game. Club officials have often used this as their escape route. Damage to the pitch etc. If it can be done at Wembley it can be done anywhere! What's to stop groups of kids, schools, junior blues, supporters clubs, playing each other before the game? Be honest what is there to do before a game, listen to the tannoy system?

Apart from seeing some "turkeys" trying to keep balls in the air at Crystal Palace years ago, being pelted with toffees at Everton, and having to endure Eddie Large hosting a joke telling competition at Luton - we lost the game, won the joke telling. What's new! I can't think of much else on offer.

Come on City lets have people playing on the pitch before the game . You can only watch people treading bits of the turf down for so long.

This is how things looked when Bristol City

were in the First Division.

Fortunately they were relegated.

* * * * * * * * * * * * * * * *

SOCCER THEORY - No 1 in a series of thousands.

It's out!!!! The thought behind the theory behind the tactic of our goalkeepers rolling the ball out of the area,sticking their haeds down and hoping to connect.While the Kippax holds their breath and waits for the day the goalie misses the ball and falls on his buttocks.

It's all to do with the wind you see.

A reliable source,who should know these things,says that if the wind is blowing strong you can get a better distance on a welly up field if you roll it out and kick it from the floor into the wind, rather than kicking it from your hands.

Do us a favour!!!!

By the next issue we're hoping to have worked out the theory behind leaving nobody up front at opponent's corner kicks.

DID WE EVER WIN AWAY ?!!

ORD RULES of U.S. CITY

As we all skipped smartly out of White Hart Lane in January '86 and were escorted back to the coaches train and cars by the police, who'd have thought that this would be our last away win for twenty months or 38 matches.

What a tortuous and tormented path we trod during that time, with very little cheer and the ignominy of a second relegation within a couple of years.

Season 85/86 faded out without the remotest possibility of a win, but the O-O draw at Anfield at the start of 86/87 gave us high hopes of an early breakthrough. Which just shows how wrong you can be when you support the Blues!

The season drifted on - if only that goal at Southend had been allowed - surely we'll win at Charlton! It was not to be, but as the season climaxed, our fans rallied round and tried to lift the team with tremendous turn-outs at Leicester, Villa, Wednesday and Everton, but despite signing Paul Stewart- not a glimpse!

We all know the story at West Ham from the last issue but could anyone have been more devastated than I? For it was me who caught the ball in the crowd and threw it to Mark Ward. He pinged over the corner for Liam Brady to make the score 2-0 and that was that.

So 1987/88 dawned bright and clear, with another new manager and dark blue socks. Off we went to Oldham where within the 90 minutes we first caught sunstroke and then pneumonia and Mels astute substitutional awareness became apparent - nil.We also (I think) got our first view of the banana!

Villa next and another enormous turn-out in my favourite away stadium where facilities and segregation for the away fans are first class. I also met an old school chum and Blue I hadn't seen since 1960! Good on you John!

Then it was Shrewsbury - this is it, a last minute penalty needless to say, the goalie saved it. Poor old Neil - will we ever.......

Leeds and then Hull and on a cold October evening when everything looked set for a Wolves giant-killing act, and without the biggest ever turn-out for the lads - a last minute John Gidman goal did the trick (first of many). Needless to say I was in the stand with the Wolves fans, and whilst delirious (well!) inside, an external low profile was required.

Next, it was Ipswich, where we hadn't scored a goal for eight years and we just managed to maintain the tradition!

Well, it just had to be Bradford didn't it? After a late start owing to floodlight failure we went 2 up, then the inevitable happened - 2-2.   Will we ever!   Then unbelievably we made it 4-2. Despite nearly breaking our necks coming down that steep stairway in the dark- shame on you, Bradford - nothing could hide our elation and relief!!
How many of you managed all 40 games and hands up all those who got themselves on the video - I was the bloke in the brown cap!!

FACTS N' FIGURES

1985/86						
0	J18	SPURS	LG	W	2- 0	◯
1	F3	WATFORD	FACR	D	0- 0	◯
2	F11	EVERTON	LG	L	0- 4	◯
3	M8	CHELSEA	LG	L	0- 1	◯
4	M22	MAN UTD	LG	D	2- 2	◯
5	M31	LIVERPOOL	LG	L	0- 2	◯
6	A12	IPSWICH	LG	D	0- 0	◯
7	A26	NEWCASTLE	LG	L	1- 3	◯
8	A28	WEST HAM	LG	L	0- 1	◯
1986/87						
9	A25	LIVERPOOL	LG	D	0- 0	◯
10	A30	SPURS	LG	L	0- 1	◯
11	S13	OXFORD	LG	D	0- 0	◯
12	S23	SOUTHEND	LC	D	0- 0	◯
13	S27	LUTON	LG	L	0- 1	◯
14	O11	N/CASTLE	LG	L	1- 3	◯
15	O18	CHELSEA	LG	L	1- 2	◯
16	O25	ARSENAL	LC	L	1- 3	◯
17	N1	SOUTHAMPTON	LG	D	1- 1	◯
18	N22	ARSENAL	LG	L	0- 3	◯
19	D6	NOTTS FOREST	LG	L	0- 2	◯
20	D21	COVENTRY	LG	D	2- 2	◯
21	D28	CHARLTON	LG	L	0- 5	◯
22	J1	WATFORD	LG	D	1- 1	◯
23	J10	MAN UTD	FAC	L	0- 1	◯
24	J24	WIMBLEDON	LG	D	0- 0	◯
25	F14	NORWICH	LG	D	1- 1	◯
26	F28	Q.P.R.	LG	L	0- 1	◯
27	M7	MAN UTD	LG	L	0- 2	◯
28	M28	LEICESTER	LG	L	0- 4	◯
29	A24	ASTON VILLA	LG	D	0- 0	◯
30	A20	SHEFFIELD WED.	LG	L	1- 2	◯
31	M2	EVERTON	LG	D	0- 0	◯
32	M9	WEST HAM	LG	L	0- 2	◯
1987/88						
33	A22	OLDHAM	LG	D	1- 1	◯
34	A31	ASTON VILLA	LG	D	1- 1	◯
35	S12	SHREWSBURY	LG	D	0- 0	◯
36	S26	LEEDS	LG	L	0- 2	◯
37	S29	HULL	LG	L	1- 3	◯
38	O6	WOLVES	LC	W	2- 0	◯
39	O17	IPSWICH	LG	L	0- 3	◯
40	O21	BRADFORD	LG	W	4- 2	◯

SUMMARY

	P	W	D	L	F	A
League	35	1	14	20	18	58
LG & Cup	40	2	16	22	21	62

How many did you manage?
Just fill in the blobs! ●

Segregation, it's not quite what you'd expect at England's premier (???) stadium.

Dave Wallace
28.3.88

Amputee Football

The primary aim of Amputee Football is to pick people up, develop an improved self-image, build confidence and prove you can have fun in the process. So says the manager of the Manchester Kestrels, England's representative in the forthcoming Amputee Football World Cup to be held in Seattle in September this year.

Amputee Football was originally introduced to this country by Bill Barry, the Coach of Seattle Sounders and now the coaching director of Amputee Football International.

Bill was so impressed with the standard of football played by the Manchester Kestrel's that he invited them to compete in America against other such teams as: El Salvador, the present holders of the trophy, Portland, Seattle, Idaho, Los Angeles, Denver and Sacramento.

Many of the players in the Kestrels have played football at a high standard, some having trials with league clubs and it shows in their play now. Dave sees Amputee Football as a step in the rehabilitation process and one which is available to the sizeable proportion of the 70,000 in England alone who have lost a limb.

As Dave says "You don't have to be 7 feet tall, weigh 15 stone or be a bloke to play it." It is open to anyone who has lost a limb.

The game is played either indoors, where Major Indoor Football League rules ore adhered to as closely as possible. Or outdoor where again F.I.F.A. rules are followed.

The modifications for Amputee Football are that players must not use their crutches for any purpose other than support. The crutch, therefore is considered to be an extension of the arm.

Goalkeepers - who are usually people who have lost an arm must not intentionally use their non-playing arm to stop, direct, pick-up or control the ball in any way. They must also remain within their goal area. For practical purposes in Amputee Football the throw-in is replaced with the kick-in. And because of the physical demands of Amputee Football unlimited substitutions are allowed to prevent over - exertion or straining of the player's leg, hand, arm or shoulder muscles and also to provide an opportunity for all the players to play.

Amputee football is presently in its infancy in Britain, however, it is hoped that it will have grown to be recognised as an Olympic Sport by 1992.

The Manchester Kestrels with their love of football are trying to encourage others, regardless of their disability to expand their horizons, believe in themselves and realise that the only handicap that exists is that in the mind. However, the cost of running such a team and competing with other teams at home and abroad is huge and the Kestrels are presently looking for sponsors and donations to help their cause.

If anybody is able to help in any way or indeed is interested in playing Amputee Football could they please contact:
David Anderson, Tel: 061-789-6997.

BANANA DRAMA...

WHAT'S ALL THIS: Giant bananas, a huge beer can and even an inflatable Frankenstein monster..... so said the caption to a photograph in the West Country Sunday Independant after City's triumph at Plymouth earlier this season. Football has never seen anything like it, how did it start?

Inflatables at City matches are nothing new. Over the years I've spotted an ET at Brighton in 1983, a large banana at Coventry in 1985 and a snake at Walsall in 1986. What is unusual is the scale of the current phenomenum. Previously no football crowd has had sufficient imagination and organisation to reach the stage where around 1000 assorted inflatables travel with City fans to their away games. The inflatables have given me some spectacular sights, humorous moments and unforgetable scenes this season. Little did I think that when I took The Banana to it's first match last year that Banana Mania would spread to such epic proportions.

In the close season I visited a friend who happened to let slip in conversation that he had a large inflatable banana. I spent the rest of the evening persuading him to lend it to me and refused to leave without it! He eventually agreed provided I proved to him that I actually took it to a game. Proof enough Alan? (I never did give it back!). The Bananas first match was the Plymouth home game last season, where it sat on the wall in the open section between the Kippax and the North Stand. I felt it was time to do something unusual to make up for being in the second division again. I went to the match with a friend, Mike Clare, who drew a face on The Banana for effect. It was a hot day so I took my City shirt off, somehow this ended up on The Banana and the first glimpse of things to come was seen.

The following week we all got soaked at Oldham where The Banana attended it's first away match. It missed several games then but reappeared at Reading. Here it was smuggled into the ground in Mark Todd's wheelchair as the police reaction was unknown. This was soon revealed as I stood on the terraces at Elm Park struggling to put a bobble hat on The Banana. A large uniformed figure approached and I braced myself for the worst. "I hope you don't have as much trouble putting a condom on as you're having with that hat" he said. After that I was quite open. It was a joy to be asked on being searched "What's that" and to be able to reply "A plastic blow up banana". They didn't know whether to believe me or not!

The next away game was West Brom. Here Mike Clare took the banana into the middle of the massed City fans and started the immortal chant: Imre Banana was born. For those of you lucky enough to have a copy of the video 'Life with the Blues' Mike's waving Imre about and I'm three to the left looking as if I'm trying to nut someone! After the West Brom game if I went to a match without Imre I always heard some comment about The Banana not being there.

Imre started going more often, to Stoke on boxing day where a kind official informed me that no banners or flags were allowed in the ground (?), Huddersfield in the FA Cup, Plymouth, Everton (who could forget the City following that night?), Huddersfield in the Cup replay and Blackpool in the next round.

At the end of February there was an important milestone in The Banana Story. At Leicester Imre turned up together with a smaller counterpart, immediately christened Baby Banana. Both also travelled to Sheffield United for the midweek match. My thanks to the City fan who loudly pointed out how Baby Banana must have been conceived! Imre's only other appearance at Maine Road was for the Liverpool match but apart from a fleeting glimpse we didn't get him on TV.

The stress of watching City was getting too much and Imre split at Barnsley. He reappeared off his sick bed heavily bandaged at Huddersfield and Middlesborough. However, help was at hand! Mike Kelly finished his editorial in BLUE PRINT (an excellent fanzine, you must get a copy!) issue 2 by saying "We urge our readers to take a blow up banana to Crystal Palace". Peter Gregory and Noel Bayley decided to jump the gun, so at Birmingham Imre Banana and Baby Banana were joined by two others and a small furry semi-peeled banana held by another City fan. The victory there was sweet after the constant baracking of debutant Neil Lennon by the Birmingham crowd who also suggested "You can shove your big banana up your arse" I didn't try but was pleased to get a mention. Fame at last!

And so to crystal Palace. I understand that every shop in Manchester that sold bananas sold out in the week leading up to the game. Despite the police trying to stop bananas entering the gates on the grounds of racism (Just because Mark Bright got Eric Nixon sent off at Maine Road) about 50 or so were smuggled in; we must have had the best endowed set of supporters to enter Selhurst Park last season! The imagination that had gone into the decoration and dressing of the bananas was marvellous to see whilst the appearance of a rhino and a penguin added a new dimension to the craze.

From little acorns mighty oaks grow, and this one's growing by the week! At one stage though I thought the phenomenum had died a death. I bought a 4ft 6in crocodile for this season thinking I'd stay one step ahead of the crowd. (How wrong I was to be proved!) At Stockport in the pre-season friendly there were just four bananas and Niccy the crocodile (named after a female colleague who snaps at everyone). At Old Trafford the situation was better but not up to the standards set at Crystal Palace. And the the season started.....

Looking at the spectacular scenes at Hull it was as if the close season was spent by City fans scouring the shops for anything plastic and blow up. Giant golf clubs, skeletons, gorilla's and pink panthers (To name but a few) were the order of the day. At Leeds the first blow up doll appeared as did an ALF and a number of sharks. Any naughty City fans who travelled to Chelsea for the midweek match may have been priveledged to see the first appearance of Frankenstein. At Barnsley a whole host of new inflatables appeared, at Ipswich I stood next to a 6ft dinasor and the sight of a multitude of bananas knocking a beachball about at half time made me laugh so much that tears were streaming down my face. At West Brom we were treated to a fight between two Frankensteins, the giant dinasor, a lilo wearing a City shirt, a 6ft diameter paddling pool, a 5ft Newcastle Brown Ale can and a 4ft diameter fried egg, whilst an authentic 7ft long rubber dingy looked on. A fine humorous touch was provided by a shark with a blow up sailing boat in it's mouth! It was a far cry from Imre Banana's appearance 11 months before, and far more entertaining than the match! It was disappointing to lose but when a car drove past with a gorilla sitting through the sunroof I had to raise a smile.

Numerous newspaper articles, a personal mention in the match program and even a TV interview (ugh!) later success hasn't changed me at all, I would have bought the Porshe and the house in Wilmslow anyway! So City now have a huge and good natured away following, an excellent relationship with the police wherever we go, acclaim

from the media and provide a spectacular scene at all the grounds we visit. Home fans at Plymouth were spotted queueing up to take pictures of the City crowd!

My personal list of different inflatables spotted now runs to over 70, but I'm sure I haven't seen them all. Why has Banana Mania caught on with City fans? It beats me, but we're having a hell of a lot of fun in the process! Whatever's next? Turn up at Stoke in fancy dress and we'll see how things go from there.....

Frank Newton

I would be very pleased to receive any press cuttings etc about Banana Mania at the address on the inside front cover.

☐ **BRILLIANT BROS: From the left Craig Logan, Matt and Luke Goss.**

Bros ● Apollo, Manchester

DEAFENED and dumbstruck, I reflected that I would rather face a herd of stampeding buffalo than get the wrong side of a theatre full of Bros fans. By comparison, A-ha's last concert at the Apollo was a vicar's tea party. Bros's support — so young that GCSEs are but a distant cloud on the horizon — can be measured on the Richter scale.

Before the appearance of the lads themselves — the Goss Bros and the other one without the Hitler Youth haircut — we were treated to a solid 40 minutes of rabble-rousing by an excitable DJ.

"Sing Luke, sing Matt, sing Craig, sing B-R-O-S," he implored. The throng of 2,700 responded by waving tee-shirts, banners, teddy bears and — more enigmatically — a large inflatable banana.

Come on who's the Bros fan?

FANCY THAT!

December 26th 1988. That date will stick in many people's memories as the day Stoke was invaded by twelve thousand plus Man City fans bearing large inflatable bananas and dressed in a bewildering array of strange fancy dress outfits. One fan described the scenes by saying that although he hadn't had a drink he felt light headed with the atmosphere generated in the ground.

It didn't start there though. In the morning there was a constant stream of traffic on the M6 southbound from Manchester, it seemed that every car had blue scarves flying out of the windows or contained a rabbit sitting next to Henry VIII or had plastic blow up bananas on the parcel shelf. One van shot past with bananas stuck to the outside, whilst a taxi arrived at a house in Manchester to be greeted by four gorillas and the muffled words 'Take us to Stoke'.

Once in Stoke and that elusive parking spot had been found, it was time to wander round to see what was happening. At the first road junction three musketeers walked past complete with swords and frilly hats. A gladiator was munching a hamburger on a street corner and a christmas tree was walking in the general direction of the ground. Every pub in the area was full with strange animals and medieval characters talking, laughing and drinking together, the atmosphere was electric. The Stoke fans seemed rather bemused by the extraordinary sight but were very friendly, whilst even the police joined in and had photographs taken with all sorts of odd characters. Reinforcements must have been called in as a Canadian Mountie was seen directing the traffic in the middle of the main street!

Inside the ground it was packed despite being given one side and an end. (we should have been given the seats behind the goal as well) There was plenty to keep me amused as I waited to greet the team. In the seats behind me was a very official looking Postman Pat and a Humpty Dumpty who insisted on sitting on the wall! A couple of convicts were nearby, very authentic looking right down to the shifty eyes! When they turned round the nametags on their backs bore the legends 'Lester Piggott' and 'Jan Molby'. It was difficult to tell if the policemen sitting near them were real or just City fans in fancy dress. Three dalmations walked by me and continued on past a group of Nazi officers complete with authentic tunics, peaked caps and long baggy white shorts with swastika's painted on them. (One tried to buy a copy of Blue Print off me with Deuchmarks!)

Then the team arrived. It was as if we had just won the cup, cheering and celebration as far as the eye could see. The players ran onto the pitch carrying large blow up bananas (a novel idea, I wonder where they got it from?) which they threw into the crowd. There were balloons floating in the air, thousands of bananas waving and other wierd and wonderful inflat ables bobbing up and down in the crowd. I just wish that someone had taken a picture of the scene at that moment, it must have been one of the most spectacular sights that football has ever produced.

The match itself has faded from my memory partly because we lost but mainly because there was so much else to take in. The interstellar branch of the City fan club was in evidence with ET sitting on the fence at half time, a crocodile and a canary seemed to be getting on intimate terms, whilst I didn't envy the rear half of the pantomime horse wandering round the ground. I wonder how much of the game he saw? I wish I'd had a week or so to walk round the crowd to take in the humour and imagination displayed by the magnificent City following.

When the game ended there was an air of disappointment at the result but still plenty of laughter as new delights appeared at every turn of the head. A rather cold looking fan wandered past wearing a snorkel and flippers and not much else, a group of pixies were spotted heading towards the car park, whilst rambo complete with machine gun (with a City scarf tied round it) walked the other way.

The following was hailed as the largest mass migration of City fans for a league match since Newcastle in '68. With the inflatables and the fancy dress I've certainly never seen anything like it. It was an experience just to be part of the scenes. The team may be in the second division but the fans are certainly top of any league!

I wrote in Issue 3 about the palace match at the end of last season: 'Just when I thought I'd seen everything in football I'm proved wrong.' Well it's happened again.

Gate Newton

The view of the match above was of necessity a personal one. If you have any overiding memories of the Stoke game why not write to Blue Print and share them with us.

Fans held own pitch check

The result was even more emphatic when you consider we were twenty goals down at half-time!

chapter 8

EAGLE EYE

crystal palace

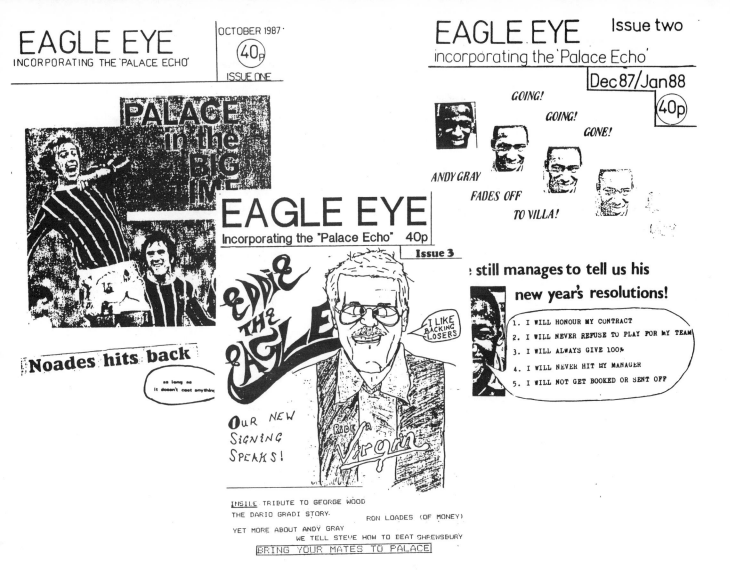

Eagle Eye began life as a result of my reading *When Saturday Comes* and *Off The Ball*. I really wanted to write, but found I could only write about Palace.

The name is really *Eagle Eye incorporating the Palace Echo* in response to chairman Ron Noades' promise of an Echo chamber on the open Holmesdale End. This, of course, has never materialised.

The first issue came out in October 1987 and was mainly me with a little help from one or two others. The Atilla The Stockbroker article in particular helped set the tone i.e. piss taking of Palace aswell as a more serious edge.

The second issue sent certain club officials up the wall, especially its cover concerning a certain Andy Gray, who left Palace for Villa in very acrimonious circumstances. We just expanded a few rumours (from very good sources!)

The third issue brought more criticism from the club. Ron Noades said we couldn't be supporters. He even thought the cover might make Virgin think they were backing a bunch of losers and pull out of their sponsorship!

All through the animosity from the club the response from other Palace supporters has been truly staggering, an endless succession of letters containing masses of praise etc. People are so pleased to see something like this in existence. The most satisfying part is getting letters from people who have never put pen to paper before, many of them now desperate to write for *Eagle Eye* and beyond. Dozens are prepared to write articles on a regular basis, so the magazine seems to have a strong future. Readership has gone up and up: the current print run is 2000 but we are confident we could sell twice that many. As always distribution remains the problem.

Where does it go from here? It needs to come out more often to respond better to current issues.

The club is taking more and more notice and is beginning to accept that we are not hooligans but a group of people worth listening to. Hopefully this means *Eagle Eye* can strive for a stronger voice **within** the club for supporters. This can only benefit both sides and put Palace where they should be - in the first division !

JOHN ELLIS

EDITORS NAME: JOHN ELLIS

AGE: 29   OCCUPATION: Computer Programmer

DO YOU/HAVE YOU EVER SUPPORTED ANY OTHER TEAM?
Bristol Rovers/ Keynsham Town.

MOST MEMORABLE MATCH EVER: Palace v Ipswich this season — I haven't got a long memory!

MOST MEMORABLE SEASON: Palace's dark age — 81 → 85.

ALL TIME FAVOURITE PLAYER: Kevin Mabbutt

WHAT SORT OF CAR DO YOU DRIVE? Don't!

YOUR FAVOURITE MUSIC: Noise — Butthole Surfers, Sonic Youth, 3 Johns,

FILMS/TV: Bladerunner, Roobarb, Black Adder.

FAVOURITE CLOTHES: Ratty tee shirts, docs, grey coats and faded jeans.

POLITICAL LEANINGS: left wing bastard

WHAT PLAYER WOULD YOU MOST LIKE TO SEE PLAYING FOR ENGLAND (SCOTLAND/ WALES IF RELEVANT)?
George Wood for Scotland now until the end of time

EDITORS NAME: Tony Matthews

AGE: 27   OCCUPATION: Too Ashamed To Say!

DO YOU/HAVE YOU EVER SUPPORTED ANY OTHER TEAM?
Fortuna Düsseldorf, Chelsea as a kid

MOST MEMORABLE MATCH EVER: Deutschland v Allied POWs — in "Escape To Victory"

MOST MEMORABLE SEASON: 1980-1 Relegation Year

ALL TIME FAVOURITE PLAYER: Gerd Muller

WHAT SORT OF CAR DO YOU DRIVE? Volvo 345

YOUR FAVOURITE MUSIC: 60's Soul / R n B / Punk - Indie

FILMS/TV: Anything with Olivia de Havilland or Ginger Rogers

FAVOURITE CLOTHES: Jeans, Trainers, Fred Perrys & Ben Sherman Shirts (bit of a Mod really?)

POLITICAL LEANINGS: None

WHAT PLAYER WOULD YOU MOST LIKE TO SEE PLAYING FOR ENGLAND (SCOTLAND/ WALES IF RELEVANT)? Tony Adams.

EDITORS NAME: Justin Williams

AGE: 21   OCCUPATION: Graphic designer

DO YOU/HAVE YOU EVER SUPPORTED ANY OTHER TEAM? Bristol City (as a kid).

MOST MEMORABLE MATCH EVER: Palace ·v· Shrewsbury (1987)

MOST MEMORABLE SEASON: 80-1 relegation.

ALL TIME FAVOURITE PLAYER: Micky Droy (a rare talent).

WHAT SORT OF CAR DO YOU DRIVE? Bus Pass

YOUR FAVOURITE MUSIC: New Order, Buzzcocks. House and the palace (when they sing!)

FILMS/TV: English social cinema (taste of Honey, Rita Sue + Bob to)

FAVOURITE CLOTHES: Hooded sweatshirt tops, docs + flowery shirts.

POLITICAL LEANINGS: Left of center'ish sort of thing.

WHAT PLAYER WOULD YOU MOST LIKE TO SEE PLAYING FOR ENGLAND (SCOTLAND/ WALES IF RELEVANT)?
Geoff Thomas.

The day a hero returned!

Set off from the Isle of Wight (south of Port smouth for those without CSE geography) to witness the return of one of the all time greats, Trevor Aylott (did you notice the hint of sarcasm there?).

Waded through the prostrate and motionless bodies of drunken mods, on the island for a scooter rally, to get to the station. Funny they reminded me of the Palace defence on a bad day.

On the Waterloo bound train greeted by horded of Pompey fans on their way to Spurs. "Hey, there's a Palace fan....you're bloody joking aren't you? Come and have a look at this then ...fuckin hell you're right, hey, lads have a look at this." Ever felt like a goldfish?

Arrived at the ground early. Read my copy of 'Palace News' (whoops, shouldn't have mentioned that!). Then the Bournemouth coach arrived and off stepped Trevor.

One young lad who obviously never saw Trevor play for Palace asked for his autograph. Chants of "donkey" and "son of Aylott" could be heard in the distance.

Made my way up to Crystals to recover from my excitment of seeing Trevor again. As usual had to put up with another Augustus Barnett sports quiz. Imagine the scene. There we are all engrossed watching Palace on the video, reliving the highlights of our spectacular 3-1 win over Oldham, then without warning the screen goes blank. When it is announced it is time for the sports quiz the room empties rapidly.

On the pitch Aylott displayed all the old touches - misplaced headers, off target shots and plenty of completely aimless running round the pitch.(see elsewhere for details!-editor).

Met the Pompey lads on the train home. They had beaten Spurs (mind you who can't). Plenty of good humoured banter.

Arrived back on the island. Went to the pub for a drink with my mates. The conversation went something like this: "You been to Palace today then Chris?"- "Yeah"- "Cor, you poor sod, let me buy you a drink".

I always knew supporting Palace must have its consolations.

Chris Errington

AYLOTT

SON OF AYLOTT

Easter saturday saw a reasonable crowd at Selhurst, no doubt everyone eager to see old favourite Trevor Aylott.

As if the two bloody big 'Eagles' poncing about wasn't enough, we had a clown on the pitch (perhaps it was George Wood in disguise?).The Palace players gave out Easter eggs as they came onto the pitch. But by the time they had been thrown into the crowd, dropped on the floor and dived on by dozens of people desperate for one, they were not worth eating. The £500 or so it cost would have been better spent on something more relevant - nevertheless it's the thought that counts.

The match itself started well enough with Ian Wright in good form. Then the referee Kelvin Morton, caused uproar by sending Ian off for no real reason.

But we had forgotten that he was penalty happy (remember the Hull game at the beg- of the season - he gave us two dubious penalties then). He promptly pointed to the spot twice more and Neil Redfearn did the honours, with a bit of help from Kelvin who let him take one again.

After half time Trevor Aylott proved he's just as crap now as he was when he played for us,missing two good chances. So we all quickly reminded him of his donkey origins!

It was interesting to note that George Graham got a bollocking from the FA a few da s later, for echoing our thoughts by saying that our mate, Kelvin, is a shit ref. How right could he be?   Iain Carruthers

Trevor's vital statistics for the Selhurst game were

Fell over - 12
Shots ballooned - 3
Headers into space for non-existent partners - 2
Hand on head after serious physical contact - 3

As the enclosure put it, give us a D.O.N.K.E.Y. and what have you got - Aylott

What's new?

CONVERSATION between Palace skipper Jim Cannon and Bournemouth striker Trevor Aylott, who used to play for Palace, during a stoppage in Saturday's game.
Cannon: "They're giving you a bit of stick over there, Trev."
Aylott: "Oh, I don't know. They used to boo me more when I played for Palace!"

from the 'Croydon Advertiser'

In the last fifteen years attendances at Football League matches have declined by an overall average of some 35 per cent. This can be attributed to many factors: the advent of television, the rise of the football hooligan and latterly the ravages of Thatcherism which have priced football out of the range of many low paid and unemployed people. In 1970 the average attendance at an English Second Division match was 14,876 but by 1985 this had dwindled to around two thirds of the above figure. One club, however, was especially hard hit by the drop in attendances. In 1985 the average Second Division crowd was 8,443 but at Selhurst Park, home of the South London side Crystal Palace, it was nineteen. N-n-n-nineteen. Nineteen. N-n-n-nineteen. And even though these brave but misguided souls had the courage to pay £2-50 or more to see what is indisputably the worst football team in the solar system, none of them received a hero's welcome. None of them: none of them. None of them received a hero's welcome. N-n-n-n-n-none of them. For ninety minutes every other Saturday afternoon for nine months of the year they were constantly exposed to fierce and merciless ridicule from the rest of the football world and many of them are still living out their experiences to this day. At the end of the 1984-85 season the number of suicidal and despairing calls made to the South London branch of the Samaritans was nineteen. N-n-n-nineteen. Nineteen. N-n-n-nineteen. N-n-n-n-n-n-n-n-n-n-nineteen. And because their level of football skill was roughly that of a paraplegic gerbil, at the end of the same season nearly all the current Crystal Palace squad were forced to leave professional football and sign on. S-s-s-sign on. Sign on. S-s-s-sign on. Being so utterly useless that they were rejected even by Peterborough, Colchester, Hull City, Grimsby Town, the Luxembourg Veteran Amputees XI and Lower Lichtenstein South Second XI Reserves, some of them ended up in Vietnam playing for a team of Hanoi toilet attendants so that they didn't have to sign on. V-v-v-Vietnam. S-s-s-sign on. V-v-v-Vietnam. S-s-s-sign on. V-v-v-Vietnam. S-s-s-sign on. V-v-v-Vietnam. S-s-s-sign on. V-v-v-Vietnam. S-s-s-sign on. REPEAT AD NAUSEAM..........

ATTILA THE STOCKBROKER

LETTERS

I have just been given, by a Spurs supporting friend a copy of Eagle Eye. I am in amazement wonder and awe. Does this mean normal, intelligent, witty humans still support Palace. This is an oasis in a desert. I thought I was the only one left, isolated in Sutton,Surrey, by friends who follow Spurs and Arsenal and a son, who after 8 years of Palace brainwashing has bought a season ticket to Spurs...and who can blame him!

Because of prices and principles(value for money) I now watch the excuses for football matches from the Sainsbury's End. I am surrounded by Geriatrics who inform me that this Johnny Byrne looks a good prospect. By sanitarium escapees, Palace must have the most! The latest who spent the Birmingham match telling the referee, whose name was Hedges, to go back to his cigarette factory. And mostly by your Daily Star, 20 pints a night, Rambo worshipping, boiled hamburger eating typical British males.

After the going's on of the last few years who can expect more!

Your mag has inspired me to ponder and recall the memories (all to few) that keep me, like a kamikaze, coming back for more.

I have just dug up the Palace promotion book "There and back again" and I eagerly await the follow-up, probably to be called "There and then so far away you wouldn't believe it" or in memory of Marvin Gaye "What (the fuck's) going on".

Oh those halcyon days. The memories flood back. Rodgers, Harkouk, Lazarus?, Hiliare, Sansom etc, etc. My personal hero - Peter Taylor - all players that made games worth wanting to go to. I'll cherish what was to me the best goal I've seen at Selhurst v Grimsby '77. Taylor took the ball from the halfway line to the byline, beating 4 players in typical fashion, finally losing the ball before crossing. He then chased the defender back to the halfway line, winning the ball back with a woderful

"Taylor" drag back tackle. Pet-
,er then repeated the run beating the same 4 players, this
time to get in a perfect cross
for Alan Whittle to brilliantly
volley home. Such ecstasy.

Nevertheless it seems I am in
accord with you in the pleasu
res of recalling the disaster
players and for sure we had
some beauties! How's this for
a hall of fame:
Borge Thorup, David Price, Per
Bartram, David "Keegan" Giles,
Tom Vansitartt, Sammy Goodwin,
Andy Higginbottom...do you
want more?

But who was the ultimate anti
hero of them all?! It is and
always was, Mel Blyth (Spirit
of Palace, as the Standard once
said). His picture first hung
in our lavatory. In his early
days he must have been the original "wally". But credit to
the man. He improved beyond
belief and crowned his career
not only with the world record
for back passes in one game.
Also something few Palace players have ever earned - a cup
winners medal. I see him now
at our tennis club, and can he
pull some weights! To me Mel
Blyth was Palace!

Your unjust criticism of the

Palace Eagles, surely cretins
is too high praise. I prefer
to call them two stupid looking bastards. Reminds me of a
previous attempt of the Selhurst ex-management to America-
nise matters. Who remembers
the Palace "dollies". About 10
of Croydon's ugliest, spottiest
teenage tarts that would dress
in Palace kit and miniskirts
to greet the teams arrival on
to the pitch. Who could play
well after a greeting from
that lot. Where are they now?
Walking the streets of Kings
Cross?! Perhaps Mrs Noades was
one and she turned our Ron's
attention to SE25.

Other images come up, such as
when I used to stand under the
directors box and spend most
of the match watching Big Mal's
expressions and hoping to catch
some cigar ash as a sovenir!

So here we are on the verge of
again of throwing away the promotion that would be a disaster
anyway. Palace lay in no-mans
land, a team and crowd worthy of
division 3 and a player capable
of playing of putting them into
division 1. Although he has scor
ed more than last year, Ian
Wright, to me, has lost that
incredible spark of last season
and any further time in the
company of our lot will take him
further to the hall of fame of
black wingers who have threatened

wonders but fade away, Remember
Coker, Chamberlain, Cunningham,
Walters. He is of course being
played as a central striker rather than the natural winger he is
so much better at being.

Do we have any youngsters at
all? If John Salako was young
player of last year - well goodbye and god bless. No! Division
one would be a minefield for us.
A yearly surge for promotion,
perhaps a narrow failure in the
play-offs would be a perfect
Selhurst season.

Perhaps I am wrong, perhaps the
ball will be kept on the ground
for more than 5 seconds, perhaps
the striped heroes (what colour
next year?) will have some shots
on target, perhaps someone will
rule midfield (have we ever had
one of these?). Oh yes! Jerry
Murphy!!! Come back Bobby Kell-
ard! Perhaps Perry is the answer
God knows how Georgie disinteg-
rated. Perhaps I can get a cup
of hot chocolate in a cup thi k
enough to keep the heat away
from the outside. Perhaps..Perh-
aps..

Perhaps I can come away from a
game as I did in the match v
Luton in 1978, saying to myself:
I've just seen the team of the
Eighties...

B.Greene

PS. Whatever happened to Mike
Elwiss?

Wood if he could

George Wood has gone to the land of leeks,
Max Boyce and singing miners. The land
which has given us great football teams
and supporters????
  George went to Cardiff because....
1. Wales has been for so many years oblivious to this great man and his skills.
George rightly thought that it was their
turn to savour his goalkeeping delights.

2. Being a keen ornithologist he had to
stay with a club with a bird as its nickname. The seagulls had seen him in action
enough times to realise he was not their
man, and the Magpies were just not quick
enough with their bid for him. So George
packed his skills in his bag and went down
the M4 to be a bluebird.

  The start was good for George, one goal
given away in 4 games. So myself and some
friends decided to go to the all-ticket
match at Leyton Orient to see this trans-
formation of a goalkeeping legend.
  At the start of the game Orient took
siege on the Cardiff goal. We were sure to
see George pick the ball out of the net.
But amazingly George leaped (well moved)
into action and made two or three good
saves and passed the ball out to his team

mates (unheard of by us Palace fans). Had
George really been reborn to goalkeeping?
Was he really Clark Kent in disguise?Or
had he just been lucky? What is the meaning
of life and why is coffee so disgusting at
football grounds? These and many other
questions I pondered. Then Cardiff scored
against the run of play. Later Orient got
a dodgy penalty which was easily converted.
So at half time the honours were shared
and as George walked off the pitch my
fiends sang Georgie is a beastie"(don't
know why) which reminded him of his Palace
days as he waved to us(well he had to do
something with his hands during the game).
He must have come out still thinking of his
Palace days. To prove this point he then
proceeded to let in 3 more goals. To be
fair, this was helped by some good work by
Steve Ketteridge (?!) and a bad Cardiff
defence.
  It was good to see George in his old form,
thankfully nothing has changed.

Jason Axell

TRAVEL AWAY
WITH THE EAGLES

DNEPR DNEPROPETROVSK
Founded: 1936
Ground: Meteor Stadium
Capacity: 34,000
Colours: Red Shirts
 and White Shorts
Address: ul Kirova 12
Dnepropetrovsk, Soviet Union

Lenin Stand

Glorious Five Year Plan Stand

Food & Drink: Cabbage or Potatoes
No Special Facilities.
Parking: Tanks and Tractors only.
Club Shop: Club shops are symbols
of bourgeois capitalist society.

Travel Details
Routes: Coaches leave at 5 a.m
for Gatwick then catch Aeroflot
flight URS123 to Moscow then by
coach to Dnepropetrovsk. £209.
Bookings will be taken in the
Club shop after today's match.

Palace have been drawn away from
home in the first round of the
Sodim Cup. Details are as above.
See you there.

WE´RE HERE
WHY CAN´T YOU SEE US?

Tuesday August 30
6.30pm. Son to father.
"Palace v Chelsea - How many will come
 tonight ?"
Father : "12,000 I suppose"

7pm Approaching ground
Father "Looks like I might be wrong -
quite a few walking"
Son : "I agree - maybe over 15000"

7.15 Parking car
Son : "We havent had to park so far from
the ground for ages !"
Father : "Yes - I bet they'll hit 20,000
tonight !"

7.25 Passing Old Stand Ticket Office
Father : "Look at the queues for tickets.
What a crowd !"
Son : "This is the most I've seen for a
long time . Must be 25,000"

7.35 Joining queue for Arthur Waite Stand
Son : "Look at the line to get in even
with tickets"

Father "I've not seen such a mob for
years. There's hundreds pouring down the
hill. Over 30,000 !"

7.45 Not in ground yet
Father : "This is chaos and dangerous.
People pushing in. Hundreds behind us in
the queue"
Son : "Must be 35,000 tonight"

7.55 In seats at last
Son : "Arthur Waite stand full.
Enclosure packed below"
Father : "Even with one Holmesdale Corner
empty, the rest is packed with others
still coming in."
Son : "The old stand's nearly full also.
Must be 40,000 here !"

9.15 Announcement over loud speakers
"Tonights attendance 17,500"

RONNIE BOY WHO ARE YOU KIDDING !
NICE LITTLE EARNER THESE LOCAL DERBIES !

                              Barrie Greene

Living on the lifeline

Croydon.
The Fairfield Halls.
Launch night of the Crystal Palace Lifeline Club.
Individual invites to a "very special evening" had been dropped through our doors.
Rumours were rife.
The "South London Press" speculated that CPFC were going public - selling shares in
the club on the Stock Exchange. Like Spurs. No way ! Wouldnt touch 'em with a bargepole.
Met my mate in the foyer. Straight from work. Hungry. Thirsty. Went for a beer.
Familiar faces in the bar. Some of the first team looking sheepish in their club suits.
Smart blazers. Embarrassed looks. Nervous shuffles. Anxious glances. Eyes on watches.
Snatches of conversation. "Whats all this about then ?". "Dunno".
Glossy leaflets. Stalls for holidays and Lada cars.
Stewards in club ties usher us into the hall. Nice place. Good seats. Free. So what's
the catch ? Money. They're after our money. No way ! Definitely not ! They can forget
it. We pay enough to get into the poxy ground and watch a match from the drafty stand.
Not to mention the expensively thin programme.
No - they could have our support, moral, vocal or otherwise.
But if they asked for money they could get stuffed.
Around us we heard similar declarations. The expectant murmur died with the houselights.
A few desultory chants of "Noades out" broke the nervous silence.
What was this in aid of ? Were we going to be merged, taken over, sold off ?
Sharing our ground was a big enough injury - was insult to be added ?
What devious plans did our dodgy Chairman have in mind ?
All was to be revealed. But first the preliminaries.
A funny man opened the proceedings with some good South London humour.
A potted history of the club (with slides) kept us amused.
Then the Directors, players and ground staff were introduced onto the stage to
differing degrees of applause and indifference from the audience.
The cold silence of Big Ron's entrance was contrasted by Coppell's ovation.
Under the bright stage lights Noades looked shiftier than ever. Would you buy a second
hand football team off this man? No ? But he'd sell it to you anyway.
And so he started selling us the Lifeline Scheme. We listened, openly sceptical.
His smooth line in patter sounded very convincing. Similar schemes had proved
successful at other clubs.
And then it struck us. He wanted our money. The bastard was after our cash. No way !
But whats this ? Steve Coppell's telling us to support the scheme. Give him the money
and he'd promise to   buy new players. Not to mention the cash prizes, cars and
holidays on offer.
My iron resolve dissolved like the Palace defence on a bad Saturday and I filled in
the glossy leaflet.
For only £2 a week I was investing in the future of my club. For only £8 a month I was
giving Steve the chance to strengthen our squad. For a mere £100 a year I was gonna
get us back in the First Division ! Yeah ! Let's go ! Sign that form. Hand it in.
Dive down to the bar for free wine care of Lada cars and Intasun.
Grab that free grub. Watch that free video of Palace beating Man Utd 5-0.
Going up. Going up. Going up uP UP. Glory days were coming to Palace again.
Outside, in the real world, empty chip wrappers blew past the Fairfield Halls.

John Pateman

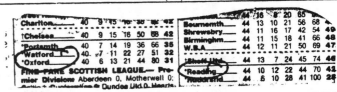

BLIND DATE

CILLA BLACK: Okay chucks, you've all met the three talented footballers who are looking for a club to play for, and now here's John Benson with a quick recap.

(Cue stupid music)

JOHN BENSON: Thanks Cilla, well will it be number one who is Bryan Robson, captain of Manchester United and England. Or how about number two, Diego Maradona, captain of World Cup holders Argentina. Or will it be number three, Brian Bason of Plymouth Argyle ?

CILLA BLACK: Thank you John. Now we're gonna meet the lucky manager who is going to choose one of these players for his team. Both he and his team have given us a lorra laffs, so let's have a big hand for Dario Gradi of Crystal Palace.

DARIO GRADI: (trips down the steps)

CILLA BLACK: Hello Dario love, ay I like your 'urr cut.

DARIO GRADI: I got Wimbledon promoted from the fourth division you know.

CILLA BLACK: Well we all wish you 'adn't bothered love but never mind. Do you 'ave some questions for our three lucky footballers ?

DARIO GRADI: Yes I have. Number one, do you score many goals in training.

BRYAN ROBSON: I'm never fit enough to take part in training. My mum says I'm not to play with Norman Whiteside because he's a rough boy. Also I can't play for Crystal Palace cause their kit's too flash (think about it!)

DARIO GRADI: Number two, did you play well in the World Cup ?

MARADONA: Ci, I theenk I have a hand een our weening the Globo Campeonsheep.

DARIO GRADI: Number three. Our flying winger has beaten five defenders and rounded the goalkeeper, he passes to you and you are left to tap the ball into the open goal from two yards, what would you do ?

BRIAN BASON: I'd pass it to Chris Jones.

CILLA BLACK: Eh oop chuck, it's a big decision isn't it Dario, love.

DARIO GRADI: No contest Cilla, I'll go for number three.

Cilla closes the show, cue stupid music.

Tony Matthews

NEXT WEEK PLAY "SCRUPLES" WITH PHILIP CARTER AND DAVID DEIN.

FOOD FOR THOUGHT

"Dining at the top of the Holmesdale End reminds one so much of La Tulipe, New York, what with the delicious hamburger nestled in the succulent bed of finely chopped onion, the piquant tomato sauce and of course the fantastic view of the Croydon skyline". So said the famous bon viveur and chef Ronnie Moady.

To be honest I can't say I always agree, for example the burger may be sometimes ok, but so far this season some of my buns have been stale and the onions cold. Due probably to the length of time left out. Most importantly though the tomato ketchup has not come up to scratch, a little runny whilst being too sharp.

By now you are muttering who is this "pretentious cretin", but I think that this attention to detail (the catering operations) can help improve our lot and may be help to attract the lost 1000's back. It is quite obvious changing the ketchup to Heinz is not going to create a dramatic change, but any improvement would show some commitment from the club towards better facilities.

Could we break away from the monotony of hamburgers and bovril (granted it is nice) and have more variety (would it be harder, honestly, to sell kebabs, fish and chips or even such delicacies like samosas!) whilst also improving the general quality and value.

The club does have scope to do this because it runs its own catering operation (concentrating on our "generous benefactor" though) unlike some supposedly larger clubs where it can be pure purgatory to eat. It's all very nice to be able to buy masterpieces of Selhurst Park, but what about something more relevant, for a start we can barbecue those bloody giant parrots and blue mouse which frolick around before kick off!

Christopher Beale

Nature spot

a strange discovery!

Ever wondered why no roof has been put on the away end loos? Why it is to allow the growth of that most rare of plants Phytobeerius pissicus (commonly known as the 'Urine slurper'. A most fortunate sighting was recorded at Home Park, Plymouth where a rich growth of these rather odd plants was seen to be happily climbing the walls. The reason for their extreme rarity is that they live on an infrequent supply of beery piss. Their growth is limited by being watered only around 22 times a year (cup games an exceptional treat!). Even then the amounts available depend upon the generosity (and numbers) of the visting donors ....and the local constabuary.

Thankfully the vist of CPFC resulted in a tremendous feast for these oddi-ties of the plant kingdom, and rest assured they will be eagerly awaiting our return next year.

Do inform us of any such sightings so that we may inform our concerned readers.

John Ellis

IT'S A STORMER TOMMY!

In the halcyon days of our inaugural spell in the first division, there were few games that could be watched towards the end of a season without nerves of iron.

One such rarity was against Everton, Palace having already clinched a place in the elite for the next season, prior to the final home game of the 1970/71 campaign.

An unusual air of jollity and bonhomie prevailed. This was embellished by the antics of Everton's full back Tommy Wright. Palace had already promised to take Everton to the cleaners in the early stages, and were a goal up by half-time.

It would be nice, we all mused, to get another and "then we can relax" and enjoy the game. A rare luxury in those days.

But Tommy was in a benevolent mood, obviously recalling the thrashings Palace had experienced over the past couple of seasons, and it was the last game of the season.

Palace were attacking the Holmesdale End, and won a corner. I seem to recall Tony Taylor, or possibly Terry Wharton took it.

There was no immediate danger to the Everton goal, especially since the lurking Gerry Queen, Jimmy Scott et al could usually be relied on to fluff the majority of chances that came their way.

But Tommy Wright had other ideas. He lauched himself into a mid air attack, flinging himself at the ball, in the direction of the Everton goal. His head connected perfectly.

The ball blurred past Andy Rankin in the Everton goal, as the Holmesdale End celebrated with roars of mirth and glee.

The match ended 2-0 in Palace's favour, but the result was secondary to the entertainment provided by Tommy boy in that split second or so of misguided athleticism - where were you Brian Moore ?

Andrew Fishleigh

OPERATION GROPE

Dozens of people have been arrested in a New Scotland Yard move to smash a notorious gang who have associated themselves with Crystal Palace F.C.

The raid, the result of months of intelligence gathering, included infiltration by police into the gang, often travelling with them to away matches.

Operation G.R.O.P.E. - Get Rid Of Pesky Eagles - began at 4 a.m when 200 officers raided addresses all over London. Norbury police arrested a total of 47 people only to discover later that they were all from Croydon police station who had set up a raid of their own and had infiltrated the infiltrators from Norbury.

Shortly after this setback a second raid was organised to catch a number of men who had been responsible for causing great distress to thousands of innocent fans, and brought the name of Crystal Palace into disrepute.

Among the arrested men was David Price, the so called "Fat Man", who was charged with inciting home supporters with his inept midfield play.

Another member of the gang was Trevor Aylott who protested his innocence to Norwood Magistrates Court by stating that "the law is an Ass", the magistrate Mr Justice Poppapill then told Aylott "So what, you are a donkey."

The court heard many horrific tales about the activities of the gang including how one fan was found unconscious on the terraces with a "calling card" pinned to his ski hat which read: "Congratulations. You have been nominated and smacked in the face by an Andy Gray penalty."

A number of weapons were seized in the raid, including scythes, a garden fork and several pairs of hedge trimmers. The owner claimed they were going to be used to help Charlton Athletic clear up their pitch.

In an exclusive interview with "Eagle Eye" P.C. Bobby Copper who was one of the undercover officers that infiltrated the gang, explained how the operation was organised.

"Well, Chief Inspector Schickelgruber wanted to find out exactly who was responsible for the trouble at Crystal Palace, and so he decided that we would have to infiltrate a team of officers into the gang. At first we found it difficult to gain acceptance, but then WPC Snottybitch suggested that we change out of our uniforms into ordinary clothes and this seemed to do the trick. We spent the next three months with the thugs and during that time gained many valuable hints and tips on how to perpretrate acts of mindless violence. We also acquired numerous weapons that will come in handy the next time we have to break up a nurses march, ooh er, I shouldn't't've said....er, you won't print that will you?"

Later in the day a similar raid which was codenamed Operation Womble proved a complete success when two traffic wardens swooped to smash a vicious gang of Wimbledon thug whilst he was having his tea. Several items were seized including a pair of carpet slippers, a yellow and blue bobble hat and a lethal signed photograph of Don Howe.

TONY MATTHEWS.

Revolutionary sponsorship deal

Crystal Palace Football Club have shaken the football world by signing a lucrative sponsorship deal with Croydon Council. Although the concept of Council sponsorship for football clubs is not new - Halifax and Millwall have already benefitted - the deal negotiated by Palace Chairman Ron Noades is nothing short of revolutionary.

Big Ron, already well known for his business acumen and eye for the "fast buck", is always on the look out for ways of bringing more money into Selhurst Park. By coming to an arrangement, or "nice little earner", with supermarket chain Sainsburys, he enabled one end of the ground to be developed to the 'mutual benefit' of both companies. Witness the packed members-only enclosure at the Sainsbury's End.

But the deal struck with Conservative and enterprising Croydon Council goes far beyond the mere piecemeal development of just part of the ground. At the same time Ron Noades has assured all club supporters that this deal in no way erodes the identity or sovereignty of the club. He will remain as Club Chairman, a post he will now share with the leader of Croydon Council Here are just some of the amazing details of this deal which incorporates all the current principles of modern Thatcherite thinking:

1. The club will change its name to Croydon Council Football Club (CCFC).

2. Manager Steve Coppell will be replaced by the Director of Recreation.

3. The club's kit colours will be changed to Tory Blue.

4. The nickname of the club shall be "The Privateers".

5. The club symbol will be a black swastika in a white circle on a red background.

6. All aspects of the club's commercial activities will be put out to private tender: from the groundstaff to the coach and his team of physiotherapists, all will be privatised.

7. The Council will set a rate at which new players may be purchased. If this rate is exceeded, penalties may be incurred, ie ratecapping.

8. Entrance fees will be replaced by a community charge, which will be a flat rate and not related to ability to pay. As a Council spokesman pointed out, "why should a pensioner or a child pay less than a family of 4 who are receiving exactly the same service - 90 minutes of entertaining football".

9. The club will become member only. All fans must register with the club where they will be issued with photo passes. All fans are eligible to join apart from members of the following proscribed organisations : The Palace Action Group, FSA, subscribers to "Eagle Eye", CND and the Labour party.

10. The turf pitch will be dug up and replaced with a synthetic surface. This will be essential as we shall be sharing the ground with 6 other clubs, each of us playing on a different day of the week. Apart from Charlton, we will obviously prefer local clubs like Wimbledon, but Marler properties, owners of Fulham, Chelsea and QPR, have also been approached and David Bulstrode has expressed "considerable interest".

11. Shares will be sold in the club on the London Stock Exchange. Application forms can be found in this weeks programme. Multiple applications will be welcome, especially from local Tory MP's.

12. The club will be able to opt out of FA control if a majority of directors vote for it. Club members will then be balloted. If the club chooses to opt out, it will not be allowed back in for 10 years. This will allow the club to set up its own "private members" cup with a number of other elite clubs. Palace will of course exit in the first round every year.

John Pateman

Some Newly Published Football Books....

1) FAR FROM THE MADDING CROWD by Thomas Hardy...A history of Wimbledon FC
2) THE RATS by James Herbert...The story of Philip Carter and David Dein
3) THE BIG SLEEP by Raymond Chandler...An afternoon at White Hart Lane
4) FLASHMAN by George MacDonald Fraser...A biography of Bryan Robson
5) SS-GB by Len Deighton...Football duty with the West Midlands Police
6) CLOCKWORK ORANGE by Anthony Burgess...Blackpool's Offside Trap
7) THE GOOD COMPANIONS by J.B Priestly...Paul Davis and Glenn Cockerill
8) SMILEY'S PEOPLE by John Le Carre...Kenny Dalglish's Liverpool
9) GREAT EXPECTATIONS by Charles Dickens...A history of Manchester United
10) FANNY HILL by John Cleland...The story of the Fulham Chairman.

Tony Matthews

Palace top of league shocker
TEAM OF THE EIGHTIES
– ITS OFFICIAL!

FIRST DIVISION

	77/8	78/9	79/0	80/1	81/2	82/3	83/4	84/5	85/6	86/7	total
CRYSTAL PALACE	50	51	49	47	34	43	42	46	57	51	462
Birmingham	55	37	58	50	53	40	39	59	30	47	468
Middlesboro	42	57	50	34	53	46	41	41	44	67	475
Stoke City	53	58	44	51	44	53	44	24	48	63	482
Wolves	51	44	58	43	32	68	27	37	57	69	486
Crewe Alex	50	43	35	48	29	53	56	65	54	70	503
Rochdale	43	47	33	60	50	55	52	55	57	54	506
Halifax T	52	39	46	44	51	59	55	42	60	59	507
Cambridge U	72	44	61	53	48	42	28	37	65	60	510
Cardiff C	51	56	41	44	45	76	53	47	53	48	514
Sunderland	67	70	69	52	38	48	42	40	47	49	522
Hereford	34	53	38	38	64	42	54	65	74	60	522
Bolton W	63	54	38	61	39	42	56	69	54	46	522
Shrewsbury	63	61	60	46	37	48	49	66	52	41	523
Blackburn	56	41	58	42	47	58	57	66	53	45	523
Oldham	54	52	49	39	50	64	47	49	62	65	531
Leicester	26	43	58	40	56	72	65	65	54	54	533
Notts County	54	48	51	49	61	55	50	48	71	77	534
Stockport	56	58	48	44	48	60	60	58	63	40	535
West Brom	62	72	54	60	46	51	48	58	35	51	537
Bristol City	49	47	37	29	40	59	70	74	69	63	537
Manchester City	74	58	43	56	49	47	66	66	43	36	538

THIRD DIVISION

	77/8	78/9	79/0	80/1	81/2	82/3	83/4	84/5	85/6	86/7	total
Preston	63	59	56	41	50	60	66	51	54	72	572
Tranmere	57	45	50	59	51	49	53	83	74	54	575
Lincoln	53	41	64	66	66	77	59	50	55	45	576
Chelsea	46	44	66	46	60	51	90	63	57	53	576
Burnley	56	51	39	60	66	56	76	60	60	53	577
Swansea	87	83	48	64	58	51	36	53	43	56	579
Bristol R	61	48	50	34	58	84	68	66	51	49	579
Peterborough	47	44	58	68	71	58	72	54	52	57	581
Arsenal	60	61	52	61	48	58	74	61	49	58	582
Grimsby	57	82	73	44	53	45	60	72	58	39	583
QPR	47	45	75	56	65	77	67	53	53	48	586
Ipswich	47	63	68	77	75	64	55	46	32	59	586
Doncaster	52	50	62	59	55	57	82	72	45	56	590
Exeter	49	61	60	62	71	81	50	57	47	53	591
Chesterfield	58	51	71	72	57	43	59	64	61	56	592
Sheffield W	50	53	81	53	55	60	62	58	63	58	593
Port Vale	46	57	56	57	56	67	51	61	67	76	594
Scunthorpe	50	54	58	60	43	71	54	83	50	73	596
Aldershot	67	63	62	43	57	61	66	56	66	64	605
Luton	54	60	66	61	86	66	53	57	61	47	611
Oxford	64	44	57	39	63	71	91	84	62	44	619
Southend	66	51	47	79	63	66	55	58	69	68	621
Newport	65	66	83	64	54	76	58	55	52	49	622
Notts Forest	69	61	63	62	42	62	76	56	69	64	624

SECOND DIVISION

	77/8	78/9	79/0	80/1	81/2	82/3	83/4	84/5	85/6	86/7	total
Brighton	63	72	47	54	43	38	69	54	64	37	541
Coventry	75	58	56	48	56	48	57	47	48	50	543
Chester	59	57	49	38	36	55	45	60	83	61	543
Leeds	63	70	46	39	39	51	55	66	58	58	545
Torquay	67	58	70	55	47	56	59	38	43	56	549
Derby	54	44	47	57	53	49	36	65	80	64	549
Carlisle	59	53	66	56	65	68	48	50	47	39	551
Rotherham	51	49	58	62	66	45	57	55	61	48	552
Norwich	52	51	58	49	64	52	48	46	64	53	557
Newcastle	42	51	53	30	52	75	85	55	67	47	557
Charlton	55	60	39	63	50	63	53	51	78	45	557
Darlington	52	49	50	65	61	61	49	66	61	45	559
Mansfield	49	51	47	58	63	61	66	41	74	52	562
Hartlepool	51	57	56	64	73	46	47	54	68	44	563
Orient	43	51	48	57	36	64	71	51	79	64	564
Hull	34	66	51	40	70	75	71	52	65	41	565
Wrexham	78	45	40	43	40	56	59	67	68	70	566
Bournemouth	41	47	52	47	62	59	63	57	65	76	569
Barnsley	61	73	53	72	59	57	57	42	47	49	570
Fulham	49	50	42	57	77	64	60	68	45	59	571
Aston Villa	57	59	51	72	55	62	59	60	51	45	571
Millwall	49	42	65	43	62	64	71	73	64	39	572

FOURTH DIVISION

	77/8	78/9	79/0	80/1	81/2	82/3	83/4	84/5	85/6	86/7	total
West Ham	52	70	54	79	66	68	60	51	74	52	626
Southampton	70	47	65	76	72	54	66	56	51	69	626
Blackpool	59	61	62	45	66	55	70	73	66	74	631
Manchester U	67	66	65	51	59	56	71	77	70	52	634
Plymouth	61	67	59	64	56	61	56	62	88	62	636
Portsmouth	41	62	91	56	55	74	73	69	69	53	643
Everton	76	52	43	55	56	66	44	88	87	76	643
Bury	62	59	45	70	80	74	61	76	63	54	644
Brentford	86	53	59	52	56	88	69	62	58	64	647
Sheffield U	62	52	60	65	94	62	86	54	64	50	649
Swindon	67	74	71	51	55	61	58	62	82	72	653
Northampton	63	64	61	65	57	65	53	53	79	103	653
Huddersfield	63	57	101	71	64	84	56	52	51	54	653
Reading	55	76	66	62	67	64	84	68	67	52	661
Gillingham	67	65	49	48	64	58	74	80	81	75	661
Walsall	61	56	75	59	51	64	68	58	90	80	662
Wigan	65	63	76	51	80	60	46	60	82	83	666
Bradford	56	62	77	53	88	68	73	77	51	62	667
York	50	51	65	47	69	88	96	70	77	55	668
Spurs	83	48	52	70	67	65	64	78	74	68	669
Colchester	55	60	64	45	82	75	69	87	88	64	689
Watford	85	83	39	50	76	74	68	81	69	67	692
Wimbledon	66	78	52	64	61	96	97	71	58	57	700
Liverpool	65	85	81	62	80	87	73	68	89	76	766

Yes! empirical evidence of the superiority of Crystal Palace FC. Now take a closer look. This is a list the goals scored by each league club in the last 10 years. Would you believe it Palace are top! Of course I do mean bottom. Yes all those great forward lines - Swindlehurst, Walsh, Langley, Aylott etc served us well. Some of you may say 77-79 are not in the 1980's. Take those away and its even worse ie.   45.1 instead of 46.2! That for stats freaks is 1.0738 goals per game throughout the whole ten years.

Jim Cannon is the only player to have seen out these glorious years of finishing 15th almost every season. He has scored 17 goals in all this time. Therefore, of the 462 goals Palace have scored, Jim has scored 3.67965% of them!

I was going to list our goal scorers over the 10 years and what goals they did get, but what's the point, hardly any of them would register.

It is rather amusing putting Manchester City and Millwall bottom of their respective divisions. Unfortunately Brighton topped the second division. Perhaps a poor season this year can put them bottom of division one?! However it was very nice to see Liverpool finishing bottom of the fourth division!

ALL ABOARD THE DRUG TRAIN

THE sad events at the Seoul Olympics, involving drug taking, have prompted "Eagle Eye's" investigative journalists to find out whether there is such a problem in the English Football League. Our findings make disturbing reading.

Picture yourself on the Holte End at Villa
With tangerine Blackpool scarves
And Gay Meadow skies

Somebody runs through
To shoot past the goalie
It's Everton's million pound buys

Lacy was more silly than Doris
Lacy was more silly than Doris
Oh, oh, oh

(Lennon & McCartney, Northern Songs)

These lyrics are taken from a song that appeared on the Beatles legendary 1967 album "Sgt Boulter's Lonely Hearts Club Band". It was a song about the drugs issue and its links with professional football and serves to illustrate how the problem has become embedded in the very fabric of the game.

If we take a closer look at the chorus we discover a hidden meaning, "Lacy was more Silly than Doris", spells out L.S.D.

It was L.S.D. that at the time was the "In" drug. Crystal Palace chairman Ron Noades recalls:

"Yeah man, I was hooked, you know what I mean? I was hooked on L.S.D. that's pounds shillings and pence. Man, all the league chairmen were into it, real heavy bread-heads. But the government brought in some new legislation called "decimalisation". L.S.D. lost one of its ingredients, they got rid of shillings. The "d" for pence was changed to a "p". Suddenly all the chairmen were after L.P.... Ken Bates wasn't the only one to end up with a huge record collection."

In fact it was in the early fifties when British soccer first confronted the problem. The then famous Wolves met CRACK Hungarian side Honved, from there on it was all downhill.

Many clubs had a problem with marijuana or "grass" as it was known. It became bad enough to cause some clubs such as QPR, Preston, Oldham Athletic and Luton Town to get rid of all their grass.

Almost as much of a thorn in the side were amphetamines, often referred to by slang names, Blues, Reds and Purple Hearts to name a few.

Reds were uppers like Liverpool, Arsenal and Manchester United. Blues however were downers, depressants. Some of the most depressing were Chelsea and Birmingham City, these blues were always going down.

At Stamford Bridge, Chelsea had to get rid of David SPEEDie when they found themselves getting too HIGH up the league table.

North of the border amphetamines were also rife. Purple Hearts changed their colours to maroon to rid Tynecastle of the scourge.

Back in the capital another problem was pot. Tottenham could never win one, despite spending millions of pounds in the attempt.

South of the river, Crystal Palace were at the forefront of the hallucinogenic revolution with their twin strikers, David Hemp and Hashish Harkouk.

Most shocking though was the scale of abuse at struggling second division club Brighton And Hove Albion. We tackled their manager Barry Lloyd. When asked about the use of dope at the Goldstone Ground he answered

"Dope ? Don't talk to me about dope, dopes more like. I've got a squad full of 'em." When he had finished grizzling we asked him about rumours that his defenders were using Steroids.

"Steroids?" he replied, "I don't know about that, but I'm convinced my defence is full of androids!"

TONY MATTHEWS.

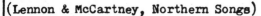

DONKEY DERBY!!

Plymouth Argyle versus Swindon Town

SPECIAL NOTICE
Would people please refrain from sending Trevor Aylott jokes.
The management

Palace v United – *a case history*

As an exiled Mancunian now living a bottle's throw from the Den, the meeting of Palace and Swindon-or rather, Coppell and Macari-was one I could not miss. Would the teams play in the image of their managers from United days-Palace tensed like a miler as the game kicked off, then giving the defence headaches with ever-imaginative running; Swindon constantly harrying, then nipping in between the defender's legs for that decisive near-post header? In the event it was Bobby Barnes who out-Wrighted Ian as man of the match, while Palace were slightly fortunate to win with a late penalty.

To mark the occasion, the programme reprinted a teamsheet from a match in which Coppell and Macari played together for United against Palace, giving the date as 17th November 1977. In a programme which elsewhere named my beloved Chairman Ron Moads and Swindon's no.7 Steve Wright, Eagles diehards were no doubt alert to the deliberate mistake: at that time Palace were just coming up from the third. I remember the meeting in November 1979 only too well: although Venables' team were doing nicely, United had not conceded a goal in five home games, so it seemed an almighty affront when the name 'David Swindlehurst' appeared on the scoreboard 12 minutes

from time. Joe Jordan saved us with one of his last-minute specials.

Palace-United matches have often had sigificance in the history of one or other club (Palace's first-ever Division One match was a 2-2 draw against Bobby Charlton and company in August '69), or indeed in my own life. One of the earliest league matches I can recall seeing on TV was our 5-3 win at Selhurst in 1970-71, where Denis Law's hat-trick included an overhead kick which inspired thousands like me to attempt neck-breaking imitations in the playground. In those days there was none of that I-want to-be-a-fireman/policeman/bus driver nonsense with me, I wanted to wear the number 10 shirt for United, but Norm beat me to it...

Two season's later the nation gasped as rock-bottom United lost 5-0 to even rocker-bottom Palace (you'd all like the video, wouldn't you, you sods?). A hundred flashbulbs caught Frank O'Farrell hiding behind the paper like a condemned criminal, a Louis Edwards vote of confidence no doubt ringing in his ears like a death knell, and the Docherty era was around the corner.

November 1st, 1980, was the fateful day of my first visit to Selhurst Park. United, having chased Liverpool to the

tape the previous spring, had drawn 8 of their first 12 games; for Palace it was Ernie Walley's first game in charge, and they were doing so badly they were 2 points behind Malcolm Allison's City. I sat in the main stand, and simply squirmed as we went down to a goal by Peter Nicholas. As if that were not enough, I'd split up with my girlfriend that morning and later found out that her first date with my successor had been a Hallowe'en Ball. Think about it.

By the following April, Palace's season had gone from bad to disastrous to cataclysmic. Burridge, Fenwick, Flanagan, Francis and Sealy had all gone the way of Venables, and in their stead came David Price, Tommy Langley, Brian Bason, Dario Gradi, uncle Ron Moads and all. United were on a 7 match winning streak that cost Dave Sexton his job, but this was one of the worst matches I've ever seen. Garry Birtles producing another of those performances which sparked speculation that here at last was the missing body of Charlie Chaplin, and Mike Duxbury (for God's sake) scored the winning goal. It was the day Aldaniti won the Grand National, and the Old Trafford tranny men drowned out the crowd. But if Selhurst '72 saw United in a slump, Stretford '81 saw Palace entering purgatory.

Brian Spurrell

A DREAM OF LEICESTER
a poem by George Wood

I leant upon a wooden post
Surveying the scene afore my eyes
Of Leicester giving up the ghost
At goals by Pennyfather and from Wright

Leicester two Palace four
From Filbert Street came the score
And Palace fans began to brag
For three more points were in the bag

I spied a Greenfinch on the stand
Such a pretty bird made me feel grand
Then came a through ball into space
I got there first to win the race

I sliced it to a Leicester man
Who tucked it home I felt so sad
And then another Leicester score
Tied it all up at four - four

George you prat
The fans all called
You're fat and senile
And you're bald

My blunder it had cost us dear
As I wallowed in my own self pity
It was the reason that I fear
They let me go to Cardiff City.

TONY MATTHEWS.

Next Week:- Dario does something stupid again!

Keith Collins

chapter 9

FLASHING BLADE

sheffield united

no. 4

Feb. '89

30p

BARGAIN HUNTING?
The *GREAT* **WEDNESDAY WAREHOUSE SALE** *IS NOW ON!*

check out these amazing prices:

MEGSON:
£250,000

BARGAIN BUYS

STERLAND:
£750,000

THESE ARE JUST A FEW!
MORE AVAILABLE ON DISPLAY!

0%
FINANCE

Order today there's nothing to pay!
NO DEPOSIT *with*
FINANCE OVER I, 2 or 3 YEARS

SALE MUST END MAY 13th
EVERYTHING MUST GO!

NO.3 December 1988.

now 32 pages

owls appoint new boss.

MAGAZINE TITLE: FLASHING BLADE

EDITORS NAME: JAMIE PIGOTT

AGE: 24   OCCUPATION: CIVIL SERVANT

DO YOU/HAVE YOU EVER SUPPORTED ANY OTHER TEAM?   NO

MOST MEMORABLE MATCH EVER: Peterbrough 0   United 4   April 1982

MOST MEMORABLE SEASON: 1981/1982 .

ALL TIME FAVOURITE PLAYER: ALAN WOODWARD

WHAT SORT OF CAR DO YOU DRIVE?   TALBOT HORIZON .

YOUR FAVOURITE MUSIC: PAST = The Jam, David Bowie   PRESENT = Then Jerico

FILMS/TV: FAWLTY TOWERS, ONLY FOOLS AND HORSES

FAVOURITE CLOTHES: Jeans + T. Shirts, anything Casual .

POLITICAL LEANINGS: Usually Conservative but now having second thoughts

WHAT PLAYER WOULD YOU MOST LIKE TO SEE PLAYING FOR ENGLAND (SCOTLAND/ WALES IF RELEVANT)?
Glenn Hoddle
Tony Agana

The idea for Flashing Blade came about during the May 1988 meeting of the Sheffield FSA. One branch member, Stuart Basson, was already producing a Chesterfield fanzine and I thought I would like to do something similar for United because the programme was pathetic and fans had nowhere to air their views.

After telling anyone who cared to listen about my ideas Brian Exford and John Middleton volunteered to become involved. And so Flashing Blade was born with a homespun issue of 500 copies. As the fanzine got more popular the contributions began to flood in, including some superb pieces by Matthew Bell. As we felt our own material was drying up we asked Matthew to join us. Fortunately he agreed and the Flashing Blade has gone from strength to strength.

Producing a fanzine can be fun but it can also take over your life. Typing, printing, selling, posting, banking money, it can become a full time job. However, when you get compliments through the post it makes it all worthwhile.

JAMIE PIGOTT

That'll Do Nicely sir

Next season to get in at beautiful down town Bramall Lane, you'll all have to be a member. This membership scheme is being forced onto the clubs, by against police advice, who with the exception of Luton, don't want it. By whom you ask, well by her majesty's government led by that well known sports minister midget Moynihan. How it will work is anyones guess, but do we really need it ?, probably not.

As a spectator, football is safer in 1988 than it was in 1978. Segregation occurs at every ground and trouble inside grounds is virtually nil. How much bother was there at the Lane last year ?. So membership can't be to reduce violence inside grounds, as to all intents and purposes it doesn't exist.

Its role can only be to prevent proven trouble makers from entering the ground. Well, envisage this scenario, young Johnny has been convicted and served his sentence (short sharp shock - so effective that he'll never sin again !) and had his card taken away from him, end of football for our Johnny ?   Well probably not - all he will need is someone elses I.D. and he's got a new card, a photo won't help as nobody will know if its his I.D. or not. The club could ban him for life, but unless he reports to a police station for life every match day the ban has no meaning. Even with closed circuit TV cameras on the crowd you can't expect the police to pick out all non-members from the crowd. Even if Johnny is prevented from entering the ground, whats to stop him turning up at 4-40 on a Saturday outside the ground to indulge in his perverse pleasure of chinning away fans.

The proposed scheme also has many administrative drawbacks. It would have to be computer operated to check each card, this would cause delays at the turnstile and mean that crowds would have to turn up the day before in order to get in !. Just think what chaos we would have had at the recent Newcastle cup tie if each and every card had needed checking, the kick off would have had to be put back to about ten o' clock !. The scheme would also have to be nationally run to account for away fans and the neutral supporter who picks his game each Saturday, and would these neutrals be allowed in the home or away end ?. Do I need to go on ? (No, but I've a feeling you will, Ed).

The whole situation just gets more and more ridiculous, and verges on a nightmare for fans whose only wish is to watch football !.

The scheme is just an idea plucked from thin air by our small (minded and sized) sports minister and it clearly illustrates his lack of knowledge of football and its crowds. He should cut his losses and abandon any idea of a scheme for 1989/90, and let clubs, fans, the FSA, and the police attempt to find a solution to the problem of hooliganism. Failing that he could at least be honest and state that his preferred solution is to ban fans from football altogether, unless of course they own executive boxes !.

For the time being the most supporters can do to oppose the scheme is to write to their M.P. Some useful points to raise in your letters are as follows:

1 - Most football violence occurs away from grounds.
2 - There are over 2000 league games every season, the overwhelming majority of which are trouble free.
3 - Costs will increase. Some small clubs have estimated that it will cost £300,000 to introduce the computer systems. Assuming 4000 card holders that works out at £12-50 per card holder.
4 - There will be congestion at turnstiles. A 50,000 crowd at a ground with 30 turnstiles will take an additional 90 mins to get in.
5 - Gates will fall. Look at Luton. A massive reduction in their average gate despite a successful season. Some small clubs could go to the wall.

YORKSHIRE AND HUMBERSIDE CUP

When the "Sheffield Star" announced in July that Sheffield United were to compete in the Yorkshire and Humberside Cup many people thought it was another Micky Mouse Trophy which United had no chance of winning.

United were drawn in Group B alongside Doncaster; Halifax; Bradford; Grimsby and Rotherham. However, each side only played three other teams in the group. United, having chosen to play each match away from home, were drawn to play at Bradford; Doncaster and Halifax.

"Typical, United being drawn in the same group as the favourites, Bradford" was the outcry from many fans. However, United looking an absolute picture in red and white shirts, yellow shorts and white socks played superb and thoroughly deserved their 1 - 0 victory with a tremendous diving header from "Stan". The only drawback of the day being the admission price of £4.50 to stand up.

The following Tuesday, United took on Doncaster at Belle Vue. The first shock was how appalling the away end was, (fences in every direction), and this coupled with a dreadful performance by United saw many fans hurrying to the exits with twenty minutes still to go. The result being 0 - 0.

However, this meant United had a great chance of reaching the final. As Halifax's ground was still unfit for spectators, (it hadn't been fit for the last twenty years) Bradford "lets rip off the away fans" City kindly allowed Halifax to stage the game at Valley Parade. However, a typical British summer's day of constant rain forced the game to be called off. This put the Y & H Cup committee in a flap and in their wisdom forced Halifax and United to play the game behind closed doors at Huddersfield. The result apparently was 1 - 0 to United with Francis Joseph scoring the goal. United were through to the final against Scarborough to be played at the McCain Oven Chip Stadium.

The big day arrived. A beautiful day in Sheffield but a typical Scarborough evening, rain, wind and cloud. However, many Unitedites made the trip on the grounds of Scarborough being another ground to knock off the grounds visited list.

After buying a programme for 80 pence and a hamburger at £1.20 the game started with John Fracis, a Garth Crookes lookalike, on trial from Exley, making his debut for United. Tony Agana put United one up in the first half but with about 10 minutes remaining Tommy Graham equalised for 'Boro'.

Another 30 minutes of rain and wind. However, all this didn't seem to matter as John Fracis scored early in the first period. After that Paul Williams hit the post with a delightful chip and Martin Pike headed out from under his own goal line.

Eventually the whistle went and the cup was ours. The crowds indicate that many people still think of it as a Micky Mouse Cup but I'm sure those loyal fans who got soaked at Scarborough enjoyed themselves.

A Barren Crop

SUBMITTED BY
DAVE BURKINSHAW.

My first glimpse of the Red and White Wizards in the flesh was at the Lane on Saturday January 16th 1965 during a goalless draw with Everton. The United team included 9 players they had developed through their then thriving youth policy; Hodgkinson, Badger, Graham Shaw, Richardson, Joe Shaw, Woodward, Tony Wagstaff, Jones and Birchenall. Alan Hodgkinson and Graham Shaw were already full England internationals while Mick Jones won his first cap at the end of the 1964/65 season. Len Badger and Alan Woodward both won Football League representative honours in their distinguished careers. This was indeed a rich crop of talent harvested from the club's youth policy and there were other products who made league appearances during the 1964/65 season; Bob Widdowson, Bernard Shaw, Cec Coldwell, Ken Mallender, Reg Matthewson, Dennis Finnigan and Barry Wagstaff. Bernard Shaw won England under 23 honours whilst with United. The following two seasons, 1965/66 and 1966/67, saw the introduction of some more highly promising youngsters namely Frank Barlow, David Munks, Mick Hill, Phil Cliff, Charlie Bell, Mick Heaton and Geoff Salmons. Hill won full Welsh caps after his transfer to Ipswich Town and Salmons became one of United's most profitable transfers when he was sold to Stoke City by Ken Furphy in 1974 for the sum of £200,000. The 1967/68 season saw no new faces introduced from the youth policy although a promising Watford youth product called Anthony Currie was signed for a fee of £27,000. United were relegated to the Second Division at the end of this season. Major factors in the club's decline were the sale of the talented Mick Jones and Alan Birchenall for £100,000 each to Leeds United and Chelsea respectively plus the failure of some of the previous seasons youngsters to develop into consistent First Division players.

The next three seasons were spent in the Second Division and the club introduced only three of its own youngsters to league football; Mick Harmston, Dave Staniforth and Ian Mackenzie. John Harris's 1970/71 Promotion winners were a team of shrewd buys plus the maturing talents of former youth products Len Badger, Alan Woodward and Geoff Salmons. At a time of great euphoria in the club's history its youth policy was starting to falter. United enjoyed some exciting moments back in the First Division but the young talent they introduced to league football was not one of them. John Harris gave opportunities to Steve Goulding, Alan Ogden, Steve Cammack, Ian Holmes, Steve Faulkner, Mick Speight and Tom Mcalister. The latter two names became Lane favourites. Mcalister may have become one of the club's all-time goalkeeping greats if it had not been for the boot of Manchester City's Rodney Marsh. Ken Furphy's only youth product was Gary France who only managed 2 league appearances in his entire career.

Ultimately the failure of the club to produce its own quality players was one of the reasons for its shameful final season (to date) in the First Division in 1975/76. Jimmy Sirrell did try to rescue the club by placing his faith in young players. Between 1975 and 1977 he gave league debuts to the following youngsters; Steve Ludlam, John Mcgeady, Keith Edwards, Simon Stainrod, Tony Kenworthy, Gary Hamson and Steve Conroy. Edwards and Kenworthy have given United great service in recent seasons with Edwards arguably being the Kop's greatest hero of the 1980s. The other Sirrell proteges I have mentioned never really fulfilled their early promise. Ludlam went on to give Chester and Carlisle good service, Mcgeady's career was ruined by injury, Stainrod has been a frustrating talent involved in several unsuccessful big money moves, Hamson's career went into decline after joining Leeds in 1979 for £140,000 and Conroy never really convinced Lane managers that he was the club's number one keeper despite brushing aside the challenges of Nicky Johns and Derek Richardson.

The Harry Haslam era saw the club's decline accelerate and its youth policy almost end when the Northern Intermediate League side was disbanded for a season. Haslam did give opportunities to some young lads namely Ian Benjamin, Phil Jones, John Flood, Richard Harwood, Tommy Smith, Imre Varadi, Trenton Wiggan, Nigel Steane and Paul Casey. Benjamin and Varadi brought the club £185,000 in transfer fees from West Brom and Everton, but the loss of Varadi in particular was regrettable.

Haslam's other youngsters hardly set the soccer scene alight. Jones has played for Boston United and Matlock Town, Flood still plays for Airdrie, Harwood drifted into non league soccer after a "Match of the Day" debut against Sunderland, Smith had an unsuccessful spell at Huddersfield, Wiggan moved to Scarborough and is currently with Gainsborough, Steane moved into non-league soccer after one substitute appearance in the G.M. Vauxhall Conference in 1988. Martin Peters gave Gary Brazil his chance during the 1980/81 season but this bold move failed to stop Fourth Division football coming to Bramall Lane. Brazil always carried the promising tag at the Lane but he never really convinced the fans he could regularly deliver the goods. His 1985 move to Preston has done his career wonders.

The Ian Porterfield era saw the club rise back to the Second Division and the youth policy did improve slightly. Mr. Porterfield gave one league game to Julian Broddle before allowing him to move to Scunthorpe on a free transfer. Richard Cooper seemed to be a bright midfield prospect but he never made the grade with the club and he moved to Lincoln on a free. Paul Smith, Bob Atkins and Gary West all showed promise but never developed into quality Second Division players. Their transfers to Port Vale, Preston and Lincoln respectively at least raised about £60,000 for the club. The two most promising youngsters Porterfield introduced to league football were Paul Tomlinson and Tony Philliskirk. Here at last were two home produced players to get excited about. Tomlinson saved a penalty on his league debut against Southend and was good enough to keep the £90,000 Keith Waugh out of the team. However, his confidence decreased and his form fell away towards the end of the 1983/84 season and he lost his first team place to Waugh and then John Burridge. Philliskirk scored some memorable goals for the club in his first season 1983/84, particularly a deft chip against Exeter and a flying header versus Rotherham at the Lane. A combination of injuries, a lack of pace and determination, a lack of physique and some poor coaching meant that this early promise was not maintained. He occasionally reminded the fans of his class in the following seasons with some tremendous goals such as against Barnsley and Huddersfield away in the 1987/88 season. Tomlinson and Philliskirk brought the club about £70,000 in transfer fees when they were sold, a major disappointment. Porterfield also gave league baptisms to the following youngsters; Lee Walshaw, Paddy Mcgeeney, Don Peattie, Russell Black, Brian Smith and Jeff Eckhardt. Walshaw and Peattie drifted out of league football after their release by United and Black has joined them after a spell with Halifax Town. Mcgeeney is currently helping Chesterfield to battle for survival while Eckhardt is a member of the reviving Fulham team after his £40,000 transfer there in November 1987. Brian Smith has emerged as a Lane favourite after finally establishing himself in the United team during the 1987/88 season.

Billy Mcewan earned himself a reputation as an able coach with young players when he was in charge of the 1985/86 Northern Intermediate League championship winning team. After his elevation to first team manager, he introduced two members of his championship winning team to league football, Clive Mendonca and Chris Marsden. Mendonca should have been given more opportunities in the team before his sale to Rotherham because of his prolific scoring record in junior soccer. Marsden failed to build upon his promising debut and became a part of Dave Bassett's clearout during the Summer of 88 when he moved to Huddersfield. Bassett has retained two more of Mcewan's discoveries, Chris Wilder and Peter Duffield, in his first team squad. Time will judge whether these two lads will become longterm United heroes.

Bassett seems keen to give youth its chance and by the end of Oct. 88 he had introduced Chris Downes, Paul Wood and Dane Whitehouse to the first team in meaningful matches. It would be great to think that Bassett will be able to unearth some outstanding young talent for the club without having to pay transfer fees. United's youth crop over the last 20 years has been very disappointing for in addition to the lads who were given first team debuts there have been dozens of other promising players who never reached that goal. Some of these "total failures" actually won England Youth Caps but were deemed unfit for the Blades.

Included in this category are W. Salkeld, R. Welch and G. Dey. There are the other "total failures" who seemed to be perpetually on the brink of a first team debut such as Simon Grayson, Chris France, Simon Copeland, Roy Hill, Nigel Williams, George Oghani, Kenny Geelan, Mark Smith, Jimmy House, Jimmy and Martyn Conroy. How I long for the day when the United team again has at least 9 youth team products playing First Division football and winning international honours for the club.

Player Profile

FULL NAME: Melvin Tarquin Nathaniel Montmorency Sterland.

NICKNAME: He with the face like a baboon's arse.

FAVE COLOUR: Whitney Houston.

QUALIFICATIONS: O'Level truancy, cycling proficiency badge.

FAVE OTHER SPORTS: Steak and chips.

FAVE ACTOR: Lawrie Madden (for his hilarious portrayal of a defender each Saturday).

FAVE ACTRESS: Gary Megson.

FAVE BOOKS: "The Subtle Art of Bribery" by Messrs Swan, Kay and Layne.
"The Wit and Wisdom of Howard Wilkinson".

FAVE RECORD: Lost in France - Lee Chapman.

WORST INJURY: Empty pot of hair gel.

LIKES: Acting the celebrity in bars and nightclubs, kicking opponents, saying you know like.

DISLIKES: Prejudice, queers, wingers with a modicum of skill as they make me look a proper chump.

HONOURS: With Wednesday ?, do me a favour.

AMBITION: None really, thats why I've stayed at Hillsborough so long.

IF YOU WEREN'T A FOOTBALLER WHAT WOULD YOU BE: Unemployed.

ADVICE TO YOUNGSTERS: Kick the s**t out of opponents.

WHO WOULD YOU MOST LIKE TO MEET: (Censored on legal advice).

Below is listed all the major honours acheived by the Owls under Howard Wilkinson:

THE NEARLY MEN

Wednesday's recent unsuccessful £750,000 bid for Palace's Mark Bright was widely reported but what didn't receive as much attention was the fact that Bright was signed by Palace from Leicester for only £80,000 three years ago and that United were competing for his signature at that time. This set me thinking about players in years gone by that United might have had had they pursued their interest, and who later made it big at the club that signed them, or were later transferred for a large fee.

In Jimmy Sirrel's time as manager he was after two little-known players from Scotland. Both were available for around £50,000 but rumour has it that the then Chairman John Hassell wouldn't sanction the money. The players? First, IAN WALLACE of Dumbarton, who was signed by Coventry and later went to Forest for £1,000,000. Second, ALAN HANSEN of Partick, bought by Liverpool for a pittance, who went on to fame and fortune at European and International level. Also in the mid-seventies United got a young striker on loan from little Banbury United, named KEVIN WILSON. However, he never played in the first team and wasn't considered good enough to warrant more than a month's trial, but later played for Derby and Ipswich and is now an important member of Chelsea's promotion chasing team and is a Northern Ireland international. Another current Northern Ireland international who United reputedly courted for several seasons but never had the money, or the courage, to buy was Kevin Wilson's namesake DANNY. He always seemed to beat United on his own when he played for Chesterfield but it was Forest who eventually signed him. He later went to Brighton and then to Luton for £200,000, where he is now an established first division player.

United's last game in the 4th division was at Darlington, who had a speedy midfield player in more ways than one - DAVID SPEEDIE. The following summer yet more rumours linked him with United but instead Chelsea snapped him up for £60,000, he scored loads of goals for them then was bought by Coventry for £750,000 and he is now a Scottish international. Promotion to Division 2 brought something more concrete then rumours about whom Ian Porterfield wanted to strengthen his team - he named names himself. Midfield was a weakness so he went for:- (1) IAN BANKS of Leicester, but £80,000 wasn't enough. He joined Huddersfield for £100,000, who in turn sold him to Bradford for £180,000. (2) PETER NICHOLAS of Crystal Palace. United's offer again wasn't sufficient so he went to Luton for £100,000, then to Aberdeen and Chelsea, both for £400,000. (3) RAY HOUGHTON of Fulham. Again United couldn't afford the required £160,000 so Oxford paid up instead. Liverpool then bought him for £800,000, turned him into an international and after he starred in last summer's European Championships Liverpool turned down a £2,000,000 offer from an Italian team. Later, Porterfield wanted a new striker to partner Keith Edwards and after DEAN SAUNDERS scored the winner at the Lane for Brighton Porterfield offered £60,000 for his services. But Brighton wanted to keep him then changed their minds and sold him to Oxford for the same fee. Earlier this season Oxford (or rather the Maxwell family) made a massive profit by selling him to Derby for £1,000,000.

But finally we must cast our minds back to 1978 for what would have been the biggest catch of all. During Harry Haslam's secret mission to Argentina his contact Antonio Rattin brought to his attention an unknown 16 year old who was for sale at £600,000. This was too much for United to gamble so they splashed out £160,000 on someone who was already an international player, Alex Sabella. As brilliant as Alex he couldn't hold a candle to the man United missed out on - none other than DIEGO MARADONA.

STOP PRESS!!!! - DEAN GLOVER - too expensive for United at £60,000, now at Port Vale for £200,000.

GEOFF'S JINX

I wonder if the date December 27th 1976 stands out in many Unitedites minds quite as much as it does in mine. This date is special to me as it was the very last time I returned from a United League away game and we had been the victors. It takes some believing but it is absolutely true, since that historic day I have travelled over 5000 miles seeing 25 games but all to no avail.

I've been a Sheffield United supporter since I saw my favourite team of the 60's (Chelsea) send the Blades into the 2nd Division in May 1968 when Peter Osgood and Tommy Baldwin scored in the second half replying to a Mick Hill goal. My second game at Bramall Lane was at the beginning of the following season, I returned as a wide-eyed 13 year old and was soon hooked. These were the glamour years under John Harris in the 2nd Division when you turned up not wondering if we were going to win, but by how many we would win by.

The 1st Division had its ups and downs until relegation in 1976. Over those years I saw United win some away games, most notably at Manchester United on the occasion of Bobby Charlton's last home appearance and at Leeds in our final year in the top flight. After watching United in the 1st Division against all the big clubs I found it difficult to visit such places as Oldham, Luton and Chesterfield in the lower divisions as my away trips suggest. Relegation in the 4th Division was to me unbelievable, and I vowed I would not watch football in that division. But of course I relented and saw both the Arsenal Cup games (lost away you will note) and a couple of home games against Bradford and Wigan, thus missing all those lovely, lovely away wins. But who wanted to visit Crewe or Tranmere when I had been used to Old Trafford or Maine Road, certainly not me! The nearest I came to seeing United win away since that famous 1976 victory was at Oxford when according to my watch they equalised in the 98th minute. Ipswich was incredible, two marvellous headers from Stancliffe and Beagrie in the first 10 minutes would surely see me break my duck but as is the norm I got let down again just a few minutes from time. Martin Kuhl put us in the lead at Palace but we meekly surrendered in the end. So we come to 1988/89 and back to Division 3. Geoff thinks to himself I'll go to some grounds I haven't previously attended like Gillingham and Aldershot where surely my hoodoo will be broken. I've witnessed the following four away games this season (I would have been at Brentford but for a wedding, but that's typical of my luck);

v GILLINGHAM - If this had been a boxing match it would have been stopped at half time to save the home team any further punishment but a free header ended my hopes that day.

v ALDERSHOT - How could I fail? Top against bottom, my miserable record was about to go on winning ties. Eventually they were drawn against Dulwich after a 12 year wait. Well as you all know we were sunk by a header (from where I stood it seemed to be from about 30 yards out and was airborne for 5 seconds).

v BRISTOL ROVERS - Didn't have high hopes for this one, but we nearly did it 2 minutes from the end. With my eyes fixed on Ian Bryson and not on the linesman's flag I was in ecstasy for fully 2 seconds before being brought down to earth again.

v CARDIFF - Another longshot but I have faith in those Red and White Wizards (or is yellow the standard colour away from home nowadays?). I don't think we would have scored if Cardiff had walked off the pitch.

Am I fated? Do I choose the wrong matches? Am I just unlucky or what? My friends all have a good laugh about my record but when will it end? My full record since that December 1976 triumph at Oldham is as tabulated below:-

Dec. 17th 1977 v Oldham	LOST 0-3		Sep. 7th 1985 v Norwich	LOST 0-4
Apr. 22nd 1978 v Blackburn	DREW 1-1		Dec. 26th 1985 v Sunderland	LOST 1-2
Aug. 26th 1978 v Preston	DREW 2-2		Oct. 4th 1986 v Bradford	DREW 1-1
Feb. 10th 1979 v Luton	DREW 1-1		Dec. 6th 1986 v Ipswich	DREW 2-2
Dec. 26th 1979 v Sheff Wed.	LOST 0-4		Jan. 24th 1987 v Shrewsbury	LOST 0-1
Jan. 5th 1980 v Chesterfield	LOST 1-2		Feb. 28th 1987 v Grimsby	LOST 0-1
Nov. 11th 1980 v Chesterfield	LOST 0-1		Dec. 13th 1987 v Palace	LOST 1-2
Aug. 28th 1982 v Portsmouth	LOST 1-4		May 15th 1988 v Bristol City	LOST 0-1
Sep. 29th 1982 v Lincoln	LOST 0-3		Sep. 10th 1988 v Gillingham	LOST 1-2
Dec. 28th 1982 v Chesterfield	LOST 1-3		Nov. 8th 1988 v Aldershot	LOST 0-1
Nov. 5th 1983 v Oxford	DREW 2-2		Jan. 14th 1989 v Bristol Rov's	DREW 1-1
Mar. 27th 1984 v Scunthorpe	DREW 1-1		Feb. 11th 1989 v Cardiff	DREW 0-0
Aug. 25th 1984 v Wolves	DREW 2-2			

THE OTHER TEAMS IN SHEFFIELD NO.1 HALLAM F.C.

The first in a new series where Flashing Blade takes a look at the other teams in Sheffield. NUMBER 1:HALLAM

As everyone knows, Sheffield FC are the world's oldest football club. However, not many know that Hallam are the world's second oldest club being formed in 1860, three years after Sheffield, and playing in a field near Crosspool. Hallam in fact still play on the same pitch, now known as Sandygate, and proudly announce via a noticeboard above their one turnstile that this is the oldest football ground in the world.

As one would expect, the ground is very basic. As stated previously, you enter via one turnstile where you are given a free twenty four page programme on entry. From the turnstile you follow a path and come to the dressing room block which also hosts the hospitality room. Next to the dressing rooms is the small terrace which holds about 200 people, is covered, and provides a good view. Behind this is a cafe where you can buy jacket spuds for fifteen pence, sausage rolls for twelve pence and cups of tea for ten pence (United take note). You can also sit down at tables here and enjoy your grub in comfort. Opposite the terrace is a cricket pitch and behind both goals is a grass walkway. However, perhaps the most unusual aspect is the pitch which has a slope like United's car park.

Hallam play in the North East Counties League along with such names as Emley, Hatfield Main and Denaby. This league has produced such players as Billy Whitehurst, Andy Barnsley and John Francis. They play before a loyal crowd of around one hundred who all stand under the terrace and go to the cafe at the same bloody time.

Although Hallam have had a rather ordinary history, heady days hit the club in 1955 when after entering the FA Amateur they kept on winning ties. Eventually they were drawn against Dulwich Hamlet, one of the non league's strongest teams at the time. It soon became obvious that Sandygate with its capacity of 2000 was going to be inadequate so much souk1 searching took place before it was announced that the tie would be played at, of all places, Hillsborough. Typically the home team lost but a crowd of 13855 meant Hallam were financially secure for many a year.

This season has been one of transition for the Hallam first team with no nickname. At the end of last season, half the Hallam first team joined Sheffield, including Craig Worsfold, who was offered a trial at Hillsborough but wanted to join a club with ambition, and star striker Jamie Kay joined Gainsborough Trinity. Not surprisingly Hallam have struggled. However, after being bottom of the table around Christmas they are now beginning to climb the table.

So next time United aren't playing why not saunter up to Sandygate and give Hallam your support. I went three times last season and can thoroughly recommend it.

GROUND DIRECTIONS:BY CAR:Travel up Manchester Road to Crosspool and turn left at the Crosspool tavern. The ground is four hundred yards on the left opposite the Plough pub. BY BUS:The number 51 to Lodge Moor stops outside.

The Rough Stuff

Greetings grapple fans:. Listed below for your delectation is the state of "The Flash-ing Blade" Foul Play Award up to and including the home game with Fulham on Nov. 12th.

FB FOUL PLAY AWARD (LEAGUE GAMES ONLY)

NAME	BOOKINGS	DISMISSALS	POINTS
PIKE	FOUR	NIL	FOUR
TODD	FOUR	NIL	FOUR
BRYSON	TWO	NIL	TWO
DEANE	TWO	NIL	TWO
WILDER	TWO	NIL	TWO
CARR	ONE	NIL	ONE
POWELL	ONE	NIL	ONE
SMITH	ONE	NIL	ONE

(Table based on one point for yellow card, three for red)

Cliff "Enoch" Powell was the first Blade to go into the ref's little black book this season following an absolutely X-certificate "challenge" on Reading's Gilkes that was straight out of the Uruguayan coaching manual. The home game with Bristol Rovers passed off as peacefully as a Quakers knees up but then the action began in earnest with Pikey reeling off a Ron Harrisesque 4 bookings in the next 5 games. Todd (twice) and "Peabo" Bryson also incurred the wrath of officialdom in the aforementioned 5 matches. Even at this early stage of the season's clogging I began to fear that Pikey would build up an unassailable lead that even Wally "The Terminator" Downes couldn't catch when he returns from injury. However, Pikey has since gone 8 games without a brandishing of the yellow card so perhaps we can put his early season exuberance down to sexual frustration or something. Whilst on the subject of Pikey,if one more of his supposed "crosses" knocks another cup of Bovril out of my hands I'll swing for him. Anyway I digress, Mark "Mad Max" Todd picked up his third caution in the Bramall Lane clash with Wolves to reduce Pikey's lead to just one point and I began to take notice of the pocket battleship in midfield. For me at least Toddy's been the surprise packet of the season's rough stuff to date - he's barely the height of a Subbuteo player (even the mascots tower over him) but he packs the punch of your average SAM missile. Blackpool away saw bookings for United's two blonde bombers Wilder and Smith (though I personally can't recollect Smithy going into the book, mind you after the pre-match session I had in the "Wheatsheaf" I wasn't sure whether I was on this earth or Fuller's so its hardly surprising my memory's a little hazy). Wigan at beautiful downtown Bramall Lane was about as violent as an episode of Blue Peter, whilst Port Vale away was hardly a re-enactment of the battle of Iwo Jima though Deano was cautioned after their ponce of a keeper feigned near fatal injuries following a challenge from our Grace Jones lookalike. Bury at home was a pacifist's dream with hardly a crude tackle to be seen but the next encounter (Hudds. away) witnessed a total of six cautions, the lion's share (four) of which went to the Blades. Sadly though for us clogging fans it wasn't that dirty a game, just a case of that well known plonker George Tyson up to his usual tricks. Georgie was inconsistent to say the least, he seemingly booked Deano for having a silly haircut and Bryson for being Scottish on a football field whilst tackles that would have made even Mr. Souness wince went unpunished. Aldershot away was next on the clogging agenda, a fixture which almost saw the return of Wally "Charles Manson" Downes!. As I munched my way through a pie that was about as warm as a penguin's posterior I pricked (?) my ears ready for the team changes over the tannoy, "Number 4 for Sheffield United....Wally Downes". After picking myself up off the floor I had visions of Wally causing mayhem as his arsenal of two lethal feet would be supplemented by a pair of crutches, but it was not to be as the nincompoop announcer had confused Chris Downes with Wally. Todd picked up his 4th caution at Aldershot to draw level at the top with Pikey but its still anybody's race. Finally, much to no my surprise no one has yet been ordered off for an early bath, I find this quite astonishing as I for one wouldn't want to use the soap after its been round Stancliffe's meat and two veg!.

——Bloody Bad—— Blades

The name Nicky Johns will undoubtedly send shivers up the spines of the 39,614 people who saw United take on Leeds in the League Cup 3rd round in October 1978.

However, before looking back at that particular match, let's look at the reasons why "Happy Harry" signed him.

It was October 1978, and United had had a pretty mediocre start to the season. We had signed John "I'm not taking the penalty against Walsall" Mathews, Steve "I'll guarantee you fifty minutes every six matches" Finneston and Alex Sabella, and hopes were high for a good season. However, even with these three signings United were still only mid-table, but they had beaten Liverpool 1-0 in the League Cup second round, and were just starting to come good with a 4-0 home victory over Burnley. The goalkeeper at the time, Steve Conroy, was playing out of his skin, and it was only the shoddy defence which was allowing opposing forwards to run through and score. Therefore Haslam should have signed a defender, not a goalkeeper.

Anyhow, on to the Leeds game. Expectations were high of a cup run because we had just seen off Liverpool in the previous round, and surely Leeds would not pose such a threat, even though Tony Currie was playing for Leeds. However, lurking at the back of one's mind was that although United had won the previous Saturday's game 3-2 against Sunderland, the goalkeeper making his debut, Nicky Johns, had been at fault for both goals and had dropped crosses galore and played rubbish.

Surely the big crowd would ensure Johns had a good game against Leeds. How wrong can you be. He was absolutely useless. He couldn't kick, couldn't catch, couldn't throw, nothing. Leeds ran out easy 4-1 winners and Johns was nowhere to be seen for all four goals. Bramall Lane was shellshocked. Harry Haslam was shellshocked, and two days later Johns was on his way back to America, never to be seen again, or so we thought.

However, near the end of the season, when United desperately needed points to avoid relegation, Charlton Athletic arrived at Bramall Lane complete with a keeper called Nicky Johns. True to form he was superb and United were lucky to win 2-1.

	Played	Won	Drawn	Lost	Goals Conceded
Nicky Johns United record	2	1	0	1	6

PORK SCRATCHINGS

Whats the difference between the Owls and a taxi ?
A taxi only lets four in.

Whats the difference between the Owls and a teabag ?
A teabag stays in the cup longer.

THE DISCIPLINARIAN.

                                              The Flashing Blade,
                                              85 Charnley Avenue,
                                              Sheffield. S11 9FR.
                                              14th. October 1988.

The Commercial Manager,
Sheffield Wednesday F.C.
Hillsborough,
Sheffield.

Dear Sir,

    It has been brought to the attention of "The Flashing Blade" that Sheffield
Wednesday are still without a kit sponsor for the current league campaign after
Finlux decided enough was enough at the end of last season.

    I'm sure you'll be delighted to know that following a recent editorial
meeting we at "The Flashing Blade" would be only too pleased to fill the void on
the front of the Owls playing strip.

    Obviously we would be prepared to pay handsomely for the privilege of being
associated with "one of the nations premier clubs" and to that end a cheque for
£13-18p will be forwarded the minute you give us the nod of approval.

    I'm sure you will agree that this deal would help cement relations between
Sheffield's two league clubs and of course give us welcome publicity, thus
killing two birds with one stone.

    Perhaps we at "The Flashing Blade" don't have the clout of a multinational
company but the longer the Owls go without major sponsorship the greater the
loss of potential revenue, and eventually you'll probably have to settle for a
mickey mouse concerns name emblazoned on the Owls "famous kit" (something akin to
"Mimi's Massage Parlour" or "Syd's Chippy, Wincobank") which would not really be
in keeping with "the great traditions at Hillsborough".

    We look forward to hearing from you in due course.

                                              Yours faithfully,
                                              Jamie Pigott,
                                              Jon Middleton,
                                              Brian Exford,
                                              Paul Cook,
                                              Richard Chatterton.

chapter 10

THE PIE

notts. county

BARCELONA.0 NOTTS CO. 4

"It looks like beer prices aren't the only thing that's going up in Nottingham this year."

SPECIAL OPEN-CLOSET EDITION

when will the fans return?

Amnesty for stay-away supporters

MAGAZINE TITLE: THE PIE

EDITORS NAME: 1) COLIN HIGGINS : 2) ANDY MARTIN : 3) JIM COOKE 4) CHRIS CURTIS 5) TONY MACK

AGE: OVER 21   OCCUPATION: 1) LECTURER : 2) PROPERTY MANAGER 3) SHOP MANAGER : 4) UNEMPLOYED 5) UNEMPLOYABLE

DO YOU/HAVE YOU EVER SUPPORTED ANY OTHER TEAM?

NO!! —Andy: Bolton as a lad.

MOST MEMORABLE MATCH EVER: LEEDS UTD v NOTTS, LEAGUE CUP 18/10/75   0-1

MOST MEMORABLE SEASON: 1970/1971 4th Division Champs.

ALL TIME FAVOURITE PLAYER: DON MASSON

WHAT SORT OF CAR DO YOU DRIVE? FAB 1

YOUR FAVOURITE MUSIC: JAZZ/SOUL/R+B. \ INDI

FILMS/TV: WILL HAY / CARRY ON's / WESTERN's : New Wave of Brit Films Late 50's early 60's.

FAVOURITE CLOTHES: FOOTBALL KIT : DOC'S : Levis (original).

POLITICAL LEANINGS: LEFT/RIGHT/CENTRE

WHAT PLAYER WOULD YOU MOST LIKE TO SEE PLAYING FOR ENGLAND (SCOTLAND/ WALES IF RELEVANT)?

MARK DRAPER

During 1986 Jack Dunnett, Notts County's chairman and main benefactor, let it be known that he would be standing down as soon as he could find someone to buy his shares. The supporters also knew that when Jack went so would Jimmy Sirrell, the man who took Notts to the First Division on a shoestring. The club was now in trouble, both on and off the field, and when it was announced that there was to be a final crisis meeting at a local nightclub, The Astoria, on the 16th of September 1986, we all feared the worst.

By 7.30 the Astoria was packed with supporters, current and ex players and club officials. Hundreds were locked out, and apart from introducing a new fund raising scheme, Life-line, the evening highlighted the deep affection the locals had for Notts.

Upon leaving the Astoria we were accosted by our first fanzine salesman, Adrian Goldberg flogging *Off The Ball*. This friendly encounter, the hysterical press reports condemning all football supporters as hooligans (it was only four months after Heysel), the then sports minister Dick Tracey talking about introducing ID cards for fans and the general disatisfaction with the Notts matchday programme nurtured the seeds that would lead to *The Pie*.

Jim Cooke started selling fanzines in his record shop and when he met up with Colin Higgins, who had access to printing facilities, on an away trip to Carlisle in December 1986, things started to move, though some thought it was a hopeless and doomed endeavour.

Colin talked to the *Orientear*, *OTB*, *Terrace Talk* and *City Gent* (who were particularly helpful) and with their guidance *Pie* 1 hit the streets of Bournemouth on January 24th 1987. When The Observer decided to invite all the fanzine editors to a Photo Opportunity Jim donned his Notts County kit and realised there was no going back.

The Pie has campaigned, along with other mags, against the ID card scheme, the Clubcall system, racism, poor spectator facilities and property speculators. We have had a go at the local media pundits, the matchday programme, the Police, the Fire Brigade and we have passionately supported the reserve and youth teams. The 'Junior Magpies' have benefitted financially during our existence and will continue to do so. What effect we have had is up to other people to judge, but we have enjoyed being involved with worthwhile causes.

Our relationship with the club has been 'up and down', even though from *Pie* 1 we have publicly stated that all profits from the mag, the quizzes we regularly hold, the sale of T-shirts and badges and the other fund raising activities we have held would be donated to NCFC. We were chucked out of the ground for selling *Pie* 2, with one of our salesmen being hauled up in front of the managing director and verbally abused. By *Pie* 4 we were on sale in the club shop and receiving good reviews both locally and nationally. *Pie* 9 led us to being banned, publicly for opposing Clubcall, but privately for writing about a player's wife. Nevertheless we continued to donate all profits to the club.

In November 1988 we approached Derek Pavis, the chairman, about organising an anti-ID card petition, which we felt would be better supported if it appeared as a pullout in the matchday programme, and we offerred to meet the total cost of this exercise. Although the meeting between our representatives and Derek Pavis began in a mutually distrustful atmosphere it ended an hour later on first name terms with the details of the petition, and other matters, agreed. Suddenly everything was hunkydory and we went about contacting Adrian Goldberg for further details of the petition and arranging press coverage. In December 1988 *Pie* 14 was published and some of the articles in it so upset certain players that we were all called to a 'summit' meeting with the players, managing director and chairman. After agreeing to destroy all remaining copies of *Pie* 14 (about 700) we regained access to the club shop and, more importantly, had our petition restored to the matchday programme. The players had insisted that the club should not be associated with us on this matter.

We are now enjoying a period of Glasnost with the club but, understandably, they are still wary about our motives and direction. They now accept our right to exist and that we are not a bunch of 'out of work bolshies'. What the future holds remains to be seen. We feel that we have given Notts County fans a focal point that is not controlled by the club and to a certain degree we act as a catalyst between club and fan. Our activities have developed to such an extent that someone described us as 'an alternative supporters club numbering some 800 to 1000 members, 0r 25% of County's average home gate'. Very flattering.

Two comments made to us during our early days will never be forgotten. John Dewhirst from City Gent told us "You will create a monster that you can't control". It nearly happened. An unpaid club official whispered to us "The more you find out about Notts the more disenchanted you will become". It nearly happened.

H.R.H. for N.C.F.C. ?

It has been hard to avoid the recent coverage in
the national press of Prince Edward's resignation
from the Royal Marines. There has been a great
deal of speculation on what he might do in the
world of 'civvy street', that is, how will he
occupy his time in a useful way?

There has also been speculation, albeit on a
smaller scale, on who will be the person to replace Jack Dunnett as Chairman of Notts County
Football Club at the end of the current season.
The search is on to find the so called 'Mr X'.

Is it beyond the realms of the fantastic that
Prince Edward could eventually prove to be this
'Mr X'? There are several good reasons for bel-
ieving this might well be the case.

I- Prince Edward, being in his early twenties, is
young enough to be in charge of the club for the
next forty to fifty years. This period in the
future could well see Notts in the First Division,
in various European competitions and, if technology is sufficiently advanced, into the Inter-
Planetary Cup Winners' Cup.

2- His father, Prince Phillip, used to watch
Windsor and Eton on several occassions. His
mother, The Queen has attended several Cup
Finals and can truthfully say she was at Wembley
when England won the World Cup in I966. Prince
Edward would, therefore, be able to carry on the
family tradition of supporting football.

3- He's not short of a bob or two. This last point
is important in any possible replacement for Jack
Dunnett. Jimmy Sirrel was very clear about this
in his memorable speech at The Astoria.

So don't be too alarmed if in the future the
Royal Standard is seen flying over Meadow Lane.
Just think about the possible increase in the
attendance figures and remember you read it first
in The Pie.

(Pie 1)

HOOK OFF

The last day of January, nineteen eighty-seven,
saw the home launch of "The Pie". From the decaying
infrastructure of eastern Meadow Lane to the
Legoland bijou cots in the west, Piemen sold their
wares in the hope of raising a few bob for County's
empty coffers and promote the old club in the
meantime. However, our man in the hat had no
sooner gone into Pete Beale mode, than the stewards
descended and banned him from spreading the word in
the environs of Our Club. On asking to see Neal
Hook, the Vendor was whisked to his inner sanctum
and given the ultimatum - if you don't pack it in
we'll call the law. Now Notts County F.C.,have
every right to limit the sale of goods within their
walls and as an 'independent' magazine we have no
reason to expect favours, but the attitude of their
spokesperson towards 'The Pie' reinforced the
feelings long held among county fans, that Notts
Board have no consideration for the punters.

Take the Lifeline launch. We were repeatedly told
that the legacy of our days in the first division
was a massive debt and if we continued to want
football at the Lane we would have to pay more for
it. Fair enough, with neighbours as successful as
Forest only a Clough*away, supporting Notts has
long been an unusual if not a downright eccentric
pastime. The rapid slide down the League has not
helped cashflow and many long-time fans have left
feeling nausea at the Glen Roeder incident among
others many of which were aired at 'question time'
at the Astoria. Old wounds were reopened and the
night was soured by answers of the 'we do what we
think best' variety to fans questions. In short,
becoming privy to current thinking on the clubs
future meant being rich enough to buy a
directorship - for the rest of us who pay good
money to see Notts at home and away in what are
cold and often unpleasant conditions we at least
have the pleasure of knowing our best interest are
being served along with the drink we are denied.

That's the last bad language in here - Ed.

(Pie 2)

NOTACLUEDO

THE TRIVIAL FOOTBALL LEAGUE BOARD GAME

The Ideal Christmas Present!!!

Simple To Play!!!!

Therefore Ideal For All Football Administrators!!!

The object behind this new board game is very topical, To bring the game of Football in to disrepute as quickly as possible.

The Rules are small minded and naturally lack any imagination.

You start the game by choosing one of the following role-playing cards:-

'Chairman of the League Centenary Committee'

'Press Baron, with Delusions of Grandeur'

'The Manager of Glasgow Rangers'

'Chelsea Supporter'

'Diego Maradonna'

'A Parrot'

The only rule of the game is that there are no rules, except the one's that you make-up and enforce arbitarily.

You begin the game by throwing away a six figure sum, bending over backwards to please nobody and reciting The Official Credo 'My only interest is in the well being of the Game' whilst laughing up your sleeve. And your off!!!

Beware of falling on to Penalty Squares such as

'New Stand Your Property Company Constructed Collapses. Go Back 4 Squares'

'You Are Interviewed by Trevor Brooking. Lose 6 Squares For Falling Asleep'

'Photographed Not Wearing A Silly Hat. Go Back To Czechoslovakia'

You travel around the board for as long as you can get away with it or until you land on the square marked

'95, Retire To FIFA Management Committee'

and you have won!!!

The fact that you know nothing about Football is not a handicap for playing this game. In fact some of the best players come from such diverse backgrounds as Catering and Property Speculation.

NOTACLUEDO is brought to you by the manufacturers of SCRAMBLE: The Allocation of Cup Final Tickets Game.

(Pie 7)

Where's That Fire?

I was not present on the day and I heard the news second-hand as "Your ground has caught fire, it's just been on the news". I had to run to the other end of the building in order to find a radio, and by the time I had tuned into Radio 2 various unpleasant fears had crossed my mind. 'Bradford' and 'I hope Old George has found someone to help him out' being only two of them.

When the report finally came through I realised that my colleague had either misheard or exaggerated the original news bulletin. However, I would not like to live through those ten minutes again, and I certainly do not want to see Notts County on the front pages of the Sunday papers because of a tragedy.

Later in the week I had absorbed most of the news reports, but I was still uneasy. My main worry was why had only two fire tenders been despatched to a reported fire underneath an occupied old wooden football stand? Hasn't anything been learnt from Bradford?

I later found out that Fire Brigade Standing Orders state that two tenders should be sent to any fire alarm originating from a 999 call. The implication is that the Fire Brigade didn't know that they were responding to a fire at a Football League ground, but was responding to a fire on Iremonger Road. Why wasn't the Fire Brigade aware of the seriousness of the alarm call?

The second cause for concern is the fact that the fire tenders were despatched from Shakespeare Street. Bearing in mind that the fire happened on the last Saturday before Christmas, and that the City Centre was bursting at the seams with seasonal extra traffic, why send out fire tenders that have to negotiate a congested City Centre, navigate the notorious "Leeming Way" outside the Victoria Centre and traverse fifteen sets of traffic lights?

Whilst acknowledging that the Shakespere Street Fire Station is in direct contact with the Trinity Square Traffic Control Centre and can therefore receive the benefit of some pre-set traffic lights on their way, it still means that the tenders would have to maintain an average speed of over 50mph in order to travel the mile and a half to Iremonger Road within two minutes. I believe this to be an impossible task at this time of year, at this time of day.

There is a Fire Station on Loughborough Road, West Bridgford, which is just two miles from Iremonger Road. There are only nine sets of traffic lights to negotiate on this route and there certainly would not be the same volume of road or pedestrian traffic hampering progress. An average speed of over 50mph would be easier to maintained on this route.

These timings may seem negligible until you take into consideration the necessity of having to summon back-up tenders and other support services, should the situation have become more serious. We all know what happened within two minutes at Valley Parade.

I am sure that both the Nottingham and Nottinghamshire Fire Brigades have discussed the response procedures with the Notts Officials concerning the outbreak of fire at Meadow Lane. I am equally sure that those procedures were adhered to on this occasion. However all feasibility programmes should incorporate flexibility, and it appears that the response to this incident was dealt with automatically rather than logically.

The outcome of this incident was not serious, but that does not mean that complacency should be allowed. Disaster control techniques should cover all possibilities and when circumstances change, so should the response.

Van Der Lubbe

(Pie 8)

BEER MATTERS by Ivor Thirst.

I don't know how many people saw Graeme 'Banzai' Souness' quote in the papers after Rangers had beaten Gornik in the European Cup that "Every round buys a player". Personally, I've always preferred the type of team where 'every player buys a round', but I suppose that's why I support Notts instead of Rangers.

Well, breathalizers came and went, but thanks to Harvey Forester for his amusing letter on the subject. As for sponsorship of the F.A. Cup, I don't know if we'll hear of this again in the near future given the amount of opposition the proposal attracted. Rumours were that Australian mega brewers Elders or their British subsidiary Courage were interested in the sponsorship (and the associated prestige) for a purported £12m over three years.

If they have lost interest, then I'm willing to enter negotiations over sponsorship of the 'Beer Matters' column. I'm not bothered with Elders, they can stick their 4X up their XXXX as far as I'm concerned, but I'm willing to listen to offers from Courage. A barrel of Imperial Russian Stout per week and a crate of Imperial Russian Stout per week and I think we can do business. Away we go.

Blackpool 28th December.

Blackpool. Depending on your point of view, Las Vegas of Lancashire and the most popular seaside resort in the country, or a national monument to commercial vulgarity at it's extreme. At least the pubs should be without the 'Couples Only' signs and the brain-dead bouncers found on the door during the summer months.

The best place to drink is round the North Railway station, very handy for those travelling from Nottm by train. First stop is the Kings Head (Talbot Rd.) opposite the station serving Higsons Mild and Bitter.

Also on Talbot Rd. are the Wheatsheaf (194) with Matthew Brown and Theakston's beers, and the Ramsden Arms (204) with Tetleys Mild & Bitter, Burton Ale and Jennings Bitter. Round the corner from the station is the Mount Pleasant (103 High St.) with another chance to try Matthew Browns and Theakstons before the two horsemen of the Apocalypse (Scottish and Newcastle) get their grubby little hands on them. The Empress (50 Exchange St.) nearby serves Thwaites refreshing Bitter and Mild.

For travellers coming from the M55, coming down Preston Rd.(A583), turning right at the roundabout onto Whitegate Drive will lead to the Saddle (286) a Bass house. However, turning left at the roundabout into Vicarage Lane (off Waterloo Rd.) will take you to the Welcome with Burtonwoods Bitter on offer. Finally, the Dog and Partridge (Lytham Rd.) serves Boddingtons about five minutes walk away from the ground. The pubs should (!)be open until 3.00

Grimsby Town 1st January.

With a bitter wind coming in from the North Sea and whistling up your kilt, what better place could there be to take your New Years Eve hangover? Yes Cleethorpes, which as every footy fan knows is where 'The Mariners' play, is a fine place for those in search of 'The hair of the Dog'. The only trouble is that some pubs may have less than regular opening hours at lunchtime.

For those wishing to drink as close to the ground as possible, and let's face it there always seems to be more delicate parts of the body on Jan. 1st, the Imperial (Grimsby Rd.) is next to the ground. It's a few years since I last visited this place but I remember it used to have jumbo photos of old Grimsby players on the walls (the photos that is). It was worth going just for these, however Bass Mild and Stones Bitter are on sale as well.

Briefly, other pubs worth visiting include; Darleys Hotel (Grimsby Rd.) serving Darleys Beers, the Swashbuckle Tavern (3 Grant St.) serves Batemans. Near the station are the Punchbowl (195 North Promenade) with Batemans and the Victoria (Grant St.) with Bass and Stones. Actually in the station, and a positive boon to the railway traveller, are the No.8 and 2 Refreshment Rooms, each with a selection of beers, though No. 2 offers the best choice. If all stations were like this, B.R. would show a healthy profit every year.

The nearby Pier Hotel (Sea Rd.) serves Tetleys Bitter and Mild, as do the Queens Hotel (28 Seaview Rd.) and the Nottingham (7 Seaview Rd.).

Finally, there is Willy's with a selection of beers on offer to the wine bar crowd.

Bristol City 16th January

Already covered (not too well) in 'Pie Issue 3.

The Blackpool forwards had been in strict training for weeks. They were taking no chances.

This time they were ready to deal with the County keeper.

What they didn't know was Micky had perfected Charlie's 'Glasgow Kiss.

And was ready for 'em!

Ducks Away

My first season down the Lane was 1964-65 and I made my debut in the old Meadow Lane stand at the Aldershot match on September 12th 1964, a week before my ninth birthday. My father had little interest in football, but my elder brother was an ardent Forest fan. Prior to my first appearance at the Lane, I had been taken by a friend's dad to see a night match at the City Ground and had not been to impressed. My companion to the Aldershot match was to be my grandma who was a County regular, both home and away. Now aged ninety, she does not attend on a regular basis although she did go to two matches last season (Port Vale and Carlisle). Gran was part of the thriving Hyson Green Supporters Club, and I was soon accepted as a member.

All Gran's friends sat in the Meadow Lane stand. They were mainly women and I soon realised I had made the right decision to follow Notts, as these kindly ladies were to spoil me daft in the seasons to come. Sweets were passed around at regular intervals, flasks of tea and coffee were on offer, as were blankets to keep the legs warm.

The match, or what I can remember of it, was a bit of a dull affair, a 0-0 draw, but Gran's crowd enjoyed it, and I was just happy to be in this good company.

My next visit to the Lane was not until five weeks later when Oxford United were the visitors. Again the score was 0-0, but it was a better match. Ron Atkinson was playing for United, but it was the first time I saw Vic Povey, a lively winger with a really cropped hair style. I had discovered a new hero, a good player and one with a hair style similar to my own, the crew cut which I had acquired during the summer. (Plus ça change! - Ed.)

Chelmsford City were the next visitors I saw at the Lane. County dispatched the non-leaguers 2-0 and we were on our way to the second round of the F.A.Cup. This was a really exciting game County's results had improved in recent weeks and a good Cup run was on the cards. After the game Gran asked me if I would like to go to Bradford City next Saturday for my first away match. What an offer. My mum was pestered as soon as I got home, and everything was duly arranged.

Waiting for the Friday evening paper to arrive seemed like a lifetime, but eventually it did and I was able to check the team.

Smith, Bircumshaw, Agnew, Sheridan, Gibson, Coates, Kavanagh, Rayner, Edwards, Docherty and Flower.

No place for Vic Povey, he was included in the reserve side who were replaying Watford at home. The A team were away at Stoke. Bradford had won only three out of their twenty league matches so far, and the previous Saturday had been knocked out of the Cup by part-timers Scarborough.

Saturday morning arrived and I set off on the 2I bus (4d to town please) meeting my grandma a few stops along the way. We were to meet the others inside the Maid Marion Café on the corner of Friar Lane. One by one they all arrived (Mr & Mrs Fish, Mr & Mrs Pitchett, the Newark girls, Roland & Eric, Mrs Walker, Evelyn, Little Billy and Cybil). There were plenty of others, mainly younger people, waiting for the coach, but this was the bulk of Gran's friends. Vic the coach driver (Netherfield Coaches) duly arrived and off we set for my first away match.

Trent also ran trips to away matches from Huntington Street, but were always a bit more expensive than the Supporters Club coach. Trent wer. charging 13/3d return to Bradford, whereas I think it was 12/- on our coach.

A sweep was organised; prizes for the highest scoring home and away teams, and the teams people had pulled out were the topic of much lively conversation as we made our way northwards. I was having great fun just looking out of the coach window, busy ticking things off in my I-Spy books. My seventeen year old cousin was also on the coach with all his pals. I remember them calling the coach the "Duck's Bus" as all the elder people referred to everybody as Duck, after you duck, are you alright duck? etc, and there was a heated debate going on about the merits of a certain Terry Bly.

We stopped for a tea on the way up and had a game of football in the Transport Café car park. On arriving in Bradford on a somewhat grim day, a pub was found where refreshment was taken before the game. Gran's friends left early so that they could chat to the players outside the ground. Players such as Alex Gibson and Tony Bircumshaw were big favourites of the ladies, and these players regularly gave them free tickets for the stands at away matches. Some money was passed to the gateman and I was hoisted over the turnstile and installed in a vacant seat.

The programme was 4d, (2d cheaper than Notts) and had a bright claret and amber cover. I read this before the kickoff and could not believe that there were so few people there. But City had been playing poorly, and at the time Bradford Park Avenue were the better supported side in the city. They were away at Barrow and had players such as Kevin Hector and Bobby Ham in their free scoring side which was pushing for promotion.

Notts won the game 2-0 and in Colin Slater's words "slogged away unremittingly for 90 minutes in the toughest action imaginable". George Smith had a cracking game in goal, and in a hard fought match both Alex Gibson and John Sheridan left the field with injuries. Dick Edwards notched the first after four minutes and Tony Flower made sure of the points in the 82nd minute. It was the first time Notts had won an away League match since Jan 18th at Port Vale, and they were now in the middle of a five match unbeaten run. Well this was the life; a good day out, good company and a good win. But it would not always be like this. My next away trip was for the Cup match at third division Brentford where Notts were well and truly stuffed 4-0. What a long journey home that was, particularly as the MI only went up as far as Northampton in those days. But for now life was great and the journey home was a happy one- made even happier by winning first prize in the sweep.

Jim Cooke.

Gone with the Wind

May I make one appeal to the new bosses at Meadow Lane. It's about something that has been missing from the ground for a good five years.

No - not First Division football - something much easier to supply than that. Namely mushy peas.

A recent trip to Goose Fair has re-awakened my taste buds (and other parts) to the green delicacy with lashings of mint sauce.

Home games have never been the same without a half-time visit to that steamy room under the main stand where women ladled gallons of the stuff out of a huge boiler. There chaos reigned, people lurched around with three or so polystyrene cups looking for spoons while others were spilling vinegar as they tried to get out.

Visitors from other clubs were incredulous.

"I've heard of pie and peas but I couldn't eat peas on their own" was a typical comment.

But we didn't mind - even if the quality was sometimes less than perfect. Gourmets may not believe this but there is an art to making perfect mushy peas. They must be soaked for just the right amount of time.

Too little results in the eater breaking teeth when they manage to catch a pea, and too much gives him nothing at all to chew on and no idea where one pea ends and another begins - looking a bit like swarfega.

When the consistency is just right they will warm much better than tea or bovril, and as Mr. Pavis has stated (quite rightly) that he has no intentions of putting a roof over the kop, this is a cheap alternative as winter approaches.

HERE WEE GO....

Being a female football supporter is not all that it could be. It's bad enough at work on Monday mornings... 'You went where on Saturday?', "Did you look round the shops?"

OK, maybe there are at large certain unenlightened members of society who don't think that "women" and "football" should be words uttered in the same breath. But I would have thought that by now "the powers that be" in the world of football would have realised that women are not just around to wash dirty kits and provide after match refreshments/entertainment. Neither does our interest in the game confine itself to admiring the players physical attributes or wondering where they get their hair done. (Ok then, maybe occasionally). We also appreciate the finer points of the game (holding our breath at hairs breadth back passes to the startled custodian), and unlike many referees and linesmen, know many of the laws of the game. (e.g. A Notts County Player can never be offside, even if his name if Charlie, when the ball goes out of play every player on the field must hold up his hand for the throw in).

Anyway to come back to the point. Thanks to 'The Pie' for the fascinating guides to local hostelries up and down the country, but I'm sorry - it's no use to me.

Why? Because I'm female and this causes two major problems a) Most bar persons don't think I actually need serving when I stand at the bar - I'm obviously just looking for somewhere to rest my elbow after applying my mascara, and b) most football clubs don't think I'm going to need a loo. If you haven't guessed by now I'm the woman who is usually standing with legs crossed talking to a steward or local bastion of law and order. It's not that I've got a thing about men in fluorescent waistcoats or blue uniforms, it's just that I'm trying to find out where the nearest ladies loo is. Having found it I often wish I hadn't. In comparison to most, our portaloo at Meadow Lane is positively palatial and inviting - except when the 'County Road Faithful' decide its more convenient to relieve themselves up the outside, whilst I'm squatting in the dark inside.

So sorry lads, I'll have to deprive you of my company in the bars before the game, or I'd miss most of the action whilst searching for the 'conveniences'. The cricket clubs seem to have got hold of the idea that women like going to sporting occasions, so why not the Football Clubs?

See you soon - you'll hear me coming either chanting through gritted teeth '2 gins and one bottle of tonic perleez', or humming to myself that well known football song 'One loo between us, there's only one loo between us, one loo between us'. I think you know the rest.

TO LOOS THE TREK

For Sale

BRITISH FOOTBALL

The Pie is proud to be able to bring to it's readers this unique opportunity to participate in the 'Share Owning Democracy' and support your favourite game at the same time. Continuing the Government's tradition of selling off things it doesn't own, you lucky readers will be able, for the first time, to buy shares in the soon to be formed company, British Football p.l.c.

Unfortunately, this means that our once glorious national game will have to undergo certain modifications which will involve a certain amount of 'streamlining'. But do not worry, this Government knows best and has determined how this will be achieved. Dear readers, you will hardly notice the difference!

How will this affect me?

Hardly at all. Naturally, B.F. will not be able to support the game with the present level of overmanning, so they envisage that some Clubs will have to go. Their advisers, stockbrokers 'Greedy, Bastards and Yuppies', have come up with the optimum League size for the maximisation of profits. They suggest a League of twelve teams would be suitable, although the Government thinks this is slightly generous. The other eighty clubs may feel the effects of this progress, but that is just unfortunate. They will be able to apply for places in many of the lower leagues if they must insist on continuing to play football.

Which are the twelve clubs?

Obviously, it will be in the best interest of potential investors that most of the teams should come from southern England, though one or two northern teams may be permitted. There are very good reasons for this division. Firstly, most B.F. shareholders will probably live in the south (after all, that's where most of the money is) and secondly, it may teach those people in the north who did not vote for this Government an important lesson. It is

for the latter reason that the Scottish and Welsh Leagues will be disbanded. If any clubs are forced into closure this is just bad luck. As most are in inner city areas, these sites will offer exciting prospects for new housing developments. Former supporters of these clubs will be found 'suitable alternatives' for Saturday afternoon activities.

How do I apply for my shares?

Simply get your secretary to fill in the form below to obtain full details.

Yes please, rush me details of this remarkable offer. ☐

I am a greedy sod eager to make some quick cash. ☐

I have already sold my Granny and am looking for other ways of making money. ☐

I am a Tory M.P. and would like ten times my share entitlement. ☐

I couldn't care less about football, but I like the idea of a quick profit. ☐

I am interested in inner city property developments. ☐

Please tick one or more boxes.

NAME.................................

ADDRESS.............................

Please post your completed coupon to:

British Football p.l.c, 221b, Greed St, The City, London, E.C.3.

Clogger's Corner

I'LL STOP HIM — FOR OOOOH!!

What's going off? – by The Ankle Tapper

Not much by the look of it.

Went to Blackpool hoping for a bit of action but was most disappointed – the odd lunge at Micky from the young ex Derby blade Garner but otherwise a clean game! Even Cunningham was well behaved unlike the racists amongst the crowd giving the lad a hard time.

In fact the season so far as been pretty quiet all round. There was a useful bit of naughty recently at Field Mill of course where Ken Worthy is alleged to have wanted a riot with the Notts fans behind the goals in the second leg of the Littlewoods Cup. My sources, as reliable as ever, tell me he beckoned to the assembled to join him on the pitch. Why? The thin blue line intervened and that was that.

Now that we've got a footballing lot down at the Lane I think I'll have to pop down the Embankment for a bit of relish – always good for a laugh – the touchline antics of the bucket and sponge brigade is brill – and no admission either. At Meadow Lane the ghost of Stubby still stalks the back four – what a player – we hope his Junior Magpie son turns out to be a chip off the old block. Norman Hunter bit your legs whilst Stubby took out the whole bod, who can forget that air of anticipation when a one on one situation occurred near the Main stand paddock, even a non-betting man like me would have to put a fiver on Notts if he was still around.

I don't know about you but I find early season football a bit iffy ... the best game of last season though wrong result was the Blackpool 2-3 in the mud. I'm looking forward to a good harsh winter when the real football is played. Come on down rain and hail for those County capers.

MOR THIRST by Beer Matters

I don't know what got into Mrs Thirst the other day, but she had an idea that hiding all my trousers would keep me away from the pub for a day or two. Well, I have to admit I was a bit flummoxed as to what to do. It did occur to me to go out wearing my Clan Sirrel Tartan kilt, an item of my wardrobe usually kept for the most ceremonial of occasions but, stone me, she'd hidden that as well. In the end I had to don a pair of particularly hideous boxer shorts, given, incidentally, as a Christmas present and kept for emergency use only. Well this was an emergency. So, with an old Nottingham Beer Festival t-shirt and a tatty pair of old walking boots, I finally made it to the local. "Just training for the Robin Hood "marathon" I said. But no-one believed me. "Ivor", said one of the regulars, "the idea of exercise must have the same effect on you as a cross on a vampire". ("or a cross on Mick Leonard" came a voice from the dart board). I ignored this unkind criticism. After all, there I was sitting in my usual seat with my first pint of the day and, in the knowledge that the score was; Mrs Thirst 1 Ivor 2, very content.

But that's enough of my domestic problems, there's a lot to get through.

(October '88)

FOOTBALL'S TV-1D

Much has been written about the validity of televised football, it's effect on gates, and the monotonous, blanket coverage of it's favourite teams. The representation of football on the box however, is rarely examined and it is in this area that I would like to open some discussion.

To watch a match in the flesh is to become involved in a spectacle which operates on a number of levels of which "following the ball" is only one. Equally important is an appreciation of tactics, a sense of contact with the reality of events and being part of a crowd of enthusiastic, like minded people. Anyone who has attended a football match will acknowledge the changes in mood on the terraces as a plan begins to succeed or fail and it is clearly impossible to reproduce such emotions in the currently vicarious medium of television. It is obvious that

television producers have conspired to create a third medium out of television and football; the notion of "televised football" which is generally mediocre, insincere and above all cheap. Recorded football matches celebrate only one icon, the Great God Goal, all else is superfluous. Instant gratification is the name of the game, sweet and sickly, and repetitive.

The technique of football presentation is ruthlessly limited and unambitious. In an attempt to capture the goals, they rigidly follow the ball with mindless camera panning which produces synthetic confining results. Devoid of all opportunity for personal interpretation on the part of the viewer, the "excitement" is "applied" in the form of the commentator's inane insincerity. Gushing with enthusiasm he informs us of; the tragedy of relegation battles, the glory of the championship chase and so on, in a melodrama of the director's making. The unwieldy "televised - football hybrid" is inadequate as a means of showing the realities of spectatorship, largely due to a lack of commitment to the game as - it - really - is at the highest levels within television, which is embodied in an unwillingness to put money into outside broadcasts.

Greater funding would allow more camera angles and imaginative editing. Ideally this would support a realistic, documentary approach, while giving room for creative individual interpretation. Literally speaking, more viewpoints would give a wider perspective, including close ups of players, intimacy with their reactions and crowd involvement.

The current compromise consists of a reliance on extended shots of distant players running with the ball, which denies this intimacy and also precludes any illustration of tactics. As a recorded game does not rely on suspense as it's chief motivator, since the score is frequently known, it is acceptable and advantageous to use the full armoury of narrative film technique. Slow motion, montage and implicit editing are all valuable weapons in highlighting the reality of football. If the concept of constructive narrative seems to football fans to be inconsistent with realism, it is surely less incompatable than cheap visuals overlaid with the screech of cliches.

To be continued..........

POLICE STATE

The police presence at the Sunderland match was pretty formidable. Delayed just off the A1 for about 2hour, escorted to Seaburn for no apparent reason and the loss of another 2hour then shepherded to Roker and marched directly to the ground. Whatever happened to civil liberties? I can't imagine a coach trip to the opera or Ascot being treated like this. Once outside the ground the Police more or less forced everybody to enter straight away. When we informed a police officer that we wished to meet some friends from "Wise Men Say"(the Sunderland fanzine)in a local pub we were warned of the evils of alcohol and that we might not be let into the game if we returned with beery breath. Most of us were still hung over from the night before, a few more beers was not going to turn us into raving psychopaths. Sunderland's policing bill must be horrific and to their credit they did not up the price to travelling supporters(as we did to theirs) The task of escorting us from the ground to our coaches was a full scale operation in itself. Countless vans, mounted police, motorbikes and officers on foot must keep the whole of the Northumbrian police force occupied on a Saturday. After the halcyon days of the Miners Strike the boys in blue must welcome this chance of a quick buck. The police escort does not end until the A1 is finally reached and we were not through then. Stopping off in Knaresborough for a couple the coach was moved on, ordered to leave by 8o'clock sharp. Bring back those laid back days of the "Ducks Bus"when we sailed through life without a care.

The response to the 'Anti-ID Card petition has been excellent. Thank you. So far we have received over 1500 signatures.... and a complaint from the Postman. We have included a copy of the petition in this issue of THE PIE. It is quite in order to photocopy the petition, but please return them to us ASAP.

The same artwork and layout that appeared in the Bolton programme was sent to Mansfield Town and Nottingham Forest. The Stags Chairman wrote back saying that he had passed the material to his Commercial Manager Stuart Burgan, asking him to include it in the next programme if possible. So far we have heard nothing.

And Forest. Not a dicky bird, even after a follow-up phone call. Now we know that things are busy over there, being a First Division Club, promoting The Sun and all that, but surely somebody can take HIS head out of the sand for five minutes and do something for their own supporters.

The attitude shown by Forest leaves much to be desired, especially when you consider Brian Clough's reported political leanings. I would have thought that the Anti-ID Card Campaign was right up his street. Maybe he feels that fighting the establishment at this time is not in his own best interests.

The reading of the Enabling Bill, The Football Spectators Bill, was introduced in to the House of Lords in mid-January. When the Bill reaches the House of Commons we will be monitoring, and reporting, the way our local MP's vote. You will no doubt recall the general hostility that occured when the initial outlines of the 'Membership Scheme' were announced. It will be interesting to see if our local Members are willing to put their political futures where their mouths are.

The proposed legislation and the opposition to it has been very well reported on the radio and in the newspapers. The same can not be said of television. So far any items broadcast have been circumspect and all shown at off-peck times. The reson for this may lie in the fact that the introduction of ID Cards will help the poor figures this seasons 'Live' games have attracted. The first, and most important, effect of introducing these cards will be that thousands of people will stop going to matches.

They will turn in to couch potatoes and watch the lacklustre fare Messrs Hill and Moore prefer.

It was pleasing to see Colin Moynihan score an own goal when he released a 'League Table' of arrests at football grounds for the 1987-88 season. He issued the figures with the claim that arrests at and around grounds had increased by 11% on the previous year. It didn't take long for Fleet Street to pull his figures to pieces and by the end of the week James Pawsey MP was quoted as saying "Many Conservatives, from both the Right and Left, don't like the Bill and there is likely to be substantial modification." Later The Referees Association came out against the proposed legislation.

Mr Moynihans figures actually proved the point that of the 17.9 million attendances at football matches during the 1987-88 season only 6147 arrests were made, for all offences inside and outside league grounds. This represents 0.04% of the total. Notts County came sixth in the Third Division 'League' with fifty arrests from a total attendance of 144,624 (0.03%). During that season Notts had the fourth highest attendance figures in the division, behind Sunderland, Bristol City and Brighton and only 17,000 behind First Division Luton Town.

The Luton attendance figures no doubt accounted for the fact that despite appearing at Wembley twice, reaching the FA Cup semi-finals and being invited to attend the Centenery weekend 'celebrations' they managed to lose £327,000. Luton, of course, operate a 'Membership Scheme' at Kenilworth Road.

On Saturday January 7th Manchester United conducted a Vox Pop at the FA Cup game against QPR. The fans were asked over the public address system to wave for and against the ID Card. The vote was a unanimous NO from 36,000 fans.

Arthur Young, the governments consultants on the ID Card scheme, have now recommended to Moynihan that the intention to implement the system before 1990 'is impractical'. Their report claims that the earliest practical date would be the start of the 1991-92 season, and then there would still be many problems to overcome

Although opposition to this ill-conceived Bill is mounting it does not mean that genuine supporters can relax their efforts. We still have one huge political hurdle to overcome, Mrs Thatcher, and when this particular legislation is abandoned something else will come along to replace it. In the meantime we urge you all to write to yoour local MP and tell him/her how you wish your views to be represented in Parliament. If any of you have any bright, practical and legal ideas that you think THE PIE should be involved in then please let us know.

(January '89)

MAGPIE MISFITS

with this season providing so little to cheer about it is perhaps time to reflect on even darker days and spotlight some of the past players who have had the misfortune to don the Back and White, albeit fleetingly. I have selected the following instantly forgettable eleven who, for one reason or another, constitute Notts' lowest appearance makers.

1) FRANK LANE Ex-Anfield custodian, prone to lapses and best remembered for his televised cock-up against Blackpool in the mid-70's.
2) JOHN RICHARDSON Arrived from Derby in 1972. Tragically broke his leg on his debut after only two minutes. Never played again.
3) GARY WOOD Hapless left back from Kettering - was not fit to lace Ray O'Brien's boots.
4) JEFF KING Stocky midfield player who spent four matches on loan from Derby. Despite the players willingness to sign Notts couldn't afford the £40,000 fee, so off he toddled back up the A52.
5) IAN LADD Lanky centre-back restricted to a single appearance in a 6-0 drubbing at Luton.
6) ANDY GRAY Could have been the final piece in Barnwell's jigsaw. Chose Tessa Sanderson and Sporting Triangles instead.
7) ALLAN MANSLEY Followed Jimmy Sirrel from Brentford in '69. Scored on his debut in a 4-0 victory. Never heard of since. A rare bad Sirrel buy.
8) EDDIE KELLY Won FA Cup honours with Arsenal. Made such an impact at Meadow Lane that during one match he threw his shin pads towards the dug out. This prompted a wag in the crowd to recommend that Kelly take himself off and leave the pads on instead!
9) GEOFF COLLIER Giraffe like centre forward signed from non-league Macclesfield for £2,000. Big Les cost half as much and hit the back of the net more times than Collier missed.
10) RICKY GREEN Precisely.
11) DECLAN EDGE New Zealand international and Jesper Olsen look-alike. Didn't really have a lot going for him did he?

Next time you feel like criticising any of the current squad just remember some of the junk we have had to put up with in the past, and be grateful for small mercies.
THE HON 'SEC

(March '89)

HOW TO HASSLE YOUR M.P.

All MP's hold 'Constituency Surgeries' at least once a month. These as for constituents to discuss local and national issues face to face with their elected member. Appointments must be booked in advance and you will be lucky to get more than ten minutes in the presence.

THE PIE deputation to see Kenneth Clarke, Con, Rushcliffe, followed the routine outlined above. As expected, we achieved nothing apart from pointing out our objections and asking how he intended to vote. Surprise, surprise, he's voting for the Bill.

One visit is not going to change any MPs mind, but if enough people make the effort then eventually the MP will realise that there is a substantial body of voters against this legislation. Those MP's with small majorities will take notice quicker.

Below you will find a list of our local MPs and how to contact them. Prime candidates would appear to be Michael Knowles and Alan Meale (who has publically stated his opposition). If you are unsure of who is your MP than contact your local library. Good Luck.

CONSTITUENCY	M.P.	MAJ	AGENT'S PHONE NO.
Broxtowe	Jim Lester (Con)	16,651	258940
Rushcliffe	Kenneth Clarke (Con)	20,839	817224
Nottm East	Michael Knowles (Con)	456	484533
Nottm North	Graham Allen (Lab)	1,665	783598
Nottm South	M. Brandon-Bravo (Con)	2,234	484533
Gedling	Andrew Mitchell (Con)	16,539	879234
Sherwood	Andrew Stewart (Con)	4,495	654867
Ashfield	Frank Haynes (Lab)	4,400	0623 554945
Bassetlaw	Joe Ashton (Lab)	5,613	0909 481933
Mansfield	Alan Meale (Lab)	56	0623 660531
Amber Valley	Phillip Oppenheim (Con)	9,500	0773 47283
Bolsover	Dennis Skinner (Lab)	14,120	0246 811244
Erewash	Peter Rost (Con)	9,754	03317 4674
Newark	Richard Alexander (Con)	13,543	0636 703269

The chances of seeing a team outside the 1st Division are going to remain slim, unless a side enjoys a good Littlewoods Cup run. Bristol City netted £122,250 from their game against the Trickies in February, the only money to leave the 'magic circle'. The balance of the money payed by ITV this season (£11 million, Index Linked and compounded) stays with the so-called Glamour Clubs. Ergo a Super League in all but name.

Forget CRIMEWATCH, CHILDWATCH, BLACKWATCH and join the......

SLIMEWATCH

Your opportunity to spot the slimiest people in football. This issue..

EMLYN 'CRAZY HORSE' HUGHES - the only football club Director who tips the opponents - and DEREK 'HORSE CRAZY' THOMPSON.

The sight and sound of Emlyn Hughes braying away on Central TV is giving me the pip. Not content with forcing this buffoon on us they add insult to injury by pairing him with Derek Thompson - the man who put the sick in sycophant - and we are all set for five minutes of assine back-slapping.

The fact that neither of them know what they are talking about is incidental. There are a lot of people on TV who have the same problem, but these two are different, they don't care and are far too busy boosting each others ego to do anything about it.

Highlights this year have included Hughes crediting John Barnwell with developing Dean Yates in to an International central defender, when we all know that Barny was trying to convert Dino in to a full back and Hughes refering to footaball fans as "Speccies". This is the first time have have heard this patronising phrase used, and I hope it's the last.

But it's the mutual back-slapping between Thompson and Hughes that really nauseates, but in the last few weeks has been eased by dispatching Hughes to a boxing gym and the snooker. Of course Emlyn made a tit of himself there, just as he did when filmed training with Chesterfield. I would have thought Paul Hart had enough problems without having the Berk of the Year hanging around. The final nail in the coffin came on Feb 17th, twenty four hours before Hull, of whom Hughes is a Director, played Liverpool in the FA Cup. Guess which team Crazy Mouth picked to win, and it wasn't Hull.

There must be someone at Central who can spot a turkey when they see one, so why are these two idiots still preening themselves on my television? Get 'em off.

TELENEWS

The announcement at the beginning of the season that the formation of a 'Super League' had been averted bought relief to all concerned. However as the season has progressed it has become increasingly obvious that a 'Super League' has emerged, developed by the games chosen to appear on ITV's shallow THE MATCH.

ITV pays £190,000 to broadcast an individual game - £145,000 to the home side, £45,000 to the visitors. Teams featured in Littlewoods Cup games receive £95,000 each. On top of this each 1st Division club receives £200,000 per season, irrespective of TV appearances. To date all the teams ITV originally approached to form the 'Super League' have appeared live; Arsenal (who will recoup £725,000), Villa (£345,000), Everton (£390,000), Liverpool (£480,000), Man U (£770,000), Forest (£485,000), Newcastle (£345,000), Sheff U (£345,000), West Ham (£340,000) and Spurs (£625,000). This is despite the poor season Spurs, West Ham, Villa, Newcastle and Sheff U have enjoyed. The fact that two of these clubs are major candidates for the 'Big Drop' doesn't discourage the TV men from inflicting them upon us.

Norwich, Millwall, Coventry, Derby and Wimbledon have spent the majority of this season in the Top Ten, but can only muster a total of four appearances between them, and only Norwich are scheduled to appear again before the end of the season. The armchair fan still thinks that Arsenal, Liverpool, Man U and Spurs are the best English teams.

Despite viewing figures of between 5.5 and 8.0 million per game the Tv bosses are unhappy with their schedules and negotiations have already begun with the League about next seasons games. The Tv companies want the fixture list primarily designed for their benefit, so that when British Satellite Broadcasting begins in Oct 89 ITV will be able to compete upfront for the available advertising revenue s.

(March '89)

chapter 11

CITY GENT

bradford city

EDITORS NAME: MICK DICKINSON

AGE: 35 (OLD SOD!)   OCCUPATION: TEACHER (OF SORTS)

DO YOU/HAVE YOU EVER SUPPORTED ANY OTHER TEAM?
WHITE HART, DENBY DALE / BRADFORD PARK AVENUE / ACKWORTH FUR & FEATHER FANCIERS F.C.
FC)

MOST MEMORABLE MATCH EVER: 1980 — 1-0 CITY LIVERPOOL (League Cup) /
(1987 WHITE HART 3 PROSPECT 1 (ME REFEREEING!)
MOST MEMORABLE SEASON: ~~1976/77~~ WINTER

ALL TIME FAVOURITE PLAYER: STUART McCALL / BOBBY CAMPBELL / SHIRLEY TEMPLE

WHAT SORT OF CAR DO YOU DRIVE? NISSAN SUNNY 1300 (WHITE - 5 DOORS AND ONE OF
THOSE FURRY THINGIES IN THE BACK)
YOUR FAVOURITE MUSIC: BLUES / ZYDECO / VAN MORRISON / THE SMITHS /
COLOURBLIND JAMES EXPERIENCE
FILMS/TV: 40 MINUTES / ONLY FOOLS AND HORSES /
→ ZEFERELLI'S ROMEO + JULIET (YOU CAN'T BE
FAVOURITE CLOTHES: ~~PINK~~ CHIFFON NEGLIGEE / SUSPENDERS / PURPLE JOCKSTRAP SERIOUS!!?)

POLITICAL LEANINGS: ~~~~ GREEN PARTY / RED PARTY / TEA PARTY

WHAT PLAYER WOULD YOU MOST LIKE TO SEE PLAYING FOR ENGLAND (SCOTLAND/
WALES IF RELEVANT)?
STUART McCALL ⎫ SCOTLAND
JOHN HENDRIE ⎭

GEOFF BOYCOTT - ENGLAND

NORMAN TEBBITT - SIBERIA

COLIN MOYNIHAN - ANTARCTICA (OR BASS ROCK)

TEAM YOU REALLY HATE: CAN'T REMEMBER THE NAME BUT SUNDERLAND
ONCE BEAT 'EM.

FAVOURITE SONG

♪ "ONE MORE WEEK TO GO
BEFORE WE — UNITED" ♪

WELLIES — GAS MASK — CLARET & AMBER MOLESKIN LEGGINGS

ASSISTANT EDITORS NAME: John Dewhirst (Initiator and former Editor of the magazine)

AGE: 26   OCCUPATION: CHARTERED ACCOUNTANT

DO YOU/HAVE YOU EVER SUPPORTED ANY OTHER TEAM?
No but I have always disliked Leeds United

MOST MEMORABLE MATCH EVER: My Wedding

MOST MEMORABLE SEASON: 1910/1911 (when Bradford City won the FA Cup)

ALL TIME FAVOURITE PLAYER: Frank Shufflebottom (BCFC 1946-48)

WHAT SORT OF CAR DO YOU DRIVE?   Lada Sports Coupee with rear spoiler and speed stripes

YOUR FAVOURITE MUSIC: Whatever Sharon plays in her Skoda

FILMS/TV: Brookside; The Unbearable Lightness of Being; Apocalypse Now;

FAVOURITE CLOTHES: Anything that I can cycle in (preferably with chamois insert)

POLITICAL LEANINGS: The Socialist Unity Party of East Germany

WHAT PLAYER WOULD YOU MOST LIKE TO SEE PLAYING FOR ENGLAND (~~SCOTLAND/
WALES IF RELEVANT~~)? Billy the Fish

FAVOURITE SPORT   CYCLING (Oxford Cycling Blue)

SALES MANAGER
~~EDITORS NAME:~~   JOHN WATMOUGH

AGE: 35   OCCUPATION: LIBRARIAN

DO YOU/HAVE YOU EVER SUPPORTED ANY OTHER TEAM? No!

MOST MEMORABLE MATCH EVER: CITY V EVERTON 14-12-89

MOST MEMORABLE SEASON: 1987 ~ 88

ALL TIME FAVOURITE PLAYER: BRUCE BANNISTER

WHAT SORT OF CAR DO YOU DRIVE? FORD ESCORT

YOUR FAVOURITE MUSIC: ANYTHING REALLY, EXCEPT FOLK MUSIC.

FILMS/TV: HORROR FILMS. / NEWS, DOCUMENTARIES, FOOTBALL

FAVOURITE CLOTHES: CASUAL

POLITICAL LEANINGS: TO THE RIGHT

WHAT PLAYER WOULD YOU MOST LIKE TO SEE PLAYING FOR ENGLAND (SCOTLAND/
WALES IF RELEVANT)? —

THE
CITY GENT

The Voice of Bantam Progressivism

The first issue of CITY GENT appeared on the Valley Parade terraces in late October 1984; on its cover a less than flattering 1967 cartoon of chairman Stafford Heginbotham.

The original motivation was due to a feeling of dissatisfaction with the standard of the Bradford City match day programme and by the fact that, newspapers apart, there was no medium for news, views and information between the club and its supporters.

The concept of a supporters' magazine based around the (independent) City Travel Club '73 (Bfd) had been discussed on a casual basis but it was City's challenge at the top of Division 3 that finally prompted pens to paper and drafts to print.

Despite being a very primitive production CITY GENT 1 was well received and by CITY GENT 6 (in April 1985) the print run had increased from 350 to 1500 - a level that reputedly outsold the matchday programme. The club's reaction to CITY GENT was that of surprise at its popularity and although official apprehension was voiced, it is to the credit of the directors and management that they were prepared to co-operate. Officials and players were the subject of interviews on a regular basis that allowed 'current affairs' to be discussed and points of view exchanged.

The basic format of the magazine was established with space also devoted to supporters' information, travel and beer guides, and readers submitting articles about Bradford City. CITY GENT was able to provide a link with the parent club for exiled supporters and this is a function of the magazine that we have always tried to encourage. Thus CITY GENT developed its own momentum and in many ways the baby turned into a monster that required an ever-increasing time commitment!

Until early 1986 CITY GENT was one of a very small number of independent magazines, but the emergence of national publications such as WHEN SATURDAY COMES brought us in touch with supporters of other clubs and helped to establish a new national readership. Over the last three seasons therefore the nature of CITY GENT has changed in some ways. From being produced originally on a monthly basis, the magazine is now once every ten weeks although larger in size (quite often 80 pages). This, combined with a policy to include as wide a range of subject matter as possible, has led CITY GENT to become more of a 'review' - although with a distinctly Bradford flavour (as epitomised by the infamous curry guides).

CITY GENT receives contributions from many sources and this has allowed a wide variety of topics to be featured. Apart from comments on the current state of the club, articles are included that deal with soccer in a national and international perspective; hopefully what we have chosen to be included in this book will give some indication of what is to be found in CITY GENT.

Since the disaster of 1985 a new club has emerged at Valley Parade and through a newly established supporters' club many of the things for which CITY GENT petitioned have been won. For example there is regular dialogue between the club and its supporters at weekly social evenings; supporters have been allowed a role in the writing of the matchday programme; the club plays in its traditional strip of claret and amber stripes and above all, the club plays at its traditional home, Valley Parade.

This era of 'glasnost' and 'perestroika' has been quite unprecedented in Bradford footballing history and accordingly, there is genuine enthusiasm for the future. 'Bantam Progressivism' was the term coined by CITY GENT to describe the rise from 14th in Division Four in 1981 to 4th in Division Two in 1988. If progress has been slow it has nevertheless been against all the

The Independent Supporters Magazine   Dedicated to the glories of Bradford City
Voted Best Magazine in the City Limits/Football Supporters Association
Alternative Football Press Awards 1988

odds; rather than allow the media to associate Bradford with disaster, CITY GENT has tried to reflect the genuine optimism and spirit that exists in the city.

The example of a football club overcoming adversity is relevant in a city that has been badly hit by recession. That a football club might inject confidence into an area and assist its recovery is a phenomenon ignored by the prophets of doom who forecast the death of the game after the events of May 1985. Unashamedly CITY GENT has tried to draw attention to what has happened at Valley Parade and encourage a favourable image of both the football club and Bradford itself.

To date there have been 23 issues of City Gent amounting to over 45,000 copies in total. In addition we we published the first beer and tourist guide to League football (Division Two 1986/87), special tributes to Lokomotive Leipzig and Super Leeds, a compilation of articles from our first six issues and we have also reprinted a rare 1927 history of Bradford City to make it accessible to supporters. Our most recent projects have been the launch of the first alternative football comic, BERNARD OF THE BANTAMS (of which there have been 3 issues to date) and a compilation of newspaper reports from City's 1911 F.A. Cup winning season.

The example of Bradford may be unique but we believe that our experience demonstrates what is possible when supporters are prepared to take the initiative and recapture the game. Long Live Bantam Progressivism!

WINNING but LOSING: 20 YEARS ON
Contemplating the Big Time with Bradford City

Some weird things have been happening to Bradford City recently. I must admit it takes a bit of getting used to. The club I've supported for most of my life has usually been struggling in the middle of the Fourth Division, occasionally climbing into the Third only to plummet back the following season. It made for awful football, but it was cosy and safe and had all the virtues of an elite. You knew everyone in your part of the ground and if you missed a game it was commented upon. After a particularly stirring performance you looked in vain for coverage in the Sunday papers, and cherished the occasional mention you managed to find. Interviews with players were unknown away from the Telegraph and Argus, and when things occasionally went right for the team you had the impression of taking on the world.

Recent successes have changed things at Valley Parade dramatically. For a start the crowds have come back in their thousands. This is a good thing for the club, of course, but not so good for the supporter. Every now and then I see a face from the old days on the kop, a face full of bewilderment and resignation as its owner is pushed and jostled in the attempt to get a clear view of the game. A good view from the kop is now almost impossible. I rarely get to see both goals, and at times the crush is overpowering. The aisles are always cluttered and a trip to the toilet and back can take half an hour. This new interest in the club is obviously a good thing, and should ensure the survival of football in Bradford for many years to come. But in gaining a successful team, supporters of long standing have lost something almost intangible, something difficult to define but infinitely real.

Following Bradford City was always a labour of love. That, indeed, was part of the appeal in a warped kind of way. The old paddock in front of the ill-fated stand was where I used to stand. A Saturday spent there was a Saturday well-spent, whatever the result. It was on the paddock that one could enjoy the kind of humour that only comes with a struggling team. Most of the regulars were either the older "faithful" who would winge and groan but would always be there whatever the weather, or else the younger masochistic fanatics who followed the team to Torquay and other footballing far-flung backwaters. At times the football was almost incidental, a kind of backdrop to the Yorkshire humour being enacted all around. I suppose it is easy to feel nostalgia for these deadening times of a few years ago. The nostalgia that I feel (if nostalgia is the right word) has much to do with the knowledge that whatever happened, we supporters were a small band who had the right to hold forth on the City because we were the only ones who went there week in and week out. I well remember being part of the smallest ever crowd at Valley Parade, a mere 1200 to watch a home defeat by bottom-of-the-Fourth Hereford. I still feel proud that I was there, and the fact makes me slightly contemptuous of most of the 13000 'hangers-on' that watch City these days.

A thing which is difficult to come to terms with is the large-scale media coverage that City now enjoy. Time was when one would search in vain through the Sunday papers for anything more than a five-line mention of a City game. The occasional giant-killing acts (such as the memorable defeat of Liverpool in 1980) brought articles worth saving if only for their novelty value. They would be described as 'plucky' or 'little', and such terms would create a feeling of "us and them" which increased the fanaticism of the supporters. Now the reverse is true. City games are often the main features in the northern editions of the Sunday papers, and the players are frequently the subject of tabloid speculation and gossip. Such coverage has changed things for the supporters in subtle ways. No longer are the feats of the team private property for the few to savour. City have 'gone public'; even armchair supporters have heard of McCall and Hendrie, and the sight of City shirts amongst the crowd in Israel for the England game reinforces the absurd impression I have that the club has somehow been taken away from its fans.

It is an absurd impression, of course. All clubs have to be forward looking, and City could not have gone on living at the foot of the Fourth Division. I am as pleased as anyone that they have achieved Second Division success. The ground, similarly, is now something to be proud of. The old Valley Parade was typically 'Ripping Yarns' with its leaky old stand and its weed-strewn kop. Until well into the seventies there was an advert for Jayne Mansfield appearing at Batley Variety Club. She had been dead several years! There was only one toilet on the paddock, and the tea kiosks had seen the best part of forty years service. Now everything is brand new. There is little doubt that the improved facilities have been responsible for the massive inrease in crowds.

The success of Bradford City has come at a time when Bradford as a city is 'bouncing back' from unemployment and recession. It has given the area something to be proud of at a time when the north generally is on the floor. But I am left wondering where all the razzamatazz will end. I keep looking at clubs like Burnley and Bolton Wanderers. Where did all their fans go when the going got tough? Back to successful clubs like Manchester United and (dare I say it?) Bradford City. I suppose that at the end of the day I'm suspicious and cynical as many other City fans of long standing. Time will tell whether the success will continue, whether the crowd figures will continue to rise, whether Valley Parade will continue to be developed. The fact remains, however, that Bradford City will never be the same. City fans like me will have to get used to their club appearing in the national papers and on television. They'll have to get used to queueing to get in the ground forty minutes before the game, and they'll have to get used to playing a proportionally minor part in the fortunes of their club. For at the end of the day, the club has been taken from its fans. It's nobody's fault, but I can't help thinking that it was a more enjoyable experience back in the Fourth. Or is that the kind of sentimentality that was responsible for the demise of that other Bradford Club, Park Avenue?

Mick Dickinson

Sports Stadia - Civic Assets or Luxury Items?

Valley Parade celebrated its centenary as a sporting arena in 1986 although it was only in 1908 that the ground was transformed from a field with rudimentary facilities to a stadium capable of accommodating over 40,000. The promoters had been motivated by the interest of local folk in soccer and, in particular, Bradford's new First division representatives.

The noble edifices that served Edwardian football, like the dark satanic mills on the surrounding hillsides, soon became dated but there was neither the ability nor foresight to bring Bradford into a modern era. The relegation of City and Park Avenue from the First Division of the 1920's, and their miserable decline into the 1970's was really no different to Bradford's industrial failings - with the same succeeding generations of half-rate businessmen presiding over the decay and neglect of both industrial mills and football stadia.

City had been formed from the Manningham Rugby League Club in 1903 and enthusiasm for soccer convinced another rugby club, Bradford FC, to change codes four years after its old rivals. The Park Avenue stadium had been established by public subscription in 1880 and in 1907, under the supervision of Archibald Leitc, it was transformed into an impressive complex to cater for Football League membership as well as a venue for county cricket.

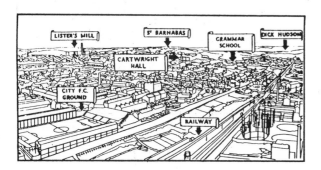

Avenue were thrown out of the League in 1970 and in 1973 acute financial problems forced them to vacate their traditional home before going into liquidation a year later. When the gates were finally closed on the football side, the city arguably lost its finest soccer stadium: in 1980, after celebrated indecision as to the stadium's future, it was demolished. The loss of the grandstand threatened the future of cricket in the city too and by 1986 Bradford Cricket Club were also forced to vacate Park Avenue.

Yet if Park Avenue and Valley Parade were in stages of terminal disrepair by the early 1980's there was at least some hope that the city's third major stadium might enjoy modernisation. Odsal Stadium began as the brainwave of Bradford's Director of Cleansing, Mr Call, as controlled tipping of rubbish began in 1923 to support a new urban roadway. The bankings formed were estimated to be capable of holding 150,000 people. The stadium was opened in 1934 with minimal facilities and twenty years later an attendance of 102,569 was recorded at Odsal for the 1954 Rugby League Challenge Cup Final replay (a further 20,000 were believed to have scaled the walls!). It had always been a pipe dream that Odsal might become the Wembley of the North and the dream appeared to have been given credence when Bradford

Council took over the running of Odsal from Bradford Northern RLFC when it was agreed that the 1985 World Speedway Championships would be held at the stadium.

Development got underway with the building of new terracing on the shale banks and the demolition of a stand, but a shift of politics and a lack of cash to continue meant that the scheme was abandoned afyter only £3.5m had been spent. The Odsal debate coincided ironically with the aftermath of the Valley Parade disaster. Would new funds be available to develop Odsal? Would Valley Parade be abandoned? Would Park Avenue be restored?

Other than the construction of segregation barriers for City's 'home' games between October 1985 and December 1986, Odsal has remained 'unfinished'. Both soccer and rugby league supporters have been unanimous in condemning the facilities that they have been provided. It was suggested that City might be persuaded by the council to share Odsal on a permanent basis but where sports followers had apathetically allowed Park Avenue to be demolished, or Odsal re-developed without adequate consultation, supporters' organisations were active in campaigning for the redevelopment of Valley Parade. The local newspaper reflected the sentiment of supporters who successfully petitioned for a return to Valley Parade. What finally clinched the matter was the availability of funds from the abolition of the West Yorkshire Metropolitan County Council. Without a doubt, the mobilisation of supporters' feelings made a return to the Valley inevitable as they became a vociferous lobby.

Admittedly the supporters' case was strengthened by the special nature of the circumstances, but had they remained silent it was not unlikely that Valley Parade would have been abandoned. With City now settled at Valley Parade there has been talk of the council cutting its losses and abandoning Odsal. Bradford Northern might have to share with City and stock car and speedway racing at Odsal would be lost altogether. Northern are presently surviving on a financial shoestring and have little muscle to flex. Park Avenue meanwhile remains semi-derelict and at one time the council even suggested that it could be used as a campsite to solve the city's gypsy 'problem'. Was it not for the concerted efforts of a small band of cricket followers, the thought of Yorkshire CCC re-estblishing a base at Avenue might have been forgotten. The position now is that pledges of commercial sponsorship have been received and there have even been suggestions that assisatance could come from the council to restore the stadium. In the last 18 months a private developer has built a Speedball cricket centre on part of the old football pitch.

A lack of political commitment to professional sports facilities in Bradford has been a feature of the city's council since the sordid Park Avenue affair began in 1973. As with other authorities the last decade has been a time of financial restraint as public spending restrictions have coincided with growing social problems. Central government is seemingly unwilling to offer funds for the benefit of sport and so any future developments will depend either on public subscription or private enterprise. Should monies not be forthcoming in Bradford, first class rugby league, stock cars, speedway amnd cricket will be lost to a district of nearly half a million people. It is a strange state of affairs that professional sport should be effectively categorised as a luxury civic amenity.

Certainly I would argue that the debate over sports stadia in Bradord has highlighted the extent to which people feel alienated from local government. The whole issue - which has focused simply upon a willingness and an ability to provide for the country's premier spectator sports in the city - has demonstrated how our elected representatives are out of touch with thousands of sports lovers. Worse still has been the politicising that threatens to make sport a party political issue in the council chamber. Funds for a football stadium have been evaluated in terms of alternative projects such as the redevelopment of a theatre or sponsorship of ethnic community schemes for example. The way the debate has been conducted has served only to heighten cultural snobbery or racial tension, which are in neither the community's interest nor that of sport itself.

It is a sad fact that if the Valley Parade disaster had not occurred, there would still be a ramshackle football stadium in Bradford with little opportunity for more than modest refurbishment. Unlike the Old Show Ground in Scunthorpe it could not be sold for retail development, or like Craven Cottage for flats, and unlike Watford there was no philanthropic millionaire. Lack of money, as well as a lack of political commitment from local authorities, could see weeds growing at more than the homes of Charlton athletic or Bradford PA. Now, more than ever before, is the time for sports followers to make themselves heard because otherwise we'll be deemed not to exist. Indeed, if we don't make ourselves heard we won't be given opportunity to exist.

John Dewhirst

"Football is the Opera of the People"

In May of last year I was coming home from a Third Division match at Orient when I heard the news from Bradford. Immediately I recalled seeing the litter under the stand. Within minutes of returning home the telephone started ringing and so began a three day marathon of interviews, articles and chat show appearances to talk about football ground design and safety.

No one likes to be wise after the event, but one comment stuck out in my mind. In a very strained, plaintive voice, Stafford Heginbotham said "Football is the opera of the people".

I felt for him. Not because I felt sympathy for him, but because he was just another victim of the pathetic mess which is English football's administration today. It is not all football's fault. Had football been the sport of lords and cabinet ministers Bradford's problems would not have existed. That Bradford should have just one, miserable (though quaint) football stadium is bad enough. That City should not have taken over Park Avenue's plot, rich as it was in potential, was sad. But that an area the size of Bradford should have no major sporting complex - for football, athletics, swimming etc is just plain nonsense.

Every opera ticket sold in this country is subsidised, on average, to the tune of £22.50. Football is not subsidised at all. On the contrary, the government takes out over £200 million a year from tax on pools at a rate of 42.5 per cent. How many cabinet ministers go to the opera? How many go to football?

In early 1983 I was at Valley Parade conducting research for my book The Football Grounds of England and Wales. At one point, having walked right around the terraces I sat down in the main stand to rest, survey the scene and tidy up my notes and sketches. It was at that point that I looked down between my legs and spotted the piles of rubbish lying underneath the stand. One only had to lift a flimsy wooden flap to see the rubbish.

One of the groundstaff told me that it was easier just to sweep the litter under the stand and then clear it all out once in a while. How this was done he didn't say. I reckoned it would have needed a huge vacuum cleaner.

In an ideal world City would never return to Valley Parade. They would move to a new, multi-purpose sporting arena (built at Park Avenue?). They would rent the stadium from the municipal authority or a private company set up amongst local businesses, sports clubs and the council.

In an ideal world the interests of the 17 million who watch football would be as closely guarded as the one million who watch opera. Heginbotham was right. Football is the opera of the people. They just happen to be the wrong people.

Simon Inglis

Simon Inglis is the author of "The Football Grounds of Great Britain" and this article originally appeared in CITY GENT # 11, April 1986.

Valley Parade before the disaster, May 1985.

AFTER THE FIRE - LIFE GOES ON

May 11 1985 is a date that has been scorched into the minds of Bradford folk. Most of them are sick of hearing about it. They're sick of the sentimentality that occurs every anniversary, and most of those who were at Valley Parade prefer to walk away rather than share their memories of that day.

But the fact remains that the fire represented a significant moment in the history of Bradford City Football Club. What happened that day marked the end of one chapter of the club, and the opening of another. Whilst it is of little use dwelling on the horrors of that day, it is worth reminding non-Bradfordians of its impact. I cannot talk in general terms. I was at Valley Parade and I can only speak personally. It would not be exaggerating if I were to say that the fire changed my life dramatically. I was fortunate enough not to be injured. I did not lose any members of my family, but I doubt that the impact of the day will ever really fade. For me the fire represents the end of innocence. That such a happy day of celebration could so cruelly turn to disaster was, for me, a betrayal of trust. I can no longer look forward without a tinge of fear and a large dose of cynicism. More significantly, perhaps, the fire put things into perspective. When Bill Shankley said those words about football being more important than life and death, he didn't know how wrong he could be!

I can remember how immediately after the fire things which had seemed important lost their significance. The whole city united in grief, and for a short time even racism disappeared. Those who make the monkey chants on the kop these days forget how the local Bangladesh community helped the survivors of the fire in little, human ways, by making cups of tea and providing blankets. At the start of the following season the brutishness of the average soccer crowd was missing, at least for the first couple of games.

I can remember, also, how important it was to feel a part of the football club in those days following the fire. So many of the older fans, those who had followed the club through their darkest Division 3 North and Division 4 days, lost their lives that it was important to stand up and be recognised as a supporter in order to make a meaning out of it all. I can remember all those City scarves at the cathedral the day after the fire. All we could do then was affirm our faith in the club.

In many ways, of course, the fire has proved to be the catalyst that has spurred City on to success. The old stand has been replaced, and the old atmosphere has been displaced by strutting confidence. The team is pushing for Division One status, and it is good to be a City fan these days. But there are times when I despair of the human capacity to learn from misfortune. The racist chanting still goes on from time to time. Winning is still apparently more important than life. There's more tension in the air, probably because we're on the brink of something big. It's when I see the memorial in the city centre, or the wreath laid by Man City fans at the ground this season, or think of an old man getting ready, as he'd done countless times before, to go to the match from which he'd never return, that I realise how much the fire changed everything. Things will never be the same.

Mick Dickinson

GIMMER GIBBER: *Coping with Radical Changes*

'Av bin watchin' futball in Bratfud fer more years than yer've 'ad 'ot curries an' ahm no spring chicken tha knaws. Ah've seen some stuff in mi day but fer the likes o' me 'ave nivver seen t'sort o' things that are gooin' on nar at t' Valley Parade. Ah'm fair brassed off. Ther wor a time when tha cud go dahn ter t'Valley an 'ave a reet gud rant. Yer cud winge yer 'art's content. There wor rubbish on t'park an' rubbish off it. Team wor crap an' so wor t'grahnd. But nar ah dun't knaw but ahm cummin' or gooin'.

Ah sumtahms wonder if t'young 'uns know owt abaht meanin' o' tradition. It's all changin' yer see. Tap rooms 'ave got carpits 'stead o' lino, an' yer can't get a decent bit o' black puddin' this side o' Barnsley. Yer gets lads wi' ear-rings an' lasses wi' muscles, an' metric measurements an' mosques. Fowk 'ave got ivverything they bluddy well want, but it's all rubbish if yo' ask me.

Now there's a lad nex' door ter mi (nowt wrong wi' 'im sept 'is pink cardigan) an' 'e's City mad. Anyroad 'e gives us a lift dahn ter t'match an' in t'car 'e's nowt but bluddy smiles! Ah jus' cuddent believe it, smilin' in Bratfud on a Satdi! Ah tried ter tell 'im that 'e wor spoilin' it fer mi, but 'e wuddent lissen. Ivverybody's serr dammed 'appy these days, it's sickenin'. Yer 'ardly ever 'ear "Wakey Wakey City" or "Bloody Rubbish City" or "I'm Never Comin' Again". Then there wor "Get Yer Finger Out" an' "I'm Not Payin' Good Money to Watch This Load o' Crap". By, but wor t'good old days!!

It's nivver bin t'same since Gary Watson left - best pillock we ever 'ad (and in 'is day we 'ad some proper pillocks, not these part-timers yer see occasionally at t'Valley nowadays.) Where 'ave they all gone? Men that could turn the best o' games into a disaster wi'out tryin', like Norman Corner, Alan Jones an' Lammie Robertson. Men that'd bring grown men to tears.

Personally ah blame t'Chairman fer ruinin' mi Satdis. Look what 'e's done fer us - 5 figure gates an' near capacity crowds, but spirit's gone somehow. There's just nowt ter moan abaht. Yer even get 'alf price pies after 'alf-time in t'kop. No more gettin' wet when yer sat in t'stand. No more fightin' ter get t'one bog in t'grahnd. No more 'oofin' an' 'opin'. No more George Mulhall an' 'is route one balls. It's a bluddy disgrace. I'm a Bratfordian born an' bred an' I've a bluddy right ter be able ter spend mi Satdis moanin'. From where ahm sittin' t'future dun't look so grand, me gooin' 'ome actually lookin' forrard ter t'next match. If it goes on like this, ah might 'ave ter get over ter t'Shay, Come back Gary Watson, all is forgiven!!!

by Mick Dickinson

Reproduced from CITY GENT # 19, December 1987

DARREN AND THE DUCHESS GO TO THE GAME

"He's welcome to her!" said Darren Slingsby upon hearing that his ex - piece had decided to try her luck with royalty - "He doesn't know what he's on for!".

Darren met Sarah while in Whitby for the pre-season friendly. "We shared chips as we sat looking out to sea. I was so impressed by her. She'd heard all about City and when she said she fancied Bobby Campbell I knew I was in with a chance of something."

Darren plucked up his courage and asked her for a date - Halifax Town, West Riding Cup away. "She seemed really keen to come along when I told her about our trendy claret and amber striped shirts."

The evening seemed to go well. "Yeah, 5-2, a great result that night. She wasn't too excited by it all but it wasn't a League game and Halifax hadn't produced much of a programme afterall. I figured that she'd let herself go at a more appropriate moment."

A more appropriate moment came when City triumphed 3-1 over Manchester United at Leeds Road. "She didn't bat a bloody eyelid - I couldn't believe it!" recalls Darren. "We'd just stuffed Man Utd - what more could she want?"

Perhaps the pre-match pie and peas hadn't gone down too well but it was still pre-season: "Yeah I figured that she was playing hard to get. You know, she wanted to see action in a proper League game."

"We didn't see much of each other for a fortnight because I was busy getting a couple of new grounds in. I told her that I wasn't too keen on those trendy Bradford discos. Too bloody expensive I told her. I wasn't dressing up like some puff when I could have a peaceful drink in Ivegate. I invited her to Carlisle but she said something about a Cambridge cocktail party. I asked her to get me a programme and told her not to go on that narrow terrace behind the goal."

Darren thought that everything was going just fine between the two of them until one evening Sarah made a passing comment about his interest in programmes. "Women! She picked up a 1964 City programme (Barrow home I think) and threw it in the bin saying that I shouldn't fill my drawers with junk and such like. Naturally I retrieved it and explained that it was worth £2."

Sarah's appreciation of antiquities didn't extend to enamel badges either and Darren tells of how she'd bend back the pins and prod him with them. "Can't understand what she was after" he admits, "she'd lie back looking soppy and there I was patiently telling her about the Rod Johnson goal back in the 1977 Bolton friendly."

Real ale didn't strike a cord with Sarah and Darren was extremely embarrassed that time she asked for a Gin & Tonic in the Boy and Barrel on Westgate: "Nowt up with the Tetleys tonight love, I told her."

The final break came at the Hull game in September. "She had the audacity to suggest that I of all people was obsessed with football" mused Darren. "It would have all been so very different if we'd played at Valley Parade. I guess that she just didn't like catching the bus across to Huddersfield and Leeds for home games."

John Dewhirst
(March 1986)

BRADFORD, bottom of the Fourth Division, were yesterday given a double boost in their struggle for survival.

Bradford City, riding high in the Third Division, are considering issuing a joint season ticket for the rest of the season while former Park Avenue chairman Mr. Leonard Evans said he would buy 500 £1 shares of the club at last night's annual shareholders' meeting.

The club chairman, Mr. Herbert Metcalfe, appealed to supporters to take up shares after revealing the club was £96,776 in the red.

He described the offer of help from Bradford City chairman Mr. Stafford Heginbotham, who offered a few weeks ago to loan three players. The two clubs, he said, were considering issuing a joint season ticket for the rest of the campaign, and for the future——probably at a slightly reduced price.

Mr. Metcalfe claimed the club's position was not as grim as it appeared, and he looked forward to the side playing in the First Division and in Europe.

Mr. Metcalfe stressed, however, that it depended on public support and told of need for the public to take up shares in the club.

"They are without value at the present time, but as our club starts climbing, they will become worth something because of their scarcity value," said Mr. Metcalfe. He listed the club's debts up to a week ago as £99,776 with funds available put at £4,356.

Of the intangible assets, he claimed the club had a third team, which was a potential source of wealth, sufficient to pay off all the liabilities.

Mr. Metcalfe said the club's liabilities would be cut to £67,459 by a proposal of the directors and other creditors to transfer their loan capital to a new issue of 38,000 shares.

He warned that if the shares were not taken up, the alternative was for the club to go out, of existence.

ZEN BANTAMISM AND THE PATH TO INNER PEACE

For so it is written, that the disciple shall meditate the paths of Bantam Progressivism at the feet of the Guru, prior to all away fixutes. Only at the feet of sri Doc Finch can the novice find the inner peace of the sublime supporter.

For so it is written, that one-ness is everywhere City go. The Master chanted softly to himself chants of meditation at the chosen holy place, beside the lockers in the Interchange, where his devout peace in Bantamism affected even the most unruly souls, far though they were from Inner Peace.

For so it is written, that the coach to Oakwell leaves at 1.30 pm precisely, thus allowing plenty of time for the communion with the Buddha before the Master and I, the humble student of Bantam Progressivism, ate our sandwiches on the journey.

For so it is written, that the disciple shall record the sayings of sri Doc Finch, in order to reveal the workings of that great sublimeness.

"It is a cold day, Master", I said.
"Speak not of the cold, Clodhopper. There shall be no cold when all art joined in the unity of the Bantam in the dress of Damart".
"Shall we take home the three points reward to advance us along the way to Bantam Perfection, Master?", I asked.
"Be calm, Clodhopper. Three years hence the sign of the goose will fly over Valley Parade, as it was seen to do three years back. The points are ours."
"Did not that goal count against us, Master?"
"In Faith is the only way to self-enlightenment."
"Master, was that not the third strike against us, and rather a good goal at that ?"
"Dolan, Dolan, Hare, Hare, we are the champions".
"Master, should we not take comfort? Is it not written that the paths of perfection are many?"
"That's as may be, lad, but losing three-nil to bloody Barnsley is not one of them."
Thus spake the Master, sri Doc Finch. Hoping that this finds you in the best of health and Bantam Awareness.

Reproducd from CITY GENT #19,
December 1987
by Tim Cooke

OVER THE WALL

With the 750th anniversary of Berlin in 1987 and the 40th anniversary of the foundation of the GDR in 1949, attention has focused upon the Berlin Wall and the division of Germany. For Germans on both sides, life has gone on and the passion for football has contiunued uninterrupted. Do we need reminding of the mighty Federal Republic World Cup fighting machine and the general efficiency of West German football clubs? Football remains the most popular participation sport in both East and West, but it has always struck me as interesting that the German Democratic Republic has been unable to achieve the sort of prominence in international soccer that its athletes have achieved in the Olympics.

We know a lot about their shot-putters and little about their ball-players. True, Scotland would admit to having found the GDR difficult opponents in representative fixtures, but the GDR is not the same force as West Germany by any means. Therefore I do not find it so ridiculous to ask what effect the building of the Berlin Wall in 1961 had on football in East Germany. Do the means of socialist construction preclude the notion of 'football uber alles'?

There are two stories about the Berlin Wall. The one adopted by revanchist Western imperialists is that the wall was constructed to stop people leaving the GDR and thereby safeguard the economy. Others of a more liberal bent have argued that the Anti-Fascist Barrier was erected to pre-empt a NATO military attack on the East and thereby safeguard the peace of Europe. As they say in the GDR, **"you choose your friend and not your brother"**. What cannot be denied is that the erection of the Berlin Wall gave the GDR a sense of permanence. Prior to August 1961, if you wanted to leave East Germany you did so via Berlin. After the Wall you had to live with your brother.

Apart from keeping the workers happy and content with their brothers' company, the leaders of the ruling Socialist Unity Party have realised that sport is a means by which the GDR can obtain a healthy working and fighting force. Since the inception of the GDR, sport has been mobilised in the service of the state and considerable investment devoted to the creation of a sporting elite.Special schools have been formed with the sole aim of improving performance and breeding winners. A separate GDR team competed in the Olympics for the first time in 1968 yet 20 years later the GDR was second only to the USSR in the medals table.

The GDR'S record at the Olymics is astonishing. And yet it is surprising that the sports facilities available to the general public are neither more plentiful nor of a better standard than those in many western countries. Leisure centres are not as widespread and swimming pools not widely accessible. The range of goods in East German sports shops is not impressive: good running shoes or cycling equipment are conspicuous by their absence. To get your equipment you have to be members of selected clubs; the state does ensure that the top sportsmen and women get what they require. Adidas equip the GDR national teams free of charge as TV offers them excellent advertising opportunities. It might seem a contradiction that the GDR allows such capitalist sponsorship, but as in many of other cases the end is believed to justify the means; the quality of the equipment is better than anything home-produced and the GDR can also save its foreign currency reserves.

In his spare time therefore, the East German is more likely to be playing football than engaging in some of the sports for which his country is famous. Why is it then that the GDR has been unable to exploit the genuine enthusiasm for football and achieve international success? There is by no means a dearth of talent in the East German Oberliga and it is ironic that the domestic league is seemingly unable to maximise the potential. Perhaps a closer look at the organistion of domestic fotball in the GDR will help provide an explanation.

The league is split into the Oberliga (DIvision One), the Liga (Division Two) and Bezirksliga (Regional Third Division). Fourteen teams contest the premier division which is made up of eight football clubs, four works teams and two others supported by state organisations. Of these fourteen probably the most famous are Dynamo Dresden, Dynamo Berlin (both army teams), Carl Zeiss Jena (works team), Magdeburg and 1FC Lokomotive Leipzig (the latter being so named because Leipzig reputedly has the largest railway terminal in Europe).

Each season the bottom two clubs are relegated to the second division, which is itself divided into two groups of eighteen teams (the winners of each gain promotion). From here on the organisation of the league differs from anything we are used to in Great Britain. None of the domestic clubs is responsible for its own finance: the cost of stadia, general expenses and such like are met by the state. Furthermore no income is available from TV recordings or advertising.

All footballers in East Germany are amateurs 'employed' by state-owned industries which allow them to train full-time. A transfer system exists, but clubs must obtain the approval of the Deutscher Fussball Verband (DFV); as a rule talented players are delegated from the lesser teams to the 'centres of excellence', such that the strength of the bigger clubs is maintained. Foreigners are only allowed to be promoted to play up to the second division; teams with foreign players are not allowed to be promoted to the Oberliga.

Usually those foreigners are students or soldiers of the Soviet Army. If the footballing prodigy wants to improve his skills in the West, the unofficial advice is for him to introduce pole-faulting into his training routine. The East German footballer is not designed for export and because the GDR requires its sportsmen and women to be

LOKOMOTIVE LEIPZIG:
the thinking fan's railway workers

suitable ambassadors, consideration for international selection requires a certain amount of making the right noises in the right places and not necessarily making private thoughts public. An East German friend of the writer refers to this as **"farting for the benefit of those who appreciate the smell"**. Presumably the defection of Frank Lippmann from the GDR (which came shortly after he had turned out for Dynamo Dresden in a Cup Winners tie at Bayer Uerdingen in 1986) was partly due to the fact that he was sick of beans. His decision is almost irreversible and unlike Poles, Hungarians or Czechs, no East German exile is 'eligible' to play for his country.

Undoubtedly this is a contributory factor in weakening the national side. Furthermore, because they only meet foreign players in European competitions, the men of the Oberliga must establish their own standards. The situation is almost akin to the 'Tykes only' policy of Yorkshire CCC where dogma has possibly been at the expense of success. Thus while the import of foreign players has helped Italian, Spanish, West German and English clubs to lift European trophies, the record of GDR teams is poor. In 1987 Lokomotive Leipzig were defeated by Ajax in the Cup Winners Cup Final after creditable performances against Sion of Switzerland and Bordeaux of France. Prior to that the only honours for East German football were an Olympic gold medal in 1976, FC Magdeburg winning the Cup Winners Cup in 1974 and Carl Zeiss Jena being runners-up in the same competition in 1981.

Another criticism which might explain the relative weakness of GDR teams is that there have been allegations of games and results being manipulated by dubious refereeing decisions. If true, then competitive standards in the Oberliga are threatened - a fact suggested by Dynamo Berlin's championship monoloply since 1979. Gates tend to average 10,000 but crowds have fallen in recent years and perhaps cynicism has been a cause. It might also explain the passion with

which the East Germans follow Bundesliga results and identify with the success of the West German national side. Arguably football has been a major element in maintaining the idea of a single Germany. This in itself is quite fascinating and anyone who witnessed the celebrations in East Berlin that followed Rummenigge's goal in the 1986 World Cup Final will confirm it. TV coverage of the Bundesliga is very popular and East Germans readily tune into western TV for football broadcasts.

The authorities have tried to discourage interest in western football as they fear the spread of 'football hooliganism' into the GDR. For this reason the state TV network discontinued its broadcast of the Heysel tragedy, although people were able totransfer to western broadcasts. Violence at matches is quite widespread and the writer's experiences do not suggest that segregation or policing tactics have been highly developed in the GDR. In order to deter any trouble there tends to be a large police presence at sporting events and a strict alcohol ban has been enforced. The state sponsored FDJ 'Youth Pioneers' movement has even attempted to co-ordinate the discipline and organisation of away travel. It should be added that Leipzig supporters were allowed to travel to Greece for the ECWC Final, which was quite a concession from a state that limits freedom to travel abroad.

It seems almost inevitable that the GDR will raise its stature as a major footballing nation and East Germany are among the favourites to qualify for the 1990 World Cup finals. However a relaxation of the dogma and paranoia that pervades many GDR institutions, including the DFV, must surely be a prerequisite for future success. The citizens of the GDR might well see the fruits of glasnost in terms of football trophies and the opportunity to attend more games in the west.

UND NUN VOLL DAMPF

This article also appeared in The Absolute Game, Issue 4, September 1987.

Fans campaign made

After the fire disaster of May 1985 Bradford City faced a future of great uncertainty and anxiety. At first there was much debate as to whether the club would have a future at all as the level of potential compensation claims was discussed. Coming only 2 years after the club had been rescued from liquidation, there were minimal financial resources despite the successful Third Division Championship season being taken into account.

Ultimately the club's insurance policies proved adequate and the Bradford Disaster Appeal also provided relief for those injured or bereaved by the fire. Nevertheless the club had no resources with which to rebuild Valley Parade and the summer of 1985 was spent considering the options available. The possibility of returning to Valley Parade depended upon public funds being made available; despite early promises it was not until spring 1986 that the club received assurances that funds would be provided.

City finally returned to Valley Parade in December 1986 after playing their 'home' games at the grounds of Huddersfield Town, Leeds Utd and Bradford Northern. In their first season back in Division Two, 1985/86, the club achieved a creditable 13th position. The strain of their nomadic existence however had an adverse effect on form and 1986/87 was spent fighting the spectre of relegation. Understandably supporters were frustrated and the following excerpts from CITY GENT reflect the mood at the time.

sure the club returned home

No-one will ever know just how good a season City would have had if they had a regular home base. Obviously the strain is telling among players and supporters alike as every match means a trip out of Bradford. This strain might be lessened had some firm plans been made for the redevelopmentof Valley Parade. So far the only succour fans can draw is from vague promises of super stadia and massive cash injections.

Perhaps my memory is failing, but I seem to remember that after the fire Mrs Thatcher promised to help rebuild the ground and I had been under the mistaken impression that work would start on the ground after the Remembrance Service. Now 6 months later with Huddersfield and Leeds only agreeing to stage three more matches each for City the need to rebuild Valley Parade is all the more urgent. Rumour has it that the Council wants to see City at Odsal permanently. If they do, they must be starting to feel lonely. Trevor Cherry, the players and fans alike have made it clear they want to return home. I'm sure that the Council would not go against our wishes and will start to turn promises into reality. I hope that the Council is not biding its time in order to force City's hand up to Odsal.

CITY GENT #9, Nov 1985

Another ingredient in the delay over re-building Valley Parade was protracted lobbying by the people who lived in close vicinity to the ground. The fact that these people were predominantly Asian resulted in football and racial issues becoming confused in the council chamber.

STRAIGHT FROM THE BANTAM'S BEAK

Residents around Valley Parade have recently expressed their wishes that City's future home will be elsewhere. One cannot help but wonder whether their views are based on

anything other than a partly understandable desire to avoid the hassle of living near a football ground. Someone is going to have to put up with the proximity of a League stadium, wherever City are to play. It hardly sees fair to add to the problems of the club at a time like this. Perhaps football stadia should not be built in residential areas but as Bradfordians we should make the most of our city and not long for some planners' dream town. Football clubs -like people- are rarely free to choose the location in which they would most like to base themselves.

I would dearly like to see a roof over the Kop at a rebuilt Valley Parade. A development such as this would be a boon to the genuine fan who has been soaked innumerable times in the noble cause of BCFC. But the money for such a venture must not come from the Bradford Disaster Fund. The victims of 11th May will no doubt be adequately provided for (as adequately as moneycanever compensate suffering) and the removal of £300,000 from the fund would probably not appreciably reduce that provision. It is even fair to say that many of the victims themselves would not object to money being used to create a practical memorial to those who died. We must remember, however, the basis on which the money was collected and seek to honour the probable wishes of those who gave it.

People from all walks of life gave to the Fund in the belief that they were directly helping victims of the fire. Should the Trustees authorise its use for construction purposes they would render many good people guilty of collecting money under false pretences. For this reason rebuilding at Valley Parade must be financed from other sources. Several of these have been less than forthcoming and we should concentrate all our efforts on attempting to slacken the right purse-strings...

CITY GENT #9, Nov 1985

HOMEWARD BOUND?

BACK TO THE VALLEY WITH THE CITY GENT

We have received a large number of letters on the subject of City's future home ground and predictably not one spoke in favour of Odsal-with everyone wanting a return to the Valley. The letters in the Telegraph & Argus have repeated this point and it would seem that public opinion has finally persuaded the council of what action to take. However we still wait for work on VP to begin and until that work is started we will not be satisfied.

CITY GENT #10, Feb 1986

Directors wanted move to Park Avenue

WHEN Bradford City's directors were first discussing the club's future after the Valley Parade fire, they favoured a move to Park Avenue.

Chairman Stafford Heginbotham and other members of the board entered into discussions with Bradford Cricket Club with the aim of buying the ground.

But such was the opposition from City supporters who wanted the club to return to Valley Parade that the move was abandoned.

Swayed

Mr. Heginbotham said: "We have always taken full account of the wishes of our supporters and the overwhelming opinion was that we should rebuild Valley Parade. The ratio was over nine to one.

"From an aesthetic point of view, Park Avenue would have been more suitable, but public opinion swayed us."

Mr. Heginbotham said the club was indebted to Bradford Northern and Bradford Metro for allowing City to use Odsal.

"They have made our stay as comfortable as possible and the ground staff have done their best in difficult circumstances," he said.

STRAIGHT FROM THE BANTAM'S BEAK

There is every reason for 1985/86 to end happily. True we haven't won the FA Cup or achieved promotion but once again we have overcome all the odds. It now looks as though City's 2nd Division status is secure and we have the money for a new stadium.

Everyone has emerged stronger after the disaster. For a few there is understandable bitterness but the club and community are stronger for having shared the experience. There is real hope and real pride in the club. In what, we are told, is a make or break season for football why don't newspapers and TV acknowledge this achievement and get the 'hooligans at football matches' story into the proper context?

Despite all the talk of a Super League we have discovered what support of an unfashionable provincial club can offer. We might not have £1m players or lavish facilities but we have real depth of character. The new development will herald a break with the past and a break with the days of Cloud-Cuckoo Land. Dreams are becoming realised and dreams are being made. Ultimate success is the most fitting memorial that we can give to the 56 who perished.

CITY GENT #11, May 1986

COUNTDOWN TO BIG DAY

VALLEY   PARADE

The countdown has begun for what should be a new and exciting phase in the history of Bradford City. It is almost 18 months since a full City side took the field at valley Parade, but it seems like 18 years! Odsal has proven to be all that it was predicted it would be - cold, uncomfortable and alien to the nature of the club. Sad memories will be stirred on December 14th. There'll be tears of recollection and, perhaps, bitterness. But there'll also be pride - for Valley Parade will stand as a symbol of triumph over adversity. It'll be an emotional occasion alright, but one that can't come too soon.

CITY GENT #14, Dec 1986

On the lighter side

FOOTBALL HOOLIGANS

While watering his garden with a hose pipe during the summer, my husband noticed that our neighbour was doing the same with his hose pipe.

They then got into a terrible argument about the merits of various soccer teams and in a sudden fury they both turned their hose pipes on at full blast and directed them at each other.

When my husband came in from the garden looking like a drowned rat he said sadly, "Football discussion isn't as friendly as it used to be, woman."

— Mrs M. S., Bristol.

DIVISION FOUR

SOUTHEND	22	HALIFAX	3
Ling (2)		Galloway, Fleming	
H.T. 0—0		Brown (pen)	

DIVISION 3

rapped in the second.

Two splendid goals by winger John Kelly earned CHELSEA a 2-2 draw at NEWPORT COUNTY.

VALLEY PARADE FAVOURITES

Three former colleagues with Leeds United, Trevor Cherry, Paul Reaney and Terry Yorath, all ended their playing careers with the 'Bantams'. Reaney won three England caps and Cherry 27. Roy McFarland spent the 1981–82 season at Park Avenue before returning to Derby.

Part-time Soccer: Is it the answer?

Bradford City's 37-years-old manager Bob Martin is not alone in his fears for the financial future of professional soccer, but, unlike many of his contemporaries, he refuses to bury his head in the sand.

He and his board have agreed, in principle, to go part-time next season— a possible solution to the problems of the ailing clubs in the lower divisions which has been put forward on numerous occasions, but, until now, has never been tested in practice.

The "Liberty" Shoe.

VALLEY PARADE,
BRADFORD,
APRIL 29th, 1908.

Gentlemen,

On behalf of the players of the Bradford City F.C. I beg to thank you for your generosity in presenting each of us with a pair of your boots in commemoration of our gaining promotion.

Yours sincerely,
GEO. H. ROBINSON.

The Liberty Boot Co.,

Bradford Agents : Crask & Co, 15 & 17. Bank Street ; Edward Hill & Co., 10. Tyrrel-st., Womersleys, 28, Carlisle Road.

Bremner described his team's showing in Saturday's goalless draw with Blackburn as "absolutely atrocious" and added: "People love to knock Leeds United."

'Thanks to the Brighton Programme City Gent can now reveal the full truth concerning Roy McFarland's departure to Derby. Our ex-player-manager was able to sever ties with City so easily because he had in fact spent the 1981/2 season at Park Avenue.

Grimsby, too seem unable to forget Park Avenue. The programme v City seems to suggest amalgamation may be a possibility...

1982: — The start of better things. Promotion from Division Four. The following year saw the club actually go into liquidation, with a new company being formed, and the Third Division taken in 1985. The fire disaster soured the success, but the Park City are again proving to be a power in football.

Beverley kit appeal

BEVERLEY Town are appealing to two League clubs for new strips after thieves stole £400 worth of kit.

Bill Oliver, manager of the club, is writing to Sheffield United and Queen's Park Rangers who wear identical colours to his team.

Can anyone tell us exactly what colours Beverley Town wear or is Bill Oliver just colour blind?

Delving in old programmes can be a rewarding exercise, as the extract opposite shows. How true it proved to be, as Mr Martin led the way in becoming a part-time businessman. And why bury your head in the sand when you can go to America and sit on it all day instead?

QUITE A VARIETY

With the Valley Road ground still out of commission Bradford have been forced to use a variety of 'home' venues which cannot have helped them settle into the higher division where they currently have 12 points from nine games played.

The Middlesbrough programme managed to add to the considerable range of grounds on which City have played lately with this amusing little invention of its own. Where next? Elland Parade?

ONE-LINER: Man. City 6 Leeds 1

Stafford is reported to have offered LIBERTY shoes to the present squad as an incentive for promotion in 1986/87 – but on condition that they beg !

OXO for Goals.

Winning teams train on OXO

OXO makes men shoot straight.

Meanwhile, the Fourth Division leaders, Northampton Town, yesterday unveiled a major scheme to move to a new 17,500-capacity stadium in the town. The £12m project — subject to approval from the local council — includes a 7,500-seater stadium, an international athletics track and provision for a dry ski slope.

Northampton Town's ambitions for a dry ski-slope should make Yeovil Town's efforts pale by comparison.

ONE-LINER:
Stoke 6 Leeds 2

"Wearing a Leeds United shirt should be the greatest thing in the world. It was to me."

sets an example

"Half the lads on the terraces would chop their right arm off to play for Leeds United.

But he gave me a shock the other day when he got the barber to shave the letters LUFC on the top of his head. He's a real fanatic.

SILLY BILLY BREMNER

Brabrooke claimed he was the reincarnated brother of Conan the Barbarian, that he was turning into an elk and had played for Leeds United. A defence psychiatrist said he was mad.

MAKING BRASS FROM FOOTBALL & WOOL

BRADFORD (PARK AVENUE) FC were voted out of the Football League in May 1970 after an ignominious series of four successive applications for re-election. The club that had once graced Division One struggled on until May 1974 as a member of the Northern Premier League before finally proceeding into voluntary liquidation.

It was a particularly sorry end for a once proud club but perhaps the inevitable outcome of a decade of recurring financial crises. The legacy of mismanagement was not only the death of a football club. The demise of the Park Avenue complex meant the loss of a valuable civic asset and the loss of a venue for first class cricket in the city. In short the death of Park Avenue was a betrayal and even as late as 1983 when Bradford City were on the verge of extinction, it was hard to believe that Bradford football had learned the lesson.

At the end of 1972/73 Avenue moved across to Valley Parade and while the rent for Park Avenue had been £336 pa the price of sharing with City became £7,000. That was possibly the final straw that broke the camel's back and certainly it did not endear Avenue fans to support City! Indeed, rather than transfer their allegiance to the traditional rival they attached themselves in the main to the likes of First Division Burnley, either of the Manchester clubs or even Leeds.

The seeds of destruction were sown much earlier. Many would argue that the transfer of Kevin Hector to Derby in June 1966 for £34,000 began the slide into oblivion. The behaviour of chairman Herbert Metcalfe did not inspire the confidence of either the Bradford public or the other League chairmen; it might also be said that it didn't help team morale. In October 1969 for example Metcalfe had told manager Laurie Brown to leave the team selection to him - Brown promptly informed the staff that he was resigning and 19 players stepped in transfer requests in support of him. Eventually social club steward Frank Tomlinson took over.

Stanley Pearson covered Avenue for the T&A between 1966 and 1970 and wrote that the club folded because at no time did it have sufficient strength of character from the boardroom down to the newest apprentice. He recollects that the "couldn't-care-less" attitude prevalent in the dressing room and the lack of spirit in a team that only won 15 matches in their last 3 FL seasons.

The late Dick Williamson (who covered Avenue for the T&A between 1946 and 1966) felt that Avenue's descent from the heights was much a matter of self-inflicted wounds as with Bradford City; "nowhere else in these islands has there been anything remotely approaching a comparable case of two League clubs in the same provincial city or town having, conjointly, been stricken with a decline of such deardful magnitude". It was his opinion that thoroughly ill-advised and irresponsible actions at board-room level in each case contributed to a shocking slump.

Avenue had been in with an outstanding chance of promotion to Division One following their Div Three North Championship success of 1927/28. They sold Walter Millership in a transfer for which the public never forgave them... and faded right out of the promotion running. After the war a succession of ill-advised moves by the Avenue board led, by gradual stages, first to relegation from Div Two and later to the final extinction catastrophe.

Surprisingly the Bradford public stood by Avenue. In 1960/61 20,000 saw them win promotion from Div Four by beating the Champions-elect Peterborough at Park Avenue. In the following season another large crowd had seen Avenue celebrate their new floodlights in a game against the Czech national team, (result 2-3). Throughout the 1960's their average gates were highly respectable when League position was taken into account: 9,147 in 61/62 (D3-11th); 8,350 in 64/65 (D4-7th). A team that won only four Leaguue games in 1967/68 still commanded an average of 3,595 and gates continued to average more than 3,100 up to 1969/70. Even the lowest-ever League crowd of 1,572 (vs Port Vale, in May 1969) would be acceptable by present day Halifax standards!

The men who held power at Park Avenue, like the city fathers, were responsible for the betrayal of the supporter and the loss of a valuable civic asset in the Park Avenue sporting complex. They took the support of the public for granted and presided over a haemorrhage of goodwill. A stadium that held a place in Bradford sporting tradition dating back to 1880 lies abandoned. Is it really surprising that the Bradford football public have been so long cynical and apathetic?

Mike Bishop
(CG#14, Dec1986)

Published in 1988, "A GAME THAT WOULD PAY" by Tony Arnold is a unique economic history of football in Bradford.

Arnold recognises the parallel decline of the textile industry and football and identifies myopic provincialism as the prime constraint to progress. In commenting on the mismanagement of football in Bradford, he points to the rationing of organisational talent and funds that had resulted from the fact that football offered little social cachet to the low-monied gentry. Besides, the Bradford woolman was hardly the model entrepeneur: "local textile manufacturers were very loathe to incorporate and were half-hearted in their responses to local issues and problems not directly connected with their trade".

And if traditional loyalties were a source of support to the identity of football clubs, in Bradford it also proved to be a barrier to progress. Arnold makes an astute observation that in Bradford internal distinctions were more important than the prospect of real success. Although many recognised that Bradford was too small to support two FL clubs, amalgamation had been resisted to the end by supporters adamant to preserve their distinctions. Identities were preserved but at what cost?

The story of success has been oft told but the story of Bradford football is probably more relevant as a representative history of the Football League. Long overdue, Tony Arnold's book is the definitive story of failure.

John Dewhirst
(CG#21, Sept 1988)

CITY GENT DIPSO WATCH

Dr Richard Kleinpfennig wrote to CITY GENT (CG#17, March 1987) to complain about the column space in the magazine devoted to 'Beer and Bantams'. Accordingly, to help the weaker-minded amongst our flock, he was so good as to draw readers' attention to those awful tell-tale signs...

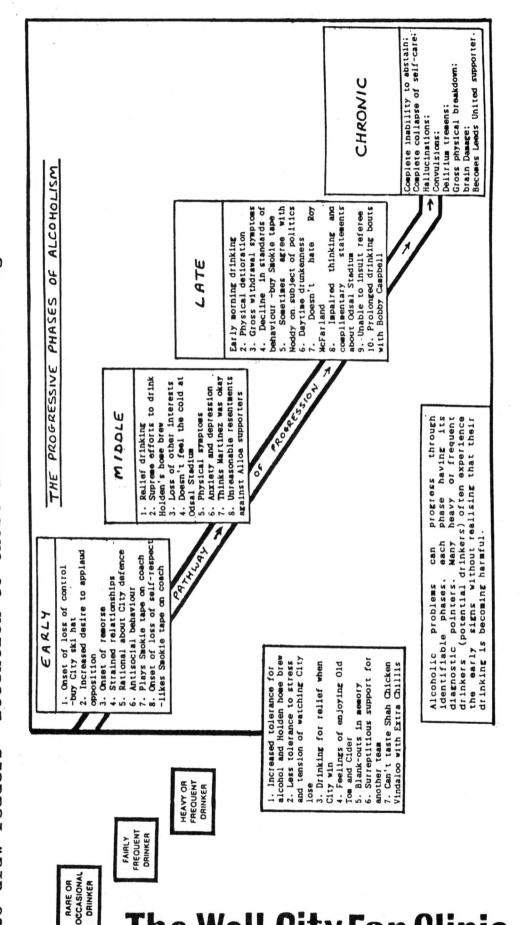

THE PROGRESSIVE PHASES OF ALCOHOLISM

EARLY

1. Onset of loss of control
   -buy City ski hat
2. Increased desire to applaud opposition
3. Onset of remorse
4. Strained relationships
5. Rational about City defence
6. Antisocial behaviour
7. Plays Smokie tape on coach
8. Onset of loss of self-respect
   -likes Smokie tape on coach

MIDDLE

1. Relief drinking
2. Supreme efforts to drink Holden's home brew
3. Loss of other interests
4. Doesn't feel the cold at Odsal Stadium
5. Physical symptoms
6. Anxiety and depression
7. Thinks Martinez was okay
8. Unreasonable resentments against Alloa supporters

LATE

1. Early morning drinking
2. Physical detioration
3. Gross withdrawal symptoms
4. Decline in standards of behaviour -buy Smokie tape
5. Sometimes agree with Noddy on subject of politics
6. Daytime drunkenness
7. Doesn't hate Roy McFarland
8. Impaired thinking and complimentary statements about Odsal Stadium
9. Unable to insult referee
10. Prolonged drinking bouts with Bobby Campbell

CHRONIC

Complete inability to abstain:
Complete collapse of self-care:
Hallucinations:
Convulsions:
Delirium tremens:
Gross physical breakdown:
brain Damage: Becomes Leeds United supporter.

PATHWAY OF PROGRESSION →

RARE OR OCCASIONAL DRINKER

FAIRLY FREQUENT DRINKER

HEAVY OR FREQUENT DRINKER

1. Increased tolerance for alcohol and Holden home brew
2. Less tolerance to stress and tension of watching City lose
3. Drinking for relief when City win
4. Feelings of enjoying Old Tom and Cider
5. Blank-outs in memory
6. Surreptitious support for another team
7. Can't taste Shah Chicken Vindaloo with Extra Chillis

Alcoholic problems can progress through identifiable phases. each phase having its diagnostic pointers. Many heavy or frequent drinkers (potential drinkers) often experience the early signs without realising that their drinking is becoming harmful.

The Well City Fan Clinic

P45s and Lawyers

"The Bantams"

The present decade has been an uneasy one for managers of Bradford City. Ever since George Mulhall walked out on the club in preference for Bolton in 1981, successive managers have left in controversial circumstances.

It is fair to say that Mulhall's departure was not the body blow that it could have been. He had been a fairly successful manager, and had laid the foundations for future triumphs, but when he left, City were in the lower reaches of Division Four. Mulhall was much lampooned by supporters for his much publicised 'route one ball' approach to the game, which in reality meant the big hoof. His departure, however, had a dispiriting effect on morale, and less then 1,300 saw City's last game of the season against Hereford. I well remember the air of gloom, compounded by the fact that City lost to a side at the bottom of the table.

Mulhall's successor was at the game. Roy McFarland heralded in the new era of 'Bantam Progressivism' by taking the club out of the Fourth Division. McFarland came as a player-manager with a superb First Divison pedigree. In his only full season with the club City finished runners-up to Sheffield United, and the future looked secure. His presence on the field was inspirational, and when he told us all at the last match of the season that - "We're going places," we all believed. McFarland waited until November of the following season, when he walked out on City in preference for Derby. The Rams eventually had to pay £10,000 compensation for 'poaching' McFarland. A lot of mud was slung, and I can remember the feeling of injustice that 'big clubs' could apparently do as they pleased. The situation seemed worse because McFarland, who had appeared loyal and committed to the club, had walked out on the eve of a big cup-tie with Manchester United.

Trevor Cherry was the next man at the helm, and he brought in Terry Yorath as his assistant from Vancouver. The partnership could do no wrong, and a superb season of fast-flowing, exciting football in 1984/85 ended with the Third Division Championship and, of course, the fire. Cherry kept the club on an even course following the fire, but it became apparent that Yorath's contribution to the success was vital. Once Yorath departed

for Swansea (after openly admitting that he wanted the manager's job at Valley Parade), Cherry's reign started to look less secure. After a disastrous run of results that saw City second to bottom in the table, the club decided to part company with its manager in January 1987. The sacking came only ten days after the club had moved back to Valley Parade, and shocked the footballing world. City's action was widely regarded as callousness in the extreme, and whether it was right or wrong, the fact remains that it reflected badly on the The Bantams.

City tried to woo Yorath from Swansea, and would have succeeded had it not been for Swans' chairman Doug Sharpe, who resisted the move. Instead, Cherry's assistant Terry Dolan (a former Avenue and City player) was given the job, a move which surprised most supporters. Dolan's introduction of the sweeper system stopped the rot, and the following season he was unlucky not to take the club into Division One. In 1988/89 however, City's league form was disappointing despite memorable victories against Everton and Spurs in cup competitions. Dolan tried to soldier on in the face of adversity, but it became obvious that he placed more belief in his own players than they had any right to expect. They let him down, and should bear some of the blamee for his eventual dismissal. I believe the club did the right thing, but once again the action does not reflect well on the good name of Bradford City.

So now we have Terry Yorath. Probably no manager has ever begun a term of office in such controversial circumstances, and we must hope that once the legalities are over the reign will be a peaceful one. But it's a sign of how far the club has come since the McFarland days that the roles are reversed and we are the club accused of 'poaching'. However pleased supporters are that Terry is rejoining the Board we must spare a thought for the Swansea supporters. It's not a nice feeling to have a club take away your manager and they have as much right to feel aggrieved as we did back in 1982. As for the future, I'd settle for a few years of managerial peace and, when the time comes, a mutually peaceful and amicable parting of the ways.

Mick Dickinson

BRADFORD CITY'S MANAGERS, 1969-1989

Jimmy Wheeler: June 1968 - September 1971;

Bryan Edwards: November 1971 - January 1975;

Bobby Kennedy: January 1975 - January 1978;

John Napier: February 1978 - October 1978;

George Mulhall: November 1978 - March 1981;

Roy McFarland: May 1981 - November 1982;

Trevor Cherry: December 1982 - January 1987;

Terry Dolan: January 1987 - January 1989;

Terry Yorath: February 1989 to date.

THE CITY LEAGUE RECORD 1968/69 to 1987/88

Season	Div	Pos		Season	Div	Pos
1968/69	D4	4th		1978/79	D4	15th
1969/70	D3	10th		1979/80	D4	5th
1970/71	D3	19th		1980/81	D4	14th
1971/72	D3	24th		1981/82	D4	2nd
1972/73	D4	16th		1982/83	D3	12th
1973/74	D4	8th		1983/84	D3	7th
1974/75	D4	10th		1984/85	D3	1st
1975/76	D4	17th		1985/86	D2	13th
1976/77	D4	4th		1986/87	D2	10th
1977/78	D3	22nd		1987/88	D2	4th

GIANT KILLERS

Despite the bitterly disappointing defeat by Bristol City in the Littlewoods Cup Quarter-Final and the 4th Round exit at home to Hull City in the FA Cup, 1988/89 has been a memorable season in the annals of Bradford City's cup exploits. Victories over two of the First Division's so-called 'Super Clubs', Everton and Tottenham Hotspur, have not only been consistent with The Bantams' reputation of being involved in cup surprises but have probably also been among their greatest achievements in cup competitions over the last twenty seasons.

The 1989 match with Tottenham inevitably brought back memories of the FA Cup 3rd Round tie at Valley Parade in January 1970. City had already defeated First Division Sunderland at Roker by 2-1 in the League Cup earlier in the season but with virtually the same team against Spurs, City were 0-2 down after 11 minutes. In claret and amber that afternoon were such individuals as Bruce Stowell, a stylish midfield player, Bobby Ham, then at his peak and the irrepressible Bruce Bannister. By half-time City had drawn level and they almost snatched a dramatic victory. The game ended all-square at 2-2, City losing the replay 0-5.

Three years later under Bryan Edwards, 4th Division City defeated Blackpool (then of Div Two) 2-1 at Valley Parade in the FA Cup, Gerry Ingram scoring both goals. This set-up a 4th Round tie against Arsenal at Highbury. Despite a lame performance by City the score was kept respectable at 0-2. The result however did not spoil a tremendous day out for City supporters and the rare thrill of being in a 40,000 crowd.

In 1974 City met Alvechurch of the West Midlands League in the FA Cup 3rd Round at Valley Parade, played on a Sunday (13,062 crowd) due to the ban on floodlight use. By the 79th minute City had taken a 4-0 lead, the third being a memorable 25 yard effort from Graham Oates, but slackness in City's defence allowed the non-leaguers to score two late consolation goals. City clung on to their lead however and were later defeated at Luton Town in the 4th Round.

In January 1976 City met another non-league club, Tooting and Mitcham United, in the 4th Round of the FA Cup - again at the Valley. City won the tie 3-1 in front of a crowd of 12,152, Don Hutchins scoring twice. In the next round City caused a major shock by beating Norwich at Carrow Road to became only one of three 4th Division sides to have ever reached the 6th Round. Unfortunately any ambitions of further Wembley glory were quashed by a single (and controversial) Southampton goal at Valley Parade.

Sensational Cup victory — McGinley is the hero
Norwich City 1
Peters 40 min
Bradford C. 2
Hutchins 39 min
McGinley 87 min
Attendance 27,047
Receipts £23,400

City continued to have the odd flirt in the cup competitions over the next few years. The 3-1 away win at 2nd Division Oldham in the 76/77 League Cup brings back fond memories and in 1978 they threw away a 2 goal lead in a League Cup 2nd Round replay against famous Lancashire neighbours Burnley, (eventually losing 2-3). A brave fight at Q.P.R. in a 1st leg, 1st Round League Cup tie in 1979 (1-2) led one Ron Greenwood to suggest that Bradford City might be the surprise team of the 1980's but that did nothing to prevent a 1-4 aggregate defeat.

After just missing out on promotion to Division 3 in May 1980 it seemed that the football world would have to wait a little longer for the ascendancy of Bradford City. However the evening of 27 August 1980 showed what regard the Paraders had for the existing aristocrats! The 1-0 defeat of Liverpool was the shock of the League Cup that season. City's hero was the immortal Bobby Campbell who knocked in a rebounded shot from Terry Dolan (later to become City's manager). Predictably, hopes of holding out in the 2nd leg soon evaporated at Anfield but the 0-4 defeat did not dampen the enthusiastic support given to City by their large contingent of travelling fans.

Bobby Campbell celebrates after scoring City's winning goal against Liverpool in the League Cup, second round, first leg at Valley Parade

In 1981 City nearly toppled the UEFA Cup holders Ipswich Town in the League Cup, beaten 2-3 after extra-time in a Valley Parade 3rd Round replay after Gary Watson had scored a deserved equaliser for 4th Division City at Portman Road. One year later in the Milk Cup, City held Manchester United to a 0-0 draw at Valley Parade and thereby earned the opportunity to visit Old Trafford, the venue at which City had won the FA Cup way back in 1911. Unfortunately the replay is better remembered for the circumstances following manager Roy McFarland's acrimonious departure; the 1-4 scoreline suitably reflected the despondancy.

In 1984/85 City tangled with two non-league clubs in the FA Cup. They demolished Tow Law Town 7-2 in the 1st Round, but their visit to Bucks Head, Telford in the 3rd Round was far from being as successful. Unable to master a deceptively sloping pitch City fell to an embarrassing 1-2 defeat, leaving the club to concentrate efforts on winning the 3rd Division Championship later that season.

More recent cup matches of note include a thrilling 4-4 draw at Ipswich in the FA Cup in 1985/86. Likewise there was a 2-0 defeat of Newcastle United at Odsal Stadium in the Littlewoods Cup in 1986/87, albeit followed by a crushing 0-5 defeat by Nottingham Forest in the 4th Round. Back at Valley Parade in January 1987 City thrashed Oldham 5-1 in an FA Cup 3rd Round replay but City were later beaten by Everton, 0-1, in the 4th.

1987/88 saw City come close to the ultimate promotion and in the same season they reached the Littlewoods Cup quarter-finals only to be beaten by Luton. The Simod Cup was relied upon to provide the glory but after disposing of Villa, Newcastle and Southampton, City succumbed to Reading. So even if cup honours have been confined to winning the West Riding Cup for four successive seasons (1984/85 to 1987/88 incl) there has been a share of glory and the dream has been kept alive!

John Watmough

They've done it before — they can do it again

Eight out of ten Finals were marred by scenes like these!

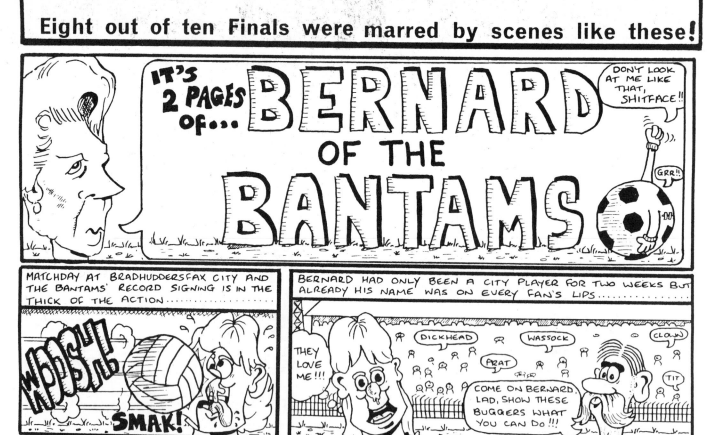

MATCHDAY AT BRADHUDDERSFAX CITY AND THE BANTAMS' RECORD SIGNING IS IN THE THICK OF THE ACTION.....

WDOSH!!
SMAK!

BERNARD HAD ONLY BEEN A CITY PLAYER FOR TWO WEEKS BUT ALREADY HIS NAME WAS ON EVERY FAN'S LIPS.....

THEY LOVE ME!!!

DICKHEAD   WASSOCK   CLOWN
PRAT
TIT

COME ON BERNARD, LAD, SHOW THESE BUGGERS WHAT YOU CAN DO !!!

CITY HAD BEEN HAVING A GREAT SEASON (UNTIL A FORTNIGHT AGO) + TODAY WAS DERBY DAY AGAINST JUMPLEADS UTD!!

WIN.
...OR I'LL HAVE YOUR TESTICLES ON TOAST!!

MANAGER BILLY BAGTHORPE HAD WOUND UP BERNARD AS ONLY HE KNEW HOW!!!

..BUT FOOTBALL, AS ONE BALD RACIST HAS LET IT BE KNOWN, "IS A GAME OLD FANNY"....

MINE!
TRAP!

....AND TRY AS HE MIGHT HE COULD NOT DO ONE THING RIGHT........

CLANG!
?
BRADHUDDERSFAX CITY

UNTIL..... ..... SOME DELIGHTFUL FOOTBALL JUST BEFORE HALF-TIME AND.........

BERNARD
THWAK!!!
IT'S A GOAL!!

HOW ABOUT THAT, TEAM-MATE? -THAT SHOWED 'EM-EH?

VERY NICE. BUT NEXT TIME PUT IT IN THE OPPOSITION GOAL YOU DAFT TWAT!!!

BRADHUDDERSFAX CITY

and now over to Bill Bothwell reporting from a damp tombstone in Nocton Parish churchyard . . . .

....AND SO NOCTON WANDERERS ARE OUT OF THE F.A. CUP - BEATEN 32-0 BY BATTLING BRADFORD CITY....

BAH, ANYBODY COULD BEAT THEM NON-LEAGUE BUGGERS !!!

LAND OF HOPE AND GLORY

1969 — the halcyon days of Yf: 2.42% unemployment as the grand old Keynesian orthodoxy semed to take care of all a nation's problems. Not that many seemed prepared to admit that there were any problems. A record balance of payments (£387 Million) was reported and self-confidence was unshakeable. British technology past and present was shown to the world; the Flying Scotsman toured the USA and Concorde had its maiden flight. (No doubt Britain had also fitted the spark plugs used in the successful Apollo landing). The red, white and blue heat of technology demanded high profile spending and development. Ronan Point (1968) had not yet ended the planners' dreams — the optimism for the future was reflected in the willingness of bulldozers to continue destroying Victorian cities and to provide that brave new world, so long overdue.

Income levels were rising and biological detergents were on sale. In the new affluent society, nearly 90% had a TV and 60% a washing-machine. Daz and Ajax were becoming household names like the Beatles and the Charltons. As prosperity rose, panties fell. Libido was hip and Abbey Road testified to the vitality of those helping to feed youth culture. Higher education was similarly opened up to those precocious youngsters and Nixon's war policy was still there to be complained about.

LSD was sending heads into the sky (as if prosperity did not provide sufficient material illusions) but 30,000,000 people had their feet on the terraces. 1969 was the year of the young pretenders — Leeds United won the championship and Swindon Town the League Cup. Talk of the terrraces south of the border was about England's brave crusade to retain the World Cup. Little England were fighting a rearguard battle, although everything seemed to be under control. Inflation was under 5%, gross profits in industry still averaged 12% and manufacturing output was growing (2.78% p.a.) The Frogs might have refused us entry to the EEC, but so what?

Alf Garnett's xenophobia appeared more credible thanks to the undeniable fact that England were World Champions. In 28 games since the glorious defeat of the Krauts in '66, England had lost only four times; in 1969 France were beaten 5-0 (up yours de Gaulle!) and the Scots 4-1. Naturally, the 1-2 reverse against Brazil in Rio was the product of unfair forces and foreign food.

The days of 1969 re-appear almost every Christmas, when the Beeb decides to screen 'The Italian Job'. Michael Caine the star, the chirpy cockney with the world at his feet (just like the rubble of his old slum dwelling). John Wayne might feed the cowboy dreamers, but Michael Caine was pumping England's delusions of glory. Against the excitable Italians, the calm intellect and originality of Caine was bound to succeed. While the wops frantically prepared for a football confrontation between Italy and England, the smart thinking English boys would steal Turins's gold — under the guise of fair-minded football supporters, complete with rattles. The impact of English football fans on Turin in the 1980s was to ensure that such an innocent welcome would never again be extended.

The film highlighted the extent to which complacent xenophobia could capture the national mood (after all, thousands of punters flocked to the cinemas to watch it). The stereotype of hot-headed, incompetent wops contrasted with the English boys who knew how to keep themselves cool. They were assured of stealing the gold, just as they were assured of England beating Italy on the pitch. The supporters minibus decorated with the praises of invincible national heroes — Moore, Bell, Charlton et al.

Lots of red, white and blue. (Union Jacks, but no flags of St.George — in GB, England predominant!). The theft of Turin's gold was executed by the mechanical superiority of the good old Austin Cooper mini. The minis put the Alfas and Fiats into place (note that in 1969 the level of UK car imports was 11%).

1969 — the end of a hot summer and the end of an age of complacent optimism? 1973 — defeat by Poland and double defeat by Italy. Growing inflation, growing unemployment, growing strikes and growing car import penetration. A total re-appraisal of national values; membership of Europe; no Leyland cars seen overtaking Fiats. In 1969 it was felt that England's golden age could continue forever, but it took just four years to show how fragile the glory of 'The Italian Job' had been. Football therefore played its part in creating a national mood which made everything so hard to bear when the chickens came home to roost in 1973.

In the sixties, Harold Wilson tried hard to identify himself with England's World Cup success, and even set the date for the 1970 election expecting that England would have beaten West Germany a few days previously. He blamed his own defeat on the fact that they lost. Was the debacle of English football in the Seventies the real reason for Margaret Thatcher's political ascendancy? Gut emotion desperately wanting to continue waving the red, white and blue? Considering that English football will be unable to take a lead role in once again stealing Turin's gold, how does Maggie intend producing 'The Italian Job II'?

John Dewhirst

KNICKERBOCKER GLORIES

Albert Shepherd F.Potts H.Walden   C.Storer J.Ewart J.Hargreaves R.Bond I.Boocock   D.Fox

The year is 1914 and only weeks after Bradford City have returned home from an all-conquering tour of Germany the wretched Huns have decided to exact revenge by playing *their* national game. For the likely lads above it would be the closing of a glorious chapter. Elected to Division Two in 1903 without ever having played a game, City were champions in 1908 and F.A. Cup winners in 1911 (also finishing 5th in Division One). In 1914/15 they finished 10th. Park Ave-

nue had joined City in Division One in 1914, after formation only in 1907, but by 1922 both clubs had been relegated within a year of each other.

Avenue dropped into the lower divisions in 1948 and by 1970 were in oblivion. City were exiled from Division Two in 1937 returning only in 1985. Whereas before the Great War Bradford had been one of the richest cities in England, by the 1920's decline had set in. The fate of the city and its football was

once inextricably bound with the sale of wool. The mills are now monuments to former glories and it is the city's remaining football club that helps provide the example for regeneration. It is the hope of Bradfordians that their grandfathers' ripping yarns can at last be replaced by tales of modern glories - thereby destroying the myth that Bradford City could only win in knickerbockers.

chapter 12

HEARTBEAT

hearts

ISSUE 3

1988-9
50p

MANCHESTER

HEARTS SUPPORTERS CLUB

MAGAZINE

IN YOUR FUN FILLED HEARTBEAT
SPORT:

STEVE ARCHIBALD EATEN BY
'ALIEN FROG!'

PLUS:

Just another old Croc or is it Peter McCloy ?

MAGAZINE TITLE: HEARTBEAT

EDITORS NAME: MIKE VAN VLECK / DES BURNS.

AGE: 32 / 31   OCCUPATION: ACCOUNTANT / TEACHER.

DO YOU/HAVE YOU EVER SUPPORTED ANY OTHER TEAM?
ALSO WATCH BOLTON WANDERERS. WHEN NOT WATCHING HEARTS. / No

MOST MEMORABLE MATCH EVER:
AUSTRIA VIENNA 0 HEARTS 1 This seasons UEFA Cup. / 1986 Scottish Cup Semi-final Hearts 1 Dundee Utd 0. Only time I have seen a team I supported win at Hampden.

MOST MEMORABLE SEASON: 1985/6 Even though it did end in disaster. / Same as Mike.

ALL TIME FAVOURITE PLAYER: Frank Worthington. / Ernie Winchester.

WHAT SORT OF CAR DO YOU DRIVE?
~~ ~~. CAVALIER. / Fiesta XR2.

YOUR FAVOURITE MUSIC: Rock / Pop.

FILMS/TV: ANYTHING ON SPORT / CAPTAIN SCARLET + EMMERDALE FARM.

FAVOURITE CLOTHES: HEARTS SHIRT. / Same as Mike

POLITICAL LEANINGS: Left. / Right

WHAT PLAYER WOULD YOU MOST LIKE TO SEE PLAYING FOR ENGLAND (SCOTLAND/WALES IF RELEVANT)?

George McCluskey. Then a few million can have a good laugh instead of just a few thousand.

Same for Both of us.

Our fanzine was first written and produced by myself in April 1986 and went under the name of *the Manchester Jambo*. I only originally produced it to get some practice on a portable computer I had acquired at work, and was inspired by the now defunct *Wanderers Worldwide*. I ran off an initial total of 25 copies and took them to Hampden for the Scottish Cup semifinal against Dundee United. To my surprise all 25 copies sold during the half time interval. Inspired by this I ran off another 50 and sold them without much trouble at the next home game. As Hearts reached the Scottish Cup final that year we decided to produce a cup final special and also decided on a change of name to *Heartbeat*. Since then the fanzine has gone from strength to strength and is now considered a cult magazine among Hearts fans. We have just issued our eleventh edition and aim to produce three per season.

Des Burns and myself do virtually all the writing, laying out and selling, but we have now managed to contract out the typing and collating to various friends for a few quid. Hearts already had two fanzines before we started, the *Hearts Review* and the *Hearts Supporter*. The *Review* concentrates more on club history, while the *Supporter* reviews current team performances plus keeping readers up to date with what the various club branches are doing. Both do a good job but we wanted to produce something independant which said what the fans thought, and also put into print our favourite pastime - taking the piss out of the Hibs.

As far as the club is concerned we have attacked them where it has been warranted, but also handed out praise where it has been earned. We have received nothing but help and encouragement from the club and players and presume they have taken our criticism as it is intended, well meaning and constructive. Our main cause for concern over the years has been the ground, which for a top club is an absolute disgrace. I could name a large number of English third and fourth division grounds which are better than Tynecastle, and the only improvements carried out since the start of our campaign are an increase in the number of turnstiles, a slight improvement in toilet facilities and a slight improvement in the woefully inadequate exit for home supporters. However, we will continue the fight to improve the ground.

MIKE VAN VLECK

ARCHIEBALLS

Some true classic quotes from the annals of soccer commentary.

"The Argentine signalling at free-kicks doesn't matter as none of the England players speak South American." David Pleat, Mexico'86

"And the French substitute is warming up underneath me." John Motson, England v France, 1982 World Cup.

"I'd resigned myself to giving up soccer, then I signed for Hibs" George Best.

"I'd like to have seen Davie Provan left on as a down and out winger." Archie MacPherson.

"Queens Park against Forfar - you can't get more romantic than that." Archie MacPherson, 1982 Scottish Cup Quarter Final.

"And there'll be more football in a moment, but first we've got the highlights of the Scottish League Cup Final." Gary Newbon, Central T.V.

"Kilmarnock v Partick Thistle, match postponed - that, of course, is a latest score." Frank Bough.

"Ayr 1 Arbroath 0 - Arbroath still without an away win of any kind." David Coleman.

"There aren't many last chances left for George Best." Archie MacPherson.

"The advantage of being at home is very much with the home side." Denis Law.

"Norwich's goal was scored by Kevin Bond, who is the son of his father." Frank Bough.

"And Bruno Conti has just collided with a photographer I fancy." John Motson, Italy v Cameroons, 1982 World Cup.

"And Southampton have beaten Brighton by 3 goals to 1; that's a repeat of last years result, when Southampton won 5-1." Desmond ("What about those Jam Tarts, Archie") Lynam.

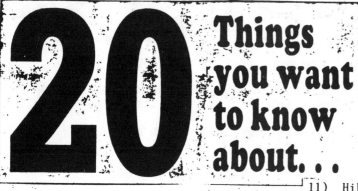

20 Things you want to know about...

THE HIBs

1) Since the Scottish League was reorganised in 1975, Hibs have scored fewer League goals than any other club in the League.

2) Although the clubs official title is Hibernian, they are better known as Hibs because their supporters cannot understand words with more than four letters in.

3) In the early days of football, Hibs nearly went out of existence when Celtic pinched all their team. Celtic must have learned the hard way because, not surprisingly, they've never been back since.

4) Their ground is called Easter Road because they're always getting crucified by their opponents.

5) Everybody assumes they play in green because of their Irish origins. The real reason they're green is because they get up everybodies nose.

6) Just to prove their lack of intelligence, there is only one word in the Oxford-English Dictionary that begins with Hibernia. There are 3 pages of words beginning with Heart.

7) In gaelic Hibernian means - 'of Irish origin.' In English it means - 'of a crap standard.'

8) The turnstiles at Easter Road are actually called 'Arseholes,' because the only thing that passes through arseholes are shits.

9) For the last 10 years Hibs have been sponsored by Tampax, because they've been going through a bad period.

10) Gordon Strachan and the Proclaimers are self confessed Hibs fanatics, and we all know what a trio of wee shites they are.

11) Hibs striker Steve Archibald had the superb scoring rate at Blackburn last season of 6 Second Division goals in 23 games.

12) The last time Hibs won the Scottish Cup, Buffalo Bill was 54 years old.

13) Hibs Joe Tortalano is the first player ever to be sent off in a testimonial match. There again it was only a wee hibee bastard he kicked - Gordon Strachan.

14) Hibs were once charged under the Trades Description Act. They were sponsored by Winalot.

15) Hibs claim to be the first Scottish club to go public. This in fact is false, as both Hearts and Rangers are Public Limited Companies, and as far back as 1905 Hearts put shares on the open market for sale to the public.

16) Hibs are a bunch of mongrals, and just to prove it here is their history. They were formed by IRISH immigrants and play in the SCOTTISH League. They have ENGLISH and WELSH born players in their team at present. Their biggest shareholder is a Panamanian firm, who hold the shares on behalf of a DUTCH firm.

17) Hibs have only won half as many major trophies as Hearts.

18) Hibs are the only club to have been beaten by all the other senior Edinburgh clubs, ie Hearts, Meadowbank, Edinburgh City, Leith Athletic, St Bernards.

19) Ex-Marillian lead singer Fish is a Hibs fan. His real name is Donald Dick - enough said.

20) Since the Premier League was formed in 1975, Hibs have only once finished in the top three, in the inaugral season.

We analysed the reasons for certain companies sponsoring certain clubs and made the following findings:-

MITA sponsor Hearts because we are the team to copy.

CROWN sponsor Liverpool because they usually produce a glossy performance.

N.E.C. COMPUTERS sponsor Everton because they are like an efficient, well oiled machine.

GUINNESS sponsor Q.P.R. because you have more chance of judging the bounce on their pitch after a few pints.

TAMPAX sponsor Hibs because they're going through a bad period!

You're Nicked !

Jimmy the Hibee and the Gogarburn Branch of the Hibs Supporters Club were travelling through to Stranraer for the big Second Division match (yes, the Hibees had finally arrived where they belong) in his ice cream van, when they were pulled over by a police patrol car.

The sergeant explained that, as they were going to watch Hibs, he could only assume that they were either drunk or just plain daft. He therefore asked Jimmy to step out of the van and take a breath test. Jimmy produced a card on which was written, "Asthmatic - please don't take breath."

"That's fine," said the bobby. "Would you mind giving a sample of blood instead?"

Jimmy showed him a second card which read, "Haemophyliac - please don't take blood."

"In that case, I must ask you to accompany me to the police station to provide a sample of urine," the sergeant told him.

Then Jimmy played his trump card, which said, "Hibernian supporter - please don't take the piss."

Jimmy the Hibee!

Jimmy the Hibee had gone out for his usual Saturday afternoon tipple. (No point in going to Easter Road). He walked into the pub accompanied by George McCluskey and a parrot. As he approached the bar the parrot, who was perched on Jimmy's shoulder, order three pints of 80/-. George McCluskey on hearing the parrot went totally mental and started smashing up the pub. The landlord insisted that Jimmy and his strange friends leave immediately. But Jimmy put his hand in his pocked and produced £1,000 which seemed to calm down the landlord. The parrot then ordered another round of drinks and George McCluskey promptly flung the Juke Box through the pub window. The irate landlord could only be placated by Jimmy producing another £1,000 to pay for damages. "What are you doing drinking with that barn stick?" inquired the landlord. "Well you see," replied Jimmy, "my fairy-godmother granted me 3 wishes. With wish 1 I asked for an endless supply of money and now when I put my hand in my pocket £1,000 appears. With wish 2 I asked for a beautiful bird - Now, I can't get rid of this bloody parrot." "What about wish 3?" asked the landlord. "Ah," replied Jimmy, "with wish 3 I asked for the biggest dick in Edinburgh and the stupid cow sent me George McCluskey!"

JIMMY

THE

HIBEE

SAYS

"THE ONLY DIFFERENCE BETWEEN A HEDGEHOG AND EASTER ROAD IS, A HEDGEHOG HAS IT'S PRICKS ON THE OUTSIDE."

SEVEN WEEKS TO BANK A CHEQUE – what a way to run a business

The recent publication of last season's accounts, showing a profit of £380,000 was an encouraging sign that Hearts are moving in the right direction. What worries me, however, is the greater profit which could be shown if the commercial department pulled its socks up.

I'm afraid that the majority of dealings we have had with that office have done little to inspire confidence.

Our first contact with the department occurred at the time of the issue of "The Pictorial History of Hearts." On phoning to enquire about the book, I was given a price and immediately sent off my order, along with a cheque for the amount quoted. Six weeks later, I received a reply stating I hadn't sent enough, so would I forward the difference?

I did so right away, but waited a further six weeks before receiving my copy of the book.

Perhaps it was just one of those things, I thought. I'm afraid not, as our continued dealings last season were to prove.

Our football team sells Hearts lottery tickets. After disposing of 800 tickets, I phoned the commercial department to ask for a further 800. Three weeks later they arrived - with only four days left until the "sell by" date. Are we so prosperous that we can throw away £200 worth of lottery ticket sales?

But read on, the worst is yet to come. We received our Cup Final tickets five days after the match, having ordered them two and a half weeks previously and enclosing a stamped, addressed envelope. Then we were asked to return them, with a promise that we'd receive a full refund in due course. That was mid-May and despite responding immediately, we are still awaiting our £36 refund in mid-August.

A friend in Edinburgh paid for his Cup Final tickets by cheque and was amazed that it wasn't banked until seven weeks later. Surely no business can afford to hold up its income for so long. Can you imagine the total amount of interest which would be lost through delays in banking cash received from sales of Cup Final tickets?

Finally, a suggestion. Nearly all the top clubs have a souvenir shop which runs as a thriving business. Hearts don't, yet it's an area which should be well tapped. Think of all the money they would have raked in during the build-up to the Cup Final alone.

Building restaurants and private boxes, running deluxe trips to Hampden and Prague are all fine. But so much potential would be wasted if Hearts continue to ignore a market which is waiting to be exploited.

Manchester United and Rangers converted their grounds into luxury stadia through efficient development associations. Let's have the same at Tynecastle.

Have you obtained your visa for Prague yet? If you have you will have noticed that you can only pay for it by cash or postal order. It would appear that the Czechs do not like cheques.

EYE —OPENER!

TYNECASTLE — stadium for the 1960's? by Des Burns

Hearts supporters, after a long wait, finally have a team of which they can once more feel proud. But can the same be said of our stadium? Don't get me wrong. I love Tynecastle dearly. But isn't there a saying that "love is blind?" If that is the case, then my eyes were opened at the recent `live' match against Aberdeen.

The Manchester Branch travelled en-masse. In our company were several Sassenachs, eager to see the cream of Scottish football in action.

They usually follow Manchester United or City - and with the same devotion with which we follow our team. They are used to the superb facilities at Old Trafford or Maine Road, and often travel to Anfield, White Hart Lane, Hillsborough and Villa Park, to name just a few.

Their first impression of Tynecastle was not a complimentary one. As we awaited the kick-off at the School End, the comments directed at me included.......

"Have you seen the state of the toilets? My new Puma trainers are soaked in Hibee!"

"God, we'll get drenched if it rains."

"Ugh! Have you tasted these awful pies I've just queued up half an hour for?"

You may well cast aside these remarks as the ravings of some "Nancy Boy" Mancunians. But, as Hearts enter Europe, with success following success, more fans of this type will be attracted to Tynecastle.

A coach full of Bradford City supporters travelled up recently; a party of 20 Bolton Wanderers supporters also attended the Aberdeen match; the supporters clubs in Manchester, Birmingham and London are thriving. So criticisms like those cannot be ignored.

I realise that the kind of money required to turn Tynecastle into another Ibrox or Old Trafford is not available, but improvements on a smaller scale are feasable and should not be dismissed lightly. Fans coming to a match at Tynecastle should at least expect to be kept dry. Even "away" fans are entitled to that.

Priority should be given to extending the cover at the School End and along the Gorgie Road terracing. The new seating in the main stand could be continued so that it flanks both sides of the players' tunnel. And why not make the Gorgie Road end all-seated?

Refreshment bars are too few and far between, and almost impossible to reach. The toilet facilities are a disgrace. While hardly adequate in the "good old days" when 7000 turned up at the ground, they certainly cannot cope now that the attendances have trebled.

Many fans are reduced to using the walls at the back of the terracing. I dread to think how the supporters of Bayern Munich, Real Madrid and Juventus will feel about this situation.

While reading this you may be wondering what it takes to satisfy some people. Of course I'm delighted that Hearts have a successful side again!

But in order to regain our rightful place at the forefront of British football, and make our mark in Europe, we need not only a quality team, but a stadium with facilities to match. Over to you, Mr Mercer.

VAN VLECK'S FUSILIERS

Our trip to Dublin started at Tuesday tea-time. Our ferry from Holyhead wasn't due to sail until 3.15 a.m. on Wednesday, so we decided to call in on the Wrexham v Bury Littlewoods Cup tie on our way. Bury had won the 1st leg 2-1 the previous week, so the tie looked finely balanced.

After a mad dash from Manchester, we managed to get to the ground about 5 minutes after kick-off. Hearts scarves in evidence and into the home supporters enclosure, but only after walking right round the ground because two sides had been closed off for safety reasons. Although I live near Bury's ground, I can't stand them because they always play such negative, boring football (the Motherwell of England), so we decided to shout for Wrexham, even though they're Welsh bastards.

The first half was predictable. Some good flowing, attacking football from Wrexham, dire defence from Bury. By half-time Wrexham were 2-0 in the lead. We spent the half-time interval throwing abuse at a group of lads in Celtic shirts. It's amazing where the scumbags turn-up.

The second half Bury broke away and scored, which took the game into extra time. Unfortunately, Bury scored again and so we decided to head for a pub-on the outskirts of Wrexham. After a few beers we hit the trail to Holyhead, and arrived for the ferry about 1.30 a.m. Looking around the line of cars we appeared to be the only Jambo's present.

Once the cars loaded onto the ferry and we get up on deck, we behold a wonderous sight; a ship full of Jambos on their way to Dublin. Although much alcohol was consumed, and we were in the early hours of the morning, all the lads behaved impeccably and impressed the other passengers with their friendliness and good behaviour. Just shows you how a bit of trust can be rewarded when you're dealing with decent fans. Are you listening Mr Mercer?

Coming off the ferry, true to form, we got stopped by the Irish customs. Anyway, after a short delay we headed for the North side of Dublin and onto the golf course. After a night without sleep, the last few holes got a bit tiring, but it

was a good course and we enjoyed the round. The trouble was, that for the last 30 hours I'd worn the same clothes, and began to stink a bit. Large groups of flies were following me round the last few holes, so as soon as we'd finished the round it was straight to the hotel.

The hotel was sound, being on Drumcondrard round the corner from Tolka Park. After a much needed shave and shower, we headed for a few beers and something to eat. We went in the Cat and Cage and there were a few Jambos already in the bar. Within an hour the place was heaving with Hearts supporters, all bursting into song. A few St. Pat's. supporters came in the bar and we were talking to them for a while. They were a good bunch of lads, as were all the St. Pat's. supporters we met on the trip.

As we headed from the bar towards the ground, everywhere seemed to be a mass of maroon and white. Hearts fans were even putting scarves on the Gardai who seemed to be taking it all in good spirit. Once on Richmond Road, and near to the ground, there seemed to be a lot of youngsters turning up wearing Celtic shirts. For a while all was normal, but ten minutes before kick-off all hell broke loose outside the home supporters turn-stiles. A group of these so called Celtic supporters had been constantly baiting Hearts fans with I.R.A. chants, and burning the Union Jack. In the end, understandably, the Hearts lads had taken enough crap from them, and proceeded to kick the shit out of them, (see Scum article for pictures and further details). It shows who the Gardai thought were to blame, as they arrested two Celtic supporters for 'provocation,' but no Hearts supporters were arrested. It should also be noted that no St. Pat's. supporters were involved.

Once inside the ground, you could see a group of Dublin Celtic supporters (about 200 of them) had congregated at the fence nearest the Hearts support, and were waving tricolours with the I.R.A. printed on, and were burning Union Jacks and Hearts scarves. To their enormous credit, the limited number of Gardai on duty, removed the I.R.A. flags and burning Hearts scarves, and were rewarded with a

MARCH ON & ON & ON ...

Post-match celebrations in the Cat and Cage Bar on Drumcondra Road. Keith (on the right), looks misty-eyed. He's obviously missing his girlfriend Magdalene Patel.

● ● ● ● ●

hail of missiles from this scum. To their credit, the Hearts supporters behaviour was impeccable and they refused to be antagonized by the Celtic scums actions.

The match itself was crap. Hearts were 2-0 up at half-time and the tie was dead. As the second half got underway a hail of missiles were thrown onto the pitch by the Dublin based Celtic scum. The referee stopped the game and collected all the objects. St. Pat's will now probably get a hefty fine for the actions of this scum, who had nothing whatsoever to do with either team on the field, and had only come with the sole intention of causing trouble.

At this point the St. Pat's fans turned on the Celtic supporters, and informed them in no uncertain terms that they were not wanted at the match. In fact the biggest cheer of the night came from the St. Pat's supporters to the Hearts fans when we said, "Celtic, Celtic, f*ck off home." Both Hearts and St. Pat's supporters cheered each other, and Hearts fans have found a new hero in St. Pat's keeper 'Hendo.' The camaradery between 'Hendo' and the Hearts fans was tremendous.

At the end of the match both sets of supporters stayed and applauded each other, and the St. Pat's team came over and applauded the Hearts fans. The scum had long since departed, knowing that if they stayed both sets of supporters would have given them a well deserved good kicking.

Later, Dublin was awash with maroon and white, as Hearts and St. Pat's fans drank and sang together in the bars. Hardly a scumbag in sight. We even bumped into ex-Jambo Pat Byrne later that night in the Cat and Cage. He's now manager of Shelbourne, but had come to support Hearts on the night.

Next day we did a tour of the football grounds in Dublin to take some Photos. We went back to Tolka Park, then to Bohemians ground Dalymount Park, and then went south of the river to Milltown to visit Shamrock Rovers old ground, which is now looking a bit derelict. Keith Fulfilled one of his life's ambitions by pissing on Shamrock Rovers pitch. I suppose it's the sectarian bigotry in him

which sets him such wonderful goals.

The behaviour of the Hearts support was superb as the final statistic reveals; Hearts fans in Dublin - 4,500; Arrests - Nil. All arrests made were of Dublin based Celtic supporters; enough said. How are we fixed for tickets for the next round Mr Mercer?

P.S.

The ferry home, late on Thursday night, only contained eight Hearts fans, but we did bump into two Cardiff supporters who had been to the Cup Winners Cup match at Londonderry. They're either very brave, or have suicidal tendencies.

YUGO TOURS 1988

FUDBALSKI KLUB „VELEŽ" — MOSTAR
UTAKMICA TREĆEG KOLA KUPA U E F-a

Velež Hearts
MOSTAR   EDINBURGH

Loža - jug 2   Red 3   Sjed. 13   £ 7

Due to various coach trips being cancelled at the last minute, Manchester Hearts attempts to get to Mostar ended in failure. We therefore bring you the following report on the eventfull trip from Dave Brunson and his mates.

After catching the shuttle to Heathrow, we were supposed to leave for Zagreb at I:00pm. In the end the plane left at 3:30pm and ended up in Belgrade! On arriving in Belgrade, we discovered that Dubrovnik airport was shut, so we had to stay the night in Belgrade. The trouble was, we had to be up at 5:30 in the morning to catch a flight to Dubrovnik, so we all got wrecked in Restaurant No.8 on crap Yugo beer and plum brandy. Most of us didn't bother going to bed, and we ended up with a steaming hangover on the nightmare flight to Dubrovnik.

After a few hours sleep in our hotel, we set off on a 3½ hour coach trip to Mostar. From the outskirts of the town we received a Police escourt, with full sirens blaring, all the way to the ground. The ground was in darkness until I5 minutes before the kick-off, and the Velez supporters were only slightly less hostile than a combination of Chelsea and Millwall supporters. There were more missiles being thrown than a biblical stoning.

We were nervous wrecks once the game had started, but Mike Galloways' goal put us all at ease. The Velez fans were real Jeckyll and Hyde characters, as one minute they were shouting and swearing at us, and the next they were waving and laughing. They got a bit upset when we started to burn their money in front of them.

At the end of the game, one climbed over the barrier into our area and headed straight towards one of the boys looking as though he was going to chin him one. But instead he planted a big sloppy kiss on his cheek. During the game, another thing that annoyed them was the Hearts supporters outsinging them, especially after Mike Galloways' goal.

After the game the walk back to the bus was akin to coming out of Parkhead after beating Celtic. One of the boys on our bus was hit by a stone which split his head open, and someone else was unlucky enough to be hit by it as it bounced off his head.

However, the Police were at hand to make sure we got back to the buses okay, and were good enough to take the boy, along with our courier, to the hospital, w

where the wound was patched-up and he was back on the bus in about I5 minutes. We were then escorted back to the outskirts of Mostar.

The courier apologised on behalf of his fellow countrymen, and passed on a message from the Police and Mostar officials, saying that hhat they were

very impressed by the Hearts' supporters behaviour and our backing of the team.

Meanwhile, back in Dubrovnik someone phones home and comes back with the news that we have resigned Robbo. This sparked off numerous orders for champagne in the hotel.

Friday, and Dubrovnik airport is closed again, which means another bus journey to Mostar, for a plane to Ljubliana, then to London, and finally the shuttle to Edinburgh. But if you think that's a long journey, spare a thought for Mike and Kenny, who hitched it there and back.

What Price Loyalty?

So 'Big-Time' European football is finally upon us. After an extremely long wait Tynecastle looks set to play host to top-class opposition on an evening which promises a capacity crowd. What a glorious sight! 'The Gorgie Road' packed with Jambos instead of 'Blue-noses, Hibees or Green backs!'

Commercially as well, it would appear to be a massive boon for the club. A bumper gate, Live T.V. fees and advertising is likely to generate income of £500,000. The Accountant must be 'laughing all the way to the Leeds!' And what about Club Chairman, Wallace Mercer, he really must be commended for his one-upmanship. What a crafty 'so-and-so' he's proved to be! Initially a rumour is spread threatening to play the tie at Hampden Park. The Hearts fans are horrified! 'Give up home advantage?' A horrendous thought. So Wallace allays all our fears and announces it will be at Tynecastle but prices will be trebled. 'Who cares what the cost is - as long as we don't surrender Home advantage' is the fans reaction.

So of course no one complains about the prices for the game. A master stroke by the senior management.

To be perfectly honest I don't think the majority of the fans object to the prices. There's a generous discount scheme for Season Ticket holders and a voucher scheme for regular attenders which offers a 30-40% reduction. So at least loyalty is reward or is it? In his recent book Mr Mercer was keen to point out what a marvellous support Hearts have even having supporters clubs based in London and Manchester. Now we travel to Tynecastle about 12 to 15 times a season, from Manchester, at an approximate cost for the day of about £20. Members travelled to Parkhead, Ibrox, Easter Road, Dens Park, Douglas Park, Dublin and surely thats loyalty. We spend between £250 and £500 a season watching our team. A season ticket is out of the question. Three consecutive home games during December and January an impossibility when you take into account the cost of the Festive season and bad weather.

We are not a bunch of loony Sassenachs! 80% of our members are Edinburgh lads who've moved South. Who's rewarded our loyalty. A drive to Edinburgh in <u>February</u>! £10 to stand on an uncovered terrace in God knows what weather! Taking a day off to go and travelling back that same night. It's nice to know your support is appreciated.

GOODNIGHT VIENNA

Well this was the trip to end all trips, with a superb Hearts' performance to round it off nicely. We'd booked on one of the Tynecastle buses and arranged for it to pick us up at the M6 near Knutsford Services. The junction is in the middle of nowhere about 15 miles from Manchester, but there is a pub next to the slip road, so we had a few beers while we waited for the coach.

When we reached the ferry at Dover one of the lads from London Hearts joined our coach, and we also met the other coaches going to Vienna. This gave us a chance to have a few drinks with our mate Adam Park, and also have a word with a couple of Hearts fans from Doncaster.

The journey to Vienna was a good laugh, the highlight of which was a stop on the motorway services in Germany. The temperature was below freezing, and we were waiting to get some food, when two Jambo's came walking in with only a pair of shorts and trainers on. They must have been freezing, but were so pissed they probably never noticed, and burst out into the Auf Wiedersehen Pet signature tune, "That's living alright," to the astonishment of a group of bemused Krauts. We all tried "not to mention the War" as well. On leaving the services a roar went up on the coach when we heard on the radio that Celtic had been knocked-out in Bremen." "No Tims in Europe, No there are no Tims in Europe" went the chant. It was also good to hear that Bolton had won at Huddersfield.

The rest of the journey to Vienna was an attempt to get as much sleep as possible in those bloody uncomfortable coach seats. We arrived in Vienna at 7.00am on the Wednesday morning and headed straight for the hotel and to bed for some much needed sleep. We awoke at noon and headed out to the nearest bar for a few beers and some scoff. We then did a tour of Vienna centre, calling in at numerous bars on the way. One thing we noticed on our tour; Austrian women are so ugly they abuse the privelage, and what a bunch of miserable bastards.

We arrived back at the hotel for 6.00pm to get the coach to the game.

The hotel was crawling with Police who were to escort us to the Praeter Stadium, but we never found out whether it was to protect us from the locals or them from us. In fact, after five minutes on our coach our police escort had taken enough of the singing and jumped off at the next set of traffic lights and into the police car in front.

Once at the stadium we all bought half-price juniors tickets and entered the magnificant Praeter Stadium. After the Nou Camp in Barcelona, this was definately the best stadium I had been in. The thousand or so Hearts supporters were congregated mainly in one end behind the goal, and here we met many old friends like Neil Stevens, Callum Anderson (ex-manager of Auld Worthies in the good days there) and Mike Buckle of Gorgie Gas.

The facilities in the Praeter were superb, and the Hearts fans were throwing down as much of the beer on sale as possible. That is until they found out it was non-alcoholic.

You've read about, and seen on T.V., the match. I'll only say Hearts were brilliant, and played the continentals at their own game, but better. During the match we met a Hearts fan from East Berlin, who had hitch-hiked to Prague and then caught a train to Vienna. There were also four members from West German Hearts at the match, and also five lads from Vienna there who supported Hearts. In fact we were stood with the lads from Vienna all through the second half, and every time a Hearts player was fouled there was a shout of "Dirty Fenian Bastard" in a Germanic accent. They also wouldn't stop singing "One Dave McPherson" every time he got the ball.

The noise made by the Hearts supporters was superb all through the game, in fact you just couldn't hear any noise from the Austrians. After the match we were kept in the stadium for half an hour. When we did eventually leave and get to the coaches, we noticed a large gathering of people, about 500, waiting beyond the park near the ground. They were Austrians waiting to have a go at any Hearts fans walking back to the centre. Those who were walking back stuck together and the Austrians didn't come near them, just being content with throwing a few firecrackers and being chased off by the riot police.

Adam Park's coach was waiting further away from the stadium than ours, and they got back to find 200 Dutch Casuals waiting for them (surprisingly it wasn't mentioned in the Sunday Post). Apparently they had travelled down from Holland just to have a battle with us British fans. Anyway the lads on the bus headed straight for them and they backed off, only returning when everyone was on the coach and they knew they were safe from attack by Hearts supporters.

Back at the hotel we watched the highlights of the game on T.V. and then went out for a celebratory drinking session in the bar behind the hotel. Here we met the lads from Oxgang Hearts and had a few beers with them One of the lads, 'Pig,' was so pissed he was having trouble co-ordinating his pint with his mouth and ended up pouring half his beer over himself and the floor. He then attempted to eat a bowl of goulash, which he knocked over the floor and table. I scraped it back from the floor and the table into the bowl, as the owner was not impressed by Pigs actions. Next time I looked round, Pig was finishing off the Goulash from the bowl again. God knows what had been picked up off the floor and table.

Once this bar closed we headed for another round the corner, where we met two lads and a girl from Manchester who were Hearts supporters we'd never seen before. After several 100% proof vodkas we then went to a street vendor for some sausages, took the piss out of two prostitutes, and went into a Turkish Working Mens Club. We were closely followed in by five Jam Rolls (poles) who sat on the next table. After a few abysmal songs from a live, (I think) Turkish band, we burst out into the Hearts song. At the end the Poles applauded us thinking it was a traditional Scottish Folk song. They then burst out into some Polish folk song which was pretty dire. When they'd finished we sang, "Solidamosc," to which the fat Lech Walesa look-alike came over and hugged us all. They then asked us to teach them a traditional Scottish folk song. After ten minutes they were in full verse with,

"We f*cking hate Hibees, We f*cking hate Hibees." If the Hibs ever draw a Polish team in Europe they could be in for a shock.

At 4.30am we eventually went to bed only to be awoken at 7.30am to get ready to depart. One of the lads from our night out, Gaz, was in such a state that he slept the next 18 hours on the coach all the way back to Calais, only waking up to throw-up into a plastic carrier bag.

On the way back they wouldn't let us out of Austria (bad losers), because they claimed the tacograph wasn't functioning correctly; and on the ferry Big Al downed half a bottle of Southern Comfort plus four pints of lager in one and a quarter hours. Needless to say, he slept for a few hours after. It turns out his job is painting the Fo'rth Railway bridge, no wonder he got so plastered.

It should also be noted that on our coach we had one lad who played for Hibs Youth Team, and another who played for Falkirk reserves. The rest of us knew how to play football.

QUIZ

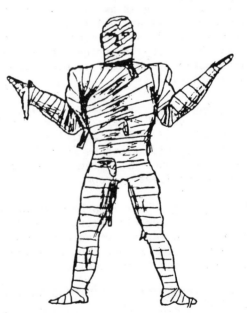

Which well known player was this reporting for pre-season training? Was it -

a) Bryan Robson

b) Trevor Francis

c) Neil Cooper

Name Pics

Many football programmes carry pen-pictures of players. Fairly predictable and often boring, they reveal mind-boggling facts such as: 'favourite food - steak and chips' or 'dislikes - getting beated.' We've decided to use definitions of the players names as an insight to their characters. Maybe Graham Blackwood and Co. would like to slide them into the Club Programme.

Henry Smith An Anglo-Saxon name for a disease of the nervous system more commonly called 'Dropsy'! There's nothing worse than an attack of the 'Henry's'.

Walter Kidd An Americanism meaning 'to move in a duck like fashion - graceful and elegant (in the water) a Walter tends to move slowly and unsurely on grass or mud.

David MacPherson David is a Hebrew word which translates as 'worrier of sheep.' This explains why it is a commonly used name in Wales. Also why 'Big Davie' is affectionately known as 'The Aberdonian!'

Roger Whittaker Roger is a French word meaning 'having it away!' Rogers tend to lack energy and bodily strength due to physical demands placed upon them. 'Give her a good rogering' shouted at Tynecastle doesn't always mean 'clear the ball upfield!'

Tosh MacKinlay Short for Macintosh i.e. A highlander who wears light coloured raincoats and offers 'Smarties' to young children. Also known as 'Big-Mac' when he first opened his raincoat in the Tynecastle dressing room!

Chuck Berry Chuck is a Lancastrian word acquired during his excursion to Bolton. It means to empty the contents of ones stomach on the floor. Possible brought on by a dodgy black pudding.

Mike Galloway Again a Hebrew word - Michael means 'tight fisted sod.' Middle name Walter thus full translation is 'tight as a ducks bum.'(see Walter Kidd). For full definition of Micky see Walt Disney or Hugh Burns.

Eamon Bannon Gaelic verb translated from - 'to aim' associated with the direction you pee in the Tynecastle Bogs, i.e. "fer crissakes watch wher' yer eamon - yer pissin on ma feet."

John Colquhoun An Americanism meaning lavatory. Name given to children who were conceived behind Public Conveniences in the Park. Also 'Dear Jean' a French Letter distributed to soldiers during World War 2.

John Robertson i.e. Son of Bob - A Yorkshire slang term for Jobbies. So when the crowd yell "Go on! Wee Robbo" they actually mean run faster you little shite!

Wayne Foster Derived from Glasgow slang word meaning 'small person' i.e. (Has anybody seen 'the Wayne'?) Thus Wayne Foster is a name given to people who drink copious amounts of Australian Lager with 'wee chaps' (thats a chaser for any numb English reading the mag!)

Alex Macdonald Gaelic name - Donald means web-footed beast! This may explain why the manager can be seen mincing through the corridors with his handbag yelling "What's up Ducky?"

By the time you've read this article the entire first team squad will probably have damaged each other in the fight to use the Club Phone to contact their solicitors either to sue us or change their name by 'deed-pole!' Our apologies to Club Captain Gary Mackay for leaving him out but we thought he'd be upset if he found out that Gary was an Urdu word meaning 'Goat's droppings!'

And finally we know you're just dying to find out about George McCluskey! Well George is an Anglo-Saxon word meaning fat and Clusk is a Welsh term meaning 'born out of wedlock!' What more can we say!

chapter 13

JUST ANOTHER WEDNESDAY

sheffield wednesday

Just Another Wednesday

An Alternative Look At Sheffield Wednesday

No. 2   AUTUMN 1988   50p

It was decided from the outset that *JAW* would not be used as a vehicle for criticism of individual players and management, as the frequency of publication would often render such criticism out of date, and Sheffield is blessed with excellent outlets for the immediate ventilation of one's feelings in the local media. Such a policy has not been without its critics, and led *When Saturday Comes* to comment "It is a criminal waste of good material".

The basic format has been A4, sixteen pages increasing to twenty-four, with a glossy front cover in the style of Private Eye, that is, a photo with speech balloons. The first issue featured a Miami Vice mock-up that was so effective that Mike Francis of *The Gooner* admitted that for a long time he did not realise that it was Lee Chapman's head and not Don Johnson's ! It was felt that the front cover should feature Wednesday players, but by the third issue it was like the chairman saying he has full confidence in the manager - a certain kiss of death. The front covers had featured Lee Chapman, Mark Chamberlain, Mel Sterland and Peter Eustace, all of whom had left. Peter Eustace in fact, on seeing the front cover of Issue 3 had remarked "If we don't win a game soon, the only place I'll be able to sit will be on the roof of the stand".

Just Another Wednesday

An Alternative Look At Sheffield Wednesday.

No. 4 SPRING 1989 50p

'Not so much a hobby, more a way of life'. This is the philosophy and driving force of *Just Another Wednesday*, whose editors are an unusual combination of father and son, Martin and Daniel Gordon respectively. Not wishing to divulge his age, Martin will however admit to not being around the last time Wednesday won the league championship, or the last time they won the F.A. Cup for that matter. For the decade of the seventies the Gordons were abroad, and the plunging of the depths was conveyed second hand through the static of the BBC World Service. They did however return briefly for Daniel to be born in Sheffield. On a Wednesday, naturally.

Daniel's first match was a 0-0 draw with Swansea City. "Boring" was his verdict, and on being informed that it was a good performance by Wednesday as Swansea were on their way to promotion, he replied "I think I'll support Swansea". Following a long harangue on the meaning of the word loyalty, Daniel has never looked back.

Later exiled on the other side of the Pennines, it was at a meeting of the Greater Manchester branch of the FSA that they first came across the world of the fanzine. Thus the idea of a Sheffield Wednesday fanzine was conceived and, following a short gestation period, the first issue of *Just Another Wednesday* appeared in the Spring of 1988, with the observation by Jimmy Greaves - "It's a funny old name".

THE THREE AGES OF DAVE BASSETT

1986   1987   1988

MANAGER

WIMBLEDON

MANAGER

WATFORD

MANAGER

SHEFFIELD UNITED

Mr Bassett's taken relegation rather badly !

BASSETT THWARTED

The Sheffield United Board has denied rumours that it has blocked one of Dave Bassett's first moves in the transfer market.

It is said that on arrival in Sheffield he attempted to sign Kenning Van Hire in the belief that he was a promising Dutch international.

The Board has issued a statement backing Mr Bassett's judgement fully and regretting that, at the time, the money was simply not available.

The emphasis of JUST ANOTHER WEDNESDAY has been firmly on humour, and much of the comment on the ills of the game have been attempted through gentle satire, rather than long in-depth analyses. In a situation such as exists in any two-team area, it is inevitable that much of the humour is directed at Sheffield United, although deliberately cruel jibes have been avoided. Interestingly, Dave Bassett has been most encouraging and has freely admitted to enjoying the fanzine.

SPITS, SPATS, STRONG MINTS AND JU-JU

Wednesday have a number of famous followers. Amongst them Joe Ashton MP, who supplied an excellent article for JAW 3, and Roy Hattersley MP whose dream ticket for season 1988/89 remained, unfortunately, just a dream.

Let's face it, if Wednesday sold off Hillsborough it would just about bring in enough cash to buy Gazza Gascoigne. And looking at the balance sheet it would take over half the season's gate receipts to sign a 31 year old left back called Mal Donaghy from Luton. To say nothing of his £75,000 signing on fee and £65,000 a year wages.

But, do not despair. There is always prayer, which costs nowt. Not that it has ever done Poland much good even though the Pope comes from there.

Yet I know for a fact that the last time the Owls got to Wembley in 1966, St Catherines Church, Burngreave took an extra £97-14-9d in lighted candle money.

What's more the priest said if only the Wednesdayites had made it a round hundred he would have personally guaranteed that the last Everton pass would not have gone through a hole in Gerry Young's foot.

In fact it is no secret that the Italian Government is confident that when the World Cup is played there in 1990 enough candles will be lit to pay off the National Debt. Providing they can get the Vatican to hand over the cash, that is.

The problem is that today we have too many youngsters on the Kop effin' and blindin' their way through Amazing Grace instead of crossing their fingers and rolling their eyes to heaven like we did.

Even goalkeepers rarely bother scratching the sign of the cross in the centre of the goal area anymore.

Although goalies in Africa know the value of it. They not only make ju-ju signs on the posts but actually spit on the penalty spot and widdle all round the goalmouth.

Some cynics say its the AIDS what frightens the strikers off not witchcraft, but nevertheless many of their teams do have remarkable defensive records.

Because there is no doubt that ju-ju works.

For instance I can't remember Wednesday scoring a last minute winner since my mate George Lee unfortunately passed away the season before last.

For some reason if ever he left bang on half past four the lads would never fail to put one in.

"Time tha went George" the whole of the North Stand would yell as they got anxious. In fact some would panic and start shouting for it at half time on a bad day. Not yet, he'd say. Don't push it.

He made many a supreme sacrifice for the club knowing he wouldn't be there to join the ecstasy himself, but having the glow of satisfaction standing at the bus stop.

I can do it sometimes by sucking a strong mint. But only if they come from that little shop on Leppings Lane. It doesn't produce a goal every time, but quite often a near miss or a corner.

And a pal of mine swore that Wednesday only got relegated in 1958 because the Corporation stopped the trams running and stopped him slairing backwards on his hobnail boots towards the Kop.

It's all gone now hasn't it ? The days when God automatically sent a club down if directors dared to spend the cash on plush seats in a new stand, instead of goal scorers for the peasants on the Kop, are long past.

And you never heard of brave self sacrificing chairmen like Jack Timm anymore. He was reputedly a pre-war boss who swore he wouldn't take off his lucky spats, socks and shoes until Portsmouth were knocked out the FA Cup (Remember how it worked against us with the Brighton manager and his lucky white shoes ?)

Anyway his team ultimately finished up at Wembley on a red hot May Day in 1939 with Jack sitting on the front row all on his own and the Queen Mother having to present the Cup with one outstretched hand while holding a bottle of smelling salts in the other.

But they won. Now why can't our directors find some ju-ju like that ?

Joe Ashton

ROY HATTERSLEY'S DREAM TICKET

FACE IN THE CROWD

On a dismal November night last year, 3756 genuine supporters turned out to watch Sheffield Wednesday play Bournemouth. Those 3756 supporters made history as comprising the lowest ever gate at Hillsborough for a first class match.

As a reward for their loyalty, we have taken a photograph of the crowd and randomly circled one of the spectators. If the lucky lady will come forward we will be delighted to present her with the £5 prize.

JUST ANOTHER WEDNESDAY also claims to have royalty amongst Wednesdayites. Admittedly the 'Face in the Crowd' had been done before, but the photo that appeared was a genuine photo of Her Majesty at Hillsborough with Bert McGee the Wednesday chairman. As for claiming Her Majesty to be amongst JAW readers, well ....

NOT THE HILLSBOROUGH NEWS

At a meeting to discuss the leadership of the Labour Party, Neil Kinnock poured a jug of orange juice over Eric Heffer, and Tony Benn rammed two bananas up Roy Hattersley's nostrils. A party spokesman described the atmosphere as tense but fruitful.

* * * *

A nasty crack appeared on the wall of the John Street Stand at Bramall Lane overnight. Workmen managed to paint it over before Dave Bassett could read it.

* * * *

After retiring from playing football, Emlyn Hughes tried work as an artist's model. However, he had to give it up as he had so little to show for it.

* * * *

A flash from the Motoring Unit - Police are advising motorists to avoid an awful hole in the middle of the M6. It's called Birmingham.

* * * *

Bobby Robson announced plans today to get the England team a better name - he is going to call them Holland.

* * * *

Emily Clarke, the midwife who delivered a bouncing Brian Clough 54 years ago, related how, on turning him upside down and smacking his bottom, he twisted round and smacked her back.

South Yorkshire Police are anxious to interview a man who has been selling defective hearing aids. Anyone who can give any information is asked to ring 999 and shout for Inspector Smith

* * * *

Lee Chapman, who was recently transferred to a French Ladies Soccer Team, made a very successful debut. He scored three times - once in the match, and twice afterwards in the shower.

* * * *

Before he left, Lee announced that he always enjoyed the second round of the Littlewoods Cup most, being particularly pleased to get the first leg over.

* * * *

Good news on the poor financial state of Sheffield United. Dave Bassett has announced that he is going to take a stand. He will be selling hot dogs on Shoreham Street on match days.

* * * *

The Scottish football fan arriving at King's Cross for the Wembley game lost all his luggage when the cork fell out.

* * * *

Police arrested a Wednesday fan at Hillsborough today for using a four letter word. He was alleged to have shouted out "Goal!".

A number of features have now become regular and popular. 'Not The Hillsborough News' is a Two Ronnies type look at the news incorporating both football and non-football subjects.

THE BUMP IN THE ONION BAG
or WOULDN'T YOU RATHER BE EMLYN

SCENE Kitchen of terraced house in Heeley Bottom
Accents Mid Shoreham Street.

FATHER Nar den son, been art as da ?
SON Ai Dad.
FATHER Wots dat egg on di forehead ?
SON Wot egg ?
FATHER (Giving it a poke with his finger) Dat bugger !
SON Ouch, dat urts !!
FATHER Dard best let di Mam put some Epsom Salts on it, else it'll gu funny.
SON (With pleading expression) Oh no Dad, nor Epsom Salts.
FATHER Ar da goin to tell us how da come to get it or do I ave to gi de another to match it !!
SON I gor it watchin United
FATHER Da's not bin scrappin at Lane, surely ?
SON No, I ad an Oxo at aif time an I dint feel to good in t'second aif, an I fainted.
FATHER So da fainted an bashed di ed den.
SON No, when I come round sun were shinin an I were runnin thru a field of buttercups in slow motion, just like soap powder ads on telly. Den it went blank agee'an.
FATHER Go on son, I'm widi.
SON Well, it seems dat in mi daze I'd jumped over t'fence an run onto pitch an run slap bang in t'other lot's near post, endin up in a crumpled ball in t'back o' t'net. When I come round I were bein put on a stretcher by two St Johns men an t'ref was saying it were a good try, but other lot were still one up !
FATHER Das made di old Dad proud, son. It's bin a long time since anybody's got carried away in front of t'goil for United. Come to think of it, if t'ball ad bin dere it would av bin a good impression of Doc Pace.
SON Dat's wot Dave Bassett said.
FATHER Old it son, da dint get to speak to im did yer ?
SON Yer I did, an e sez wi a bit of training I could be is 263rd new face this year.
FATHER By eck, das made mi an appy man. Just think, our Tarquin playin for United.
SON Do I ave to ave Epsom Salts on mi bump den ?
FATHER No son, I'll get di Mam to rub some butter on it. No expense spared for mi son the United player !!

THE END

The moral of this tale is "Even in Heeley Bottom it is not who you are, but what sort of Oxo you drink".

Dino.

A regular contributor, writing under the pen name of Dino, provides one act plays featuring a dialogue between a young Unitedite, Tarquin, and his father. It is written phonetically in Sheffield dialect and, whilst perhaps puzzling to the outsider, is highly popular with local readers.

'OWL OF PROTEST

Dear Editor:I'm not a fan
of football.And I'm not a man.
But I will tell you if I can

what I for one entirely shun.
It can't be I'm the only one
who thinks:Football isn't fun

A crowd of men with funny legs
who eat a diet of steak & eggs
of beer & cider drunk in kegs

cavort around a muddy patch
& kick,punch ,push & scratch
& frozen people sit & watch

Cheering,singing,swearing all
Grant no quarter to the ball,
Bruise,batter ,hit & maul.

Is it any wonder they
turn to thuggery next day?
Kicking is the game they play!

Is it any wonder I
switch the telly off and cry,
'Why?Why? Why ? & Why ?'

Someone who should not go free
brought your magazine to me
thinking I would like to see.

Interest in articalls
all about men kicking balls
rapidly (for women) palls.

Sheffield is a rainy city.
Not worth putting in a ditty.
Football isn't even witty.

Have I said enough to show
Think before you choose to go
Chasing leather high & low.

Think before you choose to sit
on a cold bench watching it
watching muddy men get hit.

I think I shall award a cup
to any person, man or pup
deciding to give football up.

Copyright :Deborah Freeman.

REINCARNATION

For those with doubts about re-incarnation, we present irrefutable proof of the validity of this belief.

Pictured is a sketch drawn during the first England v Scotland match that took place in Glasgow in 1872. There is no mistaking the angelic expression, the delicate pose, and the brief hint of an enigmatic smile.

Yes, Graeme Souness, even in his previous life, is instantly recognisable.

THE ULTIMATE DOUBLE

Having achieved virtually everything else, Liverpool are this season going for what has been described as the Ultimate Double.

They are aiming to appear on both 'Match Of The Day Live' and 'The Big Match Live' on the same day and against different sides. Considering their achievements so far, and the frequency of their television appearances, it is not inconceivable that they may yet perform this incredible feat.

We did wonder, however, if the pressure may prove too great even for Liverpool FC. "No problem," said Konny Dilglosh, "We just take each televised game as it comes".

Contributions have come from a variety of sources, not necessarily Wednesdayites, and not necessarily football lovers. An example of the latter was "'Owl Of Protest", written by a lady who married a Leeds United supporter and then bore him three sons. Hers is indeed a cry from the heart and, in the circumstances, perhaps understandable.

It is not just Sheffield United that is the butt of the jokes. Amongst those honoured by mention in JAW have been Graeme Souness and Kenny Dalglish. The latter article, however, was more an indictment of the excessive television coverage Of Liverpool.

HOWARD'S PARTY

As a tribute to Howard Wilkinson, a party was arranged last week to honour his successful managership.

Although no trophies have been secured, he took Wednesday in his first season into Division One, a place that has been consolidated, and there have been a number of exciting cup runs, including one semi-final and four quarter-finals.

Invitations were sent not only throughout the country, but to the four corners of the earth.

Our picture shows Howard at his party surrounded by each and every one of his many friends, admirers and well-wishers.

Whilst criticism of current players has been muted, JAW has attempted to draw attention to some of the failings of the supporters. 'Howard's Party' was trying to highlight the lack of appreciation of Howard Wilkinson's achievements, whatever his failings. Similarly, 'Where Are They Now ?' looked at the phenomenon of the floating supporter who appears from out of the woodwork at the first whiff of success, and then disappears without trace when the inevitable bad run comes along.

WHERE ARE THEY NOW ?

We don't mean Paul Hart, Lee, Tomo, Shelts or Hodgy. We know where they are. We certainly know where Lawrie is. We are talking about that packed crowd in the North Stand in the background.

Ten thousand of them.

In fact on that day, just three seasons ago, the attendance for the game against Manchester United was 48,105.

This year the corresponding game attracted, if that is the right word, just 34,105. Of those, a sizeable number came from over the Pennines.

What is the reason ? Just from the picture, it seems that we were quite defensive, even in those days. There is just the hint of a Manchester United sock intruding into the defensive wall.

Whatever the style of play, whatever the results, we should be supporting our team.

Where are all those supporters who sang "We love you Wednesday, we do." ?

Where are all those supporters who sang "We'll support you evermore." ?

Where are you now ?

ADVICE TO REFEREES

If you can keep your head while all about you are losing theirs, then you've probably missed the most blatant foul of the match.

(With apologies to Rudyard Kipling)

GENESIS In the begininng, God created the world, and on the sixth day, he divided the world's population into two. He created normal human beings and then he created football referees.

Referees of course are fair game, and although Martin himself referees regularly in local leagues, he has churned out referee jokes with gusto.

HE TOOK ME SERIOUSLY !

One of the problems with being the editor of a publication such as JUST ANOTHER WEDNESDAY is that one is never taken seriously. Notwithstanding that, I applied for the post of manager of Newcastle United. Although not appointed, it was heartening and encouraging that Mr McKeag took me seriously ....

---

11 Oct 1988

Gordon McKeag
Chairman
Newcastle United FC
St James Park
NEWCASTLE-UPON-TYNE
NE1 4ST

Dear Mr McKeag,

I wish to apply for the vacant managership of Newcastle United. I have followed the fortunes of the club since the days of that greatest of inside forwards, Bobby Charlton, and I think it is now time I did my bit to put you where you belong.

My credentials are impeccable and long, but can be summed up as follows :-

Previous Managerial Experience - I was successful manager of Wilmslow Rovers U-12's, although we could not complete our fixtures due to the number of suspensions. I take this as a measure of my success in instilling in the boys the will to win.

Dealing With The Media - At my recent court case I told the reporter present what I would do to him if a word of it got out. The story never saw the light of day.

Strength Of Character - Suffice to quote my third wife, who left me on the fifth day of the honeymoon and told the divorce judge "He is a ruthless savage".

Arthur Cox for the job ? There's no competition !!

I will be in Newcastle next Tuesday and will arrive for interview between 3.30 and 4.00 pm. There is no need to confirm - why waste postage, I always say. Also, my phone will not be reconnected until the end of the week.

Salary of course is negotiable, but I would expect around £30,000 plus a percentage of the increased gates, a percentage of any transfer fees, and of course the usual perks and backhanders.

Do not be put off by the 'Professor' at the bottom. I only use it to impress the landlady.

Yours sincerely,

Professor Martin W Gordon

Newcastle United Football Co. Ltd.

REGISTERED OFFICE · ST. JAMES' PARK · NEWCASTLE UPON TYNE · NE1 4ST · TELEPHONE: (091) 232 8361 · FACSIMILE: (091) 232 9875
REGISTERED IN ENGLAND No. 31014   R. CUSHING · GENERAL MANAGER & SECRETARY

WGM/MEC   14th October, 1988.

"Professor" M.W. Gordon,
52 Ullswater Road,
Handforth,
Wilmslow,
Cheshire,
SK9 3NQ.

Dear Professor Gordon,

Thank you for your letter of the 11th October applying for the job as Team Manager of Newcastle United.

You may be assured that your application will receive the attention it deserves.

Undoubtedly, you have all the qualities required for this position save, perhaps, experience of football management at the highest level. I say this without any disrespect to Wilmslow Rovers Under-12s.

Apart from your lack of football experience, the only reserve I have about your application is that a man of your undoubted character and qualities should feel the need to impress his landlady.

Yours sincerely,

W.G. McKEAG
Chairman

DIRECTORS - W. G. MCKEAG (CHAIRMAN) · R. MACKENZIE (VICE CHAIRMAN) · S. SEYMOUR · J. RUSH A.F.C. · SIR GEORGE BOWMAN J.P. · E. DUNN · G. R. FORBES · G. R. DICKSON

Spoof letters have appeared from time to time in JAW, but the letter to Gordon McKeag, the Newcastle United chairman showed that JAW can be outplayed and outwitted in the spoofing game. All credit to Mr McKeag who showed such humour and insight - no wonder the Football League decided he was unsuitable to be President of that august body.

AN OPEN LETTER TO JONATHAN

Dear Jonathan,

So you want to know what life is like as the wife of a fanzine editor. Memories of pre-fanzine days are hazy but I seem to remember the year divided into two, the football season and the summer. The summer was the time when we used to meet with friends like you, have a meal together and spend the day in the country. The house would be decorated, the lawns mowed, etc, etc.

Remember how we met up for a holiday in the summer of '87 ? I have paid a thousand times over for that holiday. How could a football fanatic like Martin forget that the season started a week early because of the forthcoming European Championships ? Last year when I broached the subject of holidays it was "Holidays, what holidays ? I can't take a holiday. I have a fanzine to get out for the beginning of the season." Daniel was sent off to Belgium and France for the summer to improve his French, so I thought. Instead, off he went on a tour of football grounds on the trail of Lee Chapman. The only French he came back with was "Allez les chouettes", which sounded decidedly obscene.

In the past I've asked Martin well in advance "Can you take a day off work ? The children are on holiday." The reply was inevitably "Day off work ? I can't take a day off work just like that !" (Not bad for someone who disappeared off to Mexico in '86 for five weeks.) Now suddenly it's a day off to see the printer, a day for distribution, and a day for collection. Instead of collecting Sharon from College next week, he'll probably deliver her to the printer and ask him to send her back as a poster.

Fanzine production starts when all we see is the back of his head, eyes glued to the word processor, surrounded by coffee cups and plastic folders and oblivious to the world around him. When it finally gets off to the printer he has withdrawal symptoms and for a few days the house resumes a reasonable state of tidiness. Then he starts collecting again. There was a time when his collection was just football programmes. Now it's cardboard boxes (far in excess of needs but "they may come in handy"), brown paper, envelopes, address labels and strict instructions for everyone to stay out of the spare room. Guests come at their peril !

Then, the big day when it all comes back from the printer in large heavy boxes. I'm convinced that Martin surveys the room with military precision and thinks where to put them so that
 a) they will make life for everyone else as difficult as possible.
 b) Judith will rant and rave, but will not be able to do anything because they are too big and heavy.
 c) Judith will be totally unable to reach anything more than three steps inside the room because she shouldn't be there anyway.

Eventually all these boxes are transferred to smaller ones to be distributed, and the whole family gets roped in to sell them whether we like it or not !

So when, in a couple of months, you get a letter from me to say Yael and I are coming out to spend the summer with you, you'll know why. Yes, you've got it in one. Martin has a fanzine to get out for the beginning of next season !

Judith

The final word has to be left to a long suffering wife, whose co-operation encompasses the whole spectrum from grudging to not-so-grudging. Many a wife has identified with this portrayal of life with a fanzine editor.

chapter 14

TIRED AND WEARY

No. 2   45p

XXXX ADULT VIDEOS XXXX

You screamed and squirmed at the Selhurst Slaughter -

now it's time to scream and squirm again, because

THE PALACE MALICE IS BACK

IN

NIGHTMARE ON EMMELINE STREET

It was six of one and now it's half a dozen of the other

An entire team murdered

Defence slaughtered

Keeper blitzed

Will the scoring ever stop?

WHO DARES WATCH

Out now on Birmingham City video - available from the Promotions Office

TIRED AND WEARY

NO. 4   40p

INSIDE ...
ELMDON, POLICE COSTS,
TURN OF THE CENTURY
BLUES,
GLASGOW AND EUROPEAN
TRIPS
AND LOTS MORE BESIDES !!

We used to joke that if there was a Division 1½ Birmingham City would be in it. For years the club had experienced a yo-yo existence, never quite able to survive long in the first, yet always too good for the second. But the arrival as chairman in December 1985 of Ken Wheldon changed all that. Seizing the opportunity to grab cheap shares while others hesitated, Wallsall chairman Wheldon bought out the ineffective Coombes family who'd run the club for as long as you or I could remember. He cut a fair amount of Blues' multi-million pound debt by selling the best players and replacing them with YTS lads and cheap cast-offs. He sold the training ground and apparently the cheque book too, meantime not investing a penny of his own in the club - a policy not requiring the slightest business nous. The result was never in doubt. Gone was

Division One, promotion challenges, big crowds, buying players, fans knowing what's going on. Three and a half years later and Blues are set on a new mission - to meekly go where no City side has gone before; Division Three, Associate Membership, first round of the cup, the Sherpa Van Trophy, matches against Chester City.

And as if to celebrate the club reaching the third division for the first time in its 100 year history, Wheldon sold his majority shareholding to the Kumar brothers, owners of a Manchester based fashion house, for a substantial profit. Is it any wonder the fans get angry?

Wheldon's coming however near enough coincided with the arrival on British terraces of the first national football fanzine, *Off The Ball*, which initially went on sale at the Blues v. Ipswich Town game on January 11th 1986. So City fans were among the first to be touched (financially at least) by the new thing. But it was to be a fat 20 months before they had their own fanzine. Two titles were considered: *'End Of The Road'* - the title of the club song (more commonly prefixed with the words 'Keep Right On'), and *Tired And Weary* (a phrase from it). Both possessed an ironic black humour, indicative of what was to become and essential element of the magazine. There was little to choose between the two but *Tired and Weary* won the day because it was shorter and thus cheaper to Letraset.

So, on September 19th 1987, as Blues acted out a soulless, goalless bore with Shrewsbury Town, the magazine hit the terraces and soon 500 copies had been sold, flogged for 50p each. Frankly it was rubbish, but Joe Public can be a tolerant guy and the novelty aspect, plus the fact that it was still better (and cheaper) than the club programme, counted in its favour. Issue 2 was much improved and resulted in favourable growls from the Spion Kop cognoscenti with the 600 print run going, if not like hot cakes, at least like warm ones. Since then, by common consent, *Tired and Weary* has continued to get better, digging itself a niche on the terraces and now selling 2000 per edition. The price has slipped to 40p and from Issue 4 it's been produced on an Apple Mac computer with a splash (more often a smudge) of colour and shiny paper front and back.

But no talk of *Tired and Weary*'s formative years would be complete without acknowledgement of Mr. Wheldon's invaluable contribution. Men like him are the reason football fanzines were born, and the former furrow-browed fuhrer of Fellows Park has been a constant source of inspiration. For a man who hardly ever speaks publicly we've got remarkable mileage out of him. His manner of running the club - with a secrecy a lodge of freemasons would envy - completely justifies our constant haranguing and demands for his removal. This is the man who called a press conference and then told a questioner to "Mind your own damn business".

To see and feel the utter, utter frustration of fans, their numbers now so sadly dwindled as they witness their club ruined before them, leads one to despair. Wheldon's open contempt towards supporters, mirrored by club secretary John Westmancoat, has left fans feeling numb, despondent and dejected.

Under Wheldon Birmingham City became synonymous with everything that's wrong with the way English football is run: one rich owner, self-appointed and unaccountable, PR non-existant, local community ignored, fans left in the dark and never consulted. Such circumstances make writing a fanzine simple - it's easy to strike the angry young man pose. But we've always aimed to do more than that, suggesting alternatives and encouraging readers to get active through regular promotion of the Football Supporters Association, the anti-I.D. card campaign, reviewing and listing other fanzines, encouraging the formation of an independent supporters club and the attempted distribution of club shares among fans.

For the club itself, the recent change of ownership raises many questions and possibilities. The new chairman is 26 year old Samesh Kumar, with his brothers Ramesh and Bimal and the Kumar company secretary Bryan Slater also joining the board. Disturbingly, Wheldon remains in an 'advisory' capacity as Managing Director with the new owners admitting they've little idea how to run a football club. They say they'll invest money to buy players (though the club is developing a promising youth policy with lads such as Simon Sturridge and Paul Tait showing considerable potential) and have made encouraging comments about supporter and community involvement. However that involvement apparently doesn't extend to our magazine as, during his first month in charge, Samesh Kumar twice cancelled interview appointments with us and followed that up by banning the fanzine from sale in the ground.

Exactly why the Kumars have bought Blues, apart from the prestige that comes from owning a football club, remains to be seen. They claim to be football mad and supporters of Manchester United. But however well-intentioned they may be, the takeover once again highlights the fact that football clubs - such a vital community asset - can be traded in the marketplace simply to line someone's pockets. And that's wrong.

JIM BRYANT / STEVE BEAUCHAMPE / MATTHEW COLE

Introduction - Case For The Defence

Welcome to the very first issue of Tired And Weary, a fanzine dedicated to give insight and humour and create debate on the turbulent topic of Birmingham City Football Club and football in general.

For years now football clubs have manufactured a growing band of apathetic supporters, partly through independent unpleasantaries but largely through their own major failings. Nowhere is this more true than at Birmingham where mismanagement on and off the field has led to poor playing standards and match results, unprecedented small gates, and record after record of low points in the club's history. This phenomenon has occured up and down the country on differing scales of shame leading to similar responses from passionately concerned supporters.

The miserably uninformed insight into the make-up of the supporting animal throughout the footballing media of which the club programme, riddled with adverts, excessive glossy pictures, uninteresting quizzes and worthless sparce articles is a prime example, has stimulated many excellent fanzines. Hopefully Tired And Weary can follow in their distinguished footsteps.　　　　　**Editorial Tired and Weary Issue One, September 1987**

KEN WHELDON SPEAKS SHOCK!

So Ken Wheldon was 99% certain of completing a deal with "one of the breed of new entrepreneurs... worth up to £5m... which would make Blues one of the healthiest and wealthiest clubs in the country." That was on January 4th. As I write, some 80 days later, there has not been one word from the club either to the shareholders (and Wheldon specifically promised at the AGM that he would write to all shareholders within ten days) or to the fans in general.

It has been suggested that there never were any negotiations and that the Chairman, under pressure from hostile shareholders, panicked and made up a story just to silence his critics. But that would be uncharitable and probably untrue. Wheldon read from a prepared statement and while he may have put the most favourable interpretation possible on the discussions (note the words "up to £5m") there's no evidence that he was not telling the truth (bending it perhaps).

Nevertheless, the fact is that negotiations, be they with Virgin (probably the Mail looking for a story, splashing it over the front page and pushing aside both parties' denial of any deal before then telling us that the talks have fallen through) a Branson subsidiary company or anyone else, failed long ago. Therefore, why has the Chairman not contacted the shareholders, written in the club programme or made a statement to the press.

As ever, Ken Wheldon is treating us with complete contempt, as anyone who was at the AGM should know. His outbursts against Neville Bosworth (which the old fool deserved) and Clive Wilkinson along with his refusal to say how much money he had invested in the club (his response was "I don't propose to answer that", asked why, he said "I don't

want to") show a man with no patience and even less public relations ability. Perhaps it is no surprise that talks over the mystery deal collapsed or that the Co-op were not prepared to have their name on the club's shirts (as we were told at the AGM) - trying to deal with Wheldon or elicit information from him can be a very trying and often unsuccessful process.

Add to this, that it later transpired in the meeting that Wheldon has put no cash of his own into the club, merely loaned it money (but no more than £50,000 at any one time) while converting some of the club's debts into his own shareholding (which he presumably hopes one day to sell for a profit) and we can see just how unlikely it is that a major injection of cash will be forthcoming while the present Chairman remains.

The revelation that the club and its auditors have made no contingency for paying interest on the City Council's £250,000 loan - which it seems may amount to as much as £100,000 (goodbye Steve Whitton) - shows a gross oversight by those handling the finances. Unless the loan can be extended, we're going to need to find £350,000 next May (goodbye Dicks and Overson as well) or alternatively, we could take out another loan to pay off the first loan (and then a loan to pay off the loan to pay off the loan and so on).

His retort to probing questions about the loan - that the inquisitors should shut up, because by raising the matter they were jeopardising the situation; ie keep quiet and let's hope the Council forget about charging any

interest - reflects the club's whole approach to its fans; namely, what do you know about it, stop interfering and leave it up to us, we know what we are doing - fine, look where that's got us!

So another season draws to a close and the club is no nearer to 'marching in' than last year. True, average gates are up, but only thanks to the Villa and Forest games which we won't get next season.

Unsure of survival in Division Two (though we'll probably make it in the end) and with a team that is well short of challenging for promotion, Blues are truly going nowhere.

We take no pleasure in knocking the club or the Chairman, what we'd all give to be a Liverpool or Forest, but those responsible for its administration are failing miserably to make the best of what are admittedly limited resources, but still massive potential. As Blues don't have a board as such, the main target of our complaint has to be Ken Wheldon, because he IS the board. The other two directors (Jack Wiseman and Tom Edmunds in case you'd forgotten) are merely filling supporting roles.

The AGM and the subsequent lack of activity have shown beyond doubt that Ken Wheldon is not some unfortunate guy unable to communicate and suffering from a false and undeserved public image. If he truly does have Blues best aims in mind then it was difficult to see it on January 4th, and one thing's certain, he's going about things in a very peculiar way.

****

A number of other points which came out of the AGM, but not widely reported elsewhere (if at all) were as follows:-

* Blues have shares available for general sale. There is no lower limit to the number you can buy (except zero), just contact the secretary for details. When asked to publicise this fact in the programme, the Chairman replied "I will see what I can do" (what does this mean, isn't he allowed to decide what goes in the programme?) Four home games later, what a surprise, there has been nothing in 'Blues News' about share availability (or anything else for that matter).

* We asked what were Blues doing to attract casual fans to St Andrews. After some waffle about having concentrated on the business community until now, we were informed by Commercial Manager Ernie Adkins that moves were afoot to make the membership scheme more meaningful (which is not what we asked). We were assured that ideas were constantly being considered. Since the meeting however, the club have done nothing to give members a better deal and seem to have taken no steps to attract and keep the latent support that exists.

* *When questioned about what was being done to improve toilet facilities on the Kop, Secretary John Westmancott replied that "it is a waste of time spending any money improving them as they'll only vandalised." What a way to treat fans!*

* *'Scrapper' told the meeting he hoped soon to increase the size of the board (he hasn't) and that "if anyone has £2m to put into the club I will gladly relinquish the Chairmanship" (come on then, pass the hat round).*

* *The Chairman revealed that Solihull Council had twice tried to buy Damson Lane training ground, but Blues had rejected their offers because they weren't good enough.*

* *Negotiations over the future of the Supporters Club are continuing, but following a conversation with Ernie Adkins after the meeting, it was pretty clear that Blues want to bring it completely under their control.*

* *Having failed to keep his promise, made at the last shareholders meeting, to hold future AGMs in the evening (was the choice of the first afternoon back at work after the Christmas and New Year break, when it would be hard for many shareholders to attend, just a coincidence?) the meeting voted to hold the next AGM in the evening.*

Tired and Weary Issue Threee, March 1988

_____ JIM BRYANT AND STEVE BEAUCHAMPE _____

As a Sunderland supporter I attended the game on September 17th. Despite the result I thoroughly enjoyed the day.

One thing which did upset me however was the small group of Birmingham 'supporters' who appeared to single out for abuse the two black Sunderland players. I found this amazing as Birmingham is a multiracial city with 20% of its population being black. Why do decent Birmingham supporters allow such racist abuse? Would these morons boo their own black players? I suggest that all concerned supporters should make their views known by noisily drowning out these 'supporters' the next time they direct racist abuse at a black player.

It was also surprising to see that there was considerable racist grafitti on the outside walls of St Andrews. (I also understand that in some areas inside the ground there is also grafitti.) This is particulalry true in the areas where the home fans congregate. Why don't fans write and demand its removal?

Because of the things I have mentioned it was hardly surprising that very few black people appear to watch Birmingham games. In particular, very few Asian people were at the match, despite the fact that Small Heath has a large Asian community. Has the club done nothing to try and attract Asian and Afro-Caribbean youth to the matches? How can they ignore such a large proportion of the local population?

Mark Metcalf - Hackney London

**Tired and Weary Issue Five
November 1988**

Dear TAW,
I thought I'd let you into a secret - Blues' fortunes don't rest with the ability of the team they field but with the shape of the matchday programme. Since 1978/79, Blues' programme has been two basic sizes - short and thin (as last season) and big and fat. Look now at season's performances with the different shaped programmes:
1978/79 - (short and thin) team relegated - no win till November.
1979/80 - (big and fat) - team promoted.
1980/81 & 1981/82 (big and fat) - Blues stay in Division 1. (Success for us.)
1982/83 & 1983/84 - saw the mutation of the big and fat formation with the short and thin creating the tall and thin programme. Understandably this confused the side who, as we all know stayed up when they should have gone down in '83 and went down when they should have stayed up in '84. Sanity returned in 1984/85 with big and fat format and inevitable promotion. Not having learnt their lesson in 1985/86 the powers that be at St Andrews not only returned to the short and thin but also to Division 2. They then spurned inevitable promotion by staying with short and thin for 1986/87 and 87/88 and nearly sent us into Division 3 in the process.
Our fate this season obviously rests with the programme makers. You, like me will know before a ball is kicked for the first time at St Andrews what our prospects are having just wasted 60p on Blues News.
There is only one conclusion to be drawn from all this. The Gypsie's curse extends to the short and thin programmes but not to the big and fat. If so , and if Blues return to the short and thin then perhaps they ought to put a crucifix on the cover like Uncle Ron put on the floodlights in '82.
JOHN O'SULLIVAN
Tired and Weary Issue Four August 1988

Virgin Ground

Ken's not the most talkative of fellows. Consequently, information surrounding the Elmdon training ground deal has been rather scant to say the least. What seems likely is that a consortium, including the club and Richard Branson's Virgin empire, will develop the 54 acre site if planning permission for the belt land is ever given. What this will mean for Blues in terms of hard cash is even less clear. The chairman has talked about a £5 million sum, arriving from a third share in the equity of the training ground and adjoining land valued at £15 million.

However, these figures are only speculative (due in part to Ken's silence) and hypothetical as at the moment, Solihull council seems reluctant to allow green belt land to be built on.

What also displeases is the secrecy surrounding the deal. While it is perfectly acceptable that, even when agreement has apparently been reached and the initial financial instalment (£350,000) paid that Ken still refuses to enlarge on the plans saying that shareholders (not fans, just shareholders) will be given details at the next AGM. The sale of the training ground is vital to the club's future - the chairman has said as much. It could be a terrific deal for the club and maybe we'll all want to carry Ken shoulder high down the Coventry Road and each buy him a pint in The Watering Hole. But we just don't have the facts. What happens if the planning application fails or the development is delayed? (With the rising price of real estate, it's not inconceivable that the new landowners could delay and simply let the value rise.) Where do we train if the ground is developed?

These are questions that need answering, not at the AGM but in the more public arena of a special fans' meeting, the club programme or through the media. Until we know more details of the deal, we cannot be blamed for feeling cautious.

Well, here we are, a full season on and we're little the wiser. We know that a company called Silkplan has been set up to administer the development. Planning permission must be applied for within 18 months or Blues forfeit their rights to any further profits that accrue. There's only about six months of this period left and no sign of any activity. If planning consent isn't sought we can sue Silkplan (which is owned by three companies we know bugger-all about) for compensation. But Silkplan is a holding company with assets of just £100 so legal action would be a waste of time. The EGM to give details of the deal Wheldon promised back in November never materialised, so what's happening is as clear to us as it is to you.

**Tired and Weary Issue Four
August 1988**

DON'T BELIEVE THE HYPE

It's a small world. I'd just climbed to the top step of terracing in Düsseldorf's Rheinstadion, partly to get under cover from the blazing sun, partly to enjoy a panoramic view of 'the game of the tournament' so far when a voice said "Hey, don't you go down the Blues?" The face I only vaguely recognised, a man in his late thirties/early forties with his young son. We talked on and off, both before and during the game - would we play better than against the Irish? Would Blues have given the Republic a tougher game? Were Gary P. and our beloved Ken over here scouting for some top Euro talent? And we talked to all those strangers around us, to Geordies, to Cockneys, to a lad from Manchester. We laughed and joked about how good or bad our teams were in a way that a combination of fear of violence, segregation and police behaviour doesn't allow on a normal matchday. That's one of the perversities of watching the national team and the sight of a Millwall flag draped alongside a Leeds banner is one I shan't quickly forget. And I won't forget Düsseldorf. Not just because they don't close the city down at 11 o'clock every night or because they sold white chocolate Aero, but for the excitement of being part of a festival being broadcast and reported on and around the globe, for being part of an event, for being and experiencing some-

where that wasn't England, somewhere that wasn't the Düsseldorf you read about. For, while hordes of English and Dutch undercover journalists were roaming the streets shaping up to each other, thousands of English and Dutch

TIRED AND WEARY

fans stood and sat side by side, a sea of union jacks, orange clothing and dreadlock wigs made of string. Of course there was some trouble, quite major disturbances on the night before the game and the afternoon of it, but for the most part, you didn't have to see it if you didn't want to and I, along with most other citizens and visitors to Düsseldorf, spent two pleasant afternoons and an evening window shopping in the Konigsallee, drinking in the old

town or strolling down the tactlessly named Graf Adolf Strasse (surprising the N.F. contingent didn't pinch all the road signs as souvenirs). A far cry indeed from the B.B.C. Radio News reports I'd heard on the ferry of pitched battles and the general media impression that here was Birmingham/Leeds, Luton/Millwall and Heysel all rolled into one. Contrast this with the German press, who, even in Düsseldorf, relegated the story to the inside pages and the last item on the national news. And this more realistic, relaxed approach (after all, no one was killed, only one seriously injured and less than 50 England fans charged during the whole tournament - less a series of full scale riots than a few small scale scuffles) seems to be a feature of the continent, unmasking British traditionalism and the stiff upper lip approach for the hokum that it is. And it shows in their football. While continental sides (and particularly the Dutch) play a more inventive, fluid game, changing pace, switching play and displaying far more mastery of the ball, we relied on a defence lacking a constructive thought in its collective head and displayed a tactical rigidity that years of playing to get a useful away point has ingrained into our football as firmly as the metal pins stapling together Bryan Robson's shoulder.
Not that the Dutch were that brilliant. In a

SPONSOR THE BLUES

Despite the money taken from transfer deals and land sales, Blues still need cash. To this end Tired and Weary is prepared to play its part by sponsoring the Blues to the sum of 10p for every booking we get this season and 50p for every sending off. Will you join with us in this exciting fund-raising venture by matching, or bettering our contribution? If everyone joins in we could really be going places. Remember, last season we had over 60 bookings, and an average crowd of in excess of 8,000. If we can repeat those figures this term (remembering we've got two EXTRA GAMES) - and everyone gives the minimum 10p, that's over £50,000 into the coffers - enough to cover any F.A. fine we'll incur and still leave us with money to spend on strengthening the squad.
If you're willing to join Tired and Weary in this unique enterprise, just fill in your name and address on the form below, together with the amount you're sponsoring the lads for. We'll keep you informed of the total as the season progresses and you can either send us your money in instalments throughout the season, or in a lump sum next May.   Tired and Weary Issue Four August 1988.

I agree to sponsor the Blues for............................ per booking and .... per sending off for the duration of the 1988/89 season. This to cover League, F.A. and Littlewoods Cup games only.

Signed ——————————————————
Name ——————————————————
Address ——————————————————
——————————————————

Dear Mr Downey,
We are co-editors of 'Tired And Weary', an erstwhile organ charting the everyday story of Birmingham City Football Club folk. As we're sure you are all too aware, the club currently languishes in the lower reaches of Division Two, and, with money for team strengthening at a premium, there they look likely to remain.
And Colin, here's where you come in. Tired And Weary, in conjunction with its readers, is sponsoring the team for each booking and sending-off won this season. Problems with on-field discipline, it should be noted, have dogged the club for many years now and so as the curtain went up on the current season, we all looked forward to seeing red and yellow cards brandished liberally at the 'bandits in blue' as our players are affectionately known.
Alas, after a top-notch start, when cautions exceeded one per game, things have somewhat fallen away. Obviously, in light of our enterprising sponsorship, should this trend continue, it is likely to have a dramatic effect on the club's future financial viability and the manager's team building plans.
Urgent action is required and it seems to us Colin that, via your exalted status as refereeing overlord, you are uniquely positioned to help. What we want you to do is 'have a word', so to speak, with those you appoint to officiate in Blues matches reminding them of the importance of clamping down on indiscipline.
We have enclosed a pound to help you enjoy life's pleasures. Should you feel we are people you can do business with, let us assure you that there is plenty more where that came from, if you know what we mean.
To assist in our venture, perhaps you might even persuade Clive 'The Book' Thomas himself to take up the cudgels and wet his whistle one last time. We feel sure you will respond favourably to our offer and eagerly await the results.
                              Yours sincerely,

Steve Beauchampé Co-Editor   **Tired and Weary Issue Six April 1989**

generally disappointing tournament for the football purist, they had all the luck going, right through the competition.

They're a good side, but not yet great. They'll miss Rinus Michels, but if they qualify for Italy (and they're in the same group as West Germany with only one team to go through) they should be very good. Similarly, England are by no means that bad. For all this and our national game's faults, I would contend that Bobby Robson has built the best and most skilful England side since 1970 and you could start the tournament again and get a very different outcome. Unfortunately, the best England are likely to produce at the national team level will still be below what many of our European, South American (and increasingly, African) counterparts are capable of while our coaching hierarchy is so insistant on the long-ball game and our club managers extol the virtues of work rate and hard running. Any country that insists on employing Mark Hateley as its number two centre-forward must be doing something wrong.

Back at the Düsseldorf Savoy (I wasn't staying there, but I know a man who was) we watched Ronnie Whelan's unforgettable volley and cheered Jack's lads like they were our own. In the air conditioned evening air we talked of the pleasures of visiting a stadium where the refreshment hut doesn't close when the second-half opens and where the police don't treat you aggressively or stand in a line behind you. We wondered whose idea it was to hang the flags of Europe from the roof, leaving my view of the far side corner flag blocked by Turkey's (no doubt in revenge for their 9-0 Wembley reverse during the qualifiers). We talked of how great it had been the way the stew-

ards had lain the fans own flags around the running track after every available space on the terracing had

been filled and how, between us, we'd spotted three definite Blues banners and one possible. And we wondered if there'd be trouble in the city centre that night.

In the event there wasn't, though the

armed police wisely kept a high profile well into the night. By Thursday morning, Düsseldorf was behaving like it had never had a European Championship match billed as the battle of the Euro-thugs - the bars around the station were all open again, a Chancellor Kohl speech was headline news in the papers and the big revolving Mercedes Benz sign on top of a tall square office block (all German cities have one of these) still turned relentlessly. I'd come through what the Sun had called World War 3 and lived to tell the truth. Now it was time to head for Cologne, where the Italian and Danish sections of Europe's league of football fans were converging for their Friday night encounter. The Danes would paint their faces, drink heavily and sing noisily and the Italians would chat up the local frauleins and buy them expensive perfumes while I gave the 14th century cathedral (516' high and 312 years in the building) the thumbs up and boarded the train home.

That well-known German efficiency ensured that we left twenty minutes late but my faith in myths was restored when, for the second time that week I fell asleep while passing through Belgium - it really is that boring.

As a summer's Friday broke over the English Channel, the sun-soaked white cliffs shimmered into view. My active participation in the championships was over and from now on it would be up to John, Barry and Jambok Jim or Brian and BIg Ron of the Brom, the jewellers friend, to feed me the flavour and explain how Russian kit design managed to leap forward 15 years in the space of three days. But one thing's for certain, come Italy 1990, whether England are there or not, I sure will be.

Steve Beauchampé

Tired and Weary Issue Four, August 1988

AN UNFAIR SHARE

At the last Annual General Meeting, Ken Wheldon, answering a question from Tired and Weary's Steve Beauchampé, said that it was possible for supporters to buy as few a number of shares as they like, ie that as little as one share at a time could be bought. However, in April, when I tried to do just that, I was informed by letter from Secretary John Westmancoat that the minimum number available was 100. At 50p each this is likely to be out of reach of the average fan who just wants a say in the club.

Is it right for the club to impose this minimum number? It was pointed out at that AGM that it was a lot of trouble administratively to deal with single share applications. Such small requests would no doubt create more work but if Warwickshire County Cricket Club can send an annual report and four newsletters a year to their 7,000 members, then why shouldn't Blues be able to deal with a few hundred one-off share transactions and post some extra annual reports.

Critics of such a public auction would no doubt mention that the 1983 disaster when a similar share sale failed miserably due to lack of interest. That fiasco wasn't really surprising though as the minimum investment then was £100. However, all the average fan wants is to be able to attend the annual general meeting and voice his/her opinion. The club should be grateful that so many fans are taking an interest. The supporters are not capitalists out to make a quick buck out of the club's good fortunes (ha!).

If you agree with us, then write to the Secretary, John Westmancoat, and tell him how you feel, or write to T&W and we'll pass all your views onto the club. If you are interested in buying just one share then T&W may be able to help. Send your FULL name, address and telephone number to T&W together with a cheque for £1.25 which will cover the cost of the share (50p) and all administrative and postal charges. We'll then transfer one share into your name. This may take a few weeks to complete, so please be patient.

It's always worthwhile being a shareholder, apart from gaining you admittance to the AGM it also ensures that you are sent a copy of the Annual Report and Accounts - and if you can't go along yourself you can always send someone along as your proxy. And don't forget, it's the only way to guarantee your Cup Final ticket next May!

There are lies, damn lies and John Westmancoat's excuses. We sent in all the correct paperwork five months ago. Since then we've been fobbed off by pathetic excuses why Westmancoat hasn't processed the applications. Getting to see him is an achievement in itself and, in this respect, two incidents stand out. On one visit to St Andrews, we asked to speak with him but were told that he was out, despite the fact that we could see him in the club offices. Another time, we were informed that he was in a meeting. As we left, who should we see driving up to the club, but Mr Westmancoat.

With the management seemingly intent on refusing to process the applications, we've launched a proxy exchange scheme. This means that shareholders who do not wish to or can't attend the Annual or any Extraordinary General Meeting can contact us. We'll then put them in touch with fans who have applied for a share through our scheme, who can then attend by using the form of proxy. In the meantime we're continuing our efforts to get applicants their shares.

MATTHEW COLE Tired and Weary Issue Five November 1988

The Loony In The Seats

It's said that the characters are going out of football. Gone are the Marsh's, Best's and Worthington's, the crowd pleasers - players the public would turn out in their droves to see. We've had our fair share at St Andrews over the years - Bert Murray, Trev, the afore-mentioned Frank, even Steve Whitton. But the character I miss the most never even kicked a ball in anger for the club - never even got on the pitch (though he came pretty close). He was known to me and my friends standing at the top, the top of the kop, as the loony in the seats. A man in his fifties, maybe sixties, who sat on the Tilton side of the Paddock near the dug out, never afraid (indeed only too eager) to voice his opinions on any and every refereeing decision embellishing each incident with leaps, gesticulations, mock applause and runs to the edge of the pitch.

I'd first spotted him in the late seventies when I sat with my father in Row C Seats 1 and 2 of the Railway End. But it wasn't until some years later, by which time I was watching from Spion Kop, that the singers began to take him to their hearts and watch his every move. They christened him grandad (though I persisted with the term loony) and took up the chant 'Grandad, grandad, give us a wave (which to my knowledge, he never did).

I've rarely seen a man put so much into a game. He never gave less than 110% (Saunders would have been pleased). Even meaningless, end of season matches, (on rare occasions we weren't involved in relegation/promotion battles), wet Tuesdays at home to Southampton or friendlies were treated with the same intensity. There can't have been an official on the League list who didn't dread a visit to St Andrews for fear of incurring his wrath. And he was no respector of reputations; from best to worst; from Jack Taylor to Clive Thomas, all felt the sharp end of his tongue.

Now, we're all prejudiced in favour of our team, but this man was in a league of his own. Every ref or linesman was biased or one-eyed to him we ALWAYS got a bad ref. (though unfortunately, I don't recall him ever producing a pair of spectacles with which to taunt the officials). He'd contest even the most blatant ruling if it was against Blues. An opponent's leg might have snapped off or Joe Gallagher blasted the ball into the Bull Ring and he'd still be claiming no foul, our ball or mitigating circumstances.

He'd strategically bought a seat next to the corridor about six or seven rows from the front, allowing him the space his performances demanded. his use of the gangway was inspired and provided him with easy access to the touchline from where he could harangue with gusto. He'd often be down there, still making his point about an earlier tackle when another incident would take place and he'd fair explode. I soon began to pray for decisions to go against us just to see his ire rise. Half and full times would often find him up at the tunnel (only a short journey) giving all concerned a piece of mind. I sometimes wonder whether this was why it was decided that teams and officials should use the Main Stand Railway End corner exit where it looks as if they're walking off into the city. Eventually, I decided I had to go and watch him in action close up. I had a season ticket and so, not wishing to waste it, waited until a Milk Cup Second Round First Leg Tie against Nottingham Forest (on the day Anwar Sadat of Egypt was murdered, co-incidentally). I took my seat at the rear of the Paddock and sat back. Five minutes before kick-off he arrived. Short and balding, even a little chubby, he brought with him a lady of similar age and build - his wife I assumed, though it could have been his bit on the side I suppose. They took their seats, a row or two in front of me surrounded by a fair contingent of Forest fans and everyone prepared to enjoy the entertainment. For 10-15 minutes nothing happened, and I began to feel disappointed - cheated even. Suddenly, a foul against Blues and he was off - up, up and away to the front, the sense of injustice etched in his face. As the match got dirty he became shirty. His dander was up and there was a fire in his belly. From that point on, he was a changed man, the Dr Jeckyll of the Paddock. The Forest fans loved him, cries of "who is this guy?" and "aye up, he's off again" filled the air. His lady friend just sat, embarrassed. She was, I assume, used to all this and either stomached him because of her undying love or perhaps secretly found it as entertaining as the rest of us. He sat, legs crossed, agitated, forever fidgeting, ready to rise, obviously a nervous and irritable man, always anticipating the foul, the offside, the bad decision. We lost the game 3-2, but the result was of little significance and I'd imagine that next day in a few offices and factories in Nottingham the talk was not so much of Ian Wallace's hat-trick, more of "this fruitcake in't seats in front of us." I often wondered if he was the same outside of football, running into the kitchen if the tea was late or arguing with shopkeepers if his till receipts didn't add up. I hope he didn't drive - goodness knows how many accidents he would've had. I think he was still a regular until the Leeds game, but I don't recall seeing him since. Perhaps he felt there was no point any more. After all, that day, thousands did what he never had the courage to do - run onto the pitch and try to stop the game. Indeed, I've alway maintained that the real reason that both Leeds and, earlier, West Ham fans poured from the Tilton into the Paddock was, not to fight, but to get nearer "the loony in the seats."
And frankly I don't blame them. For he was a very great man indeed.

Steve Beauchampé

Tired and Weary Issue Five November 1988

THE CUPBOARD IS NOT BARE

It's May 1982. Villa supporters are preparing to desert the city in their droves for some two-bit cup match in Rotterdam against Bayern Munich. But on a pleasant spring Sunday, Blues fans are heading for the NEC in their dozens for the inaugural Soccer 6 tournament. Little did we know that just hours later, we'd be running round the Arena with the cup.

So there were Blues, at the forefront of the football revolution, as you'd expect. Indoor soccer in an all-seater stadium on an artificial pitch with reduced team and no throw ins (sounds remarkably like 5-a-side doesn't it?) Well, it wasn't quite. There were six (count 'em) players per side and some of five-a-side's pernickity rules, like the ball can't go above head height, were scrapped, so if you looked hard, you could spot the difference. So overwhelmed by the tournament and our ultimate success was I that I can't remember much about it. I recall we played Wolves and Notts County (I missed a lot of the County game because I was answering a questionnaire). Both were decent sides in those days but I think they fielded mostly youth and reserve players while we generally used first teamers. We played Albion as well (maybe even a Villa XI) but Liverpool, Manchester United, The Arsenal and their ilk couldn't pluck up the courage to come and face us.

I remember the event being promoted as a family fun day or something but youths in pricey trainers and skinheads seemed bountiful. We certainly had more fans than all the other teams put together (which wasn't hard as the place was half empty and it was on the telly for 20 minutes or so at some ungodly hour. And I thoroughly enjoyed it (not least because we won, but I think I would have done anyway) and I was only too happy to go back the following year (when of course, we retained the trophy). The tournament started in the late morning, broke up for a couple of hours so we could all eat our tea, when most of us decided that, as Blues were in the final stages, and it was quite good fun, we might as well get tickets. These were indeed the innocent days of Soccer 6, before teams had sussed out how to play it 'properly', when tactics were fairly naive and matches ended, if not in cricket scores, at least 5-4 or something (and were those summers really hotter?) I'm writing before this year's four-day Guiness sponsored extravaganza at the G-Mex Centre, Manchester, but I'll bet that apart from games that go to penalties, they'll be very few 4,5, or more goal thrillers and most of the football will be sterile and dull. Nowadays, they don't want teams like Blues and Notts County - nor even Wolves or the Baggies. There's big money involved and the also-rans can't have it.

As I remember, after our victory, the council held a big civic reception for the new champions the following week. Unfortunately, Villa having won their game in the Netherlands, somehow muscled in on it and Blues got a bit left out. Still, I was standing at the back of the throng, calling for Dillon, Worthington and the lads to parade the cup, even if no one else was. But it was all in vain and they never showed.

Well, what did it matter, we'd bagged yet another bit of silverware and Keith Coombs was going to have to get his hammer out and build an extension to that trophy room.

Steve Beauchampé - Tired and Weary Issue Five November 1988

BLUES SILVERWARE - THE FACTS

1892/93	2nd Div Champions Shield	1919/20	Birmingham Senior Cup	1936/37	Lord Mayors Charity Cup
1904/05	Birmingham Senior Cup/Walsall Cup		Lord Mayors Charity Cup	1937/38	Lord Mayors Charity Cup
1905/06	Staffordshire Cup	1920/21	2nd Division Champions Shield	1944/45	War League Area Champions
1906/07	Birmingham Senior Cup /		Lord Mayors Charity Cup	1947/48	2nd Division Champions Shield
	Lord Mayors Charity Cup		Birmingham Senior Cup	1954/55	2nd Division Champions Shield
1907/08	Staffordshire Cup /	1921/22	Birmingham Senior Cup	1962/63	League Cup (v. Villa)
	Lord Mayors Charity Cup	1923/24	Lord Mayors Charity Cup	1978	La Linea Trophy, Spain
1908/09	Lord Mayors Charity Cup	1933/34	Lord Mayors Charity Cup	1981	Soccer 6 Tournament, NEC
1914/15	Staffordshire Cup	1934/35	Lord Mayors Charity Cup	1982	Soccer 6 Tournament, NEC
	Birmingham Senior Cup	1935/36	Lord Mayors Charity Cup	1982/83	Birmingham Senior Cup

Come on, what more do you lot want!

Hands up if you're in the supporters club. Not many of you are there? And how many of you use it for anything other than travel to away games? That's whittled the numbers down even more I'll bet. For the fact is, very few Blues fans are members of the supporters club and even fewer bother to make use of its facilities. And this is a shame because the potential benefits of a well run and organised supporters club are very great indeed, as the fans of teams such as Fulham and Walsall will testify.

Cast your mind back to May '86, and Uncle Ken's Blues/Walsall groundsharing scheme. The plot's announcement was timed to co-incide with the end of the season, thus removing fans' best opportunity to voice their opinions - home matches. In the circumstances, short of writing to the paper, or going to the Saddlers' protest meetings in Walsall Town Hall, there wasn't much that Blues fans could do, and had it not been for the strength and organisation of the Save The Walsall Action Group (centred around their supporters club) then, have no doubts, we'd by now be at least groundsharing, and quite possibly, merged. So in times of crisis, the official supporters club is usually the ONLY place that fans can turn to represent their best interests.

All of which make extremely worrying Wheldon's proposal that the supporters club are taken over and run by the football club, simultaneously moving out from under the Railway End into the executive club area.

The upshot of this will be that the supporters club will be run, not as now out of love, but out of a desire to make a profit, so you can thus expect things to get a lot more expensive than they are now if this comes to pass. Additionally, as the staff running it will be paid by Blues, it would be naive to expect the supporters club to ever criticise or take issue with the football club. This is precisely what happened at Queens Park Rangers, with the result that when the merger with Fulham was announced, the Rangers supporters club, almost unbelievably, fully supported the plan. Therefore, whatever the reason, be it to help fight off some unwanted predator, or just to organise a loss-making coach trip on a cold Wednesday night, it is important that the supporters club keeps its autonomy.

And just as importantly, the supporters club must make itself an attractive place for people to visit and get involved with, both on matchdays and at other times of the week. Unfortunately, this is not the case at present. The Committee and their helpers do sterling work, and their desire to do their best in the interests of the football club is admirable, but honestly, the thought of a night in the supporters club doesn't set one's pulse racing.

A new venue, (The Watering Hole has been suggested) an expansion of activities beyond a pool table, TV set and dart board into such areas as 5 or 11-a-side football teams, evenings with guest speakers from either Blues or the wider football world, coach trips to Wembley internationals or the staging of charity fund raising events, car boot sales etc are all activities which would make the supporters club seem more like a club, rather than as it is now, an austere, cold room at the far end of a dimly lit passageway.

There is no reason why a Blues supporters club should not thrive. Many clubs in the GM Conference have more successful social clubs than Birmingham's.

Ideally, it should be at St Andrews, but if Wheldon persists in arguing that as it's on Blues premises, then the football club should run it (and to hell with the rent he collects and the goodwill and good work of the supporters club) then a move away would be preferable, however regrettable. In the meantime, the supporters club should give its image a complete overhaul, make itself more desireable and help put a few more Blues fans in the club.

Steve Beauchampé - Tired and Weary Issue Two December 1987
Well it didn't, and Wheldon proceeded with his takeover plans , announcing that from the start of the 1989/90 season the Supporters Club would be based in the Executive Club. Meanwhile, we carried an appeal in Issue 5 (Nov '88) for the formation of an independent supporters club. A few people came forward and hopefully a truly autonomous and progressive organisation reflecting the late eighties fans' revolution can be established in time for the start of the new season.

In October, Tired and Weary wrote to Mr Wheldon asking for a meeting. We were informed that he did not, at this stage, wish to grant us an interview, but would instead write explaining his view of circumstances at St Andrews. We reprint that letter in full below.

BIRMINGHAM CITY FOOTBALL CLUB plc

Registered Offices and Ground.
ST. ANDREW'S GROUND, BIRMINGHAM B9 4NH   Telephone: 021-772 0101/2689
Secretary: H. J. WESTMANCOAT, F.F.A., M.B.I.M.   Incorporated in England No 27316

In 1985 the Directors of Birmingham City Football Club were on the point of calling in a receiver to run the affairs of the Club. The Club had debts of over Three Million Pounds a hefty bank overdraft of over One Million Pounds, the Inland Revenue and VAT departments were owed money, contributions to the players pension fund had not been forwarded to the Insurance Company concerned, the position was hopeless, and the end of Birmingham City Football Club seemed nigh.

I was asked to try and rescue the Club by the then Chairman Mr K C Coombs to which I agreed and my first task was to pay £50,000 in to the Bank to pay players' outstanding wages. There were many more problems of which you were no doubt aware.

This is now history and gone. Since then the Club has been put on a good financial footing although we are not out of the woods yet, as the Balance Sheet shows.

The results on the playing side have not been good. Season 1985/86 saw us relegated to the Second Division. Players have left the Club and other players have arrived. It is a matter of opinion regarding the ability of a player and whether he is good enough or not good enough for the Club. The sale and purchase of players is the sole decision of the Manager, as is the selection of the team. Money is available at the Club for the right Manager. He is appointed to do just that. It is part of his job. I know what has been said and written about me. Contrary to what supporters may think I care about the Club, otherwise I would not be Chairman, and as I have said before, if anyone feels they could do better I am willing to talk to them.

Success is long overdue at St Andrews. It may not be too far away especially if attendances can improve and the team receive your support.

Yours in Sport

K E Wheldon

We thank Mr Wheldon for his letter, and hope that he will feel able to meet with us in the near future, in order that we may talk more fully about the club's situation.   **Tired and Weary Issue 5, November 1988**

What makes it even more galling is that because we've published his letter in this book we're honour-bound to pay him some royalties. Sometimes life just isn't fair!

AN UNCONSTITUTIONAL SHAM

Blues Annual General Meeting, held on November 21st in the Executive Club, was an unconstitutional sham. It was probably the only opportunity supporters will get to question the man who is running our club - but Wheldon made sure we had little chance of doing that. Last time, he fell into the trap of running the meeting himself and getting into arguments with dissenting shareholders. But there was to be no repetition of that, as Wheldon surrounded himself with club and related officials and chopped and changed the agenda, stifling any opportunity for a detailed examination of his behaviour and motives. And Blues fans can point accusing fingers at the 150 or so shareholders who sat passively, letting him get away with it.

Wheldon treats shareholders with the contempt with which he treats the rest of the supporters. To him, they are an inconvenience. By law, he must hold AGM's, otherwise I frankly don't believe he'd bother with them. Shareholders were kept waiting outside in very cold weather, until 20 minutes before the start, when the main gates were finally unlocked, and many were still queuing when the meeting got underway.

Wheldon continually frustrates and ignores the wishes of shareholders, using his block vote of 831,700 to swamp any opposition. He breaks promises (ie he had previously agreed to hold this AGM in the evening - it began at 11am) and he rewrites the agenda to suit himself.

You would expect at an AGM to hear a report from the chairman - and especially so considering the club's current desperate plight - Wheldon did not give one. He surrounded himself with allies who took the brunt of the criticism aimed at him. Wilkinson and Bosworth, for all their faults (and accepting they're publicity seekers) made many valid criticisms - but they made them in the form of speeches, when direct questions were what was required. Wheldon sat impassively, letting them talk on - he'd happily of done so for hours - those speeches weren't putting him under any pressure! When he is asked direct questions, Wheldon shows his fallabilities. This was apparent on the one occasion we were able to question him. When asked about the ownership of the company Blues have signed the Elmdon agreement with he could not answer. Indeed, it took an unlikely ally in the form of Wilkinson, who had obtained a copy of the agreement, to rescue him.

Wheldon used an old ploy - that of bringing along the manager to take some of the pressure off the board. Suddenly, people who had been sitting quietly sprang to life with a whole host of questions about the team. Yes, what the manager thinks is important, and it's good for fans to be able to talk to him, but Blues problems go deeper than that and we must ask why those who were so keen to talk to Garry go silent when they are confronted by the chairman. Being a shareholder should mean more than just the kudos of turning up every year and thinking you're important.

So, when Wheldon asked "Are there any more questions for the manager?" we quite naturally expected the meeting to move on to Item 4 on the agenda, 'Any Other Business'. But no, Wheldon closed the meeting - and despite our quite legitimate protests at his acting unconstitutionally, nobody else had the guts to stand up and support us (where were you Wilkinson and Bosworth?) and the chance had gone.

Duing the entire two and a quarter hours, Wheldon said no more than a few words. His sidekick Westmancoat, ignored an earlier attempt by us to ask questions. Had Wilkinson not revealed some details of the Elmdon deal, we really wonder whether Wheldon would even have mentioned the matter. As it was, most of the questions about it were fielded by the solicitor handling the sale. At one stage, in response to Wilkinson's criticism, Wheldon tried to head off a confrontation by telling the meeting he would answer the points later, when he'd also be announcing an Extraordinary General Meeting. This, we assumed, meant later on in the meeting - it didn't and we await Mr Wheldon's words on this and pretty much every other subject regarding the club.

It's been three years now since Ken Wheldon took over the Blues. Three years of merger, mystery and suspense. Merger - in the form of the attempted Walsall groundsharing. Mystery - over what is happening (or not) at St Andrews and suspense over when the much vaunted "sunshine days" will arrive. As things stand, we can see nothing but grey skies, with the club's debt being reduced mainly by selling the family silver. We're still losing over £1,000 per week and Pendrey has confirmed we cannot compete in the transfer market. The chairman shows no signs of investing any of his own money, and the club are going to be relegated to Division Three.

Birmingham City needs new management - NOW!

Tired and Weary Insert Issue Five November 1988

TIRED AND WEARY

COMMENT

In three years Ken Wheldon has reduced Birmingham City from a First Division side which still had a chance of surviving relegation, into a third rate, Third Division club who show no signs whatsoever of turning the corner.

The day he bought control of our club, Wheldon ripped the word ambition from its vocabulary. The inevitability with which relegation has been accepted betrays the faith and loyalty of the supporters. Our best players have been pawned and replaced with a mixture of cheap cast-offs and inexperienced youngsters. Everything about Blues reeks of failure and neglect. The club has become a morgue. Dissolutionment and despondancy stalk its every fibre. It's image - to those who still care - is rock bottom. PR is non-existent. Both Wheldon and Secretary John Westmancoat are forever unavailable for comment. Wheldon's occasional public statements appear as little more than attempts to deflect criticism with promises of riches to come. Thus far they have been no more than hot air.

Throughout it all, the argument has always been put forward that if nothing else, Wheldon is a shrewd businessman who saved the club from bankruptcy. Finally, in his Walsall programme statement, he produces facts to back up this second claim. But a shrewd businessman? As far as Birmingham City is concerned, nothing could be further from the truth. It's very easy to stop spending money as a method of cutting your debts. But there's more to running a business than that. It needs initiative and enterprise, and you must take risks. For over three years Birmingham City have been running scared of this approach. In that time gates have halved to their lowest levels in living

memory and are now well below the break-even figure. The club are cemented into their worst ever League placing. And in the Third Division, revenue from all areas, particularly the TV deal and other commercial activities, will fall substantially. The result of this will be more cost-cutting, more selling of assets, less prospect of success. The team play the most appalling, unentertaining football of any Birmingham City side we can ever remember, helping to make a visit to St Andrews an ordeal rather than a pleasure. Consequently, we are losing a generation of young supporters to Villa, West Brom, Wolves, Coventry and the 'glamour' clubs.

The team is increasingly filled with inexperienced kids, employed - as is the manager - because their wages are low. Pendrey, having been forced (i.e. told) to sell our best players because they were worth a price and were earning too much, is given only a small fraction of the revenue raised and appears to have spent much of the season trying to do deals, contact players and conduct negotiations that were ultimately doomed to failure.

While admiring his dedication to the club and recognising his abilities as a motivating coach, his acceptance of the role of Wheldon's 'yes' man often makes him a pathetic stooge. As he's quite clearly not been given the tools to do the job he should have resigned and made it clear why - that way he could have kept some integrity with the fans. And it must not be forgotten that, however much he might deny it, he DID tell the AGM he'd resign if results didn't improve.

But Pendrey's managerial ability is questionable. His signings, including Trewick, Godden, Richards, Langley and Childs, have been extremely patchy, and our use of set pieces and general standard of play is woeful even given Wheldon's financial approach.

Now both the chairman and manager are using our crop of good youngsters as the excuse for not spending money. We're promised that they will not be sold and Pendrey says he won't be party to such a thing. On the management's past record of bold statements that come to nothing, anyone believing this is naive indeed. Off the field, the club's activities sometimes beggar belief. How anyone claiming to be a businessman can appoint a secretary as bad as John Westmancoat is quite fantastic. Westmancoat (for-

merly with Wheldon at Walsall) and his wife Betty (formerly with Walsall) form, in our experience, an almost impenetrable wall of secrecy around the club's affairs - and that's before you even get to Wheldon. It is hard to understand how, in the late 1980's, anybody can take such a bloody-minded attitude towards their customers as John Westmancoat does. The contemptuous behaviour he has shown supporters attempting to buy shares is indicative of the treatment he gives anything that puts him to time or trouble. His unavailability is legendary. Does he work more than an hour a week?

The club's appalling business acumen is equal to its footballing ability. And Wheldon's failure to see that the two are interdependent is the height of folly. The shirt sponsors are reportedly on the verge of deserting us in favour of an American Football team and half the first team squad don't have their kit sponsored. The club makes no attempt to sel itself in the wider community at a time when examples of the benefits this can bring are increasing. At the January 1988 AGM, we suggested that the club investigate the sort of community and business initiatives taken by Watford. It would be quite amazing for anyone working in football at secretarial level or above to be unaware what success the community developments at Watford, Preston and Milwall have created. Yet when our need to raise cash and interest in Blues has never been higher, the inactivity from the club has never been more glaring. The reason is clear and simple. It involves extra work, having to be more open with the public and SPENDING MONEY!

And Wheldon will never do that. He didn't at Walsall and he doesn't have the slightest intention of doing it at Birmingham. For he is at this club for one reason only - to make himself a lot of money. He bought Blues for a knock-down price, paying 25p per share. He's said that the club is for sale and, while it's unclear how much he wants for it, Director Jack Wiseman, in a statement at the last AGM clearly aimed at prospective buyers, said that the shares were now worth 50p. As Wheldon owns 831,700 shares (having converted some of the club's debts into shares in the hope of increasing his winnings) that's a personal profit in excess of £200,000.

Ken Wheldon has a complete

stranglehold on Birmingham City and he's choking it to death. He sells our training ground, giving no details of what, by his own admission, is one of the most important deals in the club's history. He fobs off questions about it at the AGM, deflecting criticism by claiming he's to call an Extraordinary General Meeting 'later'. Four months on, no EGM, and we're no wiser. Then he tells us there's a wind of change about to blow through the club and that he's negotiating with three parties who are interested in Blues. These morsels of information, these little hints that we might be on the verge of something big are, frankly, becoming tiresome. The fans want, and have an absolute right, to know what's going on, or if nothing is, then why not. At the moment the only sure thing is that whatever deals Wheldon's cooking up, they won't involve him in any financial risk and will only go through if they are to his benefit i.e. they up the value of his shares.

In nearly 20 years of owning football clubs, Wheldon's onfield success consists of Walsall getting promoted from Division Four once. That's it. No cups, no glory, just season after season of austerity with the odd relegation thrown in. His flouting of League regulations on club ownership at the time of the Walsall groundshare and his shady deals over Ken Armstrong and Wayne Clarke/Stuart Storer remind us that he should be watched like a hawk. His rumoured links with Wolves, which may amount to nothing more than a friendship with the owner Tony Gallagher, could possibly be turned to his benefit. After all, if he wanted to sell Birmingham in a hurry and needed to repeat his Walsall groundsharing threat in an effort to scare someone into paying over the odds for Blues he'd have a ready made accomplice.

But the bottom line is that Birmingham City can slide through the divisions 'till they're a Sunday parks team as long as Wheldon and his hangers-on feel there's something in it for them.

Patronising propaganda in the club programme that relegation to the Third Division isn't necessarily such a bad thing cuts no ice. The fans don't want excuses, they don't want austerity, secrecy, lies. They want one thing above all else - Wheldon out!

Tired and Weary Issue Six
April 1989

FOOTBALL SUPPORTERS' ASSOCIATION

This book is explanation in itself why establishing an organisation to represent the interests of football supporters was so necessary. Shoddy, incompetent administration, unaccountable decision makers, contemptuous treatment and neglect of those who are the professional game's lifeblood had all contributed to the turmoil and tragedy which marred the latter part of the 1984/85 season. The events at Luton, Birmingham, Bradford and Heysel were the inevitable consequence of the abysmal leadership football had sufferred from for decades. The fact that they all happened in such a short space of time merely heightened their sense of savagery and horror.

The authorities' response mirrored their bankruptcy of ideas. I read the newspapers and watched the television with increasing anger and incredulity as self-appointed 'experts' and talking (dick)heads came up with all the wrong answers. Most based their 'initiatives' on mass control, regulation and state-approved violence towards football fans - cage them, ban them, birch them! Meanwhile the millions who went to soccer because they loved the game remained caught in the middle, being squeezed from both sides.

Fortunately in Liverpool two soccer-mad Scousers shared my anger and decided to do something about it. Thus was born the Football Supporters Association and for the first time ever fans could cast aside club loyalties and join a national organisation with a common approach to tackling the problems afflicting the game. At the same time it offerred them a chance to celebrate football's unique place in our popular culture, its glory and its greatness.

Much of the F.S.A.'s early work involved establishing branches and establishing credibility. In the main clubs were hostile, the authorities resentful and suspicious, fans apathetic. It took the hard work of a network of volunteers, the interest and support of a few sympathetic and curious media folk and the emergence of the fanzines for the football world to start realising that here was an organisation to be taken seriously.

As the volunteers began acquiring campaigning skills results slowly started to emerge. After the success of persuading Cowdenbeath F.C. to put a light in one of their toilets, the fight in early 1987 against the proposed merger and groundsharing plans threatening QPR, Fulham, Wimbledon and Crystal Palace was childs play. The publicity and euphoria generated by the pitch and public meeting protests and then the ultimate victory helped many fans realise what collective power they had, and led to an increase in the F.S.A.'s membership and profile.

That profile has since grown enormously, helped in no small measure by the impressive manner in which chair Rogan Taylor and the Association's national and branch officers have portrayed and conducted themselves - in stark contrast to the hysterical responses of so many football administrators, politicians and journalists. F.S.A. membership, on the other hand, has grown more slowly. The organisation clearly has the backing of the vast majority of football fans but it is not (and may never be) a mass membership movement. But that's not unusual - millions support organisations such as Greenpeace and Friends of the Earth, but few become paid-up members.

In just four years the F.S.A., despite being an almost entirely voluntary body, has reached a prominence equal to that of all the other groups and associations connected with the game. Whenever a football story with a direct bearing on supporters breaks, the press and fellow fans are on the'phone immediately.

But the F.S.A.'s influence on the game's decision making process is still small. Undoubtedly important inroads have been made - the anti-I.D. card campaign has at times seen the organisation seemingly dragging the professionals into serious opposition - but there remains a strong feeling that government threats, the public shame of presiding over a monumental disaster or the knee-jerk reaction (the emphasis is on jerk) to hooliganism are more likely to stir the game's rulers from the stupor of lethargy and complacency they wallow in.

However, the sport's authorities ignore the F.S.A. at their own risk. The radical ideas (radical for football anyway) have found favour - albeit at times in watered down form - with others in the game who are increasingly taking them on board and promoting them as the national, coherent stategies they are. The stones the F.S.A. has metaphorically thrown are having a ripple effect across the whole of English soccer.

As it enters the 1990s football seems to be pulled two ways. By the government and police, whose contempt and disdain for the sport and its followers is clear, and who see the game as an excuse for experimenting with Draconian law and order tactics. And by the alternative football network, a loose assemblage consisting of the F.S.A., the fanzines and other independent supporters groups and endorsed by the P.F.A., a few directors, local councils and like-minded journalists. It is a battle on which the very survival of the professional game and our League structure depends. And it is one in which the F.A. and Football League look increasingly like irrelevant bystanders, incapable of making a helpful contribution, bereft of ideas.

Currently football's enemies are in the ascendancy, but four years on from Heysel, as the game reels from the shock of Hillsborough, my newspapers and television set are nearly as full of F.S.A. members and sympathisers talking commonsense and pushing supporters' rights as they are with idiots spewing ill thought out, unhelpful contributions. And that's a start. As with the environment, the fight to save it has started late, but there is still time - just.

STEVE BEAUCHAMPE

subscription information

ALL PRICES INCLUDE POSTAGE

Lennie Lawrence, 433 Woodham Lane, Weybridge, Surrey, KT15 3QE.
Next 3 issues £2.00.

Chelsea Independent, P.O. Box 459, London E7 8LU.
Next 6 issues £3.00.

When Sunday Comes, 2 Maybury Court, Shaftesbury Road, Woking, Surrey, GU22 7DJ.
Next 5 issues £3.00.

Leyton Orientear, 1 York Road, London E10.
Next 10 issues £6.00. Fat Fryer T-shirts £4.00.

The Elmslie Ender, 37 Grange Road, Kenton, Harrow, Middlesex, HA1 2PR.
Next 5 issues £3.50. Elmslie Ender Lynch Mob T-shirt £5.50. "We've done the double, you ain't"
T-shirt (available August '89) £6.50.

Arsenal Echo Echo, 30 Dene Road, Guildford, Surrey, GU1 4DD.
Next 5 issues £3.50.

Blue Print, 9 Lathom Street, Chesham, Bury, Lancs., BL9 6LX.
Next 5 issues £3.00.

Eagle Eye, 30 Manor Court, York Way, London N20 0DR.
Next 4 issues £2.70.

Flashing Blade, 4 Cross Myrtle Road, Sheffield2.
Next 5 issues £3.00.

The Pie, 61 Stratford Road, West Bridgeford, Nottingham NG2 6AZ.
£0.62 per issue (send £5 and they'll tell you when it's run out).

The City Gent, 46 Ainsty Road, Wetherby, LS22 4QS.
Next 5 issues £5.00. Back issues 23 and 24 £1.28 each. 'How City Won T'Cup' - Bradford City's
1911 F.A. Cup victory, £2.28. 'Classic City Gents' (Compilation from issues 1-6) £1.19. 'City
Gents: The Odsal Collection' (Compilation 7-14), available late Sept. '89, £1.28. Hillsborough
Disaster Appeal Special Issue £0.69 (or more). Bernard of the Bantams, latest issue, £0.69.

Heartbeat, 50 Bader Drive, Heywood, Lancs. OL10 2QS.
Next 3 issues £2.00.

Just Another Wednesday, 52 Ullswater Road, Handforth, Wilmslow, Cheshire, SK9 3NQ.
Next 3 issues £2.00. T-shirts £6.49. Sweat shirts £11.49.

Tired and Weary, 133 Longmore Road, Shirley, Solihull, West Midlands, B90 3EF.
Next 3 issues £1.80.

JUMA PRINTING
FIRST FLOOR
TRAFALGAR WORKS
44 WELLINGTON STREET
SHEFFIELD S1 4HD
Tel. (0742) 720915

"IT WAS EASY, IT WAS CHEAP, GO AND DO IT!"

So sang the Desperate Bicycles in their 1977 cult classic 'The Medium Was Tedium'. They were talking about making a record actually, but the ethic could and did and does apply equally to fanzines. Since 1984 Juma has printed for more than a hundred different 'alternative' magazines, around a million fanzines produced in total. We will be glad to offer information and advice if you wish to start your own magazine. On the business side we offer:

Extremely cheap prices

Good quality printing

Fast delivery

Artwork, typesetting and design services

We also print leaflets, catalogues, programmes and paperback books, such as this one.

Please contact us for a price list and information sheet.